T0326342

PEOPLE, MARKETS, GOODS:
ECONOMIES AND SOCIETIES IN HISTORY
Volume 17

Financing Cotton

PEOPLE, MARKETS, GOODS:
ECONOMIES AND SOCIETIES IN HISTORY

ISSN: 2051-7467

Series editors
Marguerite Dupree – University of Glasgow
Steve Hindle – The Huntington Library
Jane Humphries – University of Oxford
Willem M. Jongman – University of Groningen
Catherink Schenk – University of Oxford
Jane Whittle – University of Exeter
Nuala Zahedieh – University of Edinburgh

The interactions of economy and society, people and goods, transactions and actions are at the root of most human behaviours. Economic and social historians are participants in the same conversation about how markets have developed historically and how they have been constituted by economic actors and agencies in various social, institutional and geographical contexts. New debates now underpin much research in economic and social, cultural, demographic, urban and political history. Their themes have enduring resonance – financial stability and instability, the costs of health and welfare, the implications of poverty and riches, flows of trade and the centrality of communications. This paperback series aims to attract historians interested in economics and economists with an interest in history by publishing high quality, cutting edge academic research in the broad field of economic and social history from the late medieval/ early modern period to the present day. It encourages the interaction of qualitative and quantitative methods through both excellent monographs and collections offering path-breaking overviews of key research concerns. Taking as its benchmark international relevance and excellence it is open to scholars and subjects of any geographical areas from the case study to the multi-nation comparison.

PREVIOUSLY PUBLISHED TITLES IN THE SERIES ARE
LISTED AT THE BACK OF THIS VOLUME

Financing Cotton

British Industrial Growth
and Decline 1780–2000

Steven Toms

THE BOYDELL PRESS

First published 2020
The Boydell Press, Woodbridge

ISBN 978-1-78327-509-0

The Boydell Press is an imprint of Boydell & Brewer Ltd
PO Box 9, Woodbridge, Suffolk IP12 3DF, UK
and of Boydell & Brewer Inc.
668 Mt Hope Avenue, Rochester, NY 14620–2731, USA
website: www.boydellandbrewer.com

A catalogue record for this book is available
from the British Library

The publisher has no responsibility for the continued existence or accuracy of URLs for
external or third-party internet websites referred to in this book, and does not guarantee
that any content on such websites is, or will remain, accurate or appropriate

This publication is printed on acid-free paper

Typeset by BBR Design, Sheffield

To my parents and the many generations of my family
who worked in the cotton mills of Lancashire

Contents

Figures

Tables

Acknowledgements

This book has emerged from many years of research into the Lancashire textile industry, beginning with my doctoral dissertation. My choice of topic was stimulated very much by my own background and upbringing. Several generations of my family worked in the cotton mills of Burnley, Accrington and Blackburn. Although the mills have closed, the landscape and culture of the Lancashire cotton towns reflects their influence, and the men and women who worked in them should never be forgotten.

My supervisor, Stanley Chapman, played an instrumental role in developing my early academic thoughts on the history of the textile industry. The book has benefited from many helpful conversations and comments along the way and I would like to thank Bob Berry, Reggie Blaszczyk, Jean Collins, Gill Cookson, Douglas Farnie, Mike Hawley, William Hartley, David Jeremy, Brian Law and Mike Wright. I also thank Christine Gardner for her moral support and helpful suggestions.

I have published many academic papers on the subject of the industry and acknowledge the role of co-authors who have shared data, and their expertise, which have helped lay the foundations of this book. I would like to thank: Shima Amini, Matthias Beck, Igor Filatotchev, David Higgins, Steve Procter, Alice Shepherd, John Wilson and Jacky Zhang.

Much of the data has been collected from archive and record offices, and I would like to thank the helpful staff at the following locations: Courtaulds Company Archive, Coventry; Companies House, Bloomsbury, London; The John Rylands Library, Manchester; Lancashire County Record Offices (now Lancashire Archives), Preston; London Guildhall Library; Manchester Central Library; Marks & Spencer Company Archive, Leeds; Oldham Local Studies Library; Public Record Office (now The National Archives), Kew; Rochdale Local Studies Library; Rossendale Museum; Shakespeare Birthplace Trust, Stratford; University of Florida Smathers Library; West Yorkshire Record Office (now West Yorkshire Archive Service).

I would like to thank the anonymous reviewers who provided valuable commentary and constructive advice on earlier drafts, Cath D'Alton for her cartography services and Katie Toms for assistance with data analysis.

Most importantly, I would like to thank my family. I am especially grateful to Liz Toms, for providing the encouragement and support that gave me the time I needed to develop the work. My parents and previous family generations have all played a role, no matter how indirect, in making this book possible and I dedicate it to them.

Abbreviations

AP	Ashworth Papers
BCP	Birley & Co. Papers
BH	*Business History*
BHR	*Business History Review*
BPP	British Parliamentary Papers
CCA	Courtaulds Company Archive
C/DTI	Cambridge/Department of Trade and Industry
CH	Companies House
CIFD	Cotton Industry Financial Database
CP	Churchill Papers
CVR	Coats Viyella Records (company private collection, subsequently part of HCP)
EcHR	*Economic History Review*
EEC	European Economic Community
FP	Fielden Papers
GP	Greg Papers
HCP	Horrockses Crewdson & Co. Ltd Papers
IMM	Investors Monthly Manual
JEH	*Journal of Economic History*
JLP	James Lees Papers
JNPP	J. & N. Philips Papers
LCCR	Lancashire Cotton Corporation Records
M&SCA	Marks & Spencer Company Archive
MKP	McConnel & Kennedy Papers
PRO	Public Record Office
SEOI	Stock Exchange Official Intelligence (and Stock Exchange Year Book)

SER   Stock Exchange Records
TCP   Thomson & Chippendall Papers
TP   Tootal Papers
TRER   T. & R. Eccles Ltd Records
WP   Wadsworth Papers
WSCR   Werneth Spinning Co. Records

Introduction

A familiar storyline dominates the history of the Lancashire cotton industry. Factory-based textile production was at the centre of the industrial revolution in Britain, generating vast wealth, thanks in substantial part to its innovative yet avaricious entrepreneurs, wedded to the ideology of laissez-faire economics and profit maximization. Given the influence of this received narrative, and its characterization of financial behaviour and financial consequences, it is perhaps surprising that hitherto there has been no long-run financial history of Lancashire cotton firms. The performance of these firms, and the economic behaviour of their entrepreneurs, investors and managers, would undoubtedly appear to warrant substantial and systematic scrutiny, either to confirm the stereotypical account or to test the validity of alternative narratives. The purpose of this book is to present a financial history of the industry, offering precisely such an investigation.

The book concerns the British cotton industry, which was predominantly located in Lancashire and its immediate periphery. While the sizeable cotton industry in Scotland is not a prime focus, linkages between Lancashire and Scotland are investigated and found to be more significant, based on financial ties, than suggested hitherto. It is also important to note that in the second half of the twentieth century the boundary between cotton and other textiles, mainly man-made fabrics, became increasingly blurred, but even so, there are good reasons to place the Lancashire section at the centre of an analysis of the British textile industry over a long-run period. Specifically, a history focused on the financial performance of constituent firms, from the advent of powered factory production in the late eighteenth century until recent times, has the potential to highlight critical success factors driving long-run and sustainable profitability.

Histories of Lancashire textiles

Lancashire, and cotton textiles more broadly, has attracted enormous attention from historians, economists, and other scholars, which raises the question of why another study is needed. Indeed, because of the length of the period to be examined, c.1780–2000, there are naturally many overlaps between this and previous histories of the industry. Douglas Farnie's seminal account of the industry in his book *The English Cotton Industry and the World Market* is unlikely to be surpassed in terms of depth and quality of scholarship.[1] However, his account ends in 1896, leaving out further decisive phases of expansion and decline, and issues of technology adoption and industrial reorganization, which at that date, were still to be resolved. David Higgins and Steven Toms have addressed some aspects of this gap in their recent book, *British Cotton Textiles: Maturity and Decline*, which, although a collection of previously published articles, also offers an up-to-date review of research published over the last two decades on the later phases of the industry's development and decline.[2]

Other books have also dealt only with specific periods. For example, Chris Aspin's *The First Industrial Society* and John Singleton's *Lancashire on the Scrapheap* consider only the earlier and later phases, respectively.[3] Some recent books have covered the whole, more extended period, and these include Geoffrey Timmins' *Four Centuries of Lancashire Cotton* and the collection edited by Mary Rose entitled *The Lancashire Cotton Industry: A History Since 1700*.[4] The former is a relatively brief overview based on secondary sources. The latter is broad in its scope and takes a thematic approach, considering, among other things, technology, commerce, fashion and design, which intersperse the chronological chapters.

The approach taken in the present book is similar although the specific themes differ, and, unlike any previous account, the system of industrial finance is a linking theme in the narrative that helps provide a systematic interpretation of the key events and phases of growth and decline. In this respect, it has similarities with Mary Rose's *Firms, Networks and Business Values*, which is also a work of critical synthesis covering the period from 1750. The present study is not, however, concerned, like Rose, to compare Britain and the USA, and uses a single country's industry to present an extended synthesis and alternative conceptual approach, based on the linkages between technology, finance, and growth/decline. There are also similarities with Anthony Cooke's *The Rise and Fall of the Scottish Cotton Industry*, which shows how, up to 1914, cotton impacted the industrialization of Scotland.[5]

1   D. Farnie, *The English Cotton Industry and the World Market, 1815–1896* (Oxford, 1979).
2   D. Higgins and S. Toms, *British Cotton Textiles: Maturity and Decline* (London, 2017).
3   C. Aspin, *The First Industrial Society: Lancashire, 1750–1850* (Lancaster, 1995); J. Singleton, *Lancashire on the Scrapheap* (Oxford, 1991).
4   G. Timmins, *Four Centuries of Lancashire Cotton* (Preston, 1996); M. B. Rose (ed.), *The Lancashire Cotton Industry: A History Since 1700* (Preston, 1996).
5   M. B. Rose, *Firms, Networks and Business Values: The British and American Cotton Industries since 1750* (Cambridge, 2000); A. Cooke, *The Rise and Fall of the Scottish Cotton Industry, 1778–1914: The Secret Spring* (Manchester, 2010).

Perhaps the book with the broadest scope is *The Fibre that Changed the World*, edited by Douglas Farnie and David Jeremy. Within its extended time frame (1600–1990) and international perspective, it is thematically organized by geographical regions, with a focus on technology and its adoption. Other recent books taking a global perspective include Giorgio Riello's *Cotton: The Fabric that Made the Modern World*, which provides an essential and long-run account of the shifting balances of world production, trade and consumption, identifying the global preconditions and consequences of European industrialization. Sven Beckert's *Empire of Cotton* also takes a global view, offering a critical account of the politics of cotton cultivation and production, and their constant search for cheap labour.[6] Several of these themes recur in the present book, with specific and detailed elaborations in the Lancashire context. In summary, as prior studies inevitably overlap with the issues explored in the ensuing chapters, the book begins with an acknowledgement of those similarities to articulate the incremental contribution to previous scholarship.

In doing so, it is useful to specify the unique features of this book. As the above review shows, relatively few books take a long-run perspective. The period considered by this book extends over two centuries, from the earliest factories of the industrial revolution to the last surviving mills at the dawn of the twenty-first century. Over this period, the narrative draws on an original financial dataset obtained from business records of over a hundred cotton and related textile-manufacturing firms, located primarily in Lancashire. Prior studies have used similar data, most notably the collection of papers in Higgins and Toms, *British Cotton Textiles*. However, the present work draws on a more advanced version of this dataset, extended in terms of length and breadth.

The firms included, date ranges and sources of the dataset are set out in appendix 1. The dataset consists of 2,803 firm/year observations, across 115 firms, covering the years 1777–2001 inclusive. For all observations the return on capital is calculated as a key and consistent performance measure, and where useful and the data permits, further financial numbers are also included, for example: debt, total equity, fixed and working capital, and ratios between them. The dataset is drawn upon repeatedly throughout the book and is referred to as the Cotton Industry Financial Database (CIFD).

This larger dataset is used here to develop new multiple firm case studies that contrast the differential performance of firms, profit volatility and distribution through critical phases of growth, maturity, and decline. The analysis also distinguishes profits, risk and profit distribution from one period to another. In doing so, in the later chapters, it builds on the present state of knowledge

---

6   D. Farnie and D. Jeremy (eds), *The Fibre that Changed the World: The Cotton Industry in International Perspective, 1600–1990s* (Oxford, 2004); G. Riello, *Cotton: The Fabric that Made the Modern World* (Cambridge, 2013); S. Beckert, *Empire of Cotton: A Global History* (New York, 2014).

summarized by Higgins and Toms in *British Cotton Textiles*. For the pre-1880 period in particular, the book will also contribute to other literature that focuses on the specific questions addressed in the chapters that follow. These are discussed next and in turn.

New perspectives on Lancashire textiles

Economic, social, cultural and political historians have written a great deal about the Lancashire textile industry, and thanks to their efforts, much is known about capital accumulation, factory conditions and the development and decline of the towns and cities of industrial Lancashire. The historiography of the British industrial revolution almost universally recognizes the decisive role of the cotton industry. In the traditional view, cotton was the archetypal case of a gradual, broad sweep of technological discovery and modernization across several sectors.[7]

When added to this wealth of knowledge, the stories of entrepreneurs and leading firms, and measures of their financial performance provide us with a sometimes detailed portrait of this seminal case study of industrial organization. Since its inception, the cotton textile industry has been dominated by the vicissitudes of the world market and the boom-and-slump cycle of business activity. The average lifespan of the mill or manufactory has therefore been relatively short. Consequently, there have been no previous studies that examine the histories of firms as they appeared and disappeared over the full span of the history of the industry.

The purpose of this book is to conduct precisely such a long-run examination of the businesses that made up the Lancashire textile industry. This book offers a long-run critique offering new perspectives on the growth and decline of the industry. It examines how, and why, were individual firms profitable during industrialization and through the more extended cycle of industry growth and decline, and what happened to those profits?

While tracing the historiography of the industry in outline, it is essential to note that participant writers have hitherto relied on similar bodies of evidence, such as employment statistics,[8] measures of output, quality, growth and the

7   P. Deane and H. I. Habakkuk, 'The Take-Off in Britain', *The Economics of Take-Off into Sustained Growth*, ed. W. W. Rostow (London, 1963), pp. 63–82 and, for example, D. Landes, *The Unbound Prometheus: Technological Change and Industrial Development in Western Europe from 1750 to the Present* (Cambridge, 1969), pp. 77–9; E. Hobsbawm, *Industry and Empire: The Birth of the Industrial Revolution* (New York, 1968), p. 75; P. Mathias, *The First Industrial Nation: An Economic History of Britain, 1700–1914* (London, 1969), pp. 3, 13.
8   G. Timmins and S. Timmins, *Made in Lancashire: A History of Regional Industrialisation*, Manchester, 1998.

marginal profitability of investment decisions,[9] on world market share,[10] and estimates of efficiency based on measures of factor input in relation to output.[11] All of these perspectives have advanced our understanding of the development of the industry, and by adding to the body of evidence and concurrently reinterpreting major hypotheses, this study will continue the process of advancement.

Although many previous authors have addressed the broad agenda of the evolution and growth of the cotton industry, no other business history of Lancashire textiles has thus far made direct and integral use of financial and accounting data[12] to examine financial performance and commercial networks. The book uses a collation of archival and other evidence to analyse the financial performance of a large sample of textile businesses over the long run. Such evidence is of relevance to the significant areas of discussion and controversy, such as technology, entrepreneurship and the world market, as dealt with by previous histories. Studying the long-run dynamics of an industry, and its relationship with financial institutions, can, therefore, offer further insight into the evolution of this balance and how, if necessary, it might be adjusted.

Taken together, the evidence in the individual chapters shows that regardless of the size of the market, and the market share of the firms involved, firms' profits were typically highly volatile. So, although market instability was a continuous feature, profit instability reflected specific investments, which differed through time, according to ownership, industry organization and technology. The success of these investments, in turn, depended on the alignment of manufacturing and financial institutions.

Financial evidence cannot be interpreted in isolation, and the broader economic and business history literature offers relevant contexts, as do other sources of documentary evidence. Nonetheless, financial evidence complements our prior knowledge in significant ways, offering new perspectives on themes that have dominated the literature for many decades. Each chapter in the book takes one such issue, and the book's unique aspects can be summarized by briefly considering the content of each chapter.

The first issue is how the development of the cotton industry, through the main phases of industrialization, was financed. Relatedly, how profitable were cotton textile businesses during the industrial revolution, what were the

9   L. Sandberg, *Lancashire in Decline: A Study in Entrepreneurship, Technology, and International Trade* (Columbus, OH, 1974), chapter 3.
10   W. Lazonick and W. Mass, 'The performance of the British cotton industry, 1870–1913', *Research in Economic History* 9 (1984), 1–44, 5–13.
11   G. T. Jones, *Increasing Return: A Study of the Relation between the Size and Efficiency of Industries with Special Reference to the History of Selected British & American Industries, 1850–1910* (Cambridge, 1933), pp. 100–19; E. P. Brown and S. J. Handfield-Jones, 'The Climacteric of the 1890's: A Study in the Expanding Economy', *Oxford Economic Papers* 4 (1952), 266–307.
12   These include primarily the financial statements of cotton companies and capital market data in respect of their publicly traded shares.

determinants of those profits and how were those profits used and reinvested? Relatively little is known about the profitability of individual firms during the industrial revolution, although the question of profits at the aggregate level has attracted considerable attention. Neoclassical economists stress the emergence of competitive markets, in some sectors at least, including cotton, and the consequent lowering of entry barriers as the basis of rapid adjustment of profits to normal levels.[13] They also note that firms were relatively untroubled by capital market imperfections and experienced few problems accessing finance, facilitating entry and speedy adjustments to equilibrium profit levels, with the gains from technological innovation transmitted through falling prices.[14] These studies base their conclusions on analysis conducted at the macro or sectoral levels, and limited individual firm-level case histories. They acknowledge that more firm-level analysis is needed,[15] and the financial records of a range of businesses are used to tell, and in some cases retell, the stories of the leading industrialists.

Chapter 1 introduces a four-phase growth model, and, for each, examines the methods whereby firms expanded and how they financed that expansion. The model is based on the value chain, the separable processes applied to a product to increase its value and deliver it to market. A long-run case study of the firm Cardwell, Birley & Hornby, and its successor partnerships is used to illustrate investment in the value chain in each of the four growth phases. It then considers further firm-specific examples of success and failure. According to the evidence, successful expansion depended on investing in the critical stage of the value chain at the right time, while simultaneously managing the constraints imposed by adjacent unmodernized sectors.

Building on this evidence, the analysis and determinants of comparative returns to capital are the main themes of chapter 2. The evidence shows that the working capital cycle of inventory and credit was crucial, such that profit volatility reflected raw material supply and monetary conditions. Firms that were most successful in financial terms automated specific processes, using their

---

13   C. K. Harley and N. F. R. Crafts, 'Simulating two views of the British Industrial Revolution', *JEH* 60 (2000), 819–41. In the Crafts–Harley view, cotton, along with a small number of other key sectors such as iron and transportation, demonstrates specific productivity improvement, with the rest of the economy 'mired in pre-modern backwardness'. See also P. Temin, 'Two views of the British industrial revolution', *JEH* 57 (1997), 63–82; J. Mokyr, 'Editor's introduction: The new economic history and the Industrial Revolution', *The British Industrial Revolution: An Economic Perspective*, ed. J. Mokyr (Boulder, CO, 1993), pp. 1–127, at p. 2.

14   For a review, see C. K. Harley, 'Was technological change in the early Industrial Revolution Schumpeterian? Evidence of cotton textile profitability', *Explorations in Economic History* 49 (2000), 516–27.

15   Ibid. In general, at the level of the individual firm, the evidence is meagre. S. D. Chapman, 'Financial Restraints on the Growth of Firms in the Cotton Industry, 1790–1850', *EcHR* 32 (1979), 50–69.

enhanced capacity to exercise control over the remainder of the value chain and final product markets. The chapter provides previously unused archival evidence to complement prior studies and construct indices of profit and firm performance during each phase of industrialization set out in chapter 1. Bearing in mind relevant methodological issues, it compares the profitability of several cotton firms of the industrial revolution, detailing their organizational and financial structure, and examining the determinants of the profit rates observed. In combination, the evidence in chapters 1 and 2 shows that network dominance was often achieved through prior accumulations of merchant capital and the automation of specific processes in the value chain, which were significant determinants of success.

More significant investment in fixed capital in subsequent phases of industrialization meant added risk in the face of volatile markets. Entrepreneurs were pressured by such investments to impose notoriously long working hours and lobby against regulatory interventions. At the same time, long working hours and publicized abuses pushed factory regulation up the political agenda. Legislation carried out substantively in the 1830s and 1840s, inspired by Ashley in parliament and the Ten Hours movement in the country, was aimed at mitigating child labour, particularly in the textile industries.[16] Mill owners used factory discipline as a means of employing child labour and enforcing long working hours.[17]

Utilizing the business accounts of these entrepreneurs, chapter 3 considers the relationship between the rate of profit and the length of the working day. It reveals the effects of proposed changes in regulation on the profits of cotton firms and contrasts them with the rival claims advanced by both sides in the Factory Act debates. Indeed, there was a tendency for opponents of regulation to exaggerate the effects of shorter time on their profits, but their behaviour suggests that risk aversion, rather than profit maximization, was their crucial motive. Moreover, the chapter shows that before and during these debates, participants' notions of profit and profit maximization were underdeveloped and weakly conceptualized.

The chapter explains how firms' new financial structures and associated expectations about profits coloured their attitudes to the factory working hours, child labour and employment regulation during the pivotal factory reform debates.[18] Accounting evidence is used to show the effects of different regulatory regimes on the profit levels of individual firms and the consequences

16 A. Harrison and B. L. Hutchins, *A History of Factory Legislation* (London, 1903; reprinted Abingdon, 2013).
17 For further perspectives, see G. Clark, 'Factory discipline', *JEH* 54 (1994), 128–63.
18 On the wider reasons for the upsurge in child labour, see J. Humphries, *Childhood and Child Labour in the British Industrial Revolution* (Cambridge, 2010).

of legislation for subsequently realized rates of profit.[19] The chapter also compares the profitability and efficiency of Lancashire firms with international competition, which, according to some, posed an existential threat to a regulated industry. Finally the chapter presents evidence on the profits of the industry, once regulation became effective.

Regulation did not dent the profits or further growth of textile businesses, which now became a magnet for the savings of new groups of investors. Importantly, these new financial flows provided impetus to the development of financial institutions within the Lancashire region. Consequently, models of ownership varied considerably, comprising democratically controlled co-operative mills, traditional partnerships, family businesses and joint-stock corporations.

The book next considers, in chapters 4 and 5, the effects of financial networks and institutions on the characteristics of first and second phase industrialization. These chapters contrast the producer co-operative movement that evolved into a regional system of joint-stock finance (chapter 4)[20] and embryonic networks of collaborative innovation and financial connection, which developed such that the latter form became dominant (chapter 5). The differing origins of these systems had significant consequences for their long-term survival. Both chapters compare the financial performance of illustrative firms.

Chapter 4 examines the growth of industrial co-operatives and the introduction of limited liability. These developments paved the way for businesses that could effectively raise capital, providing a further model of industrial development. The chapter contrasts the financial performance and policies of co-operative and conventionally owned companies. Broadly, the co-operative

---

19   There is developing recent research on the use of accounting evidence to shape the Factory Act debates. See S. Toms and A. Shepherd, 'Accounting and social conflict: Profit and regulated working time in the British Industrial Revolution', *Critical Perspectives on Accounting* 49 (2017), 57–75; A. Shepherd and S. Toms, 'Entrepreneurship, strategy, and business philanthropy: Cotton textiles in the British industrial revolution', *BHR* 93 (2019), 503–27.

20   See Farnie, *English Cotton*, for a description of the Oldham business system, including the important aspects of co-operation up to 1896. Specific aspects of the pre-1914 system have also been examined, including their financial policies, the use of accounting information in their governance and management, the effectiveness of the Oldham stock market and the relative performance of co-operative firms to other private and joint-stock firms. See, respectively, S. Toms, 'Windows of opportunity in the textile industry: The business strategies of Lancashire entrepreneurs, 1880–1914', *BH* 40 (1998), 1–25; S. Toms, 'The supply of and demand for accounting information in an unregulated market: Examples from the Lancashire cotton mills, 1855–1914', *Accounting, Organizations and Society* 23 (1998), 217–38; S. Toms, 'The rise of modern accounting and the fall of the public company: the Lancashire cotton mills 1870–1914', *Accounting, Organizations and Society* 27 (2002), 61–84; S. Toms, 'Information content of earnings in an unregulated market: The co-operative cotton mills of Lancashire, 1880–1900', *Accounting and Business Research* 31 (2001), 175–90; S. Toms, 'Producer co-operatives and economic efficiency: Evidence from the nineteenth-century cotton textile industry', *BH* 54 (2012), 855–82.

model successfully mobilized savings from middle- and working-class investors, and generated acceptable financial returns on their behalf. In common with conventional businesses, these firms were vulnerable to the vicissitudes of the trade cycle. Co-operation and limited liability provided the basis for the emergence of independent, regionally financed business groups.

Over the longer run, the later chapters of the book contrast these regional groups with the evolution of the early partnership structures of the industrial revolution into giant conglomerates. Considering financial linkages in tandem with technological collaborations, chapter 5 reveals new dimensions and network characteristics. Networks of innovation were undoubtedly important. Increasingly though, financial interconnections dominated business relationships, and the chapter explains how these transformed cottage industries into textile trusts. Financial connections were a particularly important feature of the merger wave of the late nineteenth century, which also had the effect of consolidating long-standing relationships between Manchester and Glasgow, as financial centres, while the underdeveloped relationship with London institutions became ever more marginal.

Taking these institutional developments into account, the final two chapters (6 and 7) examine the determinants of long-run financial success, concerning how the financial system in Lancashire enabled and then stifled entrepreneurship and investment in technology. Prior literature[21] has emphasized that for the industry to remain competitive in the twentieth century, re-equipment and reinvestment were needed. However, the financial system that emerged in this period became a significant barrier. The concentration of ownership and speculative flotations and reflotations of companies restricted the capacity of the industry to turn itself around in the face of declining markets, particularly after 1920. Even so, consolidation and industrial restructuring offered survival options for some firms, but not for others, during the long phase of decline and de-industrialization.

Up to the early 1970s, the remainder of the industry enjoyed some degree of support, exercised through governmental control of international trade. These protections facilitated defensive mergers and the active exploitation of scale economies. In subsequent decades these protections were removed, leaving fewer effective survival strategies available. The final chapter, an epilogue, traces the effects of British entry into the EEC in 1973, subsequent waves of trade liberalization, and the replacement of the North West's industrial base with retail- and property-led growth. Even in this hostile environment, some firms survived, and the chapter examines the reasons.

The reasons for these differences are explored by considering the characteristics of firms that achieved financial success against the backdrop of general

---

21 Summarized in Higgins and Toms, *British Cotton Textiles*.

decline. Whereas these mergers created large corporate structures supported by regional financial institutions and networks, some authors have questioned the effectiveness of Lancashire entrepreneurship during the period of maturity.[22] Chapter 6 re-examines this literature and builds on earlier chapters by comparing the characteristics of successful and unsuccessful entrepreneurial, financial and risk-management strategies before and after the watershed of 1920. Using firm-level data, it contrasts the financial performance of firms using mule- and ring-spinning methods, and also firms that adopted vertical structures with those that were horizontally specialized. In doing so, it assesses whether and how systems of industrial finance identified in earlier chapters contributed to differential financial performance in the crisis years of the 1920s and subsequently.

Chapter 7 revisits the decline story in the decades following the immediate crisis of the early 1920s to the close of the twentieth century, using evidence from the financial performance of individual firms. Specifically, it examines cases of firms that achieved strong financial performance against a backdrop of general decline, thereby recontextualizing the institutional reasons why business leaders could not emulate these successes more widely. A necessary consequence of earlier developments was the consolidation of regional instead of national business groups. The regionalization of industry and finance explain why there was so much difficulty in galvanizing responses during the early phases of decline.

The path dependencies that emerged from the earlier growth phases led to the emergence of two models of business organization that constituted alternatives for extended survival. The first of these was the independent business group, reflecting the specialized function of individual mills based on regional financial institutions and the possibility of further specialization as defences against heightened international competition. The second was the conglomerate model, which began in the merger movement of the 1890s and formed the basis of a series of defensive reorganizations. After 1945, these responded to market constraints and overcapacity arising from post-imperial foreign policy priorities and the administration of the Sterling Area. The result was a government-subsidized, systematic mill closure programme in 1959. Surviving firms were bolstered by government planning priorities that encouraged investment, verticalization and further consolidation. A new merger wave in the 1960s was supported for the first time in the history of the industry by City institutions.

Accordingly, in the later phases, the remnants of the industry increasingly fell under the control of City-financed conglomerates and multiple retailers. Survival strategies, some of which are illustrated by the case of Shiloh plc, Lancashire's most enduring cotton spinning company, were compromised by

---

22   For a summary, see W. Mass and W. Lazonick, 'The British cotton industry and international competitive advantage: The state of the debates', BH 32 (1990), 9–65.

the further restructuring of international trade. Shiloh and other surviving textile companies, including the conglomerates, were impacted first through British entry into the EEC in 1973 and then after 1980, by moves towards liberalization and globalization of world trading systems. The epilogue explores the effects of these changes and the reasons for some successful survival strategies.

All these themes draw together the financial and industrial capital functions and promote the analysis of Lancashire cotton as a dynamic capitalist system, linking business decisions to subsequent economic outcomes. Such a systemic evaluation emphasizes linkages between technological developments and the financial investments necessary to implement them, and the resulting value creation and distribution between consumption and reinvestment. With reinvestment, the cycle begins again, and so capital accumulates. It does so within the context of evolved business practice as allowed or restricted by legal and political institutions. These relations between economic and institutional practice determine the available responses for firms during phases of industrial growth and decline. The key historical events are those which taken together alter these relations and explain development, transition and decline phases in the lives of firms and industries.

As Britain's industrial economy matured and declined, so too did the Lancashire textile industry. Throughout the long decline phase, to the present day, there has been a substantial discussion about the balance between manufacturing and finance within the British economy. The conclusion of the 2015 report by the Alliance Project[23] that the textile sector had the capacity to create 20,000 jobs in the Manchester region by 2020 begs new questions. Does it mean that historical factors symptomatic of the causes of the longer-run decline have disappeared? Alternatively, are at least some of the factors that led to earlier successful phases of industrialization still present? The historical evidence presented in this book is clear. Success depends crucially on the close alignment of manufacturing organizations and financial institutions. History offers essential lessons on the nature of such alignments and, therefore, how they might be productively adjusted in the future.

---

23   Alliance Project Team, *Repatriation of UK Textiles Manufacture* (Manchester, 2015).

PART I: EXPANSION

Industrialization and Capital Formation

From around the mid eighteenth century, innovations in technology and infrastructure transformed the textile economy of north-west England. Interacting innovations created a dynamic and discontinuous process of industrialization. Innovations impacted at different times on different stages of production and marketing of cotton textile goods. Conversion of raw cotton into marketable products can be analysed for convenience into three value chain components: spinning, weaving and distribution. The value chain refers to the stages of transformation from raw cotton into a final product for the customer. We can use these overview components for illustration, ignoring the more nuanced practical details of each component.[1]

Technological innovation, for example, jenny-spinning, typically affected only one component, spinning. Network infrastructure innovations, such as turnpike roads and canals, created development opportunities for all three, with associated opportunities for entrepreneurs to reconfigure the relationship between them. Second-generation turnpike roads used easier gradients and better surfaces to connect towns, but otherwise avoided settlements, while improvements to existing roads facilitated the operation of distributed weaving and finishing networks.[2] These structures of innovation are vital because they explain the step changes in capital requirements during industrialization. Differing rates of innovation within and across value chain stages give rise to a series of models of industrial organization. Each model persists only for a couple of decades at a time, and has differing demands on capital and its composition, in terms of fixed and working capital.

Table 1 illustrates the four such distinct models and sets out broadly illustrative time periods to describe the value chain features of each one. It uses anchors based on decades most closely adjacent to essential dates in the innovation process. For example, the transition from model 1 corresponds approximately to the period ending with the expiry of Arkwright's patents,

---

1 A more detailed elaboration of the value chain might include preparation as an antecedent to spinning, intermediate processes between spinning and weaving, and finishing, between weaving and distribution.

2 G. Timmins, *The Last Shift: The Decline of Handloom Weaving in Nineteenth-Century Lancashire* (Manchester, 1993), pp. 57–8.

Table 1. Transitional models of industrialization

	Period	Value chain component			Capital requirement
		Spinning	Weaving	Distribution	
Model 1	1750–1780	Craft production Open market purchases	Domestic outworking network	Turnpike road	Warehouse + working capital
Model 2	1781–1800	Water frame factories and jenny-spinning	Domestic outworking network	Turnpike road and canal	Warehouse + small fixed + large working capital
Model 3	1801–1830	Steam power, mule spinning	Domestic outworking network	Turnpike road and canal	Warehouse + large fixed + large working capital
Model 4	1830–	Steam power, self-acting mule spinning	Factory power-loom weaving	Railway	Warehouse + large fixed + small working capital

which had hitherto limited the supply of factory-spun yarn. The transition from model 2 in spinning likewise corresponds to the end of the Boulton & Watt steam engine patent and the rapid associated adoption of factory-based mule spinning. During these transitions, weaving remained unchanged until the technical improvement and widespread adoption of the power loom. The result was the end of domestic outworking and the transition from model 3.

As a generalization, Table 1 only refers to modes of transport that explain transitions. For example, from model 1 to model 2 with turnpike and other road improvements and the development of canal-based options, and from model 3 to model 4 with the development of the railway network. Just as important were specific additions to these network types, in the form of new routes, which presented opportunities for growth within each model.

At the commencement of the first phase of model 1, mill owners and merchants needed financial resources mostly to sustain an extended working capital cycle. They relied upon long lines of credit offered by merchants and brokers, supplemented by long-dated bills of exchange. In the late seventeenth century, London merchant Thomas Marsden set up an extended network of credit via agents using bills of exchange, discounted at rates ranging from ¼ % to 1⅔ %, and cash payments.[3] Large businesses developed, based almost entirely

3   A. P. Wadsworth and J. D. Mann, *The Cotton Trade and Industrial Lancashire, 1600–1780* (Manchester, 1965), pp. 91–6. Although these are examples are from the cotton industry, the

on circulating capital, with as many bills of exchange drawn on creditors as held on debtors.[4]

By contrast, the small-scale production mills required only modest fixed capital. From 1738, John Wyatt and Lewis Paul invented and developed the earliest method of mechanical spinning, adopted in mills not specifically concentrated in Lancashire. A few years earlier in 1733, John Kay had patented the flying shuttle and weavers widely adopted it in the 1750s. The new shuttle increased the productivity of weaving, creating a relative shortage of spun yarn. Hargreaves solved the problem of spinning productivity with the development of the spinning-jenny, which allowed a single spinner to operate multiple spindles simultaneously. He patented it in 1770 and there followed rapid expansion in the productivity of weft yarn spinning.

Thirty years after the first Wyatt and Paul factories, Sir Richard Arkwright patented a similar method.[5] The capital required for these mills was in the range of £2,000–£4,000, divided equally between fixed and working capital.[6] Wyatt–Paul and Arkwright technologies set the parameters for the scale of capital investment required in cotton mills for the next half-century. Arkwright had patented the water frame in 1769, which enhanced productivity in warp yarns.[7]

In model 2, Arkwright's water frame dominated spinning and facilitated the control of large networks of domestic workers in the weaving sector. Ease of conversion of buildings, typically from warehouses, explains the relatively low cost of fixed capital,[8] as does the relatively small scale of production in individual factory units, associated with only a particular portion of the value chain. The scale of outworking and the use of extended credit explain the more significant potential investment required in working capital. Notwithstanding the rapid growth of the industry, investments of a few thousand pounds were all that was needed to automate specific processes, while creating the possibility of controlling an expanded network of domestic outworkers.

The crucial ingredients for the shift from model 2 to model 3 were the development of steam power, the spinning-mule and their combined deployment in factories. Boulton & Watt's engines were the best and most efficient on the market. As a consequence of this technical efficiency and the Boulton & Watt

practice of using book credit to generate high implicit rates of return was quite general in the early modern period; D. North, *Discourses upon trade* (London, 1691), p. 7.

4   Chapman has also suggested that inadequate access to working capital finance stunted the growth of the cotton industry. S. D. Chapman, 'Financial restraints on the growth of firms in the cotton industry, 1790–1850', *EcHR* 32 (1979), 50–69.

5   E. Baines, *History of the Cotton Manufacture in Great Britain* (London, 1835), pp. 123–4.

6   Wadsworth and Mann, *The Cotton Trade*, pp. 479–80.

7   R. Marsden, *Cotton Spinning: Its Development, Principles and Practice* (London, 1884), pp. 226–30.

8   S. D. Chapman, 'Fixed Capital Formation in the British Cotton Industry, 1770–1815', *EcHR* 23 (1970), 235–53, at p. 252.

patent, which was established in 1773 and renewed for twenty-five years in 1775, the new engines were relatively expensive. In Lancashire, water power was less efficient, but a much cheaper alternative technology available to the industrialists of the rapidly developing cotton industry.[9] Boulton & Watt, therefore, did not try to penetrate the Lancashire market other than by contracting with the larger manufacturers, whose scale could justify the expense of the investment. Watt's son and successor, James Watt Junior acknowledged that cheaper engines, whether Newcomen, Savery, watermills or copies of Boulton & Watt designs, were available at discounts of £200 to £300. Arkwright and Simpson set up the first steam-powered cotton mill at Shudehill, Manchester in 1783.

Notwithstanding their relative expense, Drinkwater's Manchester Mill was the first to install a Boulton & Watt engine in 1789. Other factory owners installed a further thirty-two engines in other Manchester mills before 1800.[10] Crompton's mule, introduced in 1779, made possible the automation of finer counts of yarn. As mule technology developed, the water frame, which could not spin fine counts, became increasingly confined to warp spinning. By the 1790s, the mule was generating rapid productivity gains, particularly for higher count yarns. However, because of the capital outlay required, the new technique did not have a significant impact until the late 1780s.[11] Even in 1788, spinning-jennies accounted for £141,000 of capital investment compared with £55,000 for mule spinning, which in 1795 was still workshop-based. It was around this time that the earliest experiments in the application of steam power to mule spinning occurred.[12] By 1811, mules had substantially replaced spinning-jennies, and Arkwright water spinners accounted for less than 10% of total capacity.[13] The effects of these developments were highly significant. Commenting on the 'golden age' of cotton, Arnold Toynbee noted the rapid growth of the 1790s and early 1800s, and how new technology in spinning and weaving, and the application of steam power, impacted decisively.[14]

9   K. Marx, *Capital III* (London, 1984), pp. 641–8.

10   M. M. Edwards, *The Growth of the British Cotton Trade, 1780–1815* (Manchester, 1967), p. 206; A. E. Musson and E. Robinson, 'The early growth of steam power', *EcHR* 11 (1959), 418–39, at p. 423; Baines, *History of the Cotton Manufacture*, p. 226.

11   R. C. Allen, *The British Industrial Revolution in Global Perspective* (Cambridge, 2009), Figure 8.2, p. 208. Edwards, *Growth of the British Cotton Trade*, pp. 4–5. G. Timmins, 'Technological change', *The Lancashire Cotton Industry: A History Since 1700*, ed., M. B. Rose (Preston, 1996), pp. 29–62; M. Huberman, *Escape from the Market: Negotiating Work in Lancashire* (Cambridge, 1996), p. 11.

12   S. D. Chapman and J. Butt, 'The Cotton Industry, 1775–1856', *Studies in Capital Formation in the United Kingdom, 1750–1920*, ed. C. Feinstein and S. Pollard (Oxford, 1988), pp. 105–25, at pp. 109–10; Huberman, *Escape from the Market*, p. 11. R. L. Hills, *Power in the Industrial Revolution* (Manchester, 1970), p. 123.

13   Calculated from: G. W. Daniels, 'Samuel Crompton's census of the cotton industry in 1811', *Economic Journal* 40 (Supplement) (1930), 107–10, at p. 108.

14   A. Toynbee, *Lectures on The Industrial Revolution in England* (1887; reprinted Cambridge, 2011), pp. 28, 50.

Early experiments in steam-powered mule spinning were centred on Manchester and further assisted by the development of infrastructure. For example, the canal network was enhanced by the joining of the Rochdale and Bridgewater canals at Castlefield basin in 1804, which provided specific impetus to the development of Manchester as a centre of production and distribution. Canals were crucial, and adjacent factories and warehouses commanded higher values than those further afield. The new infrastructure thus facilitated the acquisition of coal and the distribution of output.[15]

Once entrepreneurs established steam-powered mule spinning, the subsequent developments and critical features of model 4 were the introduction of power looms and the development of the railway network. A further decisive improvement was the patenting of the 'self-acting' mule by Richard Roberts in 1825.[16] Self-actors made adjustments so that the speed of revolution of the spindle accorded with the diameter of the thread to produce a consistent yarn, removing the need for manual assistance. Not all spinning production switched to the mule. In coarser warp spinning in particular, continuous spinning methods developed from Arkwright's water frame, which, as steam power replaced water power, became known as the 'throstle' due to the singing noise it made when running at high speed. The throstle had the advantage of producing stronger yarns that were needed once steam power was applied to weaving.[17] For some time, productivity improvements in spinning further expanded the number of handloom weavers, which did not peak until the 1820s.[18] The firm of Horrockses, Miller & Co. of Preston developed an improved power loom in 1813, but the machine suffered mechanical problems until the early 1830s. Even so, between 1820 and 1835, power-loom productivity increased by a factor of three.[19] Chapman suggests significant imperfections and uncertainties in cotton and credit markets before 1815, which were eased subsequently by the development of bank credit and the emergence of specialist providers of finance for exports.[20] During this time, the railway network was established, which

15 P. Maw, *Transport and the Industrial City: Manchester and the Canal Age, 1750–1850* (Manchester, 2013). P. Maw, T. Wyke and A. Kidd, 'Canals, rivers, and the industrial city: Manchester's industrial waterfront, 1790–1850', *EcHR* 65 (2012), 1495–1523.

16 Marsden, *Cotton Spinning*, pp. 226–30.

17 W. S. Murphy, *The Textile Industries: A Practical Guide to Fibres Yarns and Fabrics*, vol. 3 (London, 1910), p. 68. T. Ellison, *The Cotton Trade of Great Britain: Including a History of the Liverpool Cotton Market and of the Liverpool Cotton Brokers' Association* (London, 1886), p. 32.

18 B. Mitchell and P. Deane, *Abstract of British Historical Statistics* (Cambridge, 1962), p. 376. For example, cotton spinner and handloom calico manufacturer and commission agent George Smith of the firm Jas. Massey & Son employed more handloom weavers in 1833 than he had in 1825; *Select Committee on Manufactures, Commerce and Shipping*, BPP, 1833, 690, ev. Smith, qq.9339, p. 565.

19 M. Berg, *The Age of Manufactures, 1700–1820: Industry, Innovation and Work in Britain* (New York, 2005), pp. 245–6.

20 Chapman, 'Financial Restraints'.

further reduced transport costs and facilitated the development of cotton and
yarn markets in Liverpool and Manchester.

Each model of industrialization posed differing requirements in terms of
capital. In general, firms featuring in model 1 were not necessarily smaller than
model 4 firms. The scale of model 1 firms could be equally significant in terms
of investments in working capital and warehouse capacity. Through the transitions from models 1 to 4, however, the balance of capital requirements shifted.
Working capital predominated in model 1 and to some extent in model 2, given
the relatively modest fixed capital requirements in Arkwright-type watermills
and their ability to support much larger pre-existing domestic weaving
networks. The transition from model 2 to model 3 required a substantial step
increase in fixed capital such that, for the first time, concentrated industrial
capital became dominant.

A further feature of the models in Table 1 is the role and character of entrepreneurship. The relatively rapid transition between stages provided distinct
advantages to entrepreneurs who could foresee possible trajectories, work
in tandem with inventors and engineers, and mobilize the required financial
resources. The risk was high, as once entrepreneurs had sunk capital into a
particular model, the impending next phase threatened to destroy competitive
advantage and create stranded assets. These factors combined explain the
Schumpeterian characteristics frequently attributed to early cotton entrepreneurs. However, the ownership and control features of the transitional models
offer a further dimension to these characterizations. Through command over
financial resources, associations with innovators, or the power brokers of infrastructure development, entrepreneurs could secure significant control over one
component of the value chain. Although rarely amounting to more than local
monopolization, such control could nonetheless guarantee supply or demand,
thereby stabilizing output levels and mitigating the risk of fixed cost investment.

Moreover, control of one component provided opportunities to construct
strategic alliances with those controlling other components, leading to further
stabilization and risk-sharing. Through secure networks of capital accumulation, such alliances could now influence the character of and potentially form
the next phase of industrialization. Industrial Lancashire, therefore, evolved a
serial model of entrepreneurship, in which incumbents were in a strong position
to benefit from subsequent transitions.

An accounting taxonomy is used to analyse the financial records and
financial structures of individual firms. Fixed capital can thus be broken down
into categories of land, factories and machinery, and working capital into
stocks, trade receivables and cash balances. In a similar vein, the financing
of these groups of assets can be analysed in terms of trade payables, short-
and long-term loans, and equity investments, typically in the form of business
partnerships. Credit cycles, from the production of cotton goods, through the
invoicing of customers to the receipt of cash and the payment of suppliers, can

be quantified and further analysed in terms of network connections through value chains of customers, suppliers and finance providers. Serial partnership structures allowed entrepreneurs to bypass joint-stock organization and exploit horizontal and vertical linkages with other individuals and firms. In some respects, therefore, a focus on entrepreneurs and their networks is more appropriate than on firms.

The use of accounting categories to analyse changes through time for individual firms offers several advantages and potential insights. First, it highlights the effects of technological discontinuities on capital accumulation. New inventions created opportunities for entrepreneurs, but only if they could finance the step-cost increase in fixed capital requirements. Second, these step changes in technology created disequilibrium in the productivity of different stages of production at various intervals in preparation, spinning, intermediate processes, weaving and finishing. Stages of production experiencing different levels of automation, therefore, had different requirements for financing at the same time. Automation of one stage may have required fixed capital, but simultaneously expanded the working capital requirements in an adjacent stage. Third, pre-existing networks of credit, in the form of working capital, created potential sources of finance for fixed capital investments as inventions sequentially automated production. Finally, historians commonly note the fragmentary evidence on the capital of individual firms in the pre-industrial period,[21] and the chapter addresses this deficiency. Prior studies, by contrast, often rely on aggregate data, of capital stock, number of factories, number of spindles and looms, raw cotton consumption and cotton goods exports.[22]

The detailed business history of the firm Cardwell, Birley & Hornby, its successor partnerships and broader network, offer a useful illustration of the growth stages in Table 1. The case also sets a standard of comparison for further individual studies later in the chapter. The Cardwell, Birley & Hornby story takes us through each of the models of industrial organization in Table 1 in detail and explains how the entrepreneurial successes of one phase impacted the transition to the next, covering the period c.1760–1840. There are reasonably consistent financial records surviving for the original firms and their successors during this time.

As a consequence, they have attracted some attention from other studies, most notably Edwards, with a focus on the period 1780–1815, Aspin on the 1780s and 1790s, and Clark on the period 1795–1840. By examining the long-run

---

21   For example, Wadsworth and Mann, *The Cotton Trade*, p. 250, referring to typical Manchester businesses c.1760, and Chapman, 'Fixed Capital Formation', p. 235.

22   Chapman and Butt, 'The Cotton Industry'; N. F. R. Crafts, 'Productivity growth in the industrial revolution: A new growth accounting perspective', *JEH* 64 (2004), 521–35; Chapman, 'Fixed Capital Formation'.

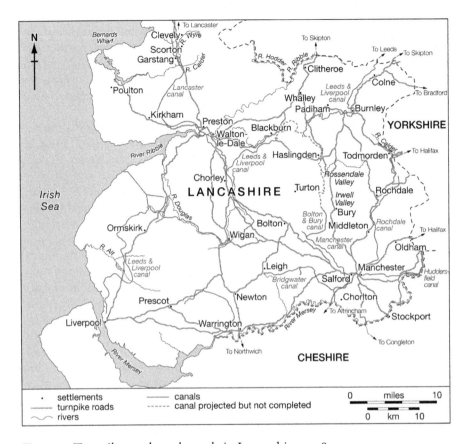

Figure 1. Turnpike roads and canals in Lancashire, c.1804

Note: Based on 'A New Map of the County Palatine of Lancaster', in *Smith's English Atlas* (London, 1804).

financial history of the firm with an emphasis on the models and transitions in Table 1, the account that follows is intended to complement these earlier studies using further archival evidence.[23] The narrative takes us on a journey from rural west Lancashire to the industrial metropolis of industrial Manchester, charting the business and financial strategies of the entrepreneurs. The maps in Figures 1 and 2 highlight the key locations that feature in this narrative.

23 Edwards, *Growth of the British Cotton Trade*; C. Aspin, *The Water-Spinners* (Helmshore, 2003); S. Clark, 'Chorlton Mills and their neighbours', *Industrial Archaeology Review*, 1978, 207–39; Cardwell, Birley & Hornby, Ledgers, stock books and inventories of Lancashire cotton manufacturers, Messrs Cardwell, Birley & Hornby of Blackburn, 1768–1858, WP, Eng. MS, 1208.

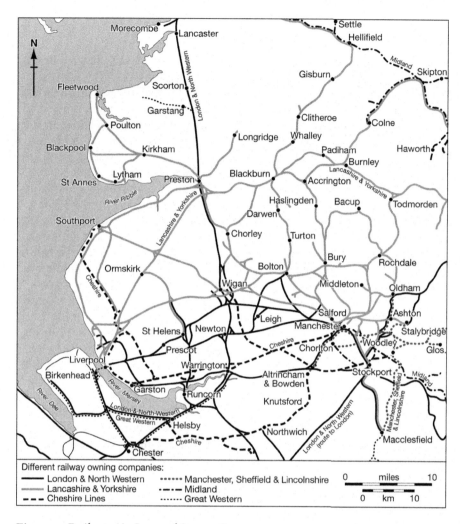

Figure 2. Railways in Lancashire, c.1890

Note: Based on "Lancashire and Yorkshire Railway and its Connections' (1915), Lancashire and Yorkshire railway map, 1998-8534, Science Museum Group Collection Online, https://collection.sciencemuseumgroup.org.uk/objects/co439974, accessed 10 January 2020.

Cardwell, Birley & Hornby, and successors, 1760–1840

In the early eighteenth century, the Cardwell family had established a putting-out network for the production of 'fustian' Blackburn checks.[24] It was a logical extension of the established flax importation and linen manufacturing business centred on Kirkham, in the Fylde. The partners thus had strong business and family connections with several merchant partnerships focused on Kirkham and also trading through associated businesses with the West Indies and the Baltic.[25] In 1767 a new partnership was formed between Richard Cardwell (1749–1824), Richard Birley (1743–1812) and 'the heirs of J. Shepherd', subsequently replaced by John Thornton, with a capital of £12,000.[26] The new partners looked to the opportunities offered by the cotton trade and moved from the Fylde to Blackburn.[27] The original features of the business thus confirm the view that, notwithstanding the low fixed capital requirements of the early industrial revolution, relatively few new entrepreneurs entered from outside the traditional textile trades such as fustians, suggesting that prior understanding of marketing and finance networks were necessary conditions for business success.[28] However, their move, unfortunately, coincided quite closely with a wave of unrest that followed James Hargreaves' invention of the spinning-jenny in 1764 and culminated in riots in the Blackburn district in 1768 and 1769, causing Hargreaves to flee to Nottingham. There were further disturbances in 1779.[29]

Notwithstanding this climate, Cardwell and Birley were keen to expand their business. Unsurprisingly their focus was on extending the pre-established network of domestic weavers. To facilitate this, the new partners were active in promoting and developing transport infrastructure. Shortly after forming the new Blackburn partnership, Cardwell and Birley both became trustees of the Skipton and Walton le Dale turnpike, formed in 1755, which received legislative approval for conversion of existing routes in the same year. They located their weaving network in villages and townships close to this route, such as Downham and Ribchester.[30] Richard Arkwright and also Claytons &

24 Fustians combined linen and cotton yarn.

25 F. J. Singleton, 'The Flax Merchants of Kirkham', *Transactions of the Historic Society of Lancashire and Cheshire* 126 (1977), 73–108.

26 Cardwell, Birley & Hornby, list of partnerships, WP, Eng. MS, 1208; Thornton was only listed as a partner for 1768 and there is no record of his involvement thereafter.

27 Singleton, 'The Flax Merchants of Kirkham', p. 101.

28 K. Honeyman, *Origins of Enterprise: Business Leadership in the Industrial Revolution* (Manchester, 1982), p. 164.

29 W. A. Abram, *A History of Blackburn: Town and Parish* (Blackburn, 1877), p. 205. Wadsworth and Mann, *The Cotton Trade*, pp. 479–80.

30 In 1767 and 1770 respectively; R. Hart, 'Financing Lancashire's industrial development' (Ph.D. dissertation, University of Central Lancashire, 2006), p. 246. The partners also led the programme of improvement commencing in 1791 (ibid., p. 247). J. Whitely, 'The turnpike era', *Leading the*

Walshman of Keighley and John Wakefield of Burneside near Kendal supplied the yarn.[31] Profitable working of the network had increased the partnership capital to £33,166 by 1784, a growth rate of 6.1% per annum, and the partners reinvested this extra capital in the further expansion of weaving capacity, with numbers of weavers rising from 205 in 1767 to 360 in 1784.[32] As Hobsbawm suggested, the apparent route to industrial expansion in the eighteenth century was not to construct factories, but to extend the domestic system.[33]

In practice, some combination of the two was advantageous. Thus far, the firm grew purely based on investments in working capital, but in 1784 entered a new phase of expansion. There were two dimensions to this: the addition of manufacturing capacity and an extended and reorganized network of domestic weavers. Like Cardwell and Birley before him, John Hornby (1763–1841) had left Kirkham in 1779 for Blackburn to train as a merchant and secured further capital following the death of his father in 1784.[34] The admission of Hornby to the partnership funded limited investment in fixed capital. Cardwell and Birley, in partnership with Joseph Feilden of Blackburn, had commenced investments in Scorton Mill, near Lancaster, in 1781, utilizing water power from the River Wyre. Hornby purchased Feilden's share in 1784 following his admission to the Cardwell–Birley partnership, at which point the implied value of the mill was £5,233.[35] The amounts invested were cautious and followed the most severe machine-breaking disturbances in Blackburn of 1779.

Further capacity, at the smaller Cleveley Mill, located on the Wyre near Scorton, was added c.1788. Insurance records showed that the firm's two mills were valued in combination at £6,200 in 1794.[36] At the time of John Hornby's admission in 1784, the partners collectively contributed a further £20,000 to the business, which included a new warehouse in Clayton Street, Blackburn,[37]

Way: A History of Lancashire's Roads, ed. A. Crosby (Preston, 1998), pp. 119–82, at p. 140; 28 Geo 2 c. 60. Cardwell, Birley & Hornby, list of weavers, balance sheets, WP, Eng. MS, 1208.

31   Aspin, *The Water-Spinners*, p. 323.

32   Calculated from: Cardwell, Birley & Hornby, list of weavers, balance sheets, WP, Eng. MS, 1208.

33   E. Hobsbawm, *Age of Revolution: 1789–1848* (London, 2010), p. 55.

34   Cardwell, Birley & Hornby, list of partnerships, WP, Eng. MS, 1208; Edwards, *Growth of the British Cotton Trade*, pp. 194, 255. G. J. French, *The Life and Times of Samuel Crompton of Hall-in-the-Wood, Inventor of the Spinning Machine Called the Mule* (London, 1862), p. 271, records Cardwell and Birley making payment to Crompton as beneficiaries of his invention. Singleton, 'The Flax Merchants of Kirkham', p. 102.

35   Feilden's 2/9 share was £1,163. Aspin, *The Water-Spinners*, p. 321.

36   Chapman, 'Fixed capital formation', p. 253. Chapman's aggregate figure is close to the separate valuation details for Scorton and Cleveley referred to by Aspin, *The Water-Spinners*, for 1792, which total £5,000 (£3,500 for Scorton and £1,500 for Cleveley).

37   Additional capital calculated from Cardwell, Birley & Hornby, Balance sheets, WP, Eng. MS, 1208; O. Ashmore, *The Industrial Archaeology of North-west England* (Manchester, 1982), pp. 186–7.

so it is clear, factoring in the Scorton investment, that the partners applied the majority of these funds to the further expansion of working capital. The number of weavers, which refers to a list of outworkers holding yarn at the stock-taking date, increased from 360 in 1784 to 770 by 1788. The evidence also suggests that the number of weavers engaged during an annual cycle was higher than at the stock-takes.[38]

The extended network of weavers posed organizational challenges for the partners. Further expansion in the 1790s was a function of the firm's organization of domestic production networks rather than manufacturing. From 1788, putting out was organized by agents, known as 'Festers'.[39] These were essentially network overseers whose roles were to distribute yarn, advance cash, collect cloth and resolve disputes, and were an organizational innovation of the 1780s/1790s.[40] From the weavers and Festers lists, it is possible to estimate the warps per weaver at around five, providing an insight into the distribution of activity across the network. The number of warps with Festers at the annual stock-take peaked in 1792 at 2,396 out of a total of 3,344.[41] The introduction of the Fester system was, therefore, a response to the increased requirement for supervision of the weaving network of distributors and domestic weavers, following the step expansion of the business with the admission of John Hornby in 1784.[42] Of the agents listed, the two most significant were William Fisher of Walton le Dale and William Haworth of Longridge. The records referred to balances held by agents like Fisher as 'Walton stocks' and 'cash in Fisher's hands'. Fisher owned a warehouse and the balances held by him increased steadily, from £3,395 to £29,596 in 1796, and at that time represented 27% of the total inventory of Cardwell, Birley & Hornby. Little else is known of William Fisher except that Cardwell, Birley & Hornby continued to subcontract with him until at least 1798, on the same scale as before, effectively financed by them and that subsequently in 1805 he is described as a 'cotton manufacturer'.[43]

These activities meant that working capital outlays dwarfed the firm's investment in fixed capital and that of other typical firms of the mid-1790s,

38   Calculations and underlying figures from Cardwell, Birley & Hornby, Balance sheets, WP, Eng. MS, 1208.
39   Cardwell, Birley & Hornby, Lists of weavers, WP, Eng. MS, 1208.
40   Edwards, *Growth of the British Cotton Trade*, p. 9.
41   Cardwell, Birley & Hornby, Lists of weavers, Festers list, WP, Eng. MS, 1208. Employment in the putting-out weaving section of the business peaked in around 1789 and, by that measure, Cardwell, Birley & Hornby was one of the largest firms in the industry: D. Bythell, *The Hand-loom Weavers: A Study in the English Cotton Industry During the Industrial Revolution* (Cambridge, 1969), p. 29. Bythell goes on to list much larger outworking networks than Cardwell, Birley & Hornby, citing Horrockses of Preston with seven thousand workers in 1816 (ibid., p. 30); *Select Committee on the State of the Children Employed in the Manufactories of the United Kingdom*, BPP, 1816, 397, ev. Taylor, p. 495.
42   Cardwell, Birley & Hornby, Festers list, WP, Eng. MS, 1208.
43   *The Monthly Magazine*, Volume 19, Issue 1.

including those investing in steam-powered mills. For the most part, premises were rented, and productive assets located in domestic workers' homes. Stocks and trade receivable balances thus grew to over £200,000 by 1797, a time when the firm's accounts showed only minimal levels of investment in fixed capital.[44]

The Fester system was short-lived. Another reason for the refocus was that there were diseconomies of scale for firms with very large putting-out networks. At around the same time, Samuel Oldknow also used 'managers' to control quality, with apparent success based on the use of accounting records that tracked the flow of goods and recorded the outcomes of visual inspections. Oldknow's network was somewhat smaller than Cardwell, Birley & Hornby, although still significant, rising from ninety weavers in 1784 to three hundred in 1786.[45]

A further fundamental problem arising from the expansion of the Fester-managed outwork system was the pressure it placed on Cardwell, Birley & Hornby's cash flow. The working capital cycle associated with outwork was lengthy[46] and the firm made significant use of bills of exchange for trade finance. The accounts reveal that between 1794 and 1795, inventory increases absorbed almost £30,000 and trade receivables a further £12,000 in negative cash flow.[47] Cash flow pressures and the change in business policy required a financial response from the partners. In the short run, there was a significant increase in the loan account by over £57,000 in 1795. Given the substantial requirement for working capital finance, Cardwell, Birley & Hornby was particularly vulnerable to credit squeezes. In 1796 there was a war-induced national credit squeeze that prompted Prime Minister William Pitt to introduce paper money the following year.[48] Cardwell, Birley & Hornby had already suffered a smaller but significant downturn in 1793 possibly as a consequence of the collapse of Smalley's Bank

44 Edwards, *Growth of the British Cotton Trade*, p. 258 and Cardwell, Birley & Hornby, Balance sheets, WP, Eng. MS, 1208, show minimal fixed capital, with the largest fixed capital balance recorded shown as 'plant' at £1,046, in the 1794 accounts, suggesting that separate books of account were kept for the Scorton and Cleveley operations at this time. Even with a valuation of £6,200, per the insurance records for the two mills (Chapman, 'Fixed capital formation', p. 253), the fixed capital was still only 3% of the total.

45 J. S. Cohen, 'Managers and Machinery: An Analysis of the Rise of Factory Production', *The Textile Industries*, ed. S. D. Chapman (London. 1997), 96–114; R. B. Williams, *Accounting for Steam and Cotton: Two Eighteenth Century Case Studies* (New York, 1997), pp. 87, 105–6.

46 For examples of similar firms, see Bythell, *Hand-loom Weavers*, p. 30.

47 Calculated from data in Cardwell, Birley & Hornby, Ledgers and Stock Book, WP, Eng. MS, 1199/1–6.

48 Invasion threats persisted throughout 1796, leading to hoarding and runs on local banks, and in turn to Pitt's abandonment of gold in February 1797. F. W. Fetter, *Development of British Monetary Orthodoxy, 1797–1875* (Cambridge, MA, 1965), p. 21. H. Thornton, *An Enquiry into the Nature and Effects of the Paper Credit of Great Britain* (1802; reprinted London, 1939), p. 97.

in Blackburn during the crisis of that year.[49] The loan capital was unsecured and depended on trust, and the ability of the firm to at least promise 5% interest, even though they missed payments in some years.[50] In response, the partners divested inventories, which they achieved by discontinuing the Festers. Under the Fester system and after its discontinuation, stocks of warps with weavers fell continuously during the 1790s, from 4,066 in 1789 to 2,687 in 1798, which would be indicative of a reduction in the number of weavers.[51] After 1795, the fall in inventory balances was more than outweighed by increases in trade receivables. In other words, the firm continued to grow but based more on direct sales to third parties and less on the control of goods through the outwork production chain. Notwithstanding these difficulties, the firm maintained an average growth rate of 7.46% in the period 1789–98, somewhat higher than in previous decades.[52]

As a result, the partners were undeterred from further investments and were able to remodel the firm in preparation for a new phase of expansion, which now relied on expanded fixed capital and streamlined holdings of working capital. After 1795 there were no further references to the Festers, and between 1795 and 1798, reduced inventories were concentrated exclusively on Haworth, and particularly Fisher, at Walton le Dale.[53] To place the new business model on a more stable financial footing and to address the issue of the increasing loan account commitment, the partners invested an additional £45,000 in the business in 1797. Some of these funds were used to expand capacity at the Scorton site, which now stood to benefit from the development of the Lancaster Canal. The investment there was increased to £12,000 in 1799, approximately doubling its 1794 value.[54]

Canal transport, in conjunction with the turnpike roads, now offered significant potential advantages to the business. Archibald Hamilton (1740–1819) of Ashton Hall near Lancaster, later the 9th Duke of Hamilton, was the MP for Lancashire from 1768 to 1772, and in 1771 petitioned parliament for the enclosure and improvement of Nether Wyresdale, which included Scorton.[55]

---

49   Chapman, 'Financial restraints', p. 51.

50   Cardwell, Birley & Hornby, Ledgers, WP, Eng. MS, 1199/1–6. The whole of the loan capital was raised from within a thirty-mile radius of Blackburn. Edwards, *Growth of the British Cotton Trade*, p. 256.

51   Cardwell, Birley & Hornby, Festers list, WP, Eng. MS, 1208. Bythell, *Hand-loom Weavers*, p. 29, notes the numbers employed in 1816 were 550.

52   Calculated from WP, Eng. MS, 1208.

53   Cardwell, Birley & Hornby, Festers list, WP, Eng. MS, 1208.

54   Cardwell, Birley & Hornby, Ledgers, WP, Eng. MS, 1199/1–6. Cardwell, Birley & Hornby accounts show £7,000 invested by Cardwell and £5,000 jointly by Birley and Hornby.

55   Sir Samuel Egerton Brydges, *A Biographical Peerage of the Empire of Great Britain*, vol. 1 (London, 1808), pp. 92–3; *Gentleman's Magazine*, January–June 1819, vol. 89, pp. 275–6; 'A petition', *House of Commons Sessional Papers*, BPP, 1791, 33, 28 January, pp. 94–5.

Subsequently, as leaseholders, Cardwell and Birley were granted surrenders by Hamilton for watercourse development at the Scorton site.[56] Once the mills were established, yarn could be sent south via the Lancaster Canal to connect with the Ribble at Preston, and Walton le Dale, where the turnpike and subsequently the Leeds and Liverpool Canal provided connections to Blackburn. There, the partnership's Brookhouse site was near to the Whalley road, turnpiked in 1776, and was subsequently close to the Blackburn–Bolton turnpike road, approved between 1797 and 1801.[57] The Lancaster Canal secured Parliamentary approval in 1792 and, when completed in 1803, featured a tramroad connecting the canal to Walton Summit and the southern section, which later became part of the Leeds and Liverpool Canal.[58] The partners stood to gain from these developments and the accounts show that surplus capital in the business was invested in the Leeds and Liverpool Canal during the 1790s.[59]

From 1799 onwards, Blackburn and particularly Manchester became the scene of the next important phase of development for the Cardwell, Birley & Hornby partners, families and associates. Cotton spinning developed rapidly in Manchester in the 1790s with the introduction of steam engines, typically supplied and installed by Boulton & Watt. An associate of the Boulton & Watt partnership, the engineer George Augustus Lee was a pioneer in the application of steam power to mule spinning.[60] In 1792 he was recruited as managing partner by the influential merchant and later politician George Philips, who had set up a water-powered mule-spinning mill in Salford a year earlier,[61] and the firm Philips & Lee commenced steam-powered production in 1794 with a capital of £21,697. New steam mills built on this model required larger fixed capital than before, reflecting the cost of engines and associated components.

The Cardwell, Birley & Hornby partners were, therefore, now contemplating investment on a similar scale. Even with the added costs relative to

56   Aspin, *The Water-Spinners*, p. 321.
57   D. Beattie, *Blackburn: The Development of a Lancashire Cotton Town* (Blackburn, 1992), p. 50; The Blackburn–Bolton turnpike was developed through a realignment of the existing route in 1797 (37 Geo. 3 c. 173) and a further Act in 1801 (41 Geo. 3 c. 123). W. Albert, *The Turnpike Road System in England: 1663–1840* (Cambridge, 1972), p. 218.
58   Westmoreland Canals Act 1792, 32 Geo. 3 c. 101; R. W. Rennison, *Civil Engineering Heritage: Northern England* (London, 1996), p. 206. Other sections of the Birley and Hornby trading empire already used the completed section of the canal to ship goods from Hull as far as Kildwick, near Skipton. Singleton, 'The Flax Merchants of Kirkham', p. 91.
59   Cardwell, Birley & Hornby, ledgers and stock book, WP, Eng. MS, 1199/1–6.
60   Lee was recognised as one of the leading managers in the trade and pioneered the use of gas lighting and Boulton & Watt engines for mule spinning: A. C. Howe, *The Cotton Masters, 1830–1860* (Oxford, 1984), p. 316.
61   D. Brown, 'From "Cotton Lord" to Landed Aristocrat: the Rise of Sir George Philips Bart., 1766–1847', *Historical Research* 69 (1996), 62–82, at p. 64. S. D. Chapman, *Merchant Enterprise in Britain* (Cambridge, 2004), p. 64. Philips & Lee, Abstracts of Accounts, DR 198/167, 1 December 1815.

Scorton, the fixed capital requirement was small in the context of their broader business interests and prior investments in working capital and domestic weaving networks. Hitherto, yarn was supplied to the partnership's Blackburn operation, inter alia by Robert Owen, and Thomas Atkinson's Chorlton Twist Mill in Manchester. In 1795, Atkinson purchased a Boulton & Watt engine on behalf of the Chorlton partnership. In doing so he requested an extended credit period from Boulton & Watt, citing the similar discount period required by customers in Scotland.[62] From 1802, in partnership with Peter Marsland, two of Richard Birley's sons, Joseph Birley (1782–1847) and Hugh Hornby ('H. H.') Birley (1778–1845), had built up a new six-storey mill in nearby Oxford Road with a Boulton & Watt engine costing £2,000 and the latest machinery.[63] H. H. in particular made significant investments in Manchester during this period. In addition to his factory developments, he also had a house and warehouse in Manchester. Following the death of Samuel Marsland in 1803, he ran, and further developed the adjacent Marsland Mills on behalf of Marsland's young sons.[64] Owen maintained his interest in Chorlton until 1809 when he moved the business to New Lanark and sold Chorlton Mill to Joseph Birley and H. H. Hornby for c.£20,000.[65] The value of Chorlton Mill was, therefore, comparable to the initial investment of Philips & Lee at Salford in 1794.

As had been the case with their earlier business models, the Cardwell, Birley & Hornby partners now set about preparing the ground for investment in Manchester by securing influence over the required infrastructure. After all, the purchase of Chorlton Mill represented a further step in the proprietorial integration of cotton production in what remained a highly dispersed geographical network. Chorlton Mill was adjacent to the new turnpike road (Oxford Street) and close to the Rochdale Canal, completed in 1804 with a connection to the Bridgewater Canal. In turn, the canal facilitated the transport of coal into Manchester.[66] These links promoted the development of the industrial suburb of Chorlton on Medlock.

In the short run, activities in Manchester complemented the more dispersed Blackburn side of the Birley & Hornby business. The transfer of yarn output from Chorlton to Blackburn was facilitated by the development of canal links

---

62   W. H. Chaloner, 'Robert Owen, Peter Drinkwater and the early factory system in Manchester, 1788–1800, *Industry and Innovation: Selected Essays W. H. Chaloner*, ed. D. A. Farnie and W. O. Henderson (London, 1990), chapter 8.

63   The development was the nucleus of what became Oxford Road Mills. Clark, 'Chorlton Mills', pp. 211–12.

64   The mill was established in 1797 by Samuel Marsland with an insurance value of £11,000. In 1801 this value had risen to £16,200, including £900 for stock and a warehouse worth £3,000; Clark, 'Chorlton Mills', p. 208.

65   The sale of the share in Oxford Road realized £21,275; Clark, 'Chorlton Mills', p. 213.

66   Maw, *Transport and the Industrial City*. Chaloner, 'Robert Owen, Peter Drinkwater and the early factory system in Manchester', p. 175.

between Salford and Bolton, which in turn offered a turnpike road link to Blackburn.[67] The death of Richard Birley in 1812 led to the creation of a new partnership of John Hornby, John Birley (1775–1831), H. H. Birley and Joseph Birley, effectively uniting the Blackburn and Manchester operations. Even so, H. H. and Joseph retained specific control of Chorlton, assisted by their new partner, engineer Benjamin Kirk. These mills were used to produce cotton yarn for onward processing at the Blackburn facility. Other significant customers included Swainson of Preston and Webster Fishwick of Burnley, who, with his brother George, had taken over Scorton Mill in 1809.[68] The Manchester Exchange, which was actively promoted among other things by H. H. Birley and John Marsland, opened in 1809 and served as a further outlet for yarn sales.[69] The partners purchased the cotton on behalf of the firm.[70]

The principal focus of the new Birley & Hornby partnership was now on the expansion of steam-powered, mule-spinning factory capacity centred on Manchester. By 1812 Birley & Hornby had £66,057 invested in Chorlton Mill, consisting of £31,161 fixed capital and £34,896 working capital. In 1813, the mill was valued at £40,000 for insurance purposes. These significant investments made sense in the context of the alternative to continue water spinning at Scorton, which still held certain advantages. Although the distance was greater, transport costs were reduced, because most of the journey was via the Lancaster Canal, which offered a lower rate per mile to locations convenient for Walton, Preston and export markets. If goods were transported on to Blackburn, a higher cost per mile via turnpike would be needed. Even if all Scorton's output was sent to Blackburn, the combined canal and road cost was lower. By contrast, in the absence of a convenient canal route, Chorlton's production could only be sent using more expensive road transport. Scorton also offered a direct saving of coal costs. Even so, these advantages were overwhelmingly outweighed by the cheaper unit cost of production at Chorlton. Birley's calculations showed 40s yarn produced at Chorlton in 1812 cost 30d/lb, and this can be compared with the open market cost of 42d. The difference per pound, extrapolated to

---

67   Manchester, Bolton and Bury Canal Act 1791 (31 Geo. 3 c. 68); This section opened in 1797, but a proposed connection to the Leeds and Liverpool Canal was never built: see P. Hindle *Manchester, Bolton and Bury Canal through Time* (Stroud, 2013).

68   Aspin, *The Water-Spinners*, p. 323; A. Hewitson ['Atticus'], *Our Country Churches and Chapels* (London, 1872), p. 524. BCP, ledger 1819, UF-1. Webster Fishwick, a tanning and textile merchant, was the son of James Fishwick of Padiham, who in the 1790s had acted as a Fester agent in the Birley & Hornby putting-out network.

69   Anon., *Copy of the Demise of the Manchester Exchange* (Manchester, 1810).

70   The point can be inferred from the accounts because in June 1828, balances from the partners account were transferred to the warehouse account. This amount represented the purchasing activities by the partners on behalf of the firm as, subsequent to the transfer, most of the balance that previously appeared to the credit of the partners appears to the credit of the warehouse account. BCP, Chorlton Mill ledger, 1824–1840, UF-2.

yarn sales and output data for Chorlton Mill No. 1, suggests an annual cost-saving of around £30,000. The additional turnpike transport cost would have been about £500.[71]

These investments and the rapid increase in asset values were a function of scale and layout, which facilitated lighting and fireproofing. A much larger engine of one hundred horsepower was installed the following year, costing £3,970, with a further £14,000 on other machinery and £5,000 on installation wages.[72] Construction began on Chorlton New Mill in 1813, which was completed in 1817, with the assistance of Kirk.[73] Kirk liaised with Boulton & Watt on the installation of the new steam engine in 1813 and also with Peter Ewart on factory equipment issues.

The partners financed the expansion from their own funds. Although 1814 had been a particularly profitable year realizing a surplus of over £26,000, the accumulated profits of the old mill were not sufficient to cover the total outlay, which required a further contribution of £46,698 partners' capital in 1817. The completed (new) mill was valued at £66,000 in 1817 and the old mill at £30,000. In 1819 the two mills were valued at £98,750. The total capital invested at this time was £161,000.[74]

Fixed capital now overtook working capital investment, with further step expansions of the mill capacity. Thus, even after the completion of the investment in the old mill in 1812, fixed capital made up less than half (47.1%) the total. By 1819 the equivalent percentage had increased to 61.5%. In the space of seven years, Birley & Hornby increased fixed capital by a factor of 3 and their personal capital by a factor of 2.5.[75] Yarn sales also increased by a factor of 3, but working capital balances remained relatively constant in the case of inventories and less than doubling in the case of other circulating capital. These numbers imply that the flow of materials and work in progress through the mills became much more efficient as a result of the new investment. Also, the credit collection period from customers was now much shorter, bearing in

---

71   Data for these estimates taken from *Select Committee into the Present State of Affairs of the East India Company*, BPP, 1830, 646, ev. J. Kennedy and H. H. Birley; Clark, 'Chorlton Mills', appendix 1; BCP, Mill Ledgers, 1811–1823, UF-1/2; C. K. Harley, 'Was technological change in the early Industrial Revolution Schumpeterian? Evidence of cotton textile profitability', *Explorations in Economic History* 49 (2000), 516–27, table 2; D. Bogart, 'The transport revolution in industrializing Britain: A survey', *The Cambridge Economic History of Modern Britain*, vol. 1: 1700–1870, ed. R. Floud, J. Humphries and P. Johnson (Cambridge, 2014), pp. 368–91, table 2. The example calculations use 40s, a relatively coarse yarn count, so given the greater advantages of mule spinning on finer counts, the cost-saving is a conservative estimate.
72   Clark, 'Chorlton Mills', pp. 213–15.
73   J. A. Cantrell, 'James Nasmyth and the Bridgewater Foundry: Partners and Partnerships', *BH* 23 (1981), 346–58, at pp. 348–9.
74   BCP, ledger, 1817–1819, UF-1.
75   The underlying figures were £31,161/£66,057 and £98,959/£161,012 respectively. BCP, ledger, UF-1.

mind that much of the output was sold within the Birley & Hornby network of connected businesses, particularly in Blackburn. Even so, the significant working capital investment required of the previous generation, in the form of bills of exchange, was now of lesser importance.

McConnel & Kennedy was another Manchester firm that invested at this time in Boulton & Watt steam engines to power mule-spun fine counts. The firm built three new mills in the period 1797–1820. Its capital increased from £1,769 in 1795 to £47,389 in 1803 and £88,374 by 1810.[76] The firm used its manufacturing capacity to specialize in fine spinning and sold its output through a network of agents and brokers using a system of inventory accounts to control assignments and discounts.[77] Even though the firm had substantial capital investments, balances on capital accounts still fluctuated wildly due to ordinary drawings by partners, their salaries and the requirement for capital withdrawals on partner retirements.

Notwithstanding these investments, and similar at other substantial concerns like Murray, the growth rate was lower than Birley & Hornby, and smaller in terms of capital, as the accounting evidence demonstrates. Birley & Hornby were also more significant than other firms in terms of spindles and employment.[78] McConnel & Kennedy has been highlighted as an example of the relative importance of fixed capital investment during this phase of the industrial revolution,[79] and the evidence of capital formation at Birley & Hornby adds weight to this conclusion.

The Birley & Hornby investments at Chorlton prompted further developments. A separate firm, Birley Hornby & Kirk, was now formed to manage the Manchester operation along with further expansion into the Orrell Mills at Stalybridge. In 1821 they went into partnership with the Orrell family, securing a share of two factories of 11,500 mule spindles combined.[80] In 1823 Birley Hornby & Kirk began their investment in power-loom weaving at Chorlton, while the Blackburn firm began its own spinning operation. At the same time, Birley Hornby & Kirk entered their partnership with Charles Macintosh to manufacture rubberized cloth. The chief implication of the Macintosh collaboration was the integration of production using power-loom weaving. The business had long been integrated through joint ownership or formal control of spinning and weaving processes. With the

76   C. H. Lee, *A Cotton Enterprise, 1795–1840: A History of M'Connel & Kennedy Fine Cotton Spinners* (Manchester, 1972), p. 167.
77   G. W. Daniels, 'The early records of a great Manchester cotton spinning firm', *Economic Journal* 25 (1915), 175–88, p. 179; P. Richardson, 'The structure of capital during the industrial revolution revisited: Two case studies from the cotton textile industry', *EcHR* 42 (1989), 484–503.
78   J. Parkinson-Bailey, *Manchester: Architectural History* (Manchester, 2000).
79   Richardson, 'The structure of capital'.
80   Cardwell, Birley & Hornby, Balance sheets, WP, Eng. MS, 1208. I. Miller, *Castle Street Mill and Tame Foundry*, 59 (University of Salford, 2016).

development of power looms and the corresponding decline of handloom weaving, the partnership now set up weaving rooms adjacent to the already established spinning mills.

During this period, the Blackburn side of the business continued to expand, albeit at a slower rate. The firm had meanwhile divested the water-spinning operation at the remote Scorton site, which had not been a success, and there is evidence that the factory was run down before being sold in 1809.[81] The Blackburn partnership now abandoned spinning, presumably because the purchase of Chorlton Mill from Owen in 1809 offered a newer and more efficient alternative source of supply. Meanwhile, the Leeds and Liverpool Canal from the Burnley direction reached Blackburn by 1810 and ran close to the Brookhouse site, then on the eastern edge of Blackburn.[82] Here the partnership now built a sizing house, from where the treated yarn could be distributed to the domestic weaving network, and added a warehouse at Walton. In 1813 Brookhouse was valued at £4,000 and the Walton warehouse at £930.[83] Despite the significant investments at Chorlton in the 1810s, in 1821 the Blackburn business was still the larger of the two in terms of capital invested. The assets of Birley & Hornby were £240,983 and Birley Hornby & Kirk £166,121.[84] Although equivalent in size, the contrast between the geographically dispersed Birley & Hornby network and the concentrated Chorlton mill complex could not have been greater.

The Blackburn partnership, therefore, had a different growth trajectory from Manchester. There was some concentration. In the 1820s, the putting-out network was dismantled and weaving operations were also now centred on Brookhouse. These investments helped increase the total capital employed from £200,000 in 1813 to £260,000 in 1827, an annual equivalent of 1.9%. Notwithstanding the developments at Brookhouse, most of this growth came from investments in circulating capital. During this time, the number of piece goods held followed a cyclical pattern but using peak-to-peak comparisons, approximately doubled, whereas the financial value remained broadly constant. The firm developed export markets in Argentina, Brazil and the Caribbean and was also involved in reciprocal trading of cargoes of sugar. In the years 1824–27 inclusive, exports accounted for 53.2% of total piece stocks held.[85] The effect of these operations was to increase the funding required for working capital even

---

81   Aspin, *The Water-Spinners*, pp. 323–4. Insurance records and physical evidence suggest that Cleveley mill was seriously damaged by fire in 1806.

82   The Leeds and Liverpool Canal, connecting Blackburn east and west, was finally completed in 1816. S. Ville, 'Transport', *The Cambridge Economic History of Modern Britain*, Volume 1, ed. R. Floud and P. Johnson (Cambridge, 2004), 295–331, at p. 299.

83   Clark, 'Chorlton Mills', p. 214; Ashmore, *Industrial Archaeology*, p. 186.

84   Cardwell, Birley & Hornby, Balance sheets, WP, Eng. MS, 1208. BCP, ledger, 1821, UF-1.

85   In 1824 the firm was trading through Buenos Ayres, Bahia and Havana. Percentage calculated from Cardwell, Birley & Hornby, Balance sheets, WP, Eng. MS, 1208.

further. In 1826, total circulating capital balances reached £313,000, mainly as a function of a steep increase in finished goods held for home demand, and most likely due to the tightening of credit that followed the crisis of 1825. Certainly, the firm sustained a large financial loss that year.[86]

At the same time, the Orrell venture recorded successive and sustained losses, beginning in July 1825, and collapsed in 1826 with bad debts. It was effectively bailed out at the cost of £25,506 and reabsorbed by the partnership.[87] In performing this venture capital function, the firm overextended itself. In 1827, £27,519 was extended to the Orrell mill business, £16,779 to McIntosh & Co., and £9,712 to 'foreign adventures'. Even without the direct investments, the firm typically granted six months' credit to customers. As a consequence of these financial pressures, and the need to revalue and reorganize the Chorlton and Stalybridge partnerships to allow Kirk to exit the partnership, the businesses were formally split in 1827. Birley Hornby & Kirk was then valued at £192,100, with Hornby taking away his share worth £61,000.[88]

Notwithstanding the failure at Orrell, H. H. Birley remained all the more committed to investment in plant and industrial infrastructure. After 1827, the Manchester firm was able to rationalize its working capital commitments by selling more of its output directly to the Blackburn operation. The Chorlton site, meanwhile, became increasingly dominated by fixed capital investments during the period 1827–42. Some of these were further direct investments in the Chorlton site, with net fixed capital rising from £69,502 in 1827 to £123,259 in 1837. Taking into account depreciation, gross investment in fixed capital during this period was £135,680, accounting for 62.1% of total assets.[89] The effect of these further sustained investments was that between 1830 and 1850, the Birley complex of mills had the highest rateable value in Manchester.[90] Oxford economist Nassau Senior, on visiting Birley's mills, commented that the principal cause of the increasing ratio of fixed to circulating capital was the displacement of labour with expensive mule spindles. Spinning and weaving were integrated on the same site, although more investment went into the former facilitating significant investments in preparatory and intermediate processes. Senior also noted: 'At Birley's, we found preparation making for a newly invented process, by which the wool was to be conveyed direct from the

---

86   Ibid.
87   BCP, mill ledger, UF-2.
88   In 1827, according to the second ledger (BCP, ledger, 1824–1840, UF-2) and Cardwell, Birley & Hornby, Stock books and ledgers, WP, Eng. MS, 1199/1–6, 1208. The owners of the successor partnership to Cardwell, Birley & Hornby were the same as Birley & Co.: i.e. John Hornby, John Birley, H. H. Birley and Joseph Birley, with Benjamin Kirk as managing partner at the latter up to 1827. By December 1827, John Hornby had left both partnerships according to these sources.
89   Calculated from quarterly and six-monthly stock accounts, BCP, mill ledger, UF-2.
90   Maw et al., 'Canals, rivers, and the industrial city'.

willow to the blowing machine, without requiring, as it now does, a whole set
of work-people for that purpose.'[91]

Despite these critical investments, the overall growth rate of capital invested
at Chorlton was unspectacular. H. H. Birley's personal capital declined significantly after 1840, notwithstanding his commitment to further investments in
machinery improvements.[92] In the twelve years between 1827 and 1840, the
average growth rate of the total invested capital was less than 1%. As Chorlton
increased its investment in plant and machinery, in similar measure, working
capital investments were reduced. Factory stocks were a small proportion
throughout, but there were large reductions in the value of goods in the
warehouse, suggesting that as the firm became more capital-intensive it also
achieved economies in selling and distribution.[93] A further reason for slow
overall growth was that the Birleys now began to diversify their investments.
Their collaboration with McIntosh & Co. led to a significant increase in capital,
from £24,346 in 1834, the year before steam power was introduced, to £115,237
in 1843.[94]

Even with these activities, by the 1830s, the Birley partnership had spare
capital with which they began to diversify their investments, and subsequently
used it to support the construction of foundries. The partners only briefly
invested in James Nasmyth's foundry at Patricroft in 1837, and a year later
shifted their support to John George Bodmer. As a textile machinery inventor
operating in adjacent premises, Bodmer was of more direct potential benefit to
the partnership and its commitment to investment in process improvement.[95]

Consistent with earlier phases of expansion, Birley and his wider business
connections once again used his political and financial influence to promote
infrastructure. In 1826 he was listed as a supporter of the Act to build the
Liverpool and Manchester Railway.[96] Also involved with the management of
the railway was Peter Ewart, who had assisted Birley and Kirk, McConnel
& Kennedy, and Samuel Greg with steam engine installations.[97] Members of
the wider Birley and Hornby families dominated the board of the Liverpool–

---

91   Clark, 'Chorlton Mills', p. 219; N. W. Senior and L. Horner, *Letters on the Factory Act, as it
affects the Cotton Manufacture, Addressed to the Right Honourable the President of the Board of
Trade* (London, 1837), pp. 5–6. While no doubt impressed by the technology, these observations
were a crucial ingredient of Senior's famous 'last hour' theory, in which capital investment created
pressure to extend working time, a theme explored further below in chapter 3.

92   Clark, 'Chorlton Mills', p. 231.

93   BCP, mill ledger, UF-2.

94   Clark, 'Chorlton Mills', p. 235.

95   BCP, mill ledger, UF-2; Clark, 'Chorlton Mills', p. 229.

96   7 Geo. 4 c. 49: *List of petitioners*.

97   M. C. Jacob, *The First Knowledge Economy: Human Capital and the European Economy,
1750–1850* (Cambridge, 2014). A. Redford, *Manchester Merchants and Foreign Trade* (Manchester,
1934), p. 230. Note also Ewart's collaboration with Kennedy in the valuation of Quarry Bank
Mill in 1831: GP, Mill valuation, C5/1/1/3.

Manchester railway before amalgamation.[98] Other family members joined boards of railways that were of strategic significance to the Birley enterprises and which in many ways mirrored the earlier turnpike road and canal-based network. These included lines connecting the Fylde and Wyre estuaries to Preston, further connections to Manchester, and connections to Blackburn and towns along the route of the Preston to Skipton turnpike road.[99]

The Blackburn side of the original partnership pursued a similar if separate, path of expansion to that followed in Manchester. The firm made significant subsequent investments in mill capacity at Brookhouse in 1828.[100] Like Chorlton, the expansion of Brookhouse, under the direction of William Henry Hornby, contributed to the industrial development of Blackburn, introducing the most significant improvements and assisting their diffusion for the wider benefit of other firms and the town as a whole.[101] The partners purchased the cotton on behalf of the firm.[102] Assisting Hornby was his partner and inventor of various improvements in weaving technology, William Kenworthy.[103] Brookhouse Mill had already benefited from its convenient location adjacent to Blackburn's main turnpike roads and canal. In 1844, a new company was formed for the construction of a railway between Blackburn and Bolton. W. H. Hornby was the founding chairman of the company and Blackburn was duly connected to the wider railway network in 1846.[104] Following its establishment by amalgamation in 1847, Hornby served as a director of the Lancashire & Yorkshire Railway Company for several years.[105]

98   *Return of Joint Stock Companies Registered under Act 7 & 8 Victoria*, BPP, 1846, 110, William Birley, John Hornby, Joseph Hornby, Hugh Hornby.

99   Ibid. The Fleetwood-on-Wyre & Clithero Railway Co.: Hugh Hornby, Thomas Birley, Thomas Langton Birley, Charles Birley, Edmund Birley, William Birley. Goole, Doncaster and Sheffield & Manchester Junction Railway Co., and Manchester, Huddersfield & Great Grimsby Direct Railway Co.: Joseph Birley. Oxford, Newbury, Andover, Manchester & Southampton Junction Railway Co.: Richard Birley. Manchester, Southampton & Poole Railway Co.: Joseph Hornby. Liverpool, Preston & North Union Junction Railway Co., now called the Preston & North Union Junction Railway Co., with an extension to Blackburn and branches to Southport and Wigan: William Birley Junior and Thomas Langton Birley. Manchester & Wigan Railway Co.: William Henry Hornby.

100   Edwards, *Growth of the British Cotton Trade*, p. 255.

101   *Blackburn Standard*, 9 March 1853.

102   The point can be inferred from the accounts, because in June 1828 balances from the partners account were transferred to the warehouse account. This amount represented the purchasing activities by the partners on behalf of the firm since, subsequent to the transfer, most of the balance that previously appeared to the credit of the partners appears to the credit of the warehouse account. BCP, Mill ledger, 1821–1844, UF-2.

103   W. Kenworthy, *Inventions and Hours of Labour: A Letter to Master Cotton Spinners, Manufacturers, and Millowners in General* (Blackburn, 1842).

104   Abram, *History of Blackburn*, p. 244.

105   See annual editions from the late 1840s and early 1850s of *Bradshaw's Shareholders Guide, Railway Manual and Directory*.

The business history of the Cardwell, Birley & Hornby partnerships, 1767–1842, provides detailed illustrations of the transitional business models set out in Table 1. The transitions between the models also reveal differential growth patterns. Early growth was a matter of expanding a pre-existing credit network utilizing improvements in mostly road infrastructure. Fixed capital was minimal and the investment required for water spinning at Scorton was not so much larger than earlier Wyatt and Paul mills. Even so, the capital growth rate was impressive and, although confined to working capital, outstripped the comparable growth rates of fixed capital investment in later phases. In part, this was because capital investment followed a step pattern and was closely concentrated in certain years. These step increases featured in the modernization of Chorlton No. 1 and the Chorlton New Mill, and were comparable at the installation of steam-powered mule spinning at Salford Mill in the early 1800s. These developments aside, investment in factory capacity further augmented working capital requirements. Small investments, which automated certain parts of the spinning process, could lead to a disproportionate expansion of the credit network. There was a spectrum of reasons for this, ranging from large and extended domestic outworking networks to dependency on long credit cycles offered to overseas customers. Independent of these features, the Chorlton accounts reveal the much lower working capital investment required when there was a specific customer within the partnership structure who could be relied upon to settle accounts quickly. Moreover, the credit cycle was speeded up to some extent by the proximity of partnership network business locations to the new road and canal infrastructure developments. These relationships suggest that had there been deep and liquid markets for their output, the cotton factories of the 1800s would have been dominated, for the first time, by fixed capital investment requirements.

'Take-off' investments: further examples

Whereas the Cardwell, Birley & Hornby example is reasonably comprehensive in terms of Table 1, most other cases are more specific to models and transitions. There are also cases of failure to transition at all. Some businesses, often centred on mills in remote or peripheral areas, did not progress from phase 2 into phase 3. Samuel Oldknow had ambitious plans, but financial mismanagement thwarted his plans for a rapid transition to steam-powered mule spinning.

In the period 1784–92, the water-powered Eccleston Cotton Mill had gross capital of £7,340, comprising fixed capital of £2,340, according to the initial outlay in 1784, and trade debtors of £5,000. The mill was sold in 1793 at a net worth of £4,200, suggesting third-party creditors of around £3,000 and a net working capital investment of £2,000.[106] The mill went through a succession of further owners before its final proprietors moved cotton production away from the St Helens area in the early 1820s.[107]

Like St Helens, in the latter half of the eighteenth century, Oldham was peripheral to the main centres of textile production and distribution. In 1760, Oldham was relatively isolated with few sources of water power and underdeveloped transport.[108] The example of James Lees and Wallshaw Mill, therefore, illustrates the trajectory of a model 1 business, with few apparent sources of competitive advantage. However, unlike Eccleston, Wallshaw sustained a series of transitions and provided further illustration of the phases of industrialization indicated in Table 1. In contrast to Cardwell, Birley & Hornby, James Lees had no access to a previously established network of mercantile connections.

Wallshaw Mill was established in 1777 and was one of the first firms to adopt 'Dutch wheels' in warp spinning. It was only several years later that the firm emerged as one of the few in the Oldham district to employ more than a hundred.[109] It was on one of the few sites that possessed access to water power, which Lees introduced after relying on horsepower in the early phases of the development of the mill.[110] In 1795 Lees insured his factory, associated fixed stock and goods for £2,050, compared with an average of £1,503 for other Oldham firms.[111] Lees was not part of a more extensive financial network, and there is nothing about this business that necessitated significant investment in working capital. So, although one of the largest firms in the area, this scale of investment compares with the mid-century Wyatt and Paul mills, suggesting relatively little growth in firm-level fixed stock investments in the latter half of the eighteenth century.

The adoption of steam power fundamentally altered these financial relationships. In 1808, James, in partnership with Robert Lees, transferred his by now more substantial investment into a new factory, financed by a mixture of accumulated capital and subsequent family relationships, which allowed James to invest in machinery using rented premises. The factory owner was Joseph Jones, whose family had accrued substantial wealth from the coal industry, and

---

106 S. Pollard, 'Fixed capital in the industrial revolution in Britain', *JEH* 24 (1964), 299–314, at p. 306. T. C. Barker and J. R. Harris, *A Merseyside Town in the Industrial Revolution: St. Helens, 1750–1900* (Liverpool, 1954), p. 121; Aspin, *The Water-Spinners*, p. 96.
107 Barker and Harris, *A Merseyside Town in the Industrial Revolution*.
108 D. A. Farnie, 'The metropolis of cotton spinning machine making and mill building', *The Cotton Mills of Oldham*, ed. D. Gurr and J. Hunt (Oldham, 1998), pp. 4–11, at p. 5.
109 Dutch wheels were horizontally positioned and could move between twelve and twenty spindles: E. Butterworth, *Historical Sketches of Oldham* (Oldham, 1856), pp. 118, 126.
110 W. M. Hartley, *An Oldham Velvet Dynasty: The Mellodews of Moorside* (Lancaster, 2009).
111 Chapman, 'Fixed capital formation', p. 245. Average size of Oldham firm calculated from appendix E.

to whom Lees was now related through the marriage of his daughter.[112] Fixed stock was valued at £17,233, including the steam engine at £8,000. In fixed capital terms, this represented an annual equivalent growth rate of 64.6%. Notwithstanding this new investment, Lees continued to operate his old factory, at least for a time, and his 1808 stock-take still records the spinning-jennies and warping machines that had been so integral to his earlier success. The aggregate value of this residual equipment totalled only around £130,[113] providing further context for the financial investment step change represented by the move to the new factory.

In the next two years, the mill achieved sales to the value of £63,450, with outstanding trade debts of £6,050. An equal balance of outstanding payments to suppliers financed the latter. These figures suggest a credit cycle of around seventy days between goods transfer and payment, a period much shorter than the twelve examples cited by Chapman, with an average of ten months, ranging from three months to two years.[114] The accounts also feature stock held for sale at Manchester, Ripponden and Sowerby, with indications of sales direct to weavers, and there are no references to bank debt, loan finance or bills of exchange. Customers included cotton manufacturers in Oldham and Manchester, and handloom weavers and their agents.[115] These features are indicative of a cash-based business, functioning outside the extensive financial and merchant networks.

Even in a rented factory, these numbers imply a proportionately significant investment in fixed capital relative to working capital and to other businesses at this time. The likely reason is that James Lees, as the son of an inventor, was an early adopter of new technology and self-made man, and whose investments did not stem from previously embedded networks of credit or involvement in the outworking system. In the Oldham of the 1770s, small firms with low capital requirements predominated, and investment in cotton created opportunities for upward social mobility, allowing James to rise from his relatively humble origins.[116] James may have been assisted by Joseph Jones' success in deploying Boulton & Watt steam engines in coal mining, and the spur given

---

112   Hartley, *An Oldham Velvet Dynasty*, p. 2, Butterworth, *Historical Sketches of Oldham*, p. 124.

113   Including three twin spinning-jennies valued at £50 in total. JLP, DDRE 1, Account book, Stock account, January 1808.

114   Chapman, 'Financial restraints', appendix 1, p. 67.

115   Individual customers can be ascertained from the list of bad debts, for example: J. Dunkerley, cotton manufacturer (*The Literary Panorama*, vol. 13, 1813); Clarke, Livesey & Co., Manchester fustian manufacturers (*London Gazette*, 1815, p. 1622). Weighing equipment is recorded alongside the stock held at these locations, with details of cash from the weavers' book. James Lees, Account book, LCRO, DDRE 1.

116   Chapman, 'Fixed capital formation', p. 244; Honeyman, *Origins of Enterprise*, pp. 95, 97; Howe, *The Cotton Masters*, pp. 46–7.

to the development of cotton manufacture in Oldham following the end of the Arkwright patent in 1783. Also, a there was a boom in turnpike roads, including a road linking Mumps with Ripponden and Sowerby, built in the late 1790s, and a reduction in wages as a consequence of influxes of displaced agricultural workers.[117] Aided by such developments, Butterworth describes him as a 'highly enterprising and spirited manufacturer' who, thanks to his efforts, had one of the largest firms in the district.[118] Notwithstanding this apparent success, Lees' involvement at Wallshaw ceased, probably around 1820.[119]

Pleasley Mill, also in a remote location, developed rapidly through investments in steam-powered mule spinning.[120] Owned by the firm Cowpe, Oldknow & Siddon, its purpose was to supply the partners' and related hosiery businesses in Nottingham using Arkwright water frames. The original capital of £4,200 in 1786 consisted mostly of fixed capital, which was typical of many similar mills supplying the hosiery trade.[121] As with other such investments at this time the mill was able to sustain a rapid increase in working capital, which rose from £700 to £15,000 by 1798, by which point it was almost double the equivalent investment in fixed capital. The firm expanded its base of customers during this period, which included supplying Lancashire weavers directly as well as through the Manchester market.[122] Cash surpluses generated by these activities allowed the firm to invest in new machinery and, in its second mill at Pleasley Vale built in 1798, install Boulton & Watt steam engines, costing £350 and £550 for eight and ten horsepower respectively. This investment resulted in a step increase in fixed capital, from £7,800 in 1797 to £12,600 in 1803. Again, working capital expanded more quickly, with a corresponding increase from just over £15,000 to £36,800.[123]

---

117 Oldham and Saddleworth Roads Act, 1795 (35 Geo. 3 c. 137). James and John Lees also had interests in the canal company: J. Foster, *Class Struggle and the Industrial Revolution: Early Industrial Capitalism in Three English Towns* (London, 1974), pp. 167–8.
118 Butterworth, *Historical Sketches of Oldham*, p. 124. On the size of the mill, see T. Osborn, *The Industrial Ecosystem: An Environmental and Social History of the Early Industrial Revolution in Oldham, England, 1750–1820*, vol. 2 (Santa Cruz, CA, 1997), p. 237.
119 Honeyman, *Origins of Enterprise*, p. 95, dates the sale of his business to soon after Crompton's survey of 1811; accounting ledger records persist to 1818, followed by some further rough profit calculations which are undated, *Account book*, LCRO, DDRE 1. Lees appears in *Pigot's Commercial Directory for 1818–1820*, p. 382.
120 S. Pigott, *Hollins: A Study of Industry, 1784–1949* (Nottingham, 1949), p. 33.
121 Richardson, 'The structure of capital'. S. D. Chapman, *The Early Factory Masters: The Transition to the Factory System in the Midlands Textile Industry* (Newton Abbot, 1967), p. 129. Thomas Oldknow, who died shortly after the partnership was formed, was the grandfather of Samuel Oldknow of Marple and Mellor. Pigott, *Hollins*, pp. 36–8.
122 Calculated from Chapman, *The Early Factory Masters*, p. 127 and table 5. On marketing, see Pigott, *Hollins*, pp. 36–8.
123 Pigott, *Hollins*, p. 39, These prices compared favourably to Boulton & Watt's general price list of £525 and £580. Boulton & Watt's pricing policy was adapted by James Watt junior in 1798 with lower prices available for customers in non-metropolitan locations. E. Roll, *An Early*

Another example of a remote firm with small beginnings, and where a relatively low initial investment in fixed capital amplified further expansion through associated working capital, was Nathaniel Dugdale & Brothers. Nathaniel began his working life as an employee of Taylor, Fort & Bury at Oakenshaw print works, and set up his own business following the dissolution of that partnership in 1795.[124] Although established rather late, other technologies such as mule spinning and steam power were at this time confined to metropolitan centres such as Manchester, so in the first phase of development, Dugdale used old technology (jenny-spinning) and a traditional domestic weaving network.[125] Given these arrangements, most of the initial investment was in working capital (£2,540), with only a small fraction invested in machinery (£215).

Despite these limitations, a strong network of connections assisted the growth and success of the firm. The start-up capital of £1,000 was divided between Nathaniel Dugdale (1762–1816) and Taylor, Fort & Bury, and later his brothers. Third-party creditors provided a similar amount. The firm was organized as an outworking network with a spinning mill centred on the small town of Padiham, near Burnley.[126] The outworking network featured places significant in the Dugdale family, including Nathaniel's family home at Great Harwood, Oakenshaw at Clayton le Moors, the site of his former employment at Taylor, Fort & Bury's Broad Oak print works, and Clitheroe, where James Thomson (1779–1850), a tenant of Lowerhouse Mill, later set up his print works.[127] By 1803 the firm's capital had increased to £6,803, and it was employing around 300 weavers, rising to 451 by 1810 and 699 by 1823. At its inception in 1797, the spinning factory, Lowerhouse Mill, was equipped with spinning-jennies, and in the period 1797–1803 twenty-four spinning-jennies were used.[128] As a peripheral manufacturer with a domestic weaving network, the choice of technology and business model was very similar to James Lees of Wallshaw. Given the high cost and difficulties in accessing and powering

Experiment in Industrial Organization: History of the Firm of Boulton and Watt 1775–1805 (London, 1930), appendix xix, p. 312, adapted list; R. Williams, 'Management accounting practice and price calculation at Boulton and Watt's Soho Foundry: A late 18th century example', *Accounting Historians Journal* 26 (1999), 65–87, at pp. 75–6.

124   B. Hall, *Lowerhouse and the Dugdales: The Story of a Lancashire Mill Community*, Burnley, 1976, p. 7.

125   Nathaniel Dugdale & Brothers, Accounts, WP, Eng. MS, 1208.

126   Nathaniel Dugdale & Brothers, Partners' Money, WP, Eng. MS, 1208.

127   Nathaniel Dugdale & Brothers, Putting Out Lists, WP, Eng. MS, 1208; Hall, *Lowerhouse and the Dugdales*, p. 6.

128   Nathaniel Dugdale & Brothers, Partners' Money, Putting Out Lists, WP, Eng. MS, 1208. In Derbyshire and Lancashire, despite its obsolescence, jenny-spinning was used for spinning coarser yarns in outlying districts: Chapman, *The Early Factory Masters*, pp. 50–1.

mule-spinning technology in the late 1790s, and limits on the productivity of handloom weaving, cheaper investments in spinning-jennies would have been sufficient to create a balanced supply.

Around the same time as James Lees, the firm subsequently did invest in a new mill and warehouse, now using mule spindles, powered by a steam engine.[129] The total investment in 1812 was £12,041,[130] which, although modest, was a step increase in the earlier incarnation of the business. In 1811 Nathaniel Dugdale & Brothers integrated forward into calico printing, taking over Lowerhouse print works from James Thomson, who then began his independent operation at Primrose Mill at Clitheroe. In 1813, Nathaniel purchased the Lowerhouse spinning mill from Peel, Yates & Co. for £7,000, payable in annual instalments. Although the firm made a high return on capital, the relatively small scale of its operation meant that generated insufficient cash flow to meet these repayments.[131]

Following the death of Nathaniel in 1816, the firm was taken over by his son John and became known as John Dugdale & Brothers. In the period 1815–23, the personal wealth of the partners invested in the business increased around fivefold. By 1824, partners' capital had increased to £68,062, a growth rate of 14.6%. The introduction of steam-powered mule spinning in 1811 was a step increase and thirteen years later, having acquired the print works, fixed capital totalled £21,563, representing a subsequent growth rate of 4.5%. Working capital investment outstripped fixed capital investment throughout, totalling £54,080 by 1824, reflecting the continued importance of the domestic weaving network. Profits totalled £68,000 in the years 1815–23 and the partners reinvested most of it.[132] So although the partners incurred further debt, they made significant investments in new capacity, including additional factories, machinery and warehouses.[133]

Some of the investment went into new printing machinery and the application of steam power to the associated finishing processes. The firm benefited from the expansion of the nearby Leeds and Liverpool Canal, the relevant sections of which opened in 1801 and 1810. A canal-side warehouse facility was constructed to take advantage of these developments.[134] Some of this investment was financed by family loans and a mortgage on the factory,

---

129   Nathaniel Dugdale & Brothers, Jennies list, 1797–1803, WP, Eng. MS, 1208. The firm was certainly using steam-powered mules in 1812: Nathaniel Dugdale & Brothers, 1812 Valuations, WP, Eng. MS, 1208.
130   Ibid.
131   Hall, *Lowerhouse and the Dugdales*, pp. 6–7.
132   John Dugdale & Brothers, Accounts, WP, Eng. MS, 1208.
133   John Dugdale & Brothers, Machinery and valuations, Partners accounts, WP, Eng. MS, 1208. In 1840, land and buildings alone were valued at £30,637.
134   John Dugdale & Brothers, Property valuations, WP, Eng. MS, 1208.

although these diminished rapidly as a proportion with the accumulation of partners' capital.[135]

As the family extended their interests through a network of connections, these debts became more sustainable. Adam Dugdale, Nathaniel's youngest brother, entered into a partnership with Thomas Hargreaves to take over Broad Oak print works, Accrington, from Taylor, Fort & Bury in 1811.[136] The association meant that during this time, until John Dugdale & Brothers repaid all outstanding debts in 1827, Adam was able to underwrite some of the loans on the Lowerhouse site.[137] Relative to partners' capital, these loans were of marginal significance, amounting to under £3,000 in 1824.[138] Hargreaves & Dugdale became successful merchants, in partnership with Salis Schwabe & Co., the rapidly expanding merchants and calico printers whose factory from 1832 was sited at Rhodes, Middleton, near Manchester. John Dugdale used the profits from Lowerhouse to expand into merchanting using connections in Liverpool and Manchester.[139] By 1840, the networked firms of Schwabe & Co., Hargreaves & Dugdale and Fort Bros. & Co. employed 2,500 staff between them.[140] John Mercer's experiments at Broad Oak with sulphur dioxide as a method of strengthening finished cloth before dyeing led to the patenting of 'mercerization' in 1850.[141] Like the Birley & Hornby network, the Dugdales, Thomson and Salis Schwabe benefited from the development of the railway network and accordingly held directorships in the relevant lines. The Clitheroe Junction line provided a new connection to Blackburn and Thomson, Hargreaves and Dugdale family members all featured on the provisional committee of directors. James Thomson and Salis Schwabe served as directors of the Liverpool, Manchester & Newcastle upon Tyne Junction Railway Company.[142]

As Birley & Hornby had provided impetus to the creation of the industrial district at Chorlton, so too did John Horrocks in Preston. Although

135   Hall, *Lowerhouse and the Dugdales*, p. 7. John Dugdale & Brothers, Partners accounts, WP, Eng. MS, 1208.

136   Ashmore, *Industrial Archaeology*, p. 179; R. Ainsworth and R. S. Crossley, *Accrington through the Nineteenth Century* (Accrington, n.d.) p. 18; G. Turnbull, *A History of the Calico Printing Industry of Great Britain* (Altrincham, 1941), p. 97.

137   Hall, *Lowerhouse and the Dugdales*, p. 7.

138   John Dugdale & Brothers, Accounts, WP, Eng. MS, 1208.

139   Chapman, *Merchant Enterprise*, p. 148; Hall, *Lowerhouse and the Dugdales*, p. 11; T. W. Freeman, H. B. Rodgers and R. H. Kinvig, *Lancashire, Cheshire and the Isle of Man* (London, 1966), p. 117.

140   The figure excludes those employed at Lower House by John Dugdale, that in capital terms was about half the size of Broad Oak, which itself employed 1,040: Turnbull, *History of the Calico Printing Industry*, pp. 170, 468.

141   Calico Printers' Association, *Fifty Years of Calico Printing* (Manchester, 1949), p. 14.

142   'Clitheroe Junction Railway', *Railway Chronicle*, 17 May 1845. *Return of Joint Stock Companies registered under Act 7 & 8 Victoria*, BPP, 1846.

coterminous with the activities of Philips & Lee in mid-1790s Manchester, his rapid expansion of manufacturing capacity predated Birley & Hornby by a decade, showing that the conditions for transition between models 2 and 3 in Table 1 were present in the 1790s. The scale and speed of the expansion of Horrocks's business at this time were indeed 'remarkable'.[143] He invested in the automation of preparation and spinning processes, at first using carding engines and quickly moving on to steam-powered mule spinning. In the space of a decade, he established ten new factories, some of which replaced previously installed capacity, and by 1816 he had six steam-powered mills with over 100,000 spindles and employing around 704 workers.[144] Horrocks had only commenced business in Preston in 1791, operating out of single-room workshops, but still outstripped Birley & Hornby's operation, which by 1816 employed 549 in Manchester and Preston.[145]

From the start, Horrocks developed a capital-intensive business, which corresponded closely to model 3 characteristics in Table 1. Growth was very rapid in the 1790s, from a rented room requiring capital of £600 in 1791, to four factories with an aggregate insurance value of £16,350 by 1796.[146] In 1800 the capital of the firm was around £173,000, comprising £145,000 in fixed capital and factory stock, and £28,000 in working capital. These activities were financed in approximately equal proportion by third-party debt and partners' capital. Between 1799 and 1815, partnership capital grew somewhat more slowly than in the take-off years of the 1790s, from £105,000 to £185,000, an annual rate of 3.5%.[147]

Production on this scale required access to a large warehousing and outworking network. As with Birley & Hornby, where the scale of the outworking network and associated management problems imposed limits on growth, John Horrocks and his partners experienced similar issues with their much larger network, which they addressed partially by erecting large sheds for handloom weaving adjacent to their other sites in Preston.[148] Even so, the firm's accounts record balances held at warehouses in Blackburn, Bolton, Chorley, Darwen, Garstang, Kirkham, Leyland, Manchester, Longridge, Ormskirk,

---

143   J. G. Timmins, 'John Horrocks', *Dictionary of National Biography* (Oxford, 2004). https://doi.org/10.1093/ref:odnb/13807 [accessed 19 September 2019].

144   T. C. Dickinson, *Cotton Mills of Preston: The Power Behind the Thread* (Lancaster, 2002), p. 9, suggests that Horrocks had 107,000 spindles in 1812 in eight mills. The average of 13–14,000 spindles per mill is somewhat larger than the investments made at the same time by Philips & Lee and Birley & Hornby in Manchester.

145   R. S. Fitton and A. P. Wadsworth, *The Strutts and the Arkwrights, 1758–1830: A Study of the Early Factory System* (Manchester, 1958), p. 195. The completion of Chorlton New Mill in 1817 effectively doubled these numbers.

146   M. Burscough, *The Horrockses: Cotton Kings of Preston* (Lancaster, 2004), pp. 12, 14.

147   Calculated from HCP, Ledgers, DDHS 1–2.

148   Burscough, *The Horrockses*, p. 16.

Plumpton, Preston and Wigan.[149] Stocks held at these depots were occasionally substantial, for example, £19,247 held at Bury in 1804, but more typically were in the £200–£2,000 range. Notwithstanding the predominance of fixed capital in its financial structure, the firm employed around seven thousand domestic outworkers in 1816, or ten times the number employed directly in factories.[150] Operation of the mills and the domestic network was facilitated by the Douglas Navigation, connecting Preston to the Wigan coalfield, and later the Lancaster Canal and its extensions in the early 1800s.[151] Turnpike roads assisted distribution through the warehouse network, which, as the above list suggests, had much in common with the location of the Birley & Hornby sites.

There were several reasons for the speed and overall success of the Horrockses operation. First, Horrockses was one of several firms that managed to acquire imitation Boulton & Watt engines at a lower cost relative to the patented versions in 1796. By 1801 they were operating 'six or seven' Boulton & Watt-type engines in as many mills.[152] John Horrocks was also an early experimenter in weaving automation, which he patented.[153] Second, Horrocks exploited a significant gap in the market. Samuel Oldknow's financial difficulties and the uncertainty associated with the French Revolution had led him to withdraw from fine muslin production, which Horrocks now stepped in to supply.[154] Horrocks's entrepreneurial personality reinforced these opportunities. He had been quick to see the openings offered by mule spinning in the production of fine counts of yarns, but also the threats posed by the vagaries of the credit system. A contemporary diarist records how he was left with a large stock of unsold goods at Hamburg, following the resumption of war in May 1803. His response was to prioritize creditworthiness over profit, selling at a loss to ensure timely payment.[155] An entry in the accounting records notes that the decision and consequential losses were down to Horrocks alone, thus insulating the other partners from the effects.[156] It was by such means that Horrocks built a reputation for trustworthiness, which he valued over and above short-term

149   HCP, Ledgers, DDHS 1–2.

150   *Select Committee on the State of the Children Employed in Manufactories of United Kingdom*, ev. William Taylor, p. 492; Bythell, *Hand-loom Weavers*. Fitton and Wadsworth, *The Strutts and the Arkwrights*, p. 195.

151   Burscough, *The Horrockses*, p. 17.

152   The engines were the subject of a legal investigation under the Boulton & Watt patent: Burscough, *The Horrockses*, pp. 17–18. Dickinson, *Cotton Mills of Preston*, p. 8.

153   Anon., 'Mr Horrocks', *The Repertory of Arts, Manufactures and Agriculture* 25/2 (1814), p. 1.

154   G. L. Craik and C. MacFarlane, *The Pictorial History of England during the Reign of George the Third* (London, 1848), p. 699.

155   J. Grieg, *The Farington Diary*, vol. II, 28 August 1802 to 13 September 1804 (London, 1923), p. 147.

156   For example, the large loss in 1803 arising from adverse price movements was charged to Horrocks alone: HCP, Ledgers, DDHS 1.

financial profit or loss. Indeed, such losses were bearable, given his diverse customer base, which was expanded further following the establishment of a London office in 1798.[157] Success in these respects was, therefore, attributable to his reputation for trustworthiness with his creditors and by working closely with his suppliers, also to ensure high quality. As a consequence, Horrocks's firm, now managed by Samuel Horrocks, won a massive contract as a monopoly supplier of muslins to the East India Company in 1807.[158]

The scale of investment, in both factory capacity and the associated domestic outworking system, required significant financial support. Temporary partnerships with Thomas Greaves and Richard Newsham provided initial capital, but as the business grew, Horrocks used his resources and reputation to lever substantial lending from a close network of business contacts. Longer-term partners, including his brother Samuel, admitted in 1797, and John Whitehead and Thomas Miller, admitted in 1801, provided only small capital sums relative to that from Horrocks.[159] By contrast, a small number of significant long-term, third-party investors provided the funds needed to sustain the business through its expansionary phase in the 1790s and early 1800s. These were metropolitan collaborators in the supply chain and included John Whitfield of Whitfield & Co., Manchester merchants, who had £35,446 outstanding in 1804 on a loan account that was typically in the £20,000–40,000 range year on year. Other investors with similar levels of commitment were Thomas Martin (£32,111 in 1804), a Liverpool merchant, and also Rowlandson & Burra, Manchester warehousemen in London, who had £22,084 outstanding in 1800. It was through these connections that Horrocks was able to secure his supply of American cotton, confirming his reputation for quality. Smaller, although still significant amounts were borrowed from local banks, most notably Atherton & Co. Bank, comprising banking partners Atherton, Greaves and Dennison, known in Preston as the 'Old Bank'. There were also loans from Thomas Greaves in a personal capacity.[160] Greaves had previously been a partner at the inception of the business and provided Horrocks with the funds to purchase the first mule

157   R. G. Thorne, *The House of Commons, 1790–1820*, IV (London, 1986), p. 247; Grieg, *The Farington Diary*, p. 147. Lancashire customers: for example, Preston-based manufacturers Sidgreaves & Leighton, and John Rostron, calico manufacturer of Edenfield: HCP, Ledgers, DDHS 1.

158   Burscough, *The Horrockses*, pp. 18–19.

159   The agreed division of profits in the post-1801 partnership was: John Horrocks 6/10, Sam Horrocks 3/10, John Whitehead and Thomas Miller 1/10: HCP, Ledgers, DDHS 1; Timmins, 'John Horrocks'.

160   For details and amounts of creditors, see HCP, Ledgers, DDHS 1, 1799–1805. For the importance of connections to Liverpool and Manchester merchants as suppliers of American cotton, see Burscough, *The Horrockses*, p. 18. For background on Whitfield, Rowlandson & Burra, Martin and Atherton & Co., see respectively, S. Haggerty, '*Merely for money*'? *Business Culture in the British Atlantic, 1750–1815* (Liverpool, 2012), p. 94; A. Calladine and J. Fricker, *East Cheshire Textile Mills* (London, 1993), p. 38. H. Kent, *Kent's Directory for 1803* (London,

spindles in 1792.[161] Smaller lenders included other local businesses, such as cotton mill owners Riley, Paley & Co., who had previously collaborated with Horrocks in machine making and, more substantially, John Goodair.[162] Of all these investors, Martin and Whitfield were the providers of the more significant part of long-term finance.

As noted earlier, Horrocks successfully exploited a gap in the market vacated by Samuel Oldknow. The question arises, therefore, why did Horrocks succeed where Oldknow did not? Certainly, Oldknow was successful for a time, making profits from muslin manufacturing totalling £34,000 per year in 1789 and 1790, and was aware, along with other leading entrepreneurs including Arkwright, Drinkwater, Owen and Philips, of the significant potential profits to be made from fine spinning. These factors prompted Oldknow to consider investing in steam-powered mule spinning, planned for his large Stockport factory, with an associated network of domestic outworkers, warehouses and finishing centres. The already substantial scale of this plan was complemented by a water-spinning factory at Mellor for coarser counts, but investment in the surrounding landed estate went well beyond what was needed to sustain cotton production.[163] Oldknow was highly dependent on London buyers, who were demanding according to the vagaries of fashion, forcing frequent changes in required production and also vulnerable to changes in international market conditions such as the crisis that struck continental trade in September 1792.[164] The Horrockses, on the other hand, first John and then Samuel, developed a broad customer base, which before 1807 was centred on Lancashire manufacturers responding to new demand for high-quality cotton products. Unlike Oldknow, they were able to access the East India market from a position of strength to secure further steady growth. Horrocks cultivated trustworthy creditor relations, whereas Oldknow tested them, again and again. Thus, although Oldknow had some patient creditors, including the Arkwrights, his attempted transition from model 2 to model 3 was unsuccessful. By 1795, he had abandoned all but the Mellor site[165] and therefore failed to accomplish the step increase in fixed capital associated with steam-powered mule spinning.

Whereas some ventures, like Oldknow's, were failures, business restructuring was frequently necessary due to the nature of partnerships. These were

1803), p. 172; C. Hardwick, *History of the Borough of Preston and its Environs: In the County of Lancaster* (Preston, 1857), p. 456.

161   Timmins, 'John Horrocks'.

162   HCP, Ledgers, DDHS 1: Goodair had £10,880 outstanding in 1805; Dickinson, *Cotton Mills of Preston*, p. 8.

163   G. Unwin, *Samuel Oldknow and the Arkwrights* (Manchester, 1968), pp. 124–5.

164   M. Berg, 'Quality, cotton and the global luxury trade', *How India Clothed the World: The World of South Asian Textiles, 1500–1850*, ed. G. Riello and T. Roy (Leiden, 2009), 391–414, at p. 406.

165   Unwin, *Samuel Oldknow*, p. 156.

typically short-lived and reflected changes in business strategy and changes in family circumstances, including a series of multiple partnerships, sometimes with the sons of the family and sometimes with established trading concerns linked through marriage. The activities of Samuel Greg and his associates are a useful illustration. There were three main series of partnerships traceable through various successions, the first two related to export and marketing, and the third to manufacturing, illustrated in Figure 3. Thomas Greg (1718–96), Samuel's father, had established the firm of Thomas Greg & Co. which became one of the most successful broking, underwriting and discounting firms in the mercantile transatlantic trade, and whose clients included cotton manufacturers J. & N. Philips, during which period the business was managed from London by Samuel's brother, also called Thomas (1752–1832).[166] Samuel Greg meanwhile took over Hyde & Company, then one of Manchester's largest merchant manufacturers in 1782. He then inherited £10,000 from Robert Hyde and formed a new, albeit short-lived, partnership with John Middleton of Tideswell.

These pre-existing business structures and inherited capital allowed Samuel Greg to enter cotton spinning directly, using a model 2-type structure. In 1783 he established Quarry Bank Mill to guarantee a regular supply of yarn, using water-powered frames. Most of the output was sold in the Manchester yarn market, with the remainder sent for handloom weaving in Derbyshire. Greg owned a hand-weaving shed at Eyam and a warehouse at Broadheath on the Bridgewater Canal.[167]

The features of Greg's pre-existing network and his inheritance seemingly reduced any pressure to transition to model 3 and steam-powered factory production. The merchant network was readily expandable through family and marriage connections. Further capital was obtained through marriage when Greg's sister married Thomas Hodgson, a Liverpool merchant with spinning mills at Caton. Greg attempted to manage Quarry Bank Mill himself, but in 1796 offered a partnership to the engineer Peter Ewart, who spent ten years making technical improvements.[168] Even so, because Quarry Bank Mill was water-powered, and in a remote location, it was more dependent on child labour than steam-powered mills in urban areas. Greg was, therefore, one of the last employers to use the factory apprentice system.[169] On Ewart's admission to the

166 M. Janes, *From Smuggling to Cotton Kings: The Greg Story* (Cirencester, 2010); Chapman, *Merchant Enterprise*, p. 64. The relationship with the Philips family was long standing. In 1824, Robert Hyde Greg married Mary, the daughter of Robert Philips: S. Gremson, I. Pringle and D. Winterbotham, *Philips Park: Its History and Development* (Bury, 2011), p. 11.

167 F. Collier, *The Family Economy of the Working Classes in the Cotton Industry* (Manchester, 1964), p. 38. M. B. Rose, *The Gregs of Quarry Bank Mill* (Cambridge, 1986); J. H. Hodson, *Cheshire, 1660–1780: Restoration to Industrial Revolution* (Chester, 1978), p. 85.

168 Rose, *The Gregs of Quarry Bank Mill*, p. 23.

169 The practice of hiring child apprentices ceased in 1847. Rose, *The Gregs of Quarry Bank Mill*, p. 57. The child labour issue is addressed in detail below in chapter 3.

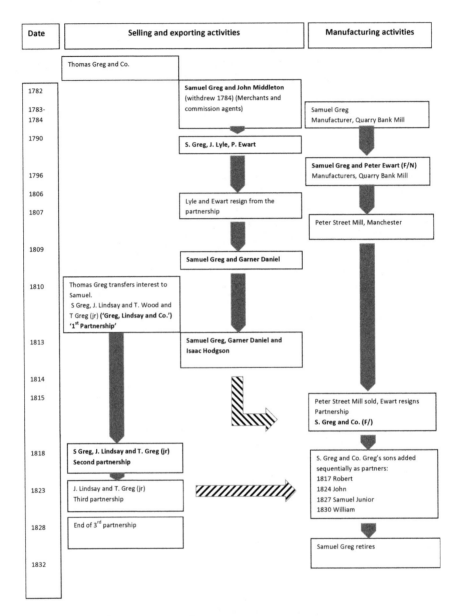

Figure 3. Samuel Greg partnerships, 1783–1832

Notes: Bold text indicates new business involving Samuel Greg. Solid arrows indicate partnership activities involving Samuel Greg. Shaded arrows indicate Greg's resignations from partnerships and refocus on manufacturing.

Sources: GP, C5/1/2/2–4; Rose, *Gregs of Quarry Bank*, chapters 2 and 7; Janes, *From Smuggling to Cotton Kings*, chapter 7.

partnership, the capital was £17,655, the vast majority of which was invested in working capital.[170] The mill, which was rented to the business, had 2,425 spindles by 1796 and had initially cost £3,000 to build and equip. In 1798, the value of machinery can be estimated at a similar amount.[171] Of total capital of just over £20,000, therefore, about £6,000 was invested in fixed capital and the balance (70%) in working capital.

In the early 1800s, as Birley, Horrocks and others engaged in substantial investment in fixed capital, Greg committed to a relatively modest investment in Manchester. In 1806, he acquired land for this purpose at Peter Street, Manchester. A steam engine was installed in 1811, costing £1,901 to power mule spindles, spinning typically coarse 40s yarn.[172] By this time the mill had 12,400 spindles and had cost £23,981 to build and equip.[173] Working capital amounted to around £20,000 if a large accumulated cash balance is excluded.[174] In line with other steam-powered mule mills, the majority of the total investment was now in fixed capital.

Notwithstanding these investments, Greg's attention remained focused on merchant networks and overseas markets. A related partnership of Greg, Lyle & Ewart was set up to trade in the USA, Italy and Russia.[175] Following bad debt problems in these markets, Lyle and Ewart left the partnership after 1806. Greg formed a new partnership in 1809, this time aimed at continental cloth markets, with Garner Daniel and also later his wife's nephew, Isaac Hodgson. In 1811, Thomas Greg retired and passed his share of the partnership to Samuel with the new partnership taking the name Greg, Lindsay & Company.[176] Greg was the senior partner, entitled to one-third of the total profit, with James Lindsay, Thomas Wood, and Thomas Greg each entitled to one-third of the remainder.[177]

Viewing Samuel Greg's activities as a whole, factory production was a relatively small component of a wider web of activities. In 1814, the total value of the investment at Peter Street was £44,355 and at Quarry Bank £20,000, out of overall investments valued at around £190,000.[178] Fixed capital perhaps accounted for about 20–25% of the total, applying the proportions calculated

170 GP, Partnership Book, Account of First Partnership, C5/1/2/2 and 4 (where 'first partnership' refers to that of 1810–18).
171 For the initial value, see Rose, *The Gregs of Quarry Bank Mill*, p. 20. The value of machinery was not shown separately in the accounts but can be estimated from the £231 depreciation charged in the year to September 1798, assuming a rate of 7.5% (GP, Partnership Book, C5/1/2/2).
172 GP, Memorandum, C5/1/2.
173 Rose, *The Gregs of Quarry Bank Mill*, p. 24.
174 GP, Partnership Book, Account of First Partnership, C5/1/2/4.
175 GP, Assets and liabilities, C5/1/1.
176 Janes, *From Smuggling to Cotton Kings*, pp. 27, 53. GP, Partnership Book, Account of First Partnership, C5/1/2/4.
177 GP, Partnership Book, Account of First Partnership, C5/1/2/4.
178 GP, Assets and liabilities, C5/1/1.

earlier. The remainder was in a portfolio of investments, including estates at Reddish and in the West Indies. Financial investments included Consols and shares in the Rochdale and Grand Union canals, both of which were of direct importance to Greg's trade in cotton. With such healthy cash surpluses, Greg had little need for external financing.

From this strong financial position, Greg now concentrated on expanding manufacturing as an immediate family business. In 1815 the partnership with Ewart was terminated, and Ewart took Peter Street Mill into a new partnership with McConnel & Kennedy. Greg first refocused on Quarry Bank, which used throstle spinning, followed by major investment in a new mill 1817–21. During this period, in 1817, he acquired Caton Mill in settlement of a debt from Isaac Hodgson.[179] This partnership lasted until 1818 following Wood's retirement. The new 'second' partnership lasted until 1823 when Samuel withdrew, giving way to a third partnership of Thomas Greg and James Lindsay that was finally dissolved in 1828.[180] By 1824, Greg's total wealth had increased to £223,000, a steady equivalent annual growth rate of 1.6%.[181] Most of the growth came from a new network of mills, centred on Quarry Bank, and devolved to the management of Greg's sons on admission to the partnership. Robert joined in 1817, John in 1824, Samuel Junior in 1827 and William Rathbone in 1830.[182] By the time of Samuel's retirement in 1832, as Figure 3 illustrates, there had been no fewer than twelve documented new businesses or partnerships, and the Quarry Bank Mill business alone went through seven changes.[183] All of the Greg mills had fixed to working capital ratios of around 1:1 by this time.[184]

J. & N. Philips was, as Greg and Horrockses, a leading example of a merchant-manufacturing firm. It was one of the most influential early textile businesses, established in 1748 and expanding rapidly in the second half of the eighteenth century. In 1755, the capital in tape manufacture was £4,800, which had increased to £7,500 ten years later.[185] The firm used Dutch looms to weave ribbon at Tean Hall in Staffordshire, supported by a rapidly expanding network of loom shops and domestic workers in surrounding villages. It also

---

179   Rose, *The Gregs of Quarry Bank Mill*, p. 17. Janes, *From Smuggling to Cotton Kings*, chapter 7.
180   GP, Partnership Book, Accounts of Second and Third Partnerships, C5/1/2/4.
181   Calculated from GP, Assets and liabilities, C5/1/1, 1814 and 1824.
182   Rose, *The Gregs of Quarry Bank Mill*, p. 49.
183   The Quarry Bank partnerships were: S. Greg/Middleton (1783–84); S. Greg (1784–96); S. Greg and Peter Ewart (1796–1815); S. Greg (1815–17); S. Greg and R. H. Greg (1817–24); R. H. Greg and J. Greg (1824–27); S. Greg, R. H. Greg, J. Greg and S. Greg (1827–30); R. H. Greg, J. Greg, S. Greg and W. Greg (1830–32). The total excludes other short-lived partnerships formed for specific investment opportunities, for example Greg's speculative land purchase in partnership with William Hibbert in the early 1800s (Janes, *From Smuggling to Cotton Kings*, p. 30).
184   *Factories Inquiry Commission*, BPP, 1833, 450, ev. R. H. Greg.
185   Wadsworth and Mann, *The Cotton Trade*, pp. 290–1.

produced fustians and small ware at Radcliffe and Whitefield, Manchester. In its earlier phases of growth the firm developed a customer base using canvassing tours of East Anglia, Scotland, Bristol and Exeter, allowing them to avoid reliance on London, then the main market for selling small ware and hats, and the high charges imposed by merchants.[186] When the firm did sell into the London market, it did so through a diverse range of customers. In 1750, access to London was available via turnpike roads at Tittensor, ten miles away, and after 1771 via the canal network.[187]

In the 1790s, the firm entered a new phase based on spinning automation and export markets. These developments were co-ordinated by George Augustus Lee at Salford in partnership with George Philips, and came a few years earlier than Birley & Hornby's comparable investments at Chorlton. To the initial capital of £21,697 in 1794, Lee commenced a programme of expansion in 1800, increasing the capital to just over £51,000 by the end of 1803. Working capital at this time can be estimated at around £15,000, or 30% of the total.[188] Between 1794 and 1814, the capital of the Philips & Lee partnership increased from £21,697 to £179,991.[189] During the war years and after, most investments were now into working capital as Philips & Lee sold the mill's output to overseas customers requiring extended credit terms.[190] By 1814 the firm was the third-largest in the area, even though there was no new investment in fixed capital.[191]

In a similar vein to Cardwell, Birley & Hornby's expansion to model 3, from 1794, Philips & Lee's factory at Salford provided automated yarn spinning for the wider family network. From there, yarn could be supplied to N. & F. Philips, fustian, and small ware manufacturers at Whitefield, Thomas Philips & Co., hat and tape manufacturers, Dolefield (off Bridge Street in central Manchester), and the J. & N. Philips small ware manufactory at Tean. From there, the orientation of the network was to the south, via Tean, and to customers in London and export markets.[192]

So, although the Philips network was significant in the industrialization of Manchester, the main focus of the firm was the expansion of international

---

186 Thomas French & Sons Ltd, 'Smallwares and Narrow Fabrics. Historical Sketch (to 1944)', *Journal of the Textile Institute* 41 (1950), 751–99, at p. 767.

187 Albert, *Turnpike Road System*, p. 35.

188 Philips & Lee, Abstracts of Accounts, DR 198/167, 1 December 1815. The fixed and working capital can be estimated using the depreciation charge, assuming it was applied at 8% per annum to arrive at a capital equivalent value.

189 Ibid.

190 Howe, *The Cotton Masters*, p. 25. Chapman, *Merchant Enterprise*, p. 66.

191 Philips & Lee, Abstracts of Accounts, DR 198/167. *Select Committee on the State of the Children Employed in the Manufactories*, pp. 374–5. Measured by total employees, Philips & Lee at 937, were behind A. & G. Murray (1,215) and McConnel & Kennedy (1,020).

192 W. Pitt, *A Topographical History of Staffordshire: Including its Agriculture, Mines, and Manufactures* (Newcastle-under-Lyme, 1817), pp. 221–2. JNPP, Ledgers, 1806–1922, M97/2/1; Brown, 'From "Cotton Lord" to landed aristocrat'; Chapman, *Merchant Enterprise*, p. 64–5.

markets. George Philips was a founder of the Manchester Exchange and a political Whig, described as the 'unofficial MP for Manchester'.[193] During this period, Philips was able to use his political influence to assist his manufacturing concerns, lobbying to open up international markets. He won a series of export contracts by building up a network of agents and later developing his own merchant business. The Philips firm exported its output to America, first with the assistance of Greg and, after 1800, through the partnerships of Philips, Cramond & Co. and subsequently Boddington and Sharp.[194] Under these new arrangements, connections with London houses were much more important, not least for accepting bills drawn on slow-paying American customers.[195] The firm expanded significantly based on this model, increasing the number of weavers to between two and three thousand by 1817, operating from three nearby sites with an associated bleach works, by which time they were the most extensive tape manufacturers in Europe.[196]

Through these stages of evolution, J. & N. Philips had similarities with Cardwell, Birley & Hornby and other manufacturer-merchants. These firms typically supported a dispersed set of activities based on family connections, of which textile manufacturing was just one component, which provided the basis for supplying a much larger downstream network. Of the step increases in capital, steam-powered mule spinning in the 1790s and steam-powered weaving in the 1830s, only the first involved a substantial net increase in total capital.

Surviving accounting records suggest that the firm had achieved this scale at least a decade earlier. Partnership capital invested at the Tean Hall, Whitefield, and Manchester sites were £105,000, £13,000 and £8,000 respectively in 1814, with these figures almost unchanged when compared to 1807. At the same time, the capital for the firm as a whole, which reflected interests beyond weaving, doubled from £122,000 to £243,000.[197] Nathaniel Philips died in 1808 and full control passed to his two sons John and Robert, and their cousin George Philips, of the Manchester firm, Philips & Lee.[198]

Likewise, the partnerships under the umbrella of the J. & N. Philips firm prioritized other matters over fixed capital investment. Sir George Philips blamed high taxes and lower wages on the continent.[199] He feared the spread of Luddism and factory reform, devoting his energies in Parliament to limiting

193   Howe, *The Cotton Masters*, p. 92.
194   Chapman, *Merchant Enterprise*, p. 65. Cramond was based in Philadelphia. Brown, 'From "Cotton Lord" to landed aristocrat', pp. 67–8.
195   *Orders in Council*, 1808, BPP, 10, pp. 1–13, ev. Wood and Philips.
196   Pitt, *A Topographical History of Staffordshire*, pp. 221–2. Wadsworth and Mann, *The Cotton Trade*, pp. 290–1.
197   JNPP, Ledgers, 1806–1922, M97/2/1.
198   Gremson *et al.*, *Philips Park*.
199   *Hansard*, 'Exportation of cotton yarn', c.237, 7 May 1817.

interference through regulation.[200] In 1830 they acquired an interest in the firm of James Chadwick & Brother of Eagley Mills, a more remotely located site near Bolton, cotton spinners, and thread-makers. A year later in 1831 on Philips's retirement, the firm was taken over by Holland Hoole.[201] Even before then, as Brown notes, Philips was interested mainly in using business wealth to acquire landed status.[202] The business records of the firm tend to support this view, showing the integration of landed properties at the senior family seat at Heath House and Heybridge at Tean, and at Snitterfield Park into the financial accounts.[203] The latter was a large country estate in Warwickshire acquired by Robert in 1815.[204] The capital of the firm fell significantly after 1815 when George Philips withdrew £50,000 to lend to the Duke of Norfolk and to finance his land acquisitions. Philips personally diversified away from manufacturing, such that by 1820 his income from land exceeded that from his interests in Philips & Lee and J. & N. Philips.[205] Although George remained a large investor, the total capital of the J. & N. Philips firm declined further, returning to its 1807 level by 1832.[206] The accounts reveal that after 1813 the capital employed at manufacturing sites at Whitefield was being quickly run down.[207] At Tean Hall, total capital remained constant, but the trend masked significant changes. In the early 1820s, the firm sought the advice of George Augustus Lee on the conversion of the Mill to steam power. Lee projected the cost of the modernization, which would replace four hundred outsourced handlooms in the surrounding area, at just over £20,000. In the event, in 1824, the firm went ahead and ended the outworking system, but did not use Lee's designs and instead made two smaller investments at Cheadle and Tean.[208] The Philips example demonstrates that weaving investment in the 1820s involved something of a like-for-like replacement, in monetary terms at least, of fixed capital for working capital.

A similar pattern was observable at the firm of Ashworth Brothers. John Ashworth, in partnership with his brother Edmund, had established New Eagley Mill at Turton near Bolton in 1802 to spin fine counts of cotton using water power. The mill was relatively small and increased its capacity only slowly,

200 J. L. Hammond and B. Hammond, *The Town Labourer, 1760–1832* (London, 1925), pp. 64, 161, 163.

201 Howe, *The Cotton Masters*, p. 13. The firm was known as Lambert, Hoole & Jackson.

202 Brown, 'From "Cotton Lord" to landed aristocrat', p. 63.

203 JNPP, Ledgers, M97/2/1.

204 Gremson *et al.*, *Philips Park*, p. 11.

205 Brown, 'From "Cotton Lord" to landed aristocrat', p. 70, table 1.

206 Ibid., p. 69. Howe, *The Cotton Masters*, p. 92. JNPP, Ledgers, M97/2/1.

207 JNPP, Ledgers, M97/2/1. See also the summary of withdrawals in Howe, *The Cotton Masters*, appendix 2, p. 317.

208 Wadsworth and Mann, *The Cotton Trade*, p. 291; Thomas French, 'Smallwares and Narrow Fabrics', p. 777.

from 4,500 spindles in 1802 to 5,084 in 1811. A Bolton warehouse, close to the canal, was used as a centre for handloom weavers, selling to mostly local customers. Like Cardwell, Birley & Hornby, the Ashworth Brothers encountered problems associated with supervising the outworkers and bad debts arising from extended credit and challenging conditions in the Manchester market.[209] Of customer and weavers book debts totalling £4,957, the firm estimated that £1,545 were doubtful and expected to realize only half of that value in the 1817 valuation. At that time, the business was at a fairly low capital intensity, rooted in a model 2-type business structure. Fixed capital of £3,481 represented just over a third of total capital of £9,803, with only a small fraction of the total financed by third-party creditors.[210]

After 1817, as at Quarry Bank, there was an extensive programme of fixed capital investment. In 1818 Henry Ashworth, son of John, became senior partner, and was subsequently joined by his brother, Edmund, admitted in 1821, and the brothers became sole partners in 1831. The partners commenced a second mill and dye-works in the late 1820s at nearby Egerton, and modernized and expanded New Eagley, equipping it with the most modern and productive spinning mules. George Bodmer, who later advised Birley & Hornby, was instrumental in the site design for these investments in the late 1820s. Other engineering contacts, such as George Branson of Manchester, could also provide useful advice on the application of steam power to manufacturing. By November 1831, fixed capital accounted for almost two-thirds of the total capital of £57,790.[211]

The firm had relied initially on canal transport and from the 1830s, benefited from new rail connections. However, these were partial and delays caused problems securing steady supplies from Liverpool, resulting in the mills standing idle. The firm invested its surplus cash in the new Blackburn to Bolton line from 1844, and Henry Ashworth lobbied for the construction of a new line connecting Bolton and Liverpool, completed in 1849. Another line built at around the same time connected Turton to Bolton and Blackburn, of which Henry was vice-chairman.[212]

Ashworth's strategy differed in certain essential respects from the archetypal growth stages set out in Figure 1. Expansion within model 2 was limited by problems with credit, outworking and working capital. When the firm made its step increase in fixed capital investment, in the 1818–31 phase, it did not

---

209   R. Boyson, *The Ashworth Cotton Enterprise* (Oxford, 1970), pp. 6, 8.
210   AP, J&E Ashworth Stock account, 1817, Eng. MS, 1201.
211   Boyson, *Ashworth Cotton*, pp. 13–23, 40–2; AP, Quarterly stock books, Weaving accounts. George Branson's estimate of the cost of power for weaving, Manchester, 23 August 1850, Eng. MS, 1201.
212   Boyson, *Ashworth Cotton*, pp. 40–2. AP, Henry & Edmund Ashworth Stock Accounts, November 1844 *et seq.*, Eng. MS, 1201.

concomitantly expand circulating capital to accommodate the extra output into its network. Instead, rather than revisit earlier difficulties, the firm abandoned weaving and built a network of agents in Manchester and Glasgow to sell its yarn output directly. Terms of trade nonetheless dictated extended credit and the typical period for settling accounts was 150–200 days. In other words, for every £2 of yarn sold, a £1 investment was required for working capital. Some customers were local, such as Horrocks & Jacson of Preston, but the accounts suggest that larger customers included Glasgow agents Bogle, Douglas & Co., Oswald Stevenson & Co. and John Shepherd & Co., also based in Manchester. As the firm evolved, these Scottish connections became increasingly important. Stevenson, in particular, became more significant and then, in 1853, the Ashworths began selling to another Scottish customer, J. & P. Coats.[213] Chapter 5 revisits these connections in more detail.

From 1841, the firm also began to produce and sell its cloth using a small weaving shed of ninety-six power looms at New Eagley,[214] necessitating a new set of contacts to access markets. John Slagg & Co. of Manchester and Rathbones of Liverpool provided opportunities in export markets, albeit with mixed results. In 1845 the Ashworths reached an agreement with Atkinson, Tootal & Co., also of Manchester, who agreed to 'furnish a market for the whole of our manufacture of cambric and jaconet cloth', with profits shared equally.[215]

The agreement represented a significant opportunity. Atkinson Tootal was a profitable firm and used its money and influence to promote railway connections from Manchester to the Midlands and London. One partner, Edward Tootal, increasingly focused on railways in collaboration with Edward Watkin, who had a significant influence on the development of the wider network.[216]

At New Eagley, the agreement stimulated investment in weaving capacity. Before the agreement, in 1845, the annual equivalent value of cloth production was £7,912, using fixed capital worth around £4,000 and 96 looms. After the deal, in 1848, the comparable figures were £16,118, £7,485, and 180. Wages also increased in the same proportion, from £442 to £895.[217] These figures suggest that productivity gains from the introduction of power looms were small. Moreover, poor quality control resulted in the breakdown of the arrangement

213 Customer account settlement periods calculated from yarn sales and amounts owing for yarn, AP, Quarterly stock books and Henry & Edmund Ashworth Stock Accounts, November 1831 et seq., and 1853, Eng. MS, 1201. By 1839, Oswald Stevenson & Co. were taking over 50% of the yarn output. Boyson, Ashworth Cotton, p. 57.

214 AP, Quarterly stock books, Weaving accounts, 1841 et seq., Eng. MS, 1201. Boyson, Ashworth Cotton, p. 60.

215 Boyson, Ashworth Cotton, pp. 40–2; AP, Weaving account, third quarter, 1845, Eng. MS, 1201.

216 D. Hodgkins (ed.), The Diary of Edward Watkin (Manchester, 2013).

217 AP, Quarterly stock books, Weaving accounts, Eng. MS, 1201.

with Atkinson Tootal after only a year, with a small net loss on the contract. After that, the output of the weaving shed was sent directly to a warehouse in Booth Street, Manchester. These difficulties attenuated the Ashworths' commitment to expansion in weaving and they failed to realize their earlier plans for a shed of six hundred looms.[218]

Unlike the step increase in fixed capital with the introduction of steam-powered mule spinning in the early 1800s, the subsequent conversion to steam-powered weaving typically involved lower growth rates. As noted already, the growth rate of the Birley partnership centred on Chorlton slowed during this period.

Continuing the story of Wallshaw Mill provides a further illustration. Once steam-powered mule spinning was established there, looms were added sometime between 1818 and 1825. In 1847 the mill was still owned by Joseph Jones and had a total fixed capital of £30,742, excluding factory buildings, which were rented, and employed four hundred workers. Compared to 1808, the capital had approximately doubled, at an equivalent annual growth rate of only 5.0%, but wage costs had increased by a factor of around three, or an annual equivalent of 8.1%.[219]

These changes contrasted with Lees' business model c.1816 when his firm usually worked shorter hours than the Manchester average. Enhanced productivity in spinning and a market that typically oversupplied the weaving section, particularly in remoter hubs of handloom weaving, had reduced pressure to work longer hours.[220] As a consequence of productivity imbalances between spinning and weaving, working hours were increased in 1826. Following the restrictions on child working hours in the 1833 Factory Act, the firm was one of many to adopt the relay system. A summons for offences against the Act, including working under-13s longer than the legislated hours and falsifying the time book, provides further evidence of intensification during this period.[221]

A similar pattern of growth through the four stages can be observed at Fielden Brothers of Todmorden. Here, small water-powered mills provided output for an extensive domestic weaving operation, which, after 1794, could be

218   AP, Quarterly stock books, Manufacturing account, arrangement with Atkinson, Tootal & Co., 1847, Eng. MS, 1201; Boyson, *Ashworth Cotton*, pp. 42–4, 59–60.

219   Assuming an average weekly wage of 123d in 1808 (G. H. Wood, *The History of Wages in the Cotton Trade During the Past Hundred Years* (London, 1910), table 41, p. 127) and 137d in 1844 (this and other figures and assumptions for 1840s per Foster, *Class Struggle*, p. 296).

220   *Select Committee on the State of the Children Employed in the Manufactories*, ev. Thomas Whitelegg, p. 383. *Factories Inquiry Commission*, 450, D1, ev. Nanny Wolfenden, p. 706.

221   E. Baines, *History, Directory and Gazetteer of the County Palatine of Lancaster*, vol. 2 (Liverpool, 1825), p. 447. *Factories Inquiry Commission*, 450, D1, ev. Nanny Wolfenden, p. 706; *Return of Mills in Lancaster and York, in which the System of Relays of Children has been Observed, since July 1836*, BPP, 1837, 50, p. 195; *Return of Number of Persons Summoned for Offences against the Factories Act, 1835–36*, BPP, 1836, 50, p. 9.

sent to Manchester via the Rochdale Canal.[222] By 1811, the firm had 2,280 mule spindles and 864 throstle spindles at Waterside Mill and 2400 mule spindles at Lumbutts mill, suggesting a total fixed capital value of £4,000 to £5,000. A large sixty-horsepower steam engine intended to power eight hundred new looms was scheduled for introduction in 1825, in a new shed which was then the largest in the world. By 1832, manufacturing assets, including smaller mills, totalled £92,739.

Notwithstanding these investments, in 1832 most weaving was still done by handlooms. Measured according to business scope, the number of mills and the size of the payroll, Fielden was the biggest cotton manufacturer in England at that date. As with previous examples, such rapid growth was fuelled primarily by the application of steam power to mule spinning. Estimates of fixed capital between 1811 and 1832 suggest an annual equivalent growth rate of 13.2%. Such sizeable investment was sustained by the success of their policy of direct selling on consignment to Manchester merchants selling into Latin America such as Hodgson Robinson, and also their transatlantic partnership with Hebden and Pickersgill, and related businesses.[223] These involvements, coupled with the retention of some handloom capacity, meant that although heavily invested in factory plant and equipment, the fixed capital element constituted only around 22% of the total.

As a function of parallel increases in fixed and working capital require-ments, total financial capital investment increased substantially in the early decades of the nineteenth century. Although investment in fixed capital had the potential to increase the turnover time of capital,[224] progress was slow. By 1831, circulating capital still made up around 53% of the total capital invested at Quarry Bank Mill.[225] Robert Hyde Greg estimated the turnover of the total

222 E. Baines, *History, Directory and Gazetteer of the County Palatine of Lancaster*, vol. 1 (Liverpool, 1825), p. 126.

223 B. R. Law, *Fieldens of Todmorden: A Nineteenth Century Business Dynasty* (Littleborough, 1995), p. 20. Baines, *County Palatine of Lancaster*, vol. 2, p. 565. In terms of spindles, the growth in fixed capital was 9.5%, but this comparison excludes the introduction of power looms from 1825. Capital calculated from Law, *Fieldens of Todmorden*, tables III and VI, pp. 38, 65, the propor-tions were £61,000 fixed capital at the main site at Waterside Mill and the smaller mills, out of total capital of £277,000. Scale and wealth measures: see S. D. Chapman, 'The Fielden Fortune. The Finances of Lancashire's most Successful Ante-bellum Manufacturing Family', *Financial History Review* 3 (1996), 7–28, tables 1 and 7, pp. 8–9, 26.

224 P. Hudson, *The Industrial Revolution* (London, 2014), pp. 25–6.

225 GP, Partnership Accounts, 31 March 1831, C5/1/2/3–4: floating capital, £16,299, total capital £30,634. The sunk capital was rented to the business by Samuel Greg and not shown on the balance sheet. To estimate its value, fixed capital additions were depreciated at the rates declared by Robert Hyde Greg at the *Factories Inquiry Commission*. In 1833 the ratio was 50–60%: GP, Partnership Accounts, C5/1/2/3 and statement of sunk and circulating capital, C5/8/32. Greg's numbers suggest the ratio to be 59.09%; if, however, more conservative valuations are used (see chapter 3), the figure would be close to 50%.

capital of the business as about once per year.[226] When the Dugdale partnership began in 1797, fixed capital was 12.47% of the total; by 1823 it had increased to 31.56%.[227] Corresponding figures for McConnel & Kennedy were 31.82% in 1797 and 55.14% in 1827.[228]

Capital structure and industry growth

In summary, the examples detailed in this chapter, illustrate why the literature lacks clarity in terms of the capital structure of textile firms in the industrial revolution. Some authors have suggested that firms could access modest amounts of fixed capital relatively easily but placed voluntary restraints on further growth due to supervisory and managerial problems associated with a grander scale.[229] Chapman suggests that accessing working capital was more problematic than fixed capital, noting that Cardwell, Birley & Hornby, Fielden Brothers and Horrocks Miller & Co. all experienced problems obtaining finance for exports to Latin America and the Orient. Richardson's study of McConnel & Kennedy and Cowpe, Oldknow & Siddon shows that fixed capital requirements were higher than previously thought by Pollard and others, suggesting a ratio of 1:1. These arguments are not incompatible, since, as Mokyr points out, circulating capital increased in tandem with fixed capital formation. More broadly, Mokyr's 'growing up' model suggests a long period of disequilibrium, during which old and new technologies coexist with 'quasi-rents accruing to the new sector.[230] The evidence from the cases in this chapter broadly confirms this view.

It also shows that interpreting the build-up of capital, and its fixed and circulating components, depends crucially on the choice of census date and whether the firm is defined purely as a production site or as a more extensive network of associated business partnerships. Chapman has suggested that before 1815 the previously estimated ratio of fixed to working capital of 1:2 was probably too low and that 1:3 was perhaps more realistic, factoring the higher investment in marketing and distribution of the larger firms. Indeed, this was

---

226   *Factories Inquiry Commission*, 450, D2, ev. Greg, p. 784, Appendix A, No. 1, Second Mill. The figures contained in this table also correspond to a handwritten 'Statement of Sunk and Floating Capital' (GP, C5/8/32).

227   Nathaniel Dugdale & Brothers, Valuations, WP, Eng. MS, 1208.

228   Richardson 'The structure of capital', table I, p. 493.

229   V. Gatrell, 'Labour, power, and the size of firms in the second quarter of the nineteenth century', *EcHR* 30 (1977), 95–139. R. Lloyd-Jones and M. Lewis, *Manchester and the Age of the Factory: The Business Structure of Cottonopolis in the Industrial Revolution* (London, 1988).

230   Chapman, 'Financial Restraints'; Richardson, 'The structure of capital'; Mokyr, 'Editor's Introduction: The New Economic History and the Industrial Revolution'.

true for firms such as Fielden and also Thomson & Chippendall.[231] Chapman also cites Horrockses, which had a more substantial working capital than fixed capital in the 1830s (for example 1:1.6, fixed:working captial in 1836).[232] However, the evidence from the period in question, taken from Horrockses accounting records, suggests the choice of date is crucial. Before 1815, fixed capital predominated as a proportion of total capital, suggesting two significant take-off growth phases, first in fixed capital, then subsequently an expansion of working capital in the form of investment in marketing and distribution to attack overseas markets. Philips & Lee was perhaps a better example of Chapman's figure as a first-mover in steam-powered mule spinning in the 1790s, which generated a steep rise in working capital on the back of the initial fixed capital investment. Other firms, such as Dugdale and Thomson & Chippendall, experienced similar patterns, but somewhat later in terms of step increases in fixed capital, as they emulated the pioneering firms. When Nassau Senior toured Lancashire factories in 1829, he found examples of capital intensification: 'At Orrell's splendid factory, we found a new blower enabling three persons to do the work of four. At Bollington, we found a new machine, which transfers the sliver direct from the cards to the drawing-frame, and thus dispenses with another class of attendants.' The net effect of all these changes was to increase the fixed and reduce the circulating proportions of total capital. Improved transport linkages meanwhile lowered the requirement to hold stocks, thereby further increasing the ratio of fixed to circulating capital.[233] As a result, by the 1830s, there were more firms with higher fixed capital ratios, around 1:1, like the Ashworths, Wallshaw Mill and the Greg mills, as suggested by Baines in 1835 concerning the industry as a whole and endorsed subsequently by Pollard.[234]

For these reasons, the four-stage model proposed in Table 1 is useful for retelling the story. In terms of fixed capital requirements, these naturally were small in the first stage, although it is worth noting that there was not much difference between Wyatt and Paul-type factories of the 1750s and the Arkwright-type water spinners of the 1790s. Investment in these technologies nonetheless promoted a significant expansion of domestic outworking, which was more readily available to well-capitalized and established merchants, now able to expand into manufacturing. Even for larger firms, such as Cardwell, Birley & Hornby, there were diseconomies of scale associated with managing

231 Thomson & Chippendall had built up its investments in land and estates, and to a greater extent than industrial capital, suggesting Chapman's estimate of the fixed to working capital ratio was perhaps if anything too high. See TCP, Primrose works, Ledger accounts, CYC 3/46–48.
232 Chapman, 'Financial Restraints', p. 64 and appendix III.
233 Senior and Horner, *Letters on the Factory Act*, pp. 5–6.
234 Baines, *History of the Cotton Manufacture*, p. 413. Baines estimated fixed capital invested in cotton manufacture in 1832 at £15 million, with an equivalent sum invested in floating capital. Baines' definition of floating capital includes stock and necessary sundries (p. 342) and therefore excludes net investment in trade receivable balances. Pollard, 'Fixed capital'.

these networks. Smaller industrial capitalists, such as James Lees, meanwhile relied much more heavily on cash-based markets. The step increase in fixed capital came in the period 1795 to 1815, which witnessed the transition from model 2 to model 3, and the development of steam-powered mule-spinning factories. During this time, fixed capital doubled and trebled very quickly. In turn, this created further pressures to expand the handloom sector, warehouse facilities and distribution networks. These developments also absorbed significant fixed capital, in terms of cottage building, conversions and warehousing facilities, estimated at between £1 and £2 million, which was in some cases provided by building societies.[235]

During the take-off phase, firms thus expanded working capital disproportionately, reflecting the increased productivity in spinning. For established merchants, ready access to working capital provided sources of finance for further expansion in mill capacity. Technology, limited at this stage mainly to steam power and mule spinning, was less of an entry barrier than access to markets and production capacity through networks, including weaving and outworking, as well as direct export of yarn. Markets, including credit markets, remained fragmented, which allowed simultaneous investments in old and new technology and created vulnerability to long credit cycles and the effects of sudden contractions in trade. The typical debt collection period for firms such as Birley & Hornby and Ashworths was around six months. Other evidence confirms that credit was more than twelve months in many cases and rarely less than three months.[236] Chapman provides further evidence of significant imperfections and uncertainties in cotton and credit markets before 1815, which were eased subsequently by the development of bank credit and the emergence of specialist providers of finance for exports.[237] The introduction of joint-stock banking in 1826 and the boom in new banks during the 1830s offered new sources of funding and reduced dependency on bills of exchange.

The transition from model 3 to model 4 involved a more gradual rate of growth in capital. Whereas the introduction of steam-powered mule spinning had a complementary relationship with working capital, the introduction of the power loom was substitutive. In other words, as new looms were installed in factories, firms could divest their domestic networks and associated long credit cycles in equal measure. J. & N. Philips and the Ashworths illustrate this point. Moreover, the evidence from the 1830s and 1840s shows that factory production was becoming relatively more labour-intensive during this period, due to the absorption of weaving, and reflecting a stagnation of wages as a percentage of

---

235 G. Timmins and S. Timmins, *Made in Lancashire: A History of Regional Industrialisation* (Manchester, 1998), pp. 97, 137 and appendix.
236 Chapman, 'Financial Restraints', p. 56; and appendix I; Ellison, *Cotton Trade of Great Britain*.
237 Chapman, 'Financial Restraints'.

total output in the first half of the nineteenth century.[238] In sum, these pressures resulted in a slower rate of capital growth, notwithstanding the application of steam power in the weaving section and much more rapid capital formation in adjacent sectors such as railways.

As a by-product, individual entrepreneurs accumulated capital rapidly in the period c.1760–1830. Their behaviour was mercantilist rather than profit-maximizing. As will be discussed in chapter 3, the notion of profit maximization was underdeveloped before 1830. Even so, substantial profits were to be made and were indeed necessary as the motive force shifting firms through the different stages of the growth model. The next chapter examines the profitability and its variation through time and firm to firm.

238 On wage stagnation and wages as a share of surplus, see R. C. Allen, 'Engels' pause: Technical change, capital accumulation, and inequality in the British industrial revolution', *Explorations in Economic History* 46 (2009), 418–35.

2

Industrialization and Profitability

When we walk the streets of large commercial towns, we must be struck with the
hurried gait and care-worn features of the well-dressed passengers.

Charles Taylor Thackrah on health issues of
Merchants and Master Manufacturers, 1831.[1]

Economists have extensively examined the performance of the cotton industry
during its take-off period and early phases of the industrial revolution. Positive
financial performance can generally be assumed for a take-off industry but
cannot be expected to apply evenly. The boom-slump cycle was a prominent
feature of the industry. Recent scholarship has downplayed the disruptive aspects
of industrialization, arguing that it was a more gradual and local phenomenon
than previously thought. These interpretations have been predicated on the
prior and independent dominance of the commercial and financial services
sectors, and their elites of 'gentlemanly capitalism'.[2] Cotton, along with a small
number of other vital industries such as iron and transportation, are regarded
as instances of specific productivity improvement, with the rest of the economy
'mired in pre-modern backwardness'.[3] These discussions have centred on the
Schumpeterian view of rapid growth, based on a disequilibrium model in which
capital market imperfections allow innovative firms to restrict entry, thereby
earning long-run super-normal profits. Neoclassical interpretations, in contrast,
argue that firms were relatively untroubled by capital market imperfections and
experienced few problems accessing finance, facilitating entry and rapid adjustments to equilibrium profit levels, with the gains from technological innovation

1   C. T. Thackrah, *The Effects of the Principal Arts, Trades and Professions and of Civic States
and Habits of Living on Health and Longevity* (London, 1831), pp. 84–5.
2   P. J. Cain and A. G. Hopkins, *British Imperialism: 1688–2000* (London, 2014).
3   P. Temin, 'Two views of the British industrial revolution', *JEH* 57 (1997), 63–82; J. Mokyr,
'Editor's Introduction: The new economic history and the Industrial Revolution', *The British
Industrial Revolution: An Economic Perspective*, ed. J. Mokyr (Boulder, CO, 1993), 1–127; N. F. R.
Crafts and C. K. Harley, 'Output growth and the industrial revolution: A restatement of the
Crafts–Harley view', *EcHR* 45 (1992), 703–30.

transmitted through falling prices.[4] The evidence above, reviewed in chapter 1, shows that there is some truth in all these explanations since the transition from one model to another typically relied on the modernization of only one section of the value chain at a time. Within each model stage of development, innovation and traditional business practice coexisted.

Questions about which firms were particularly profitable, when and why, therefore offer a potentially useful new perspective on the industrial revolution in the cotton industry. For example, how different were profits in the four stages of development? Were transitions between the models motivated by the offer of potential additional profits? Were such profits readily accessible to all firms? Answering these questions builds on previous studies of individual firms, which have identified several reasons for likely business success at the entrepreneurial level. The role of technology has traditionally been an important explanatory factor.[5] Indeed the positive pay-offs from such investments are almost a truism since if they were not profitable, they would not have been emulated, and the take-off would not have occurred. New profit-making routes offered new possibilities for upward social mobility.[6] Entrepreneurship played an important role, but the favourable business environment meant that poor decisions based on inadequate accounting went unpunished.[7] Finance for investment came from plough-back of profits rather than third-party loans.[8] The competitive climate placed business leaders in a dynamic that forced them to invest in order to maintain their position.[9] Notwithstanding the variety of interpretations, the prevalence of competition, particularly in an atomized industry such as cotton textiles, had rarely been questioned.

However, other non-market factors were also at work. More recent literature has identified the importance of access to external economies of scale and particularly network connections.[10] Political connections and the development of ideology meant that Lancashire cotton masters were the leading entrepreneurial group of the industrial revolution.[11] Pre-industrial business practices

---

4   For a recent review see C. K. Harley, 'Was technological change in the early Industrial Revolution Schumpeterian? Evidence of cotton textile profitability', *Explorations in Economic History* 49 (2000), 516–27.

5   A. E. Musson and E. Robinson, 'The early growth of steam power', *EcHR* 11 (1959), 418–39; T. S. Ashton, *The Industrial Revolution* (Oxford, 1969); F. Crouzet, *Capital formation in the Industrial Revolution* (London, 1972); R. C. Allen, *The British Industrial Revolution in Global Perspective* (Cambridge, 2009).

6   K. Honeyman, *Origins of Enterprise: Business Leadership in the Industrial Revolution* (Manchester, 1982).

7   P. Hudson, *The Industrial Revolution* (London, 2014), p. 23.

8   Ashton, *Industrial Revolution*, p. 97.

9   Hudson, *The Industrial Revolution*, p. 25.

10 M. B. Rose, *Firms, Networks and Business Values: The British and American Cotton Industries since 1750* (Cambridge, 2000).

11 A. C. Howe, *The Cotton Masters, 1830–1860* (Oxford, 1984), pp. 48, 310–11.

persisted, for example, with the putting-out system in the substantially unmechanized weaving sector.[12] As the putting-out networks became larger, control became more complicated, and embezzlements a more significant problem. Thus, entrepreneurs adopted the factory system, with its machine-based division of labour, because monitoring costs were high in putting out, not because the factory system offered greater technical efficiency.[13] Innovation in factory production was gradual and not sufficient to overcome the advantages of handloom weaving in finer, higher-quality cloth production until the 1840s.[14] Indeed, the putting-out system presented severe problems for the drapers and other cotton merchants. In such a system, there were significant opportunities for producers to embezzle, substitute inferior materials, or otherwise renege on agreements.[15] A residual and vital question is just how profitable were these alternative arrangements?

What limited quantitative data exists has been repeatedly examined to develop numerous interpretations based on the rate of growth, its productivity and the innovations of its entrepreneurs. Less is known about the profitability of the individual firms involved. Yet this is an essential dimension of the industrialization process, which links the availability and investment of capital by entrepreneurs, their relative success and the process of subsequent capital formation. The examination of the individual firm's profits also allows linkages to be made between quantitative evidence on financial performance and qualitative evidence about the role of entrepreneurs and firm-specific circumstances.

To address the question of profitability, the financial performance of a group of firms in and around the nascent Lancashire cotton industry during the industrial revolution is examined. This chapter begins with a review of the issues and evidence concerning the average rate of profit during industrialization. It will thus illustrate the long-run pattern of profitability in the period 1797–1860 and offer some explanation of profit trends compared with

12   J. H. Clapham, *An Economic History of Modern Britain*, vol. 1: *The Early Railway Age, 1820–1850* (Cambridge, 1930).

13   S. A. Marglin, 'What do bosses do? The origins and functions of hierarchy in capitalist production', *Review of Radical Political Economics* 6 (1974), 60–112.

14   For example, the weft stop motion invented by Kenworthy and Bullough. G. Timmins, *The Last Shift: The Decline of Handloom Weaving in Nineteenth-Century Lancashire* (Manchester, 1993), p. 23.

15   S. Pollard, *The Genesis of Modern Management: A Study of the Industrial Revolution in Great Britain* (Harmondsworth, 1968); Marglin, 'What do bosses do?'; E. P. Thompson, 'Time, work-discipline and industrial capitalism', *Past & Present* 38 (1967), 56–97, at p. 73. D. Landes, *The Unbound Prometheus: Technological Change and Industrial Development in Western Europe from 1750 to the Present* (Cambridge, 1969), p. 59. D. A. Reid, 'The Decline of Saint Monday 1766–1876', *Past & Present* 71 (1976), 76–101; S. Toms, 'Financial control, managerial control and accountability: evidence from the British Cotton Industry, 1700–2000', *Accounting, Organizations and Society* 30 (2005), 627–53; F. F. Mendels, 'Proto-industrialization: The first phase of the industrialization process', *JEH* 32 (1972), 241–61.

trends in prices, productivity and innovation. The chapter also considers the strategies and performance of a selection of individual firms based on similarities and differences, including the adoption of steam-powered mule spinning, that explain differential and superior performance. Such financial comparisons through time and with other firms allow the consequences of entrepreneurial effort, and associated risk, to be quantified. The purpose of the analysis is to cast further light on contrasting interpretations by showing how firms using old and new technology performed, and how they accessed and used finance to fund their growth. By conducting such an investigation, further insights can be gained into recent debates and different interpretations of the industrialization process.

Profits and profit calculations

The chapter draws on firms' financial records, based on the above review, covering the period 1767–1860. During this period, the financial records of the first twenty-four firms listed in the CIFD (appendix 1) are used to compute the return on capital. The characteristics of the sample were determined first by their survival in the archive and second by the capability of the records to support calculations of return on capital.[16] The sample was supplemented by sources in the secondary literature. These sources were used either to corroborate figures and estimates from the archival record or to enhance the sample using data collected in tables or appendices.

The characteristic feature of the individual firms discussed so far is that all have surviving archives that allow rates of return on capital to be calculated. Successful firms were often the innovators, and the durability or otherwise of their profits therefore provide a useful test of the Schumpeterian hypothesis and its alternatives. At the same time, survival bias in this sample is inevitable. Firms that failed typically did not have their archives saved, and those belonging to influential social networks were more likely to have their archives preserved. Even so, individuals operating in networks of partnerships had the opportunity to withdraw from those ventures where business was not going well, and some of these failures are reflected in the sample. For example, Samuel Greg abandoned his partnership with Lyle after an accumulation of bad debts in 1809. Later, the Greg partners withdrew from the unsuccessful Ancoats mill after a string of heavy losses in 1827. Through their involvement in multiple business partnerships, the Gregs survived these sporadic misfortunes, and

---

16   Return on capital is defined as net profit plus interest paid to partners and partners' salaries (all firms are partnerships). Capital is defined as net assets, i.e. fixed assets plus current assets minus current liabilities, which is equal to and also measured by partners' permanent and accumulated capital plus long-term liabilities.

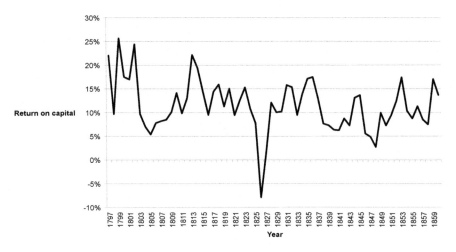

Figure 4. Long-run profitability, 1797–1860

Note: Return on capital is the ratio of profit before interest divided by total partners' capital plus long-term loan capital.

Sources: See appendix 1.

elsewhere in the industry, the bankruptcy rate declined steadily from an annual peak of 3% in 1806 to well under 1% by 1835. The effect of these statistics would be to overestimate the average profit of the industry by approximately 1.9% per year, based on surviving firms only.[17]

For each firm in the sample, return on capital was calculated by taking the profit before interest divided by total partners' capital including, where applicable, partners' loan accounts. Managerial salaries, which were paid to partners in some cases, were also added back to profit. In isolated cases, for example, Cardwell, Birley & Hornby, there was additional third-party loan capital, which was included in the denominator with the associated interest added back to profits. In the more general case, total capital corresponded to partners' capital. The return on capital, therefore, typically measured the total profit generated for the partners as a ratio of their total investment.

Data requirements for these calculations and the partial nature of the archival records determined the number of observations. Firm-level data was typically only available for shorter periods within the overall frame of the study, leading to an unbalanced panel. Using all available data, the number of observations

---

17   P. M. Solar and J. S. Lyons, 'The English cotton spinning industry, 1780–1840, as revealed in the columns of the *London Gazette*', *BH* 53 (2011), 302–23, at p. 307. Calculated assuming that the sample rate of profit is representative of surviving firms and that bankrupt firms record a loss in the year of bankruptcy equal to total capital, i.e. −100%.

Table 2. Profitability by growth phase and trade cycle interval

		Period	Average return on capital %	Standard Deviation %
A. Growth phase	Models 1 & 2	1777–1796	11.31	16.23
	Model 3	1797–1825	13.38	5.40
	Model 4	1826–1860	9.97	5.35
	Whole period	1777–1860	11.47	9.17
B. Growth phase by firm	Models 1 & 2		15.45	7.22
	Model 3		13.62	5.17
	Model 4		9.29	7.24
C. Peak-to-peak cycles		1777–1790	14.96	9.89
		1791–1798	6.06	22.57
		1799–1812	12.71	6.11
		1813–1822	14.28	2.59
		1823–1830	7.48	6.02
		1831–1835	14.32	2.33
		1836–1844	9.69	3.42
		1845–1852	8.23	3.92
		1853–1860	12.29	4.77

Note: Return on capital is the percentage of profit before interest divided by total partners' capital plus long-term loan capital.

Sources: Calculated from CIFD.

up to 1860 was 511. The median number of firms was only seven per year, although, in some years, there were twelve firms in the sample.

The unbalanced nature of the sample is most problematic in the earlier years, mainly 1777–85, for which there was only one firm, Cardwell, Birley & Hornby, and 1786–96 when they were joined by Cowpe, Oldknow & Siddon. From 1797 the number of firms builds up with most years in the period 1810–50 featuring eight firms or more. In this period, the sample features several mills owned by Samuel Greg & Sons. These mills were managed as independent profit centres by Samuel Greg's four sons, engaged in different activities using different technologies, and their financial results were reported separately. Their performances were, therefore, representative of the diversity of the industry. Figure 4 shows the financial performance of the sample firms and illustrates the rate of return on total capital for the period 1797–1860. The years 1777–96 are not shown due to the small number of firms. Table 2 shows the average return and standard deviation by period and groups of firms. Panel A takes the average return on capital of all firms by year and aggregates them by period, determined with reference to the expected dates of technology availability and adoption set out in chapter 1. For example, the inception of steam-powered mule spinning (model 3) is taken to be 1797. Panel B re-examines the data by assigning individual firms to model growth phases according to dates of actual technology adoption by that firm. Panel C examines the long-run time trend set out in Figure 4, using trade cycle peak-to-peak measures of average profitability. The patterns in Figure 4 and Table 2 are used as benchmarks to inform the discussion in the ensuing sections.

Early phase financial performance

The evidence in Table 2 suggests that early phase growth models were highly profitable. However, this conclusion relies on limited evidence from a small number of firms. The Cardwell, Birley & Hornby archive offers a rare glimpse of profitability in what could be definitively referred to as a phase 1-type putting-out network. The firm's trading performance from 1777 to 1784 followed a cyclical trend, with profits averaging 19.12% per annum. At such rates, profits were more than sufficient to expand working capital, leaving around £26,000 for division between the partners. These accumulations, inside and outside the business, were enough to insulate the partnership from the vicissitudes of the trade cycle and the risks associated with further significant investments. The firm experienced considerable volatility in profits, with a standard deviation of return on capital of 7.81%.[18] Unfortunately Cardwell, Birley & Hornby aside, there is little further evidence of model 1, firm-level financial performance.

In Table 2, therefore, models 1 and 2 are aggregated due to the small number of firms. Panel A shows that profits averaged 11.31% during the years 1777–96 when models 1 and 2 predominated. Panel B shows that the average profit for firms accommodating model 1 and 2 strategies, regardless of the year of adoption, was 15.45%. Such a high average rate of profit implies that model 2 firms could be financially successful because profit rates were higher for all firms in the early nineteenth century.

The experiences of individual firms explain the specific reasons for these early profit premiums. For Cardwell, Birley & Hornby, the model 2 phase came after 1784 with the automation of spinning, which, as explained in chapter 1, facilitated the further expansion of the putting-out network and associated warehouse and distribution facilities. Compared to model 1, however, the

18   Figures calculated from Cardwell, Birley & Hornby, Ledgers, 1777–1784, WP, Eng. MS, 1208.

results were disappointing. Up to 1792, the firm experienced sharp fluctuations in profits, which averaged only 10.57%. Cowpe, Oldknow & Siddon experienced a similar pattern. Rates of return averaged 9.6% in the ten years after 1786 and were highly variable. During this time, the firm accessed new markets and benefited from a general boom in trading conditions in 1789–90.[19] These developments paved the way for the installation of steam power, which helped further improve the firm's position after 1797.

For Cardwell, Birley & Hornby, the outbreak of war exacerbated these trends and the profit rate fell further to an average of 3.71% up to 1809. Some of these problems may have been attributable to the management problems of large putting-out networks highlighted in chapter 1. However, significant investments in working capital also increased the firm's vulnerability to market dislocations in the war years and the associated accentuation of the trade cycle, placing pressure on cash flow during the downturns, including reliance on loan accounts, and leading the partners to increase their investments. For a time, this included the expansion of the water-spinning mills at Scorton.

Increased productivity in spinning meant that a relatively small capital investment could sustain a more extensive network of outworking handloom weavers. Small outlays in fixed capital and the self-financing nature of circulating capital tended to increase the returns on capital from this strategy. Nathaniel Dugdale & Brothers sustained high returns on capital in 1797–1808 (23.5%). These profits were remarkable, in contrast to Cardwell, Birley & Hornby, and given its relatively small scale and primitive technology. Even so, low-cost spinning-jennies could supply a much more extensive weaving network and also external yarn markets.

Another reason for Nathaniel Dugdale & Brothers' strong financial performance was that as a peripheral firm, well away from the main markets, it was better able to exploit price differences locally. Consequently, the firm achieved a short-run competitive advantage in certain yarn counts through price differentials. The position was quickly lost, though, leading the firm to shift progressively into finer counts. For example, the count range in 1797 was 21/28s compared to 28/74s in 1803, creating the opportunity for more significant premia. In 1803 the firm was able to sell 74s yarn for 396d/lb at a time when the market price for 100s was only 85d.[20] Although not necessarily achieving such premia on every transaction, it may have helped the firm to attain short-run excess profits arising from product market imperfections.

The broader strategy was similar to Cardwell, Birley & Hornby, in that Nathaniel Dugdale & Brothers was able to use increased productivity in spinning, and road and canal infrastructure development, to control an expanded weaving network. As a smaller business, it had the potential to

---

19   Pigott, *Hollins: A Study of Industry, 1784–1949* (Nottingham, 1949), pp. 36–7.
20   Nathaniel Dugdale & Brothers, Yarn prices, WP, Eng. MS, 1208.

grow without experiencing the diseconomies of managing a more extensive network or face exposure to risk from large working capital holdings during trade cycle fluctuations. The examples of Cardwell, Birley & Hornby and Nathaniel Dugdale & Brothers show that in models 1 and 2, infrastructure development and then automation of spinning facilitated step expansion of working-capital-intensive businesses, but did not at the same time guarantee sustainable abnormal profits.

Steam-powered mule spinning and profitability

In their model 1 and 2 expansion phases, firms like Nathaniel Dugdale & Brothers and Cardwell, Birley & Hornby used technology to modify traditional networking arrangements. Others integrated it much more closely in their business models. These firms included McConnel & Kennedy, Cowpe, Oldknow & Siddon, Birley & Co., Horrocks Miller, Philips & Lee, and Greg & Ewart.[21] All were early investors in steam power and mule spinning, typically in urban locations. From the early 1790s, the mule was generating rapid productivity gains, particularly for higher-count yarns,[22] so the expectation would be that firms making these investments would secure above-average profits. Even so, as late as 1833, evidence given to the *Factories Inquiry Commission* suggested that there was no definitive advantage for steam, as coal costs for steam-powered firms balanced the risks of drought for watermills.[23]

The evidence indicates that firms investing in steam-powered, mule-spinning factories experienced significant but short-term boosts to their profits. On average, firms installing steam-powered mule spinning achieved profit rates 3.9% higher than a benchmark average return in the first ten years following their introduction.[24] The experience of individual firms corroborates this pattern, most strikingly for McConnel & Kennedy. In the period of its most

---

21   The Greg & Ewart partnership was based on Quarry Bank Mill and, from 1807, Peter Street Mill in Manchester. In 1815 Samuel Greg sold his interest in Peter Street Mill to Ewart: GP, Partnership Accounts, C5/1/2/3–4.

22   Allen, *British Industrial Revolution*, figure 8.2, p. 208.

23   *Factories Inquiry Commission*, BPP, 1833, 450, D1, ev. H. H. Birley and H. Hoole, pp. 729–30.

24   Computed using all sample firms and a ten-year window for each firm installing steam-powered mule spinning: Cowpe, Oldknow & Siddon, McConnel & Kennedy, Horrocks, Birley & Hornby and J. Lees. For each firm the abnormal rate of return was calculated as the difference between the return on capital for the year of installation (time $t_1 \ldots t_{10}$) and subsequent years of operation (time $t_1 \ldots t_{10}$) for that firm minus a benchmark based on the average return for all other firms for each year. The benchmark only included observations from firms that did not install mule spindles during the same window. The abnormal returns were then averaged for the window $t_1 \ldots t_{10}$.

significant investments in steam-powered mule spinning[25] between 1797 and 1807, McConnel & Kennedy averaged profits of 21.1%, which in turn was a profit above 10% relative to a benchmark of other cotton firms in the same period. However, profits declined quickly thereafter. As the scale of the operation increased, particularly between 1819 and 1820,[26] the firm demonstrated relatively poor performance, suggesting that the strategy of investing in steam-driven fixed capital did not necessarily lead to permanent competitive advantage, even where previous investments provided the basis for further expansion. McConnel & Kennedy's profits declined from an average of 21.1% between 1797 and 1808 to just 3.8% between 1813 and 1827, a pattern that suggests the rapid loss of initial abnormal profits attributable to innovation. Birley & Hornby had a similar experience with returns averaging 27.7% in the period 1811–15, which directly followed on from the significant investments in new buildings and mule spinning at Chorlton.[27] During this time Birley's mills outperformed the benchmark average of other cotton firms by a considerable margin of 12.1%. Profits declined after 1816, notwithstanding further investments.

Horrockses Miller was another firm that achieved a boost in profits in the years immediately after installing steam-powered mule spindles. Between 1799 and 1803, profits averaged 26.4%, which was 11.0% ahead of the benchmark. Again, these profits declined rapidly thereafter. Following a similar investment at Pleasley Vale in 1798, Cowpe, Oldknow & Siddon also experienced a surge in earnings for the next three years, but again like the other firms, suffered lower returns over the longer run.[28]

The most likely reason for short-term sharp increases in profit was the much cheaper unit cost of production. Evidence from Chorlton, analysed in chapter 1, shows that production costs per pound were almost 30% lower than the prevailing market price in 1812.

Although most firms achieved significant boosts to profitability in the years immediately following the introduction of steam-powered mule spinning, profits in the long run tended towards the average for other firms and the industry as a whole. Returns of 9–13% were typical. Cowpe, Oldknow &

25 G. W. Daniels, 'The cotton trade at the close of the Napoleonic War', *Transactions of the Manchester Statistical Society* (1918), 1–29, at p. 19.

26 P. Richardson, 'The structure of capital during the industrial revolution revisited: Two case studies from the cotton textile industry', *EcHR* 42 (1989), 484–503, table I, p. 493. Between 1819 and 1820 the value of gross fixed capital increased from £55,023 to £80,297.

27 See also Stone's analysis, which shows that for a similar period at Chorlton Mills, average profits were very high and in excess of 100%. W. E. Stone, 'An early English cotton mill cost accounting system: Charlton [*sic*] Mills, 1810–1889', *Accounting and Business Research* 4 (1973), 71–8.

28 In the ten years after 1798, the firm averaged a rate of return of 2.5% ahead of the benchmark average.

Siddon averaged 11.2% profit in the period 1796–1813, supplying the domestic market. For similar reasons, James Lees & Son did not experience the high rates of return offered by new spinning technology. In its earlier expansion phase, the firm built excellent connections with local customers. The subsequent next-generation partnership between James and Robert Lees, established in 1808, averaged 10.71% profit in the period up to 1818 following the introduction of steam-powered mule spinning, which was well under the average reported in Table 2, and much less than other Oldham entrepreneurs of this time such as James Gledhill. Although the partners were well connected within the locality, its small scale, its specialization and the relative underdevelopment of the district seemingly limited the firm's competitive position.

The financial advantages of investments in new technology, therefore, appear to be short-lived, offering no guarantee of high returns. The short-run cost advantage for the steam-powered mule mills meant that innovative firms could penetrate markets quickly and cause them to be oversupplied. Developing export market presence was, therefore, crucial for keeping the newly installed machinery operating at full capacity. However, the significant investments in these new factories occurred in the period 1792–1815, coinciding precisely with a period of war and market dislocation. Had the new mule-spinning factories been able to access foreign markets unhindered, the periods of extraordinary profits may have lasted beyond the years immediately following their installation.

As it was, the external market acted as a significant constraint on the realized rate of profit. Limitations in the home market and instability in export markets meant that profitability in cotton, as shown in Figure 4, was strongly correlated with the known features of the trade cycle over this period. The years 1797–1802 saw volatile but generally above-average profits, during which time, according to Daniels, the cotton trade made 'considerable but unsteady progress', associated with rapid expansion of cotton exports.[29] Speculative buying based on the rapid development of the industry ensured that 1799 was also the year in which the raw cotton price reached its long-run peak. Although severe credit conditions persisted,[30] Horrockses Miller, McConnel & Kennedy, Nathaniel Dugdale, and Greg & Ewart all recorded profits above 20% on capital. Only the first two of these companies had thus far made significant investments in fixed capital, suggesting that conditions prevailing in export markets were an equally important determinant of financial profitability. Glasgow merchant, Kirkman Finlay, described

29   G. W. Daniels, 'The cotton trade during the Revolutionary and Napoleonic wars', *Transactions of the Manchester Statistical Society* (1915/16), 53–84, at p. 61; A. D. Gayer, W. W. Rostow and A. J. Schwartz, *The Growth and Fluctuation of the British Economy, 1790–1850* (Oxford, 1953), p. 767; Daniels, 'The cotton trade at the close of the Napoleonic War', pp. 18–19; M. M. Edwards, *The Growth of the British Cotton Trade, 1780–1815* (Manchester, 1967), p. 72.
30   Gayer, Rostow and Schwartz, *Growth and Fluctuation*, p. 71; Daniels, 'The cotton trade during the Revolutionary and Napoleonic wars', p. 61.

the profits in spinning as being at their highest in 1802,[31] and although he did not quantify profitability, the average in Figure 4 reveals this to be 24.4%.

In the period 1803–08, by contrast, profits were below their long-run average. There was a dislocation of markets caused by the resumption of war, with one cotton manufacturer citing 1803 as the end of 'a golden age' and, in the two years that followed, failures in the cotton trade became increasingly numerous as profits 'fluctuated violently at lower levels'.[32] This period of low profits coincided with the expansion of Napoleon's continental system to include much of northern Europe and Russia, following the Treaty of Tilsit in 1807 and the imposition of the American embargo in the same year.[33] Indeed, the year 1807 was a low point for most firms in the industry.

This conclusion is borne out by the relatively poor performance of firms concentrating primarily on merchanting during the war years. Samuel Greg was engaged in several activities during this period, including his cotton-spinning partnership with the innovator Peter Ewart.[34] At the same time, Greg and Ewart formed a partnership with James Lyle to sell manufactured cotton goods in foreign markets.[35] In a period comparable with the innovative manufacturers, 1798–1809, the Greg, Lyle & Ewart partnership achieved average profits of only 5.1%; in the same period, Greg's manufacturing partnership with Ewart made 13.2%. Although offering little that can be generalized about the relative profitability of the two sectors, the comparison is illustrative as the firms shared common management teams. Greg, Lyle & Ewart's operation in foreign markets created high risk, as revealed by the higher standard deviation of its returns on capital. An important reason was that the firm suffered significant losses from bad debts in the American, European and particularly the Russian market.[36]

The level of bad debt in export markets that had been experienced by Greg, Lyle & Ewart was a testimony to the lack of both trust and contractual enforceability in export markets. Alliances with controllers of market networks were, therefore, crucial for firms engaged in upstream manufacturing if the abnormal returns from new technology investments were to be realized and sustained. Notwithstanding their earlier investments, Horrockses performed particularly

31 *Select Committee on Manufactures, Commerce and Shipping*, BPP, 1833, 690, ev. Finlay, q.649, p. 41.
32 William Radcliffe, quoted in E. Baines, *History of the Cotton Manufacture in Great Britain* (London, 1835), p. 338; Edwards, *Growth of the British Cotton Trade*, p. 23; Daniels, 'The cotton trade during the Revolutionary and Napoleonic wars', p. 61.
33 Edwards, *Growth of the British Cotton Trade*, p. 56; Daniels, 'The cotton trade during the Revolutionary and Napoleonic wars', p. 77.
34 A. E. Musson and E. Robinson, 'The origins of engineering in Lancashire', *JEH* 20 (1960), 209–33.
35 M. M. Edwards, 'The development of the British cotton industry, 1780–1815' (Ph.D. dissertation, University of London, 1965), pp. 508–9.
36 Edwards, 'The development of the British cotton industry'.

badly in 1806–08 following the introduction of the continental blockade. J. & N. Philips refocused on Manchester after 1794 and exported to America, first with the assistance of Greg and, after 1800, through the partnership of Philips, Cramond & Co.[37] During this time, as noted in chapter 1, the firm had access to the political influences of George Philips and built up its export contracts.[38] Philips & Lee returned steady profits during the war years and up to 1821, which also necessitated high capital investment given the long credit periods extended to overseas customers.[39] Consequently, the firm's return of 13.5% in the period 1794–1815 was close to the average, notwithstanding the advantages of an urban location associated with access to labour and local external economies of scale and scope. Other longer-established branches of the Philips business, at Whitefield and Tean Hall, contributed to a similar overall rate of profit for the J. & N. Philips partnership of around 12% during the war years.

Philips and other firms benefited from a revival of trade after 1811. A small upturn in that year was followed by a rapid advance in prices in the final quarter of 1812, assisted by peace between Russia and Turkey, the reopening of Levantine trade and the rapid re-establishment of trading relations with several European countries in 1813. Horrockses' profits recovered strongly after 1813. Even so, domestic unrest, the American war and slow progress towards peace in Europe resulted in gloomy assessments by many cotton traders.[40] As a consequence, although average profits were significantly above their long-run average in the period 1813–15, some firms continued to suffer low profits, including James Lees of Oldham, Cowpe, Oldknow & Siddon and Greg & Ewart. Speculators overestimated the demand for manufactured goods in post-war Europe, resulting in a wave of bankruptcies in 1816, including associated bank failures.[41]

The effects of the commercial crisis on the cotton industry were short-lived, and although average profits dipped in 1816, they quickly reverted to above long-term trend in 1817. Returns on capital mirrored the revival in trade in 1817–18, the slump of 1819 and the recovery of 1820. For Horrockses, investment in quality and customer focus contributed to longer-run and sustainable abnormal returns, particularly after the war years. Returns varied sharply, with a substantial increase in the period 1812–15, over and above the longer-run average of 16.9% in the period 1799–1815. After the war, the firm

---

37 S. D. Chapman, *Merchant Enterprise in Britain* (Cambridge, 2004), p. 65. Cramond was based in Philadelphia.
38 JNPP, Ledgers, 1806–1922, M97/2/1. Philips lost interest in the business and the firm floundered after 1815. The average profit at J. & N. Philips in the period 1807–32 was only 6.45%.
39 Howe, *The Cotton Masters*, p. 25. Chapman, *Merchant Enterprise*, p. 66.
40 Edwards, *Growth of the British Cotton Trade*, pp. 62, 72; Daniels, 'The cotton trade during the Revolutionary and Napoleonic wars', pp. 80–2. Daniels, 'The cotton trade at the close of the Napoleonic War', pp. 14–17.
41 Daniels, 'The cotton trade at the close of the Napoleonic War', p. 25.

retained the essential ingredients of superior performance. The Ashworth brothers enlarged the scale of the existing factory at New Eagley, recruited new operatives and increased the width of mules, enhancing their productivity. As a consequence, in the period 1818–22, their profit averaged 17.0%, well above the firm's longer-run average of 10.7%.

Although the Ashworths used water power, these profits were commensurate with those achieved by steam-powered firms in the same period. Notwithstanding the short-run, early advantage for steam-powered mills, some watermills, such as Quarry Bank, were particularly profitable in the 1820s. Despite the apparent disadvantages of the remote location, the profitability of Quarry Bank Mill was impressive. The average return in the period 1816–31 was 19.01% compared to 10.2% for the whole industry. For all years except 1820 and 1825, Quarry Bank's profits were higher than the benchmark average. An important reason, noted in chapter 1, was the significant re-equipment and capacity increases at this time.

The post-war years marked the beginning of a secular trend of declining profit margins.[42] Of all the downturns in the period, the sharpest was that of 1825–26. The investment boom of 1824–25 resulted in a significant addition to capacity and, according to some commentators, caused a persistent depression thereafter.[43] However, the evidence in Figure 4 suggests that the industry recovered substantially and that the depression of 1826 was acute but quite short. The unusually sharp fall in profit resulted from the effects of a broader financial crisis, during which the Bank of England and provincial banks ceased to discount bills of exchange. As credit dried up, businesses were forced to sell goods at half their cost.[44] At the same time, there was considerable speculation in cotton, significantly increasing raw material costs.[45] As Figure 4 illustrates, the effect was that margins evaporated and most firms incurred losses or meagre profits during the downturn, with an average loss across the sample of 7.90%. The crisis penalized the section of the industry that had gone furthest in automation, the specialized spinning mills, as a function of the most underdeveloped and traditional aspect of business organization: reliance on discountable bills of exchange for trade credit. Exceptions included the Ashworths, who supplied yarn to a local network of handloom weavers on a cash basis and used minimal trade debt.[46]

42   Gayer, Rostow and Schwartz, *Growth and Fluctuation*, pp. 154–5.
43   *Select Committee on Manufactures, Commerce and Shipping*, BPP, 1833, 690, ev. Smith, qq.9321–4, p. 565.
44   J. B. DeLong, 'This time, it is *not* different: The persistent concerns of financial macroeconomics', *Rethinking the Financial Crisis*, ed. A. S. Blinder, A. W. Lo and R. M. Solow (New York, 2013), pp. 14–36, at pp. 18–20.
45   *Select Committee on Manufactures, Commerce and Shipping*, BPP, 1833, 690, ev. Smith, qq.9096–8, p. 555.
46   R. Boyson, *The Ashworth Cotton Enterprise* (Oxford, 1970), p. 59.

Another method of surviving downturns such as the 1825 crisis, for factory owners, was to diversify. For the Gregs, cotton manufacturing was only part of a diversified set of activities. Also, by holding a portfolio of mills with different capabilities, they were able to hedge risk. Thus, although there were losses at the Greg mills at Caton, Lancaster and severe losses at their Ancoats mill, Quarry Bank recorded a profit, benefiting from the slower decline in cloth prices compared with yarn markets.[47] Such risks may have created further portfolio-based incentives for integration into manufacturing, particularly given the low fixed-capital requirements in the early 1800s. Network connections offered the opportunity for such investments and family connections were potentially a critical conduit. Diversification of investments then did not mean that funds were transferred from less successful to more successful branches of business. Although closely connected, often through family ties, the Greg mills were mostly independent businesses. Birley & Hornby maintained similar arms-length arrangements, even though the Manchester firm used its links with Cardwell, Birley & Hornby in Blackburn for buying cotton and selling its output.[48]

Profits in the mature growth phase

In the next phase of development, new opportunities arose through the automation of weaving and the development of rail transport. As noted in chapter 1, because the mechanization of weaving had a substitutive effect on existing capacity hitherto provided by handlooms, there was no step increase in growth rates during this phase. Many investments were incremental rather than step changes. These included new product developments in rubberized cloth with Charles Macintosh but although a patent was granted in 1824, it was not until 1829 that manufacturing commenced.[49] Horrocks Miller developed an improved power loom in 1813, but the machine suffered mechanical imperfections until the early 1830s. Even so, between 1820 and 1835, power-loom productivity increased by a factor of three.[50] In the same period, Horrocks's use of handloom weavers declined, leading to a reduction in wages.[51]

As power-loom weaving developed, handloom weavers became more vulnerable to the effects of the trade cycle. Because spinning output increased in

47   M. B. Rose, *The Gregs of Quarry Bank Mill* (Cambridge, 1986), pp. 52–3.
48   R. S. Fitton and A. P. Wadsworth, *The Strutts and the Arkwrights, 1758–1830: A Study of the Early Factory System* (Manchester, 1958), p. 195; BCP, ledger, 1824–1840, UF-2 and Cardwell, Birley & Hornby, Stock books and ledgers, WP, Eng. MS, 1199/1–6, 1208.
49   Clark, 'Chorlton Mills', pp. 215–19.
50   M. Berg, *The Age of Manufactures, 1700–1820: Industry, Innovation and Work in Britain* (New York, 2005), pp. 245–6.
51   *Select Committee on Handloom Weavers' Petitions*, BPP, 1835, 341, ev. Hitchin, p. 237.

the late 1820s and early 1830s, there was little downward pressure on aggregate numbers of handloom weavers. The slow pace of improvement in power looms up to 1840 meant that their adoption was limited.[52] Thus, factory owners could use power looms for most of their production and employ handloom weavers during booms to cover additional orders, laying them off as soon as demand fell.[53] During this period, the handloom weavers enjoyed little bargaining power in the value chain and suffered accordingly. Beginning in the 1820s, and more decisively after 1840, the opportunities for locally specialized networks based on traditional relationships, supplemented by limited and non-integrated technologies, were disappearing with the decline of handloom weaving. Firms following the outworking strategy increasingly encountered problems due to such changes. From the 1820s, mill owners following this strategy, such as James Massey & Son and James Grimshaw, faced a permanent squeeze on weaving margins.[54]

Following the crisis of 1825, there was a recovery in profits, peaking in 1831 and 1832 (Table 2). Underlying activity in the cotton trade in this period was punctuated by relatively rapid fluctuations between boom and slump.[55] Several cotton manufacturers, along with other industry representatives, complained of falling profits in the Parliamentary Committee hearings of 1833.[56] Kirkman Finlay attributed the decline in earnings to the investment in capital and extension of the industry brought about by the 'high rate of profit of former times'.[57] However, the evidence does not support the proposition of a general slump in trade. Finlay's evidence related mainly to the fortunes of the Scottish cotton industry, while other commentators referred to the prosperity at Manchester, Liverpool and Glasgow, due to the expansion of the domestic market.[58] James Thomson, of the Clitheroe firm Thomson & Chippendall,

---

52 Timmins, *The Last Shift*, p. 91.

53 J. S. Cohen, 'Managers and Machinery: An Analysis of the Rise of Factory Production', *The Textile Industries*, ed. S. D. Chapman (London. 1997), 96–114., p. 103.

54 *Select Committee on Manufactures, Commerce and Shipping*, BPP, 1833, 690, ev. Smith, tables 1 and 2, p. 568; ev. James Grimshaw, qq.10120–10121, pp. 606–7.

55 For example, a slump in the finishing trade in 1829 and 1830. *Select Committee on Manufactures, Commerce and Shipping*, BPP, 1833, 690, ev. Thomson, q.3905, p. 246.

56 Gayer, Rostow and Schwartz, *Growth and Fluctuation*, pp. 221–2; 226. *Select Committee on Manufactures, Commerce and Shipping*, BPP, 1833, 690, ev. Loyd, qq.475, 596, pp. 31, 38.

57 *Select Committee on Manufactures, Commerce and Shipping*, BPP, 1833, 690, ev. Finlay, q.622, p. 39. Regarding the poor state of Glasgow trade, see also: ev. Houldsworth, q.5191, p. 313; ev. William Graham, qq.5365–6; attributed to over-investment in the Glasgow mill-building boom of 1825, qq.5527–9, 5536, pp. 325, 334; unfair competition from Lancashire on working hours, q.5514, p. 333.

58 *Select Committee on Manufactures, Commerce and Shipping*, BPP, 1833, 690, ev. James Cook, q.1617, p. 107 and John Ewart, qq.3991, 4057, pp. 250, 253; ev. William Haynes, qq.4937, 5022, 5033, pp. 300, 305. For a more pessimistic view, see also: ev. Loyd, qq.563–4, p. 35; ev. George Smith, q.9030, p. 552.

reported the cotton printing trade to be in a prosperous condition.[59] The trade superseded the linen and mixed fabric branches, and also benefited from the repeal of duties on printed goods in 1831. Immediately before the repeal, the average profit margin in printed products was 14.3%.[60]

Fluctuations in export activity suggest that trade recovered in 1830 following a slump in the previous year, but with a new downturn in 1831–32. As with prior recessions, all firms did not uniformly feel the effects and average profit rates were not significantly affected. George Smith of the firm James Massey & Son in Manchester, commented that firms more dependent on credit and with older machinery were typically those with no profit, whereas more profitable firms were those that had combined spinning and weaving activities.[61]

Several cotton firms, Birley & Co. and the Greg mills at Bury (Hudcar Mill) and Lancaster, recorded profits over 20% during the years 1831–32.[62] Averages at New Eagley and Quarry Bank were much lower, and it was the stated profits of these mills, perhaps unsurprisingly, that featured prominently in the lobbying against the Factory Act by Ashworth and Greg.[63] The boom of 1833–36, driven by rapid growth in exports,[64] had the effect of boosting average profits once again (Table 2), particularly for Birley & Co. and the Ashworth Brothers, including their new mill at Egerton.

These developments spurred investments in power-loom weaving, although the resulting returns were somewhat disappointing. In the decade following their installation at the Ashworths' New Eagley mill in 1841, profits averaged only 4.5%. In 1835 Bashall and Boardman began erecting a new weaving shed at Farington. During a similar period, 1838–51, profits averaged 8.10%, a disappointing performance in part explained by the downturn of 1837–42.[65] Wallshaw Mill, the successor firm to James Lees, which had expanded into weaving in the 1820s, achieved somewhat better performance and the average rate of profit was 13.2% between 1844 and 1851.

To some extent, these firms were dragged down by the generally poor trading conditions. For all firms, profits only averaged 8.1% in the decade after 1841.

---

59 *Select Committee on Manufactures, Commerce and Shipping*, BPP, 1833, 690, ev. James Thomson, q.3539, p. 225.

60 Before interest and depreciation. Calculated from Baines, *History of the Cotton Manufacture*, p. 284.

61 *Select Committee on Manufactures, Commerce and Shipping*, BPP, 1833, 690, ev. Smith, qq.9134, 9160, pp. 557–8.

62 A cotton factory at Ashton was reported to be fully employed and making good profits: *Select Committee on Manufactures, Commerce and Shipping*, BPP, 1833, 690, ev. Gurney, q.139, p. 12.

63 *Factories Inquiry Commission*, BPP, 1833, 450, the summary report, p. 45; *Factories Inquiry Commission*, Supplementary Report, BPP, 1834, 167, p. 490.

64 Gayer, Rostow and Schwartz, *Growth and Fluctuation*, p. 263.

65 O. Ashmore, *The Industrial Archaeology of North-west England* (Manchester, 1982), p. 203. Howe, *The Cotton Masters*, p. 25.

Fielden, the firm that had installed what was then the largest single-room weaving shed in the world, achieved below-average profits in the late 1830s and 1840s. J. & N. Philips likewise had disappointing returns on capital following weaving automation. Indeed, the investments in power-weaving did not result in the same abnormally large profits accruing to steam-powered mule spinning in the late 1790s and early 1800s.

These investments coincided with the onset of a protracted period of below-average profits in the late 1830s and early 1840s. In the years 1838–43, profits fluctuated around the 5% level and the effects of the depression seem to have been universally felt. Although less pronounced than the downturn of 1826, the slump in profits was more protracted. All firms suffered reduced earnings in these years, with few instances of profits over 10% in even a single year. Manufacturers attributed these low profits to the threat of increased foreign competition and the high price of bread, and renewed their agitation for the repeal of the Corn Laws. The only years of the 1840s during which cotton firms made above-average profits were 1844 and 1845, corresponding to an upturn in industrial activity at that time.[66] Political lobbying, by the Whig opponents of the Ten Hours Act, played its part in opening up China to imports of opium from India, so that Indian merchants could obtain cash to import Lancashire goods and for the direct export of textiles to China.[67]

If the purpose of British policy in accessing the Chinese market was to stabilize the cotton sector of the economy, as suggested by Singleton,[68] it did not succeed, at least in the short term. The Chinese Treaty of 1842 indeed prompted some of the associated mill building and exports, but these subsequently resulted in significant losses in 1846–47.[69] Citing Factory Inspectors' reports, Marx also attributed the high investment and prosperity of 1845 to the low cotton price, which as Figure 4 shows, coincided with a high rate of profit, only to be reversed in 1846 by an advance in the cotton price. The removal of cotton duties along with the Corn Laws in the same year boosted underlying profits but did not obviate the stronger effect of the cotton price on the cyclical pattern of profits. A much sharper slump came in 1847, with a new credit

66   As manifested by rises in imports and exports of cotton goods, Gayer, Rostow and Schwartz, *Growth and Fluctuation*, p. 263.
67   W. T. Hanes and F. Sanello, *The Opium Wars: The Addiction of One Empire and the Corruption of Another* (Naperville, IL, 2002), pp. 22, 158.
68   J. Singleton, 'The Lancashire cotton industry, the Royal Navy, and the British Empire, c.1700–1960', *The Fibre that Changed the World: The Cotton Industry in International Perspective*, ed. D. Farnie and D. Jeremy (Oxford, 2004), pp. 57–84, at p. 65.
69   Treaty of Nanking. *Supplemental Appendix to Reports from the Secret Committee on Commercial Distress*, BPP, 1847–48, 395, ev. R. Gardner, qq.4872–4. Notwithstanding these setbacks, China became a significant new market, accounting for over £1 million in cotton exports by 1850; D. Farnie, *The English Cotton Industry and the World Market, 1815–1896* (Oxford, 1979), p. 91.

crisis, accentuated when some cotton manufacturers drew bills on their banks, and each other, for speculative investments in railway shares. A related cause was the fraudulent discounting of bills by merchants.[70] When the crisis broke, discount rates rose sharply, and many merchants and manufacturers, such as Fielden Brothers, could not discount their bills at all.[71] The Bank of England responded by printing money,[72] which marked the inauguration of a new period of relatively high profitability up to 1860.

After 1846 profits fell back to levels experienced in the late 1830s and early 1840s. Exports declined up to 1848, to be followed by a new investment boom, which was driven by domestic demand, based on an increase in real wages, rather than exports. For this reason, relatively few firms made large profits in this period. The recovery in profits did not lead to a rise in average earnings until 1852. By 1853 export demand was once again buoyant,[73] and average profits peaked at 17.4%, a rate not seen since 1814.

Profits fell the following year, coinciding with the onset of a depression and industrial unrest centred on Preston. Notably, Horrockses Miller, still the dominant Preston firm, enjoyed a very high rate of return on capital (25.5%) in 1854. Commentators attributed the profits to Horrockses Miller's exploitative attitude towards their workers and the crisis to overproduction, caused by the 'great increase in the number of mills'.[74] Investment in new capacity continued in 1854 despite falling export demand,[75] and as Figure 4 shows, it resulted in a decline in overall profitability. A possible reason was that investors believed new factories would be remunerative in the future, notwithstanding current poor conditions. In the short run, mill owners managed to survive through collusion and organized short time.[76] The long-run average rate of profit of 11.1%, which was often exceeded during the 1850s, suggests some support for the notion of justified investor optimism. Following the commercial crisis and Indian mutiny of 1857, the cotton industry enjoyed a new, export-led revival and entered a

---

70   *Second report from the Secret Committee on Commercial Distress*, BPP, 1847–48, 584, J. Kinnear, q.6022; J. Anderson, qq.6224, 6225, pp. 523, 534. *Supplemental Appendix to Reports from the Secret Committee on Commercial Distress*, BPP, 1847–48, 395, ev. R. Gardner qq.4872, 4888. *Report from the Secret Committee of the House of Lords Appointed to Inquire into the Causes of the Distress*, BPP, 1847–48, 565, ev. J. Lister, qq. 2444, 2500.

71   Ibid., ev. J. Lister, q. 2481, p. 336.

72   K. Marx, *Capital III* (London, 1984), pp. 124, 408; *Reports of Inspector of Factories*, BPP, October 1845, p. 13; *Reports of Inspector of Factories*, BPP, October 1846, p. 10.

73   Farnie, *English Cotton*, p. 131; J. R. T. Hughes, *Fluctuations in Trade, Industry, and Finance: A Study of British Economic Development, 1850–1860* (Oxford, 1960), p. 79.

74   M. Huberman, *Escape from the Market: Negotiating Work in Lancashire* (Cambridge, 1996), p. 53.

75   Hughes, *Fluctuations in Trade*, p. 81.

76   Hughes, *Fluctuations in Trade*, pp. 82–3. Short time was inaugurated in 1857. Huberman, *Escape from the Market*, pp. 113–24, dates the practice to the depression of 1841 and charts its continuation through subsequent downturns.

period of 'unprecedented prosperity', manifested by higher mill margins,[77] which by 1859 had pushed profit rates up to a new, forty-five-year high.

In the Birley & Co. case, and others, family connections facilitated the development of substantial business empires. The business groups that emerged were analogous to mergers, based on informal business connections rather than stock exchange finance. The rationale for such mergers was control: vertical control of the value chain and, to a lesser extent, horizontal control of the market. These motives for strategic alliances were unsurprising, given the relative underdevelopment of markets, which, in the case of weaving, for example, relied very much on traditional business practices up to 1825 to sustain a large number of handloom weavers.

Business groups, often reinforced through family connections, could exercise network power and access capital to invest in new technology. The most successful in financial terms whose strategy, as noted above, combined networking with forward integration into technical and design-led innovation in printing, was the Dugdale–Chippendall group. An essential source of competitive advantage for the firm of Thomson & Chippendall was its investment in technology and design. Its leading partner, James Thomson (1779–1850), a former manager of Peel's calico print works at Church, near Accrington, combined a detailed understanding of both the technical aspects of production and export markets.[78] Thomson developed new dyeing techniques and secured the patent for the Turkey Red process. He also employed Lancashire-based artists, secured copyright protection and undertook visits to shops in Paris.[79] As a result, Thomson & Chippendall returned an average of 22.03% on its capital in the period 1811–25.[80] The trends in the profitability of Thomson & Chippendall were partly explained by the healthy growth of printing as a branch of the cotton industry, particularly in the Indian market, after the East India Company gained total control over India.[81]

Like Horrockses, the firm's investment in quality, penetration of overseas markets and its customer focus contributed to long-run and sustainable

77   Farnie, *English Cotton*, pp. 105,138, 140; Hughes, *Fluctuations in Trade*, pp. 96–7.
78   D. Jeremy, 'The International Diffusion of Cotton Manufacturing Technology, 1750–1990s', *The Fibre that Changed the World: The Cotton Industry in International Perspective, 1600–1990s*, ed. D. Farnie and D. Jeremy (Oxford, 2004), pp. 85–127, provides examples based on Thomson's writings in Rees's *Cyclopaedia* between 1808 and 1812, at pp. 88–91.
79   *Select Committee on Manufactures, Commerce and Shipping*, BPP, 1833, 690, ev. Thomson, qq.3831–2, 3868, 3870, 3880–7, pp. 244–5. See also Baines, *History of the Cotton Manufacture*, p. 285.
80   TCP, Primrose works, Ledger accounts, CYC 3/46–48.
81   At the same time, in 1813, under the East India Company Act (53 Geo. 3 c. 155), the East India Company lost its trade monopoly on most goods. Between 1814 and 1825, the amount of exported printed calicoes subject to duty increased from 3,324,160 to 6,662,368 pieces. *Select Committee on Manufactures, Commerce and Shipping*, BPP, 1833, 690, ev. Thomson, q.3893; Calculated from Baines, *History of the Cotton Manufacture*, p. 283).

abnormal returns. By 1850, the linkages created a significant horizontal presence in the printing and finishing trade to which the Manchester connection added connections and expertise in export markets. The profits of Nathaniel Dugdale and Thomson & Chippendall were consistently high, whether based on this integrated model or the primitive jenny manufacturing and outworking model of Nathaniel Dugdale's original incarnation. As late as 1823, the Dugdale partnership was still earning an overall rate of profit of 30.4%.[82] As handloom weaving declined, the firm emulated Thomson & Chippendall by concentrating on printing, which as the latter's performance demonstrated, offered significant profit opportunities.

The case study evidence, taken together, demonstrates several overlapping routes to achieving superior returns. Featured firms exploited specific opportunities but were also subjected to similar constraints, associated with prevailing technical and market conditions. Networks and technological innovation offered alternative routes to competitive advantage for cotton firms in the industrial revolution, certainly before the mechanization of weaving. The former appeared to be more enduring. Before drawing overall conclusions on the determinants of profitability, it is, therefore, useful to assess the systemic determinants of profit for the sample as a whole during all the transitional phases of industrialization.

Long-run profitability and the trade cycle

For the whole period, profitability averaged 11.0%, with a standard deviation of 5.7%. Investment in cotton, therefore, appears to compare favourably with the broader economy. An index of London stock prices for the period 1811–50, comprising mainly utilities and financial services (and excluding mining), increased from 72.9 to 88.6, an average annual return of less than 1%. These index numbers exclude the effects of dividends, but even if it is assumed that all quoted firms paid yearly dividends of 5%, their average return was still substantially below the cotton average of 10.1% for the corresponding period. The standard deviation of cotton returns in the same period was 5.4% compared with 9.6% for returns on the London index.[83] These contrasting returns are suggestive of a disaggregated regional cotton economy, offering different investment opportunities with significantly favourable risk-adjusted returns when compared to alternatives. They explain why Lancashire attracted substantial investment during the period, notwithstanding the declining rate

---

82   Calculated from CIFD.
83   All London figures calculated from A. D. Gayer, A. Jacobson and I. Finkelstein, 'British share prices, 1811–1850', *Review of Economic Statistics* 22 (1940), 78–93, using December index values (June 1840 = 100).

of profit and regular complaints of low earnings from cotton entrepreneurs before 1846.[84]

The strongly cyclical nature of the industry posed a significant risk for entrepreneurs committing increasing amounts of fixed capital. Using the cotton industry to illustrate the long-run characteristics of the trade cycle, Karl Marx noted that periods of stagnation became more prolonged and more severe. He pointed out that in the 'period of monopoly' from 1770 to 1815, there were only five years of crisis and stagnation. In contrast, during the period of 1816–63, characterized by increased international competition and struggles for markets, twenty-eight years were marked by stagnation and only twenty years by prosperity.[85]

The data in Figure 4 broadly support this argument. The average profit up to 1815 was 14.0% and 10.6% thereafter.[86] Earnings in the earlier period were somewhat more volatile.[87] Although there is a secular downward trend in the data to 1846, there is little evidence in Figure 4 that slumps were becoming more persistent or more prolonged. The long-run decline in profitability in the period 1797–1846 supports the neoclassical view of average profits being competed away by new entrants, but the downward adjustment is sufficiently slow to suggest some support for the Schumpeterian view of persistent abnormal profits as a return to innovation.

The above narrative, together with the long-run trends evident in Figure 4, provides potential support for the Marxian, Schumpeterian and Neoclassical interpretations in the literature. Profitability is strongly correlated with the known features of the trade cycle and demonstrates a steady downward trend, at least until the mid-1840s. Profits were typically higher in the earlier period, particularly in the war years up to 1815. The average profit for the whole period was around 11%, but typically nearer 13% up to 1825 and about 9% after that point. The period 1826–46 witnessed not just low profits but also high volatility. The ratio of return to risk, as measured by standard deviation in Table 2, was at its lowest during this period. Volatility, rather than a decline in profit, is the dominant feature. The data in Table 2 suggest a positive and linear relationship between risk and return, with an average, risk-adjusted abnormal return of 3.8%.[88]

Several countervailing factors serve to modify all three interpretations. The first of these was that cotton and yarn prices both declined at a relatively constant rate. These trends are summarized in Figure 5, which shows that the steady decline in yarn margins in pence per pound was not associated with

---

84   The extent to which the presentation of high production costs and low profits to parliamentary regulators constituted an organized lobbying position is the subject of chapter 3.
85   K. Marx, *Capital I* (Harmondsworth, 1976), pp. 583–4; Marx, *Capital III*, pp. 124–37.
86   The differences were statistically significant at the 95% confidence interval.
87   Standard deviation up to 1815 was 6.33% and 4.84% thereafter.
88   The intercept term in a simple cross-sectional regression of average return and risk by firm.

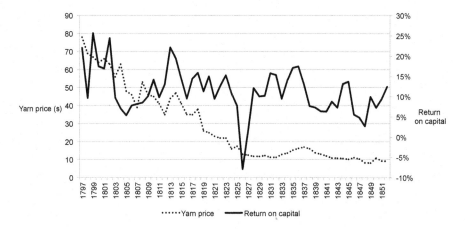

Figure 5. Yarn price and return on capital, 1797–1852

Note: Figures are based on current prices.

Sources: Prices, 1797–1826, 40s warp, C. K. Harley, 'Cotton textile prices and the industrial revolution', *EcHR* 51 (1998), 49–83, Table A1.1, p. 74, and 1822–52, M. Huberman, *Escape from the Market: Negotiating Work in Lancashire* (Cambridge, 1996), p. 101. Return on capital calculated from sources in appendix 1 (this volume).

anything like such a steep decline in the rate of profit. An important reason for this trend was that although prices declined, margins remained relatively constant. In other words, although the price of yarn fell, so too did the cost of raw cotton.

Figure 6 shows the gross margin percentages for spinning and weaving. For spinning, it is calculated as the ratio of gross profit per pound to the sales value of yarn per pound. For weaving, it is the ratio of profit per yard to selling price. In weaving, margins rose steadily during the period. Interpreting margins in percentage terms rather than in price terms explains mathematically why the rate of return on capital decline was slower than the decrease in margins expressed purely in terms of falling prices on a pence per pound basis.

At least this is true as far as spinning was concerned. As the trend line for spinning shows, margins declined steeply to 1800 and fluctuated after that but hardly declined at all up to 1830. Interpreting these figures, the rapid expansion of the supply of raw cotton in the 1790s, first in the West Indies and then in the USA, should be borne in mind. Indeed the decline in raw material price, and the concentration of buying power in Liverpool, created an advantage for Lancashire that lasted for the whole of the nineteenth century.[89] The implied

---

89   S. Beckert, *Empire of Cotton: A Global History* (New York, 2014); Farnie, *English Cotton*, pp. 82–3.

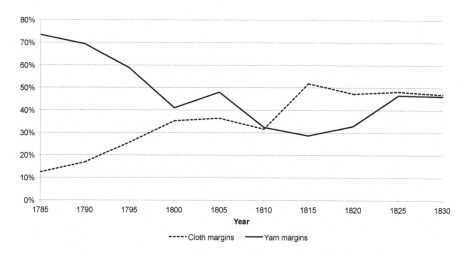

Figure 6. Cloth and yarn percentage margins, 1785–1830

Source: Calculated from deflated cost components in Harley, 'Was technological change in the early Industrial Revolution Schumpeterian?', Table 3.

gain in productivity[90] was 5.01% per annum between 1785 and 1800, and 6.01% per annum between 1785 and 1815, but with no net gain after that. Individual mill accounts, where price data is also available, show that percentage margins were indeed relatively constant after 1825. For example, at Quarry Bank Mill in the period 1827–31, both the gross margin (revenue minus cotton costs divided by revenue) and operating margin (revenue minus all running expenses divided by revenue) remained quite steady, as indicated by the low standard deviation.[91]

A further reason for the relatively slower decline in return on capital in spinning was the possibility of achieving higher throughput from invested capital. New investment, in the form of widening mule lengths, factory extensions, the introduction of self-actors after 1830,[92] and new larger mills provided opportunities to counteract the effects of declining d/lb margins. Thus, more productive technology with higher throughput reduced the capital required to generate a given unit of sale, thereby increasing the turnover of capital and slowing the decline in overall profitability that would have otherwise resulted from lower d/lb

90 Following the approach in D. McCloskey, 'The industrial revolution, 1780–1860: A survey', *The Economic History of Britain since 1700*, ed. R. Floud and D. McCloskey (Cambridge, 1981), pp. 103–27, at pp. 110–11.

91 Gross profit margin 42.6% (standard deviation 2.3%), operating profit 12.2% (standard deviation 2.1%). Calculated from GP, Partnership Accounts, 1827–1831, C5/1/2/3–4.

92 Berg, *Age of Manufactures*, p. 155. Mill capacity increased by eight times between 1797 and 1833, and 1.6 times between 1833/4 and 1850; S. D. Chapman, 'Financial restraints on the growth of firms in the cotton industry, 1790–1850', *EcHR* 32 (1979), 50–69, at p. 50.

margins. In his critical digest of evidence from Lancashire mill owners presented to the Factories Inquiry Commission in 1833, John Welsford Cowell showed that significant productivity gains could be achieved through mule widening.[93]

Given the steadiness of the profit margin, bearing in mind constant real wages, and the relatively rapid rise in productivity during the period, it is perhaps surprising that the rate of profit, as a function of these two factors, nonetheless declined slowly over the long run. As illustrated in chapter 1, in the early 1800s, large-scale operations were possible with relatively small investments in fixed capital. High returns were, therefore, achievable on small monetary investments by entrepreneurs already commanding large networks of both credit and outworkers. Improving productivity came from machines that were relatively more expensive and capital requirements were added to by the continuing need for circulating capital. Frequent recessions meanwhile limited the realization of profits from more expensive machinery, contributing to a gradual decline in the rate of profit. Where further investment was needed to achieve improvements in fixed capital productivity, incumbent firms might also suffer a competitive disadvantage. Cotton entrepreneurs like George Smith thought that declining margins in d/lb terms were indeed a problem, citing the low values available to pay wages and profit, particularly for more marginal firms.[94]

Entrepreneurs were wary of the risk associated with fixed capital investments, which became a more dominant concern with the decline in handloom weaving. Indeed the trend volatility in Figure 4 shows that their fears were justified. Average profits, therefore, needed to be sufficiently high to justify risky fixed capital outlays, and this outcome was achieved by suppression of union activity, and hence wages, in the period before 1850. Parliament and the courts were aggressive in preventing combinations, and this may have benefited the factory masters.[95]

A further countervailing effect on profit decline came from developments in weaving. After 1815 weaving margins were constant (Figure 6), due to a relative lack of automation and indeed the number of handloom weavers, which increased until the 1820s.[96] Increasing fixed capital investments and output in spinning therefore created bottlenecks in weaving, consequently increasing weaving margins. As Figure 6 shows, cloth margins increased steadily between

---

93 *Factories Inquiry Commission, Supplementary Report*, BPP, 1834, 167, Cowell's Preface Report, pp. 387–8. Mill A, 25 pairs combined into 13 pairs of 636 per mule, 12 of the 25 adult spinners dismissed and 9 additional piecers employed; Mill B, 20 pairs of mules combined into 10 pairs of 648 per mule, 10 adult spinners dismissed and 7 additional piecers employed; Mill C, 103 pairs of mules combined into 50 pairs of 648 per mule, 53 adult spinners dismissed and 41 additional piecers employed.
94 *Select Committee on Manufactures, Commerce and Shipping*, BPP, 1833, 690, ev. Smith, qq.9030–45, p. 552. See also *Factories Inquiry Commission*, BPP, 1833, 450, ev. R. H. Greg and H. Hoole.
95 Cohen, 'Managers and Machinery', p. 109.
96 B. Mitchell and P. Deane, *Abstract of British Historical Statistics* (Cambridge, 1962), p. 376.

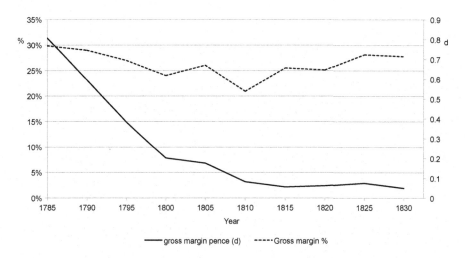

Figure 7. Gross spinning and weaving margins, 1782–1830

Notes: Gross margin (pence) price of cloth minus price of cotton (d/lb); gross margin percentage calculated as the price of cloth minus price of cotton divided by price of cloth.

Source: Calculated from deflated cost components in Harley, 'Was technological change in the early Industrial Revolution Schumpeterian?', Table 3.

1785 and 1815, and declined only slightly from their peak in the 1820s. Because of the sharp decline in cloth prices in the absence of productivity improvements, the cost of maintaining profits for integrated firms fell exclusively on the net earnings of the weavers.

Consequently, profit declines were more pronounced in firms that remained dependent on handloom weaving after 1830. George Smith, whose firm invested in new spinning machinery but continued to manufacture calicoes by hand, recorded no profit from the activity in 1831 and small profits in 1832 and 1833, commenting that of thirty-two handloom manufacturer acquaintances, twenty-eight had failed in the period 1812–26.[97]

Firms combining spinning and weaving, even if not in the same factory, were insulated from the decline in yarn margins, benefiting from the general rise in weaving margins up to c.1820, at least. Figure 7 shows the gross margin on spinning and weaving combined. As Figure 7 illustrates, percentage gross margins (combining spinning and weaving) were typically constant, fluctuating around 25% and were higher in 1830 than in 1815, notwithstanding the rapid decline in profit per yard up to 1815 and the steadier decline thereafter. The

97 *Select Committee on Manufactures, Commerce and Shipping*, BPP, 1833, 690, ev. Smith, qq.9269–75, 9278, pp. 562–3.

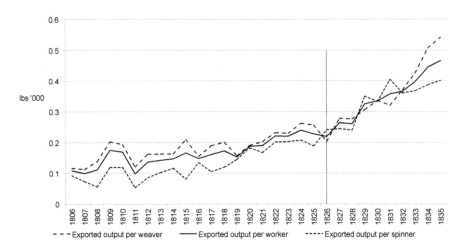

Figure 8. Productivity, 1806–35

Source: Mitchell and Deane, *Abstract of British Historical Statistics.*

lack of automation in weaving resulted in annual growth in productivity for spinning and weaving of 3.4% between 1785 and 1815, roughly half of the rate of improvement in spinning alone.

The generally flat trend in profit margins meant that overall profit in the industry did not demonstrate a sharply declining tendency. Up to 1820 profitability was assisted by the improvement of margins in the relatively unmodernized weaving section. After the mid-1820s, however, further automation helped both branches through productivity improvements.

Productivity trends in spinning, weaving and for all cotton workers are shown in Figure 8. There were undoubtedly productivity gains during the whole period, as the trend in Figure 8 shows. Allen's data show that the decisive improvements in productivity arising from spinning-jennies, water frames and mules occurred in the 1780s and 1790s, with the downward trend in unit costs tending to level off in the 1800–25 period.[98] However, the productivity increase is only marginal before 1826 and speeds up thereafter. Up to that date, firms had substantial working capital commitments arising from investments in the outworking system and were unable to take decisive advantage in weaving automation.

A structural break in the mid-1820s would be consistent with the next wave of technological developments, which coincided with a recovery in the trade cycle after the banking crisis of 1825. Before then at least, profits were in a state of disequilibrium and did not adjust downwards decisively. After a series

---

98   Allen, *British Industrial Revolution*, figures 8.1 and 8.2, pp. 188 and 208.

of partially successful experiments, power looms were sufficiently improved by 1825 and likewise the self-acting mule by 1830.[99] These developments then led to the dominance of productivity-driven factory production after 1830. In the fifteen years following the crisis, power looms were increasingly adopted, but the expansion of spinning during boom periods, including the boom of 1836, was sufficient to sustain or in some districts even increase handloom weaving.[100] Cloth exports assumed the lead in driving the growth of the industry after 1843.[101]

In summary, the trends taken in conjunction with the rest of the evidence in this chapter and the previous one, suggest significant structural breaks. The first, between c.1795 and 1815, was associated with the transformation of production using steam-powered mule spinning and the transition from model 2 to model 3. The effects were to improve the profitability of early adopters and enhance productivity, driving down unit margins, but increasing fixed capital turnover via higher throughput, tending to stabilize the trend, but not the volatility of the rate of profit. The second, in the mid-1820s, was associated with the automation of the weaving sector and further refinements on spinning. Further productivity gains were again sufficient to offset the effects of falling unit margins and also, by replacing handlooms with power looms, to diminish the required investment in working capital. The rate of profit, although under some pressure from the general effects of the trade cycle, did not, therefore, suffer unduly relative to the earlier phases of growth.

Growth and profitability

In models 1 and 2, network dominance, for prior accumulations of merchant capital, together with selective automation of a single aspect of the value chain, namely spinning, had the hallmarks of a successful strategy. Nathaniel Dugdale & Brothers used this strategy to good effect, achieving healthy profits in the early phases, even with relatively primitive technology in a remotely located network. In model 3, steam-powered mule spinning resulted in very large but relatively short-run profits. The leading and most profitable firms, McConnel & Kennedy, Birley & Co. and Horrockses Miller, enjoyed higher profits following significant investments in capital equipment. These opportunities were not repeated in model 4 mature phase expansion with the automation of weaving when profits were relatively disappointing. During this and earlier phases, the Horrockses and

99   T. Ellison, *The Cotton Trade of Great Britain: Including a History of the Liverpool Cotton Market and of the Liverpool Cotton Brokers' Association* (London, 1886). George Smith suggested that power-loom weaving began to increase considerably from 1825. *Select Committee on Manufactures, Commerce and Shipping*, BPP, 1833, 690, ev. Smith, qq.9418–20, p. 569.
100   Timmins, *The Last Shift*, p. 93.
101   Farnie, *English Cotton*, p. 89.

Thomson & Chippendall cases also illustrate that market positioning based on a reputation for product quality, was an essential reason for success.

As shown in chapter 1, these and other firms making investments in steam-powered mule spinning experienced rapid step-growth rates in fixed capital, with concomitant increases in working capital. These investments resulted in concomitant increases in profitability, with a premium of around 3–4% over and above firms that did not make the same investments. As the profit rate for cotton as a whole fluctuated around an average of 11%, the total returns for innovative firms in the six to ten years following steam-powered mule investments were more than 14%. These returns were also high in the context of those available from investments in the broader economy.

However, because automation was specific to certain parts of the value chain, and technologies like water spinning and steam-powered mules could coexist profitably in expanding markets, the competitive advantage of innovating firms was tenuous. A 3% premium may have been sufficient to deter many from making significant fixed investments for several reasons. Profits were subject to the vicissitudes of the trade cycle, amplified by the disruptions of the war years and ongoing uncertainty in overseas markets after that. Deep pockets were needed to finance related working-capital expansion, providing a competitive advantage to those controlling pre-existing merchant networks, relative to entrepreneurs from humble origins and in smaller factories. Premium profits from steam-powered mules could potentially be competed away by new entrants, for whom 11% profit was still handsome, with the added appeal of avoiding the fixed costs of larger factories. As weaving was automated, profits became even less certain and attracted no similar premium, notwithstanding the expanded scale of production. The larger mills were also vulnerable to mob attacks, for example Birley's Manchester mills during the Plug Riots of 1842.

The character of these investments, therefore, goes some way towards explaining the business and political attitudes of cotton factory owners in the early nineteenth century. On the one hand, high profit rates secured rapid capital and private wealth accumulation and social status. On the other hand, their investments were subject to high levels of risk from business competitors, at home and overseas, as well as from social classes thus far excluded from the direct financial benefits of industrial expansion. Whether such thoughts troubled H. H. Birley, as he considered how he and the yeomanry might respond to the gathering at St Peters Field in 1819, is a matter for speculation. A few years later, in the first book to be published on the subject of occupational health, Charles Thackrah noted the worried disposition of the typical businessman.

These concerns came to a head in the debates on factory regulation, which punctuated the first half of the nineteenth century with increasing intensity. The fixed costs of investments and the resulting profits were crucial in framing these debates, and having examined their nature in the previous two chapters, the next chapter discusses how they impacted on policy debates and regulation.

3

The Factory Act Debates: Financial Perspectives

The saddest news is, that we should find our National Existence, as I
sometimes hear it said, depend on selling manufactured cotton at a farthing
an ell cheaper than any other People. A most narrow stand for a great Nation
to base itself on.[1]

A stark feature of the British industrial revolution, particularly in the textile
industries, was the enforcement of long hours through factory discipline, including
hours worked by children.[2] There were many examples of labour exploitation
in the early cotton mills. The worst of these stirred public opinion and created
increasing pressure for legislation.[3] Employment of children was widespread, not
because of the low cost of child workers, but as a result of labour shortages, and
the survival of older legislation and its accommodation to the factory system.
These justifications, along with the technological features of industrialization
discussed in previous chapters, particularly the model 2 phase of development,
combined to shape the characteristics of entrepreneurial opportunity.

Litton Mill in Derbyshire during the 1780s is perhaps the best-documented
example and illustrates in a single case the negative factors that tended to
promote child exploitation. In the second half of the eighteenth century,
parishes in the south of England were facing escalating costs for maintaining
paupers, particularly children, and new employment opportunities in the north
presented a convenient solution.[4] Child apprentices were sent in batches from
the southern districts, including London, to mills such as Litton. Although
there were abundant sites for water, first in Derbyshire and then more decisively
in Lancashire, reliance on water power created labour shortages, as the best
streams were often in remote valleys.[5] Child apprentices were a convenient

1 T. Carlyle, *Past and Present* (London 1843), p. 228.
2 For a discussion of alternative perspectives, see G. Clark, 'Factory discipline', *JEH* 54 (1994),
128–63.
3 J. L. Hammond and B. Hammond, *The Rise of Modern Industry* (London, 1911).
4 M. B. Rose, 'Social policy and business: Parish apprenticeship and the early factory system,
1750–1834', *BH* 31 (1989), 5–32.
5 G. Timmins, *The Last Shift: The Decline of Handloom Weaving in Nineteenth-Century
Lancashire* (Manchester, 1993), p. 57. There was pressure to keep the mills working, particularly

solution to this problem, which entrepreneurs such as Ellis Needham at Litton were keen to exploit. Needham, like others in the area attracted to the opportunities offered by industry, came from a landowning family that provided the necessary capital. Margins were generous and new entrants were encouraged by the prospects of high profits, as the evidence in chapters 1 and 2 has shown. Such benefits were rather more elusive in the remote mills, due to high costs associated with transport, and supervision and maintenance of the child workforce. In Needham's case, Litton mill was disadvantaged for all these reasons, and financial difficulties set the context for his brutal treatment of child workers such as Robert Blincoe.[6]

As child labour diminished as an issue, agitation for shorter working time increased. Changes in attitude can be mapped approximately onto the transition from model 2 to model 3. As steam-powered mule spinning was introduced, there was more significant pressure to enforce longer working hours due to the increasing capital intensity of textile production. Although model 2 and model 3 growth phases overlapped until the 1820s, child labour was in decline by the 1830s.[7] Also, as the previous chapters have shown, the typical mill of the 1830s was far more capital intensive than the conventional mill of the 1790s and early 1800s. Consequently, the chief source of risk faced by mill owners, in the form of commodity market instability, was now complemented and increasingly overtaken by risk arising from the scale of sunk investment in productive capital.

Against the backdrop of these changes, arguments about fixed costs and relative profitability had a substantial impact on the national debates concerning the length of the working day and the ethics of child labour. These debates, which raged for much of the first half of the nineteenth century, were highly charged cocktails of moral outrage and hard-headed accountancy. For a public shocked by revelations of factory conditions, ethical considerations were paramount. For prominent mill owners, economists and, crucially, legislators, the chief concern was profit and loss. For a time, at least, financial justifications prevailed. Unsurprisingly then perhaps, author and social commentator Thomas Carlyle's reaction, quoted above, was one of frustration at the factory system's lost moral compass.

Shifts over twelve hours contrasted with what had gone before under the more leisurely cottage-based outworking system.[8] The ten-hour day, with

where groups of mills along a river were mutually dependent on steady flows. J. Waller, *The Real Oliver Twist, Robert Blincoe: A Life that Illuminates a Violent Age* (Cambridge, 2006).

6   J. Brown, 'A Memoir of Robert Blincoe' (1832), reprinted in *The Ten Hours Movement in 1831 and 1832: Six Pamphlets and One Broadside*, ed. K. Carpenter (New York, 1972); Waller, *The Real Oliver Twist*.

7   C. Nardinelli, 'Child labor and the Factory Acts', *JEH* 40 (1980), 739–55.

8   On the transition, see, S. Pollard, *The Genesis of Modern Management: A Study of the Industrial Revolution in Great Britain* (Harmondsworth, 1968); S. A. Marglin, 'What do bosses do? The origins and functions of hierarchy in capitalist production', *Review of Radical Political*

associated better protection for younger and female workers, was the principal demand of the Ten Hours movement, a coalition of labour organizations and MPs. Parliamentary advocates included Richard Oastler and Lord Ashley (later Lord Shaftesbury). Those mill owners also prepared to engage in the political process, figured on both sides of the resulting debates. In favour of regulation were most notably Robert Owen, John Fielden and William Kenworthy. Henry and Edmund Ashworth, John Pooley, Robert Hyde Greg, Hugh Hornby Birley, Holland Hoole and associated political lobbyists led the opposition.[9] In making their case, both groups of employers relied heavily on financial evidence.

To add further ideological strength to their lobby, opponents of factory reform opened a dialogue with leading representatives of the newly emerging discipline of political economy. To fulfil their commission, the leading economists, including George Poulett Scrope and Nassau Senior, attempted to both rationalize the rate of profit and justify long working hours. Most famously, Senior's theory suggested that all profit was made in the *last hour* of the working day.[10] To help the economists elaborate on their theories, mill owners supplied them with figures from their business accounts.[11] Evidence from these sources was also presented to parliamentary commissioners to influence legislation, and in pamphlets and speeches to influence public opinion.[12]

Instead of finance, however, the extensive literature on factory legislation has been particularly concerned with the ethics of child labour and associated disputes over alleged misrepresentations of the harshness of factory working conditions.[13] Recent analysis has complemented this literature by considering

---

Economics 6 (1974), 60–112; E. P. Thompson, 'Time, work-discipline, and industrial capitalism', *Past & Present* 38 (1967), 56–97, at p. 73; D. Landes, *The Unbound Prometheus: Technological Change and Industrial Development in Western Europe from 1750 to the Present* (Cambridge, 1969), p. 59.

9   R. G. Kirby and A. E. Musson, *Voice of the People, John Doherty, 1798–1854: Trade Unionist, Radical and Factory Reformer* (Manchester, 1975); M. Berg, *The Machinery Question and the Making of Political Economy 1815–1848* (Cambridge, 1982), pp. 232–6.

10   Berg, *The Machinery Question*; G. M. Anderson, R. B. Ekelund Jr and R. D. Tollison, 'Nassau Senior as economic consultant: The Factory Acts reconsidered', *Economica* 56 (1989), 71–81.

11   As part of this dialogue, Senior was invited to tour the factories. N. W. Senior and L. Horner, *Letters on the Factory Act, as it affects the Cotton Manufacture, Addressed to the Right Honourable the President of the Board of Trade* (London, 1837), pp. 4–5.

12   For example: ibid.; Anon. (attributed to John Doherty), *Misrepresentations Exposed in a Letter Containing Strictures on the Letters on the Factory Act etc.* (Manchester, 1838); Lord Ashley, *Ten Hours' Factory Bill, The Speech of Lord Ashley M.P.* (London, 1844). R. H. Greg, *The Factory Question* (London, 1837); H. Hoole, *A Letter to the Rt. Hon. Lord Althorp* (Manchester, 1832); 'Proofs that Wages on the Continent are not lower than in England', *Mechanics' Magazine Museum, Register, Journal, and Gazette* 21 (1834), 52–7; W. Kenworthy, *Inventions and Hours of Labour: A Letter to Master Cotton Spinners, Manufacturers, and Millowners in General* (Blackburn, 1842); R. Oastler, *Fleet Papers* (London, 1842).

13   Kirby and Musson, *Voice of the People*, p. 396. Anon., *Misrepresentations Exposed in a Letter Containing Strictures on the Letters on the Factory Act*, contrasted real conditions in factories

competing financial arguments, noting a tendency of entrepreneurs lobbying against regulation to understate profits and exaggerate their fixed costs, with those entrepreneurs favouring legislation taking a more optimistic view of their finances.[14] Motivations of the rival groups in presenting these views seem clear and intuitive, but it is worth examining their sensitivities further for several reasons. For example, it may have been an exaggeration to suggest, as some leading mill owners did, that a small reduction in working hours would ruin the industry. At the same time, there must have been a minimum level of prescribed working time that would indeed have effectively wiped out the mill owners' profit. To ascertain the sensitivity of profit to changes in working time, the analysis below uses accounting data drawn from the business records of the mill owners on either side of the argument and the financial evidence presented for parliamentary scrutiny in the course of the debates.

Of central concern to either side was not merely the sensitivity of mill profits to changes in working time, but also the risk arising from entrepreneurs' commitment to fixed-cost investments. Evidence suggests that by the 1830s, such risk was indeed an essential consideration for mill owners opposed to factory regulation, an issue that this chapter will explore in more detail. If the level of risk can be quantified, so too, in line with financial theory, can the corresponding expected rate of profit.[15] Hence the question can be answered: what would be a reasonable rate of profit that entrepreneurs could expect on their investments? The answer to this question was at the forefront of contemporary economic thinking. Debates on the factory question were paralleled by a discussion within political economy about what constituted profit and what the rate of profit should be. Relatedly, was there some reduction in the working week that would have been compatible with also earning what contemporary observers considered a reasonable rate of profit?

The answer to these questions allows the legitimacy of the claims of political economists and the Ten Hours movement to be re-evaluated, as well as their ethical standpoints. A financial focus avoids the problem of moral relativism that bedevilled the legislators, who, when confronted with evidence of harsh conditions at one mill, were often presented with counterbalancing examples of better conditions elsewhere. To make matters worse for legislators, employer

with Senior's account based on biased information from employers. Some accounts from the supporters of regulation, such as, for example, William Dodd, may have also been misleading: see J. Humphries, *Childhood and Child Labour in the British Industrial Revolution* (Cambridge, 2010), p. 17. See also, A. Harrison and B. L. Hutchins, *A History of Factory Legislation* (London, 1903; reprinted Abingdon, 2013); A. P. Robson, *On Higher than Commercial Grounds: The Factory Controversy* (New York, 1985).

14   S. Toms and A. Shepherd, 'Accounting and social conflict: Profit and regulated working time in the British Industrial Revolution', *Critical Perspectives on Accounting* 49 (2017), 57–75.

15   For a summary of the relevant financial theories, see S. Toms, 'The labour theory of value, risk and the rate of profit', *Critical Perspectives on Accounting* 21 (2010), 96–103.

pressure had the potential to distort operatives' testimonies. Moreover, the modern reader naturally interprets nineteenth-century employment practices anachronistically. Financial relationships nonetheless temper moral arguments through the provision of appropriate yardsticks. Poor working conditions might be easier to justify in conditions approaching bankruptcy than where the rate of profit was more than enough to satisfy the requirements of the typical mill investor. Such parameters apply as much in today's business contexts as to the politically charged atmosphere of the factory debates.

Economic arguments were thus crucial ingredients of the legislative process, and the chapter subjects them to detailed scrutiny. The arguments of supporters and opponents of regulation featured in contemporary pamphlets and evidence to parliamentary committees. A third, neutral stance, can also be established by conducting an independent examination of surviving accounting records taken from the archives.[16] These and other examples are used to generalize the underlying relationships between firms' cost structures, the rate of profit and the length of the working day. These parameters are used to reframe the political debates, for example, illustrating the effect on profit of carrying out the legislative programme of the Ten Hours movement in contrast with the status quo, and claims and counterclaims about the threat of foreign competition.

The chapter provides some brief background on the history of factory legislation. It then considers the nineteenth-century origins of the notion of profit and its relation to investment in fixed capital, and the economic motives of the supporters and opponents of legislation. The significant elements implied in these debates, the specification of the employment contract, cost behaviour, risk and the rate of profit, are combined to structure the analysis of accounting data. The relevant evidence can be assessed from a pro-regulation, anti-regulation and neutral standpoint, such that the relationship between the length of the working day and the rate of profit can be quantified. Implicated in these trade-offs is the role of fixed costs, particularly with reference to Senior's theory of the 'last hour', which is re-evaluated with reference to business records. The cost and profit position of British firms can also be assessed to test the claims of the cotton masters that the trade would be ruined by foreign competition if legislation further restricting working time were allowed. It will be argued that factory legislation did not pose a threat to profitability on the scale that employers feared and that a shorter working week was consistent with acceptable rates of profit. Even so, although profit rates were high, mill owners faced significant risks arising from their investment in fixed capital.

---

16   The dataset of business-level accounting records on which this book is based is well suited for such a purpose, as it includes the accounting records (see AP and GP) of inter alia the most prominent lobbyists, the Ashworths and the Gregs.

Factory regulation

In the 1790s, opposition to long hours and child labour came from medical practitioners such as Thomas Percival and his colleagues on the Manchester Board of Health.[17] In the period 1800–30, political moves to regulate the working day, and hours worked by children, in particular, achieved only tentative results. The regulation was the subject of intense political controversy, in which, as a general rule, the manufacturers opposed to legislation followed the Whig interest and supporters the Tory interest. The latter group consisted of landowners resentful of the rising manufacturing class and also philanthropists genuinely appalled by factory conditions. Some regarded factory legislation as the only solution to the practice of child exploitation. Sir Robert Peel, the Elder, had been surprised to learn of the widespread employment of children in his factories and, with insufficient time to address the problem personally, introduced an Act of Parliament to do it for him.[18]

This first Factory Act of 1802 was an extension of the Elizabethan poor law and applied only to apprentices.[19] Based on the principle that parliament could not legislate parental responsibility for children, it placed *in loco parentis* responsibilities on Masters employing orphans but was widely regarded as ineffective.[20] The employment of children did not diminish as a consequence of the new system of inspection introduced after 1802.

Meanwhile, new divisions of labour and deployment of machinery intensified work. In mule spinning, the number of motions that had to be completed per minute more than trebled and the average distance walked by the piecer increased from twelve miles to nearly thirty between 1814 and 1840.[21] The evidence in the previous two chapters has shown that model 3 and model 4-type investments typically intensified the use of labour.

In response, some mill owners, such as Peel and Owen, promoted the regulation of cotton mills, but there was strong resistance from others. Opponents felt that regulation would advantage steam-powered over water-powered mills because the latter required more continuous operation.[22] A

---

17 Harrison and Hutchins, *A History of Factory Legislation*, p. 9.

18 Ibid., pp. 16–17; Pollard, *The Genesis of Modern Management*, p. 165.

19 Harrison and Hutchins, *A History of Factory Legislation*, p. 2.

20 Health and Morals of Apprentices Act 1802, 42 Geo. 3 c. 73. Harrison and Hutchins, *A History of Factory Legislation*, p. 17.

21 J. Foster, *Class Struggle and the Industrial Revolution: Early Industrial Capitalism in Three English Towns* (London, 1974), p. 91. The piecer's role was to monitor the machines and repair broken threads. For a contemporary description of the role of the piecer and associated harsh employment conditions, see W. Dodd, *A Narrative of the Experience of the Sufferings of William Dodd: A Factory Cripple* (London, 1841), pp. 7–12.

22 *Select Committee on the State of Children Employed in the Manufactories of the United Kingdom*, BPP, 1816, 397, ev. W. Sidgwick, p. 117.

subsequent Act of 1819 stated that no children under nine were to be employed and that the working day was limited to twelve hours for children aged nine to sixteen.[23] In 1825 Sir John Cam Hobhouse's Bill proposed a working week of 66 hours, amended by the House of Lords to 69 hours, following recommendations from Robert Hyde Greg and another master spinner.[24] In 1831 Hobhouse brought in another bill proposing to restrict weekly hours worked by children to sixty-four, which resulted in a further compromise Act, limiting the working day to twelve hours for all those under eighteen and night work to those aged twenty-one and over.[25]

Notwithstanding the relatively minor effects of earlier legislation, the centralization of production in metropolitan areas diminished the significance of child labour as an issue per se. Attention was now increasingly focused on the working hours of all operatives and had become a divisive political issue by the 1830s. It was the focus of a series of debates over factory legislation in the British parliament in the 1830s and 1840s, culminating in the Factory Act of 1847, which broadly resolved the issue in favour of the operatives' key demand, for a regulated maximum ten-hour day. Up to then, although the Great Reform Act of 1832 had enhanced the political power of the manufacturing classes, represented by the Whig party and the Anti-Corn Law League, their political demands were resisted by the landowning classes. For some, at least in the Tory party, the poor employment practices of the mill owners were a suitable target. The Ten Hours movement was therefore led in parliament by Tories, most notably Sadler and subsequently Ashley, while drawing on wider political support from radical and working-class organizations. Although less prominent, child labour was still an emotive issue and the movement accordingly combined demands for regulation of the working week with further restrictions on child labour.[26] Pressure for new legislation came from outraged sections of the public, influenced by the publication of the Robert Blincoe memoirs,[27] the operatives, represented by the Short Time committees and also from Tory radicals such as Oastler, suspicious of rapid industrialization.[28]

Public and parliamentary campaigns to reduce the length of the working

23   Cotton Mills and Factories Act, 1819, 59 Geo. 3, c. 66. The House of Lords recommended an eleven-hour limit, but the Commons amended it to twelve.

24   *Factories Inquiry Commission*, BPP, 1833, 450, ev. R. H. Greg, p. 781. The 1833 Act also established a partial holiday on Saturday and provided penalties for offences against the Act.

25   Labour in Cotton Mills Act, 1831, 1 & 2 Will. 4, c. 39. None of the laws passed before 1833 contained procedures for enforcement.

26   For a detailed analysis of the politics of regulation, see Robson, *On Higher than Commercial Grounds*.

27   Brown, 'A Memoir of Robert Blincoe'. The memoirs were made public in increments beginning in 1830; see Waller, *The Real Oliver Twist*.

28   R. Gray, *The Factory Question and Industrial England, 1830–1860* (Cambridge, 1986), pp. 7, 66.

day thus reached new levels of intensity. As a consequence, in 1832, a new bill sponsored by Sadler and Ashley that proposed restricting the working day to ten hours, including for adults, was then introduced. As Chairman of the Parliamentary Select Committee on the Bill, Sadler used his position to inflame opinion further by hearing evidence mainly from victims of poor employment practice and publishing what his opponents regarded as a one-sided report.[29]

To frame a financial analysis of the debates, some account needs to be taken of what is already known about the motivations of the pro- and anti-regulation groups. Although led by Ashley, the pro-regulation lobby received support from certain mill owners, most famously Robert Owen and John Fielden MP. A possible reason why some mill owners supported regulation was experimental evidence showing that it was in the interest of *all* employers to curtail labour hours beyond a certain point. These experiments suggested that there were diminishing returns from increases in working hours.[30] Moreover, they were conducted, in some cases at least, to deliberately further the lobbying process in favour of regulation. For example, Gardner's shorter time experiment in Preston commenced in April 1844, with no reduction in the *rate* of wages and coincided with a petition presented to Ashley by Sir George Strickland MP in support of the Ten Hours Bill.[31]

Meanwhile, manufacturing interests, in cotton and other textile industries, argued that long hours were essential to the profitable operation, and indeed their mills' survival, in the face of threats from overseas competition. Opponents of regulation like Robert Hyde Greg and the Ashworth brothers had good reason to respond to Sadler's evidence, which among other things, noted that in country areas, there was a tendency to work longer hours to evade restrictions.[32] Consequently, Greg, the Ashworths and other mill owners lobbied successfully for a new Royal Commission (The Factories Inquiry Commission) to visit the manufacturing districts and take further evidence. These mill owners would prove to be prominent witnesses at the Commission hearings.[33] Supporters of

29 *Report from the Committee (Sadler Committee) on the 'Bill to regulate the labour of children in the mills and factories of the United Kingdom'*, BPP, 1831–32, 706.

30 For example, the short-time experiments conducted by Robert Owen at New Lanark, Arkwright and Strutt in Derbyshire, and by Swainson, Gardner and Horrocks & Jacson in Preston, typically reported efficiency improvements and no overall loss of output. See, respectively, J. Minter Morgan, *Remarks on the Practicability of Mr. Robert Owen's Plan to Improve the Condition of the Lower Classes* (London, 1819); Anon., 'Answers to Certain Objections made to Sir Robert Peel's Bill', *The Factory Act of 1819*, ed. K. Carpenter (New York, 1972); *Preston Chronicle*, 27 April 1844. See also Ashley's argument, *Ten Hours' Factory Bill*, p. 15, that workers were only 50% efficient in the last hour of the working day.

31 *Preston Chronicle*, 27 April 1844. Strickland was the MP for Preston.

32 Greg, *The Factory Question*, pp. 128–9; *Sadler Committee*, BPP, 1831–32, 706, ev. J. Longstone, qq.9379–81.

33 Greg, *The Factory Question*, p. 8. Henry Ashworth (1794–1880) and Edmund Ashworth (1800–81), along with John Pooley, were deputed by the Master Spinners to give evidence to

regulation accordingly described Greg and the Ashworths as '[f]oremost in this movement of importing children from the agricultural districts' and opposing the Ten Hours Bill.[34]

Evidence from Lancashire was collected by two subcommittees (D1 and D2) of the Commission, chaired respectively by John Welsford Cowell and Edward Carlton Tufnell.[35] The two chairmen took very different attitudes to the issue in question. There is evidence that in carrying out this function, Tufnell, on the one hand, colluded closely with Greg and the anti-regulation lobby. Perhaps as a consequence, Greg had the 'last and longest word in this group … supported by elaborate calculations about costs and returns on investments'.[36] Cowell, on the other hand, was strongly critical of the evidence presented by 'Messrs Pooley, Birley, H. Hoole, Ashworth and Greg', and particularly 'the statistical documents furnished by the latter gentleman'.[37]

As the Sadler Committee had been regarded as swinging too far in favour of regulation, the Commission was now regarded by supporters of regulation as rigged against it. Consequently, Greg's opponents in the pro-regulation lobby now refused to participate in what they referred to as a 'Commission for the perpetuation of infanticide'. They expected a whitewash on behalf of the employers.[38] Greg's evidence to the Commission, based on an analysis of the cost structure of the Greg partnership's main businesses, particularly Quarry Bank Mill, formed an important part of the manufacturing interest's case against regulation. Greg aimed to build on earlier lobbying successes. He had been instrumental in framing the Lord's amendment to Hobhouse's 1825 Bill, mitigating its effects from the employers' point of view.[39] The outcome of the Commission hearings shaped the ultimate Factory Act legislation of 1833.[40]

Cowell's Committee, *Factories Inquiry Commission*, BPP, 1833, 450, pp. 678–83. R. Boyson, *The Ashworth Cotton Enterprise* (Oxford, 1970), pp. 158–9.

34 P. Grant and A. Ashley Cooper [Earl of Shaftesbury], *The Ten Hours' Bill: The History of Factory Legislation* (Manchester, 1866), p. 54.

35 *Factories Inquiry Commission*, BPP, 1833, 450. The two committees collected evidence in parallel during the second half of 1833 and are listed as D1 (Cowell) and D2 (Tufnell) in the full report, and below.

36 Toms and Shepherd, 'Accounting and social conflict'; Gray, *The Factory Question*, p. 71.

37 *Factories Inquiry Commission, Supplementary Report*, BPP, 1834, 167, Cowell's preface, p. 136, also cited in Greg, *The Factory Question*, p. 100.

38 'Commission for the Perpetuation of Infanticide', *Fraser's Magazine for Town and Country* 7/42 (1833: June), 707–15. H. P. Marvel, 'Factory regulation: A reinterpretation of early English experience', *Journal of Law and Economics* 20 (1977), 379–402, at p. 382.

39 *Factories Inquiry Commission*, BPP, 1833, 450, D2, ev. R. H. Greg, p. 781.

40 Grant and Ashley Cooper, *The Ten Hours' Bill*, p. 53. The Factory Act of 1833 (3 & 4 Will. 4, c. 103) was commonly referred to as Althorp's Act. No children were to work in factories under the age of nine (though by this stage, numbers were few). The Act also required children under thirteen to receive elementary schooling for two hours each day. Even so, the Act established a maximum working week of 48 hours for those between nine and thirteen, limited to eight hours a day; and for children between thirteen and eighteen, work was limited to twelve hours daily.

The final Commission report referred to the economic arguments of the entrepreneurs and coupled that with limited recommendations on child labour and inspection. Lord Althorp, as Leader of the House, now used the Commission report as the basis of a new bill, which was carried by a large majority. Ashley and his followers were frustrated and now forced to surrender the original Ten Hours Bill.[41]

Some of the literature has tried to explain the differences of opinion between Ashley's group and the anti-regulation group led by Ashworth and Greg by highlighting their divergent economic interests. Marvel proposes an 'industry capture' argument, suggesting that the purpose of the regulation was to increase the cost of production for the smaller mills, thereby causing them to curtail their output. The result would naturally be higher textile prices and thus increased quasi-rents accruing to capitals least affected by the Act, specifically metropolitan steam-powered mills.[42] Support for reform was indeed higher in mule-spinning regions where demand for adolescents was higher than demand for juveniles or women.[43] According to Nardinelli, violators of the Factory Acts were owners of small, isolated mills.[44]

Even so, the weight of evidence in support of this hypothesis has not been sufficient to resolve the debate. Rose rejects the argument that rural water-powered mill owners were the principal opponents of factory legislation, arguing that their main concern was foreign competition.[45] Rose, Taylor and Winstanley also suggest that larger firms needed to work longer to make sufficient output to cover their higher fixed costs.[46] Although it is the case that larger firms would have higher fixed costs, the role of fixed costs and the relationship to the working day has not been hitherto fully explored. In now doing so, the chapter illustrates how accounting arguments were used to justify the political objectives of this element of the liberal economic discourse in the 1830s and 1840s.

41   Grant and Ashley Cooper, *The Ten Hours' Bill*, p. 53. Viscount Althorp, John Charles Spencer, 3rd Earl Spencer (1782–1845), used his position as Leader of the House to promote the new bill. Grant refers to Althorp as the Prime Minister. Chadwick, the chair of the Royal Commission drafted Althorp's bill, which naturally embodied most of the Commission's recommendations; see Marvel, 'Factory regulation', p. 383.

42   Ibid., pp. 387–8, 393.

43   Gray, *The Factory Question*, p. 105.

44   C. Nardinelli, 'The successful prosecution of the Factory Acts: A suggested explanation', *EcHR* 38 (1985), 428–30.

45   M. B. Rose, *Firms, Networks and Business Values: The British and American Cotton Industries since 1750* (Cambridge, 2000), pp. 143–4.

46   M. B. Rose, P. Taylor and M. J. Winstanley, 'The economic origins of paternalism: Some objections', *Social History* 14 (1989), 89–98.

Ideological theories of profit

The role of fixed costs, their impact on profit and the length of the working day were indeed of great interest to contemporary opinion. Mill owners meanwhile were amassing wealth from new sources, which lacked ideological justification. They needed a consistent lobbying position, which was now given to them by leading political economists.

These issues provided a particular focus for the emerging discipline of political economy, which now became the ideological expression of the anti-regulation group. Early-nineteenth-century writers on political economy paid considerable attention to theories of profit and profit accrual, in which they made implicit but important assumptions about cost behaviour. Feudal regulations against usury and in favour of just prices had tended to limit the notion of profit to rewards commensurate with risk or the physical and mental labour of the undertaker. The ordinary rate of profit, implying no risk, was, therefore, the official interest rate, which until the 1850s was commensurate with the usury laws. Upward adjustment for risk, arising, for example, from overseas trade in politically unstable regions, had long been accepted.[47]

In the meantime, however, mill owners and other entrepreneurs were amassing vast fortunes from their purely domestic activities.[48] They, therefore, needed a justification for these profits, which became urgent as more stringent factory regulation threatened.[49] There were two particularly useful standpoints from the employers' point of view. First, there was the ideological argument of laissez-faire, with its roots in Smithian economics. To admit to any regulation was to surrender this, their leading principle.[50] Earlier Factory Acts, in 1802 and 1819, notwithstanding their limitations, directly challenged the doctrine. Although the Factory Act of 1833 did not concede the main demands of the Ten Hours movement, its passage nonetheless represented a defeat for the laissez-faire principle, particularly after 1836, when the inspection system was more rigorously enforced.[51] The emphasis of political economy now, therefore, shifted to a second, related issue, which was the challenge of theorizing the rate of profit. Ideologically, this meant opposition to Hodgskin, Saint-Simon and Owen, who advocated the right of the labourer to receive the whole produce of labour.[52] With the transition towards greater investment in machinery, political

---

47 W. J. Ashley, *English Economic History* (London, 1892); S. Toms, 'Calculating profit: A Historical Perspective on the Development of Capitalism', *Accounting, Organizations and Society* 35 (2010), 205–21.

48 Cotton spinners, for example, sold directly to the market in Manchester, not to the ultimate overseas customer.

49 Berg, *The Machinery Question*.

50 Robson, *On higher than Commercial Grounds*.

51 Including rights of access and fines for non-compliance; Boyson, *Ashworth Cotton*, pp. 165–6.

52 Berg, *The Machinery Question*, pp. 115–16.

economists now looked to the nature of fixed capital, to understand the sources of increasing returns, and to the state to nurture its development.[53]

Scrope identified two particular reasons why the rate of profit should be high in manufacture. The first, also advocated by Rae and Ramsey,[54] was as a reward for entrepreneurial labour, which was mental or knowledge labour rather than manual labour and, in addition to the ordinary rate of profit on capital, there should be reward for skill and trouble, according to the standard of remuneration 'generally expected of his class'.[55] Second, Scrope argued that risks in manufacture were greater than in agriculture because fixed capital was more likely to be superseded by new inventions. In this sense, depreciation, or wear and tear, was viewed as an appropriation of profit, as part of the insurance value of employing fixed capital. Embryonic theories based on capital maintenance promoted this approach, or the need to recover capital advanced, plus a commensurate return. Further compensation, in Scrope's scheme, arose from the risk peculiar to the trade in which the capital was engaged. The remainder, the return obtained without labour or risk, was the net profit, comprising compensation for sacrifice of personal gratification and insurance against the risk of loss of property.[56]

The threat of legislation also promoted attempts to relate the accrual of profit to the length of the working day. A reinterpretation of laissez-faire was needed that allowed for the regulation of child labour but resisted the more general demands of the Ten-Hour committees.[57] Senior was invited to visit the mills and his observations led him to develop his 'last hour' theory. Senior argued that profit was a specific fraction of total cost and, therefore, any revenue was required to cover total cost before any profit could be registered. It followed that all profit was earned in the last hour of the working day and, therefore, any reduction of the working day would eliminate the profit.[58] Although flawed, Senior's arguments carried temporary weight because the 'fixed cost' problem was poorly understood.[59] Moreover, although the argument itself was incorrect, since reducing the working day would also eliminate cost in some proportion,

---

53   Ibid., pp. 124 and 139.
54   J. Rae, *Statement of some new Principles on the Subject of Political Economy: Exposing the Fallacies of the System of Free Trade, and of some other Doctrines Maintained in the 'Wealth of Nations'* (Boston, 1834), p. 195; G. Ramsay, *An Essay on the Distribution of Wealth* (Edinburgh, 1836).
55   G. P. Scrope, *Principles of Political Economy* (London, 1836), pp. 209–11.
56   Ibid., p. 158.
57   Robson, *On higher than Commercial Grounds*, pp. 151–2.
58   Senior and Horner, *Letters on the Factory Act*, pp. 4–5.
59   For example, the 'fixed cost' problem, as identified by R. S. Edwards, 'Some notes on the early literature and development of cost accounting in Great Britain', *The Accountant* 97 (1937), 193–5. Edwards concluded that whereas accounting methods were adequate for the purposes of the putting-out system, once production had been internalized in factories, there was a subsequent failure to resolve the fixed-cost problem.

the implied relationship was partially true insofar as some of the costs were fixed. The argument was good enough for Henry Ashworth, who in 1833 changed his position on the required working day from eleven hours to twelve in line with Senior's arguments.[60]

The last-hour theory thus precisely suited the agenda of the anti-regulation lobby and complemented further practical considerations. Laissez-faire ideology also conveniently accommodated the need to respond to competitive pressures, and perhaps in some cases, concern about wealth transfers in favour of real wages at the expense of capital accumulation. Also, a further motive that has not been examined in detail before might have been risk aversion of entrepreneurs in the face of increasing fixed capital commitments. Senior enlisted the arguments of Henry Ashworth who suggested: 'when a labourer lays down his spade, he renders useless for that period a capital worth 18 pence. When one of our people leaves the mill, he renders useless capital that has cost £100.'[61] In other words, the investment in fixed capital procured on behalf of the operative confronted the mill owner with a substantial risk in the event of restrictions on the working day.

Additionally, entrepreneurs benefited from an environment where profit and capital measurement were poorly understood, and poorly monitored, enabling them to present and indeed manipulate financial evidence to support their case. Regulators were unable to scrutinize factory accounts and business records[62] so that the possible financial consequences of regulation were subject to interpretation and distortion. As a consequence, the pro-regulation lobby presented a consistent and pessimistic line on the profitability of the mills and the risks faced by their enterprises. Nonetheless, the argument was more of a lobbying position than a statement of economic reality.

Summarizing the opposing points of view, it is clear that the rate of profit and the extent of fixed costs were important parameters that helped frame arguments for and against restrictions on the hours of labour. In light of these differing positions, there is an opportunity to analyse the data and model the implied assumptions. Conducting such an analysis reveals the nature of contemporary assumptions about the relationship between fixed costs, the rate of profit and the length of the working day. Setting up a model of the implied relationships, using the figures presented in the debates before parliament and its committees, and from contemporary business accounts in the archives, provides the opportunity to reassess employer justifications for the length of the working day.

---

60 *Factories Inquiry Commission*, BPP, 1833, 450, D2, q.1104; Boyson, *Ashworth Cotton*, p. 162.
61 Ibid., p. 7.
62 There is no record of visitors having inspected Quarry Bank under the stipulations of Peel's 1802 Act, notwithstanding Greg's being one of the largest employers of child labour. Rose, 'Social policy and business', p. 22.

Financial evidence in the lobbying process

The first instance of accounting data being used to underpin a lobbying position was in the evidence presented to the Factories Inquiry Commission in 1833. Robert Hyde Greg, the managing partner of Quarry Bank Mill, which was part of the Samuel Greg partnership, supplied much of this evidence. Because Quarry Bank was a remote location and water-powered, the mill was more dependent on child labour than steam-powered mills in urban areas. Greg was, therefore, one of the last employers to use the factory apprentice system.[63]

Along with other water spinners, he also had further specific reasons for objection to regulation. These included exemptions to work for extra time lost to interruptions caused by drought. Further remediation was needed because wages in remote locations were already low, such that further reductions would lead to migration into the towns. High rents for leasehold access to water-courses were also cited as giving rise to higher costs.[64]

If Robert Hyde Greg opposed the principle of regulation on economic grounds, from a practical point of view he favoured measures that equalized the working day for adults and children at twelve hours, opposing night work, and increasing the age of admission and the provision of universal education. For Greg, the inequality between regulated working days for different age groups working in the same teams was inefficient, although he later recognized that this was preferable to lower hours for all groups, as agitated for by the Ten Hours movement.[65]

Greg and other objectors to Sadler's Ten Hours Bill also argued that Britain's advantage over continental competitors arose from the possession of better machinery so that more work was done in the same length of time with the same plant.[66] Restricting the hours of labour would, therefore, limit the advantage arising from more efficient technology. Specifically, they argued that time for stopping and starting the mill would increase the proportion of unproductive to productive labour time, and that restriction on the time an individual was allowed to operate his machinery was an infringement of liberty.[67]

---

63   Gray, *The Factory Question*, p. 9. Consistent with earlier practice, Greg was foremost among employers seeking to recruit new apprentices following the Poor Law Amendment Act of 1834 (Grant and Ashley Cooper, *The Ten Hours' Bill*, p. 54) and apprentices were used at Styal until 1847; see M. B. Rose, *The Gregs of Quarry Bank Mill* (Cambridge, 1986), p. 78.

64   *Factories Inquiry Commission*, BPP, 1833, 450, D2, evidence R. H. Greg, p. 784.

65   Greg, *The Factory Question*, p. 20.

66   *Factories Inquiry Commission*, BPP, 1833, 450, p. 42, referring to the evidence of William Rathbone Greg. Cf. G. Clark, 'Why isn't the whole world developed? Lessons from the cotton mills', *JEH* 47 (1987), 141–73. Clark shows that labour efficiency was higher in Britain than, for example, in Switzerland, therefore compensating for apparently lower wages.

67   *Factories Inquiry Commission*, BPP, 1833, 450, D2, evidence R. H. Greg, pp. 784 and 786, Appendix B.

Greg gave evidence to the second Lancashire committee of the Factories Inquiry Commission chaired by Edward Carleton Tufnell, while H. H. Birley and Holland Hoole, Edmund Ashworth and John Pooley gave evidence to the first Commission, chaired by John Welsford Cowell. Their submissions contained strong similarities, and each presented evidence showing their perceived scale of fixed charges analysed by main category and scenarios showing the effect of these charges on profits and wages, assuming pro rata reductions in outputs, in line with Senior's theory. When the debates on Ten Hour legislation resurfaced in the 1840s, anti-regulation lobbyists, including the Ashworth brothers, undertook similar calculations. These calculations were made on a separate sheet in one of Ashworth's ledgers and were intended as a response to a pro-regulation pamphlet published by William Kenworthy.[68] John Fielden MP, although himself a cotton entrepreneur with access to cost and profit data from his own firm, based his parliamentary speech in 1844 on Kenworthy's figures. Ashley's earlier 1844 address used other examples based on more comprehensive data, including the case of a spinning establishment comparable to Greg, Birley and Hoole, Pooley and the Ashworth brothers' examples.

To conduct an analysis showing the impact of fixed costs on the rate of profit, allowing output to vary according to different assumptions about the length of the working data, requires data on production, the perceived split of total cost into fixed and variable components, and the amount of capital invested. Further detail, on depreciation, interest, wages and other sundry components of cost are also helpful, as is data on the split between fixed and circulating capital. For these reasons, three anti-regulation sets of evidence were selected based on sufficient data: Greg's submission and also that of Birley and Hoole to the Commission in 1833, and Ashworth's calculations in response to Kenworthy in 1844.[69] The pro-regulation evidence consists of only one dataset, taken from Ashley's speech in 1844.[70] Although the selection of evidence is somewhat unbalanced in this respect, the Ashleyites appear to have relied less on accounting data than the anti-regulation lobby. Such imbalance is perhaps unsurprising as the discourse of the Ten Hours movement was based on the sense of moral outrage over child labour and overwork,[71] whereas the laissez-faire mill owners based their arguments on the threat of apparently cheaper overseas competition.

68   AP, Quarterly Stock Accounts, 'Calculations for Ten Hours Bill', p. 111, Eng. MS, 1201; Kenworthy, *Inventions and Hours of Labour*.
69   *Factories Inquiry Commission*, BPP, 1833, 450, D2, ev. R. H. Greg, pp. 780–4; ibid., D1, pp. 729–30; AP, 'Calculations for Ten Hours Bill', Eng. MS, 1201.
70   Ashley, *Ten Hours' Factory Bill*, p. 9.
71   For example, Oastler, *Fleet Papers* and the periodical entitled *British Labourer's Protector and Factory Child's Friend* (reprinted New York, 1969).

The third set of evidence, taken from the archives, is used as a means of auditing the evidence used by the pro- and anti-regulation lobbies. The Greg and Ashworth papers both contain sufficient data to extract the measures for comparative analysis, which is done by reperforming their publicly disclosed data with comparable data from their private business records.[72] For Greg, the averages of the previous five years' data, 1827–31 inclusive, are used and for Ashworth, the profit and loss account for the quarter ended in November 1845.[73] These figures are appropriate because they appear in the ledger directly opposite the Kenworthy calculations and provide a very detailed contemporaneous analysis of costs.[74] No comparable archival records are available for the Birley and Hoole case, although their evidence appears to be a generalized abstraction rather than a specific firm. Even so, the Birley and Hoole figures can be reworked using assumptions consistent with the information shown in the Greg and Ashworth ledgers.

Table 3 shows a collation based on the underlying records summarizing each political position (columns [1] and [2]) and data extracted from archival documents, which is intended to represent an objective position (column [3]). The table shows the required level of output necessary, expressed in hours per week, to achieve specified levels of profit ranging from 5% to 15%. These figures can then be interpolated to compute the implied rate of profit for hours per week reflecting the status quo (69 hours, as favoured by the anti-regulation lobby) and the 58-hour week implied by a Ten Hours Bill.[75] The table also shows the weekly fixed and total costs, with the proportion of fixed cost to total cost as a percentage, allowing the perceived scale of fixed cost between pro- and anti-regulation lobbies to be evaluated.

The results in Table 3 follow a clear pattern. The opponents of regulation estimate high levels of fixed cost, which appears to justify the requirement for a long working week to earn a reasonable rate of return. High fixed-cost estimates also lead to a high operating leverage ratio, but even accepting this is an overestimate, the notion of a 'reasonable rate of return' might be in the order of 10%, in view of the presence of some fixed costs and the pronounced nature of the trade cycle affecting the cotton trade.[76] In contrast, the pro-regulation lobby

---

72   AP, Quarterly Stock Accounts, Eng. MS, 1201; GP, Partnership Book, C5/1/2/4.

73   It is appropriate to use aggregate examples from the 1830s and 1840s because the terms of the debate, on the Ten Hours question, continued following the 1833 Act. All example cases are therefore based on cost structures of firms working a 69-hour week. It should be borne in mind that the fixed capital of a typical 1840s mill was larger than a 1830s mill, a point discussed in more detail below.

74   AP, Quarterly Stock Accounts, pp. 111–12, Eng. MS, 1201.

75   For details of the proposed hours, see Grant and Ashley Cooper, *The Ten Hours' Bill*, p. 101.

76   J. J. Siegel, 'The real rate of interest from 1800–1990: A study of the US and the UK', *Journal of Monetary Economics* 29 (1992), 227–52. Siegel calculates the average arithmetic rate of return on equity for the period 1800–1990 as 7.81%. However, the differential between equity and bond

Table 3. Comparative costs and profits

	Anti-regulation[1] [1]	Pro-regulation[1] [2]	Archival evidence[1] [3]
Working week (hours) required to achieve profit on capital[2] of:			
5%	47.8	23.0	32.3
10%	68.8	46.0	55.2
15%	89.8	69.0	78.0
Implied rate of profit on capital[2] of:			
69-hour week	8.25%	15.00%	15.02%
58-hour week	6.10%	12.83%	10.27%
Total cost (£ per week)[3]	334.01	175.00	371.48
Fixed cost (£ per week)[3]	117.55	19.25	85.43
% Fixed cost	35.19%	11.00%	23.00%

Notes:
1 [1] and [3] average of Greg, Birley and Hoole, and Ashworth based on Factories Inquiry Commission and archive sources, respectively; [2] based on figures given by Ashley.
2 After depreciation and before interest charges.
3 Costs are shown in decimal equivalent values.

Sources: Compiled from respectively [1] *Factories Inquiry Commission*, BPP, 1833, 450, D1, ev. H. Birley and H. Hoole, pp. 729–30; ibid., ev. Greg, D2, pp. 780–4; AP, Quarterly Stock Accounts, 'Calculations for Ten Hours Bill', p. 111, Eng. MS, 1201; [2] Ashley, *Ten Hours' Factory Bill*, 10 May 1844, p. 9, spinning establishment; [3] GP, Partnership Book, C5/1/2/4; AP, Quarterly Stock Accounts, Profit and loss account, 1845, p. 112, Eng. MS, 1201; *Factories Inquiry Commission*, BPP, 1833, 450, D1, ev. H. Birley and H. Hoole, pp. 729–30.

produced low estimates of fixed cost and also higher levels of profit. In some cases, these were overestimated.[77] The corresponding figures computed from archival data suggest an average range of outcomes for these variables. As the

returns was much lower in the earlier part of the nineteenth century (ibid., figure 5). Long-run estimates of the premium on risky investments suggest that a range of 3–8% over and above the risk-free rate of investment, which c.1840 can be taken as 3.5%. On the premium, see E. Dimson, P. Marsh and M. Staunton, 'Equity Premiums around the World', *Rethinking the Equity Risk Premium*, ed. P. B. Hammond Jr, M. L. Leibowitz and L. B. Seigel (Charlottesville, VA, 2011), 32–52; on British interest rates in the 1840s, see S. Homer and R. Sylla, *A History of Interest Rates*, 4th edn (Hoboken, NJ, 2011), chart 6, p. 179.
77 Ashley, *Ten Hours' Factory Bill*. In the calculation on p. 7, the net effect of all reductions was to reduce the total cost per pound of fixed charges for a 60-hour week compared to a 69-hour week. The result seems to arise from cumulative rounding errors applying pro rata reductions,

data in Table 3, column (3) show, shorter hours were possible in combination with reasonable rates of profit. A 58-hour working week implied a 10% return on capital, with fixed expenses representing less than a quarter of the total cost, suggested low vulnerability to downturns in the trade cycle. In contrast to Senior's theory, these calculations show that a substantial proportion of costs (c.80%) varied with output.[78]

Table 3 is suggestive of other reasons why mill owners, in general, would not welcome legislation, notwithstanding their political differences. Most importantly, the rate of profit on capital can be seen to be sensitive to assumptions about the cost of production concerning enforced reductions in output. The relationships of the neutral position set out in column [3] suggest that the working week could be set as low as 55 hours per week and still allow 10% profit, which seems to be a suitable compromise, but from the mill owners' point of view, would represent a cut of around 5% in the rate of profit achievable under the same conditions with a 69-hour week. A reduction of one-third in the rate of profit would perhaps provide a compelling reason for at least some employers to oppose the measure, particularly those such as water-powered mills that were subject to output restrictions arising from weather-related risk, and for those more specialized mills most vulnerable to volume-based variations resulting from the trade cycle.

The pro-regulation lobby assumed that only a small proportion of costs were fixed (11%), such that the effect on profit of shorter hours was proportionately less. Also, naturally, they presented a higher rate of profit (15%) for their purposes, although such an estimate is reasonable. Factory inspector Leonard Horner, writing to Senior, provides some support for the notion of 10% as the minimum average rate of profit:

> I am not clear as to the accuracy of your statement on the rate of profit in the cotton trade. It is very possible that, at the particular time of your inquiry, ten percent may have been the average net profit, on spinning, coarse and fine, and power-loom weaving; but the vast fortunes which have been made in the course of a few years, and in so great a number of instances, in all parts of the country where the cotton manufacture is carried on to any extent, by men who began without a shilling, and entirely on borrowed capital, for which they had to pay a heavy interest, prove to my mind that the average rate of net profit, in any period of five years since the cotton trade rose into consequence, must have greatly exceeded ten percent in well-managed factories.[79]

which was not the case in the other spinning establishment example used by Ashley, *Ten Hours' Factory Bill* on p. 9 (and in table 1).

78   Average fixed costs in columns (1)–(3) are 23%.

79   Leonard Horner (Senior and Horner, *Letters on the Factory Act*), provides some support for the notion of 10% as the minimum average rate of profit.

In short, both Horner and the analyses of Ashley, Fielden and Kenworthy were more consistent with the archival evidence reviewed, which itself is based on the business records of the anti-regulation lobby.

Effects of fixed costs

As Table 3 shows, an important reason for differences between pro- and anti-regulation positions arose from their assumptions about cost behaviour. Ashley and others argued that specific categories of cost that the mill owners assumed to be fixed were actually variable. They included depreciation on plant and machinery, which they claimed was related to usage, not merely the passage of time.[80] The mill owners argued for high depreciation charges that remained constant, regardless of use, because the rate of technical progress tended to increase obsolescence rates of sunk capital investments.[81] The second area of disagreement over fixed cost was the charging of interest on capital. The anti-regulation lobby argued that interest was a necessary cost of production, although their business records showed that it was a method of appropriation to the partners' capital accounts. The pro-regulation lobby argued that interest on the floating part of the capital was a variable cost of production since the reduced output following from a shorter working week would lead to a corresponding reduction in the circulating part of the capital. Fielden (using Kenworthy's figures) used this argument in the debates of the early 1840s.[82]

John Welsford Cowell made a similar point in response to the evidence presented by Pooley and Ashworth, Greg and others to the 1833 commission. Although not of Whiggish sympathies, to begin with, Cowell was unimpressed by the mill owners' apparent knowledge of business and forced them to concede that reduced hours would cause a parallel reduction in floating capital investment.[83] Cowell commented in the minutes:

---

80   Ashley, *Ten Hours' Factory Bill*, p. 7, pro rata reductions in wear and tear allowance in tabulations; Kenworthy, *Inventions and Hours of Labour*: 'amount of wear and tear ... will be lessened in the same proportion', p. 12; also cited in a speech by J. Fielden, *Hansard's Parliamentary Debates*, 18 March 1844, vol. 73, c. 1236.

81   For example, *Factories Inquiry Commission*, BPP, 1833, 450, D2, ev. Jackson, p. 779 and R. H. Greg, p. 782. See also K. Marx, *Capital I* (Harmondsworth, 1976), p. 333, notes 64 and 70, quoting authorities from the 1860s (*The Times*, 26 November 1862; *Reports of the Inspectors of Factories*, BPP, 31 October 1862, p. 19).

82   Toms and Shepherd, 'Accounting and social conflict'; J. Fielden speech, *Hansard's Parliamentary Debates*, 18 March 1844, vol. 73, c. 1236.

83   *Factories Inquiry Commission*, Supplementary Report, BPP, 1834, 167, Cowell's preface, pp. 119–45) and footnotes in *Factories Inquiry Commission*, BPP, 1833, 450, D1, ev. E. Ashworth and J. Pooley, pp. 679–80, H. H. Birley and H. Hoole, p. 727, and Q1, p. 726.

The answer to no. 9, as Mr. Ashworth observed, took more than an hour ...
It struck me as singular that gentleman should be so well acquainted with the
rate of wages on the Rhine and in the Netherlands, and yet require so long
a time to settle a rough proportion between the fixed and circulating capital
employed in their own business.[84]

A possible reason why Ashworth and Pooley discussed responses among
themselves was that they wished to present a common view of the evidence
most favourable to their case, rather than reflect actual business practice.

Archival evidence provides a means of analysing the claims of the pro- and
anti-regulation lobbies in more detail. Table 4 shows a detailed breakdown of
the costs for the Ashworth Brothers in November 1845. Data per the accounts,
which reflected a 69-hour week is shown in the first three columns, split between
variable (1) and fixed costs (2), together with the total costs (3). The next
three columns show the effect of reducing the working week to 58 hours, split
into variable costs (4), fixed costs (5) and total costs (6). The classification
of individual expense accounts into their fixed and variable components is a
detailed process and provides the means of splitting costs, following similar
assumptions in general contemporary accounting practice.[85] This is with
reference to relatively small cost classifications, such that although some
assumptions are necessary, their individual effect is relatively small, thereby
producing a potentially more accurate audit of cost behaviour. There would
undoubtedly be greater accuracy when compared with the aggregations into
more generic cost categories used in the parliamentary debates.[86] The total fixed
cost for the quarter evidenced in Table 4 was £625, or an annual equivalent of
just over £2,500.[87] For this calculation, variable costs are adjusted pro rata to
an output reduction implied by reducing from sixty-nine to 58 hours per week,
whereas the fixed expenses are held constant. The increase in cost per pound
arising from the restriction can then be calculated. The table shows that the
increase in cost would be from 10.123d/lb to 10.475d/lb, or a 3.447% increase
(⅜d). The difference in cost of ⅜d/lb corresponds closely to the difference
of ⅜d articulated in parliament by Fielden, based on the figures supplied by
Kenworthy. Fielden castigated his opponents for inflicting the suffering on
child workers for such a small financial return. In summary, evidence from

84   *Factories Inquiry Commission*, BPP, 1833, 450, D1, ev. E. Ashworth and J. Pooley, pp. 679–80.
85   For examples of these practices, see Toms and Shepherd, 'Accounting and social conflict'.
86   For example, excluding labour and raw material, Ashley and Greg used only four cost
categories; Ashley, *Ten Hours' Factory Bill*, 10 May 1844, p. 9; *Factories Inquiry Commission*,
BPP, 1833, 450, D2, ev. R. H. Greg, p. 784.
87   Boyson, *Ashworth Cotton*, p. 59, refers to a calculation by Henry Ashworth that such were
the overheads in a 52,000-spindle mill, it did not pay to stop the mill until losses exceeded £6,334
a year. See also *Report from the Select Committee of the House of Lords on the Burdens Affecting
Real Property*, BPP, 1846, 411 II, pp. 336–7.

Table 4. Ashworth accounts analysis

	Data per Accounts (69 hours)			Effect of 58 hours		
	(1) Variable £	(2) Fixed £	(3) Total £	(4) Variable £	(5) Fixed £	(6) Total £
Quarter total cost	2787	626	3413	2343.00	625.64	2968.64
Annual equivalent cost	11149	2503	13652	9371.99	2502.56	11874.55
Output lbs			80916			68016
Annual equivalent output lbs			323664			272065
Cost (d/lb, decimal)			10.123			10.475
Cost (d/lb, fraction)			10⅛			10⅛
Cost increase (%)						3.477%

Note: Costs related to the volume of spinning are assumed to be variable, i.e. cotton carriage inwards and brokerage, direct conversion costs in carding and spinning, production wages paid by the piece, interest on floating capital and machinery depreciation. Residual, non-volume-based costs are assumed fixed: supervisors' salaries, warehouse costs, other salaries and travelling, engineers' salaries, interest and depreciation on land and buildings. Assumption-based calculations are shown in italic.

Source: AP, Quarterly Stock Accounts, November 1845, Eng. MS, 1201.

the Ashworth archive seems to support the assertion of marginal impacts on production costs.

If the effects were marginal, however, the strident opposition of some mill owners to legislation remains to be explained. Some have argued, as noted earlier, that opposition came from the owners of more peripheral water-powered mills who would have suffered competitive disadvantage in the event of restriction on hours,[88] but there seems to be no correlation between the type of mill and the attitudes of lobbyists on either side. Indeed, Greg and Ashworth relied on water but were nonetheless leading concerns in terms of the scale of their investments. Hoole, meanwhile, was the proprietor of a steam-powered mill in Manchester, at the metropolitan centre of British industrialization.

88 Ashworth's opposition was based on water-power dependence according to Boyson, *Ashworth Cotton*, p. 160. J. Foster, 'The making of the first six Factory Acts', *Bulletin of the Society for the Study of Labour History* 18 (1969), 4–5, argues that Scots mill owners, largely water-powered, specifically charged the Lancashire mill owners with rigging the Act in their own interest.

Fielden, on the other hand, was in a remote location, although a significant investor in steam power.[89]

If the archival evidence is to be believed, then the conclusion is that the *ex ante* assumptions about the profit rate under existing conditions made by the Ashleyites were relatively accurate, as was their assumption about the cost of production. However, they underestimated the incidence of fixed costs, which, although only a small proportion of total costs according to the archival evidence, were even so proportionately higher than suggested by the pro-regulation lobby, suggesting that the mill owners were motivated in part by the risk associated with their fixed investments.

Foreign competition

In addition to the direct effect on profit that would arise from restrictions on working hours, the anti-regulation lobby also repeatedly cited the danger of international competition. With lower wages and even greater efficiency, continental manufacturers posed an existential threat to the Lancashire cotton industry. Coupled with that, the recalcitrance of British workers created a case for increased factory discipline and if they were given shorter hours, they would only use the time in antisocial activities. Such was the general narrative of mill owners in their lobbying against regulation. These arguments prefaced similar stories of blame, explored in later chapters, for the apparent decline in the performance of British cotton and manufacturing generally, in the 1890s and the 1970s.[90]

In the early 1830s, a consistent argument made by the cotton factory masters in their evidence to the Commission was that wages in their mills were higher than those paid by foreign competitors. Greg furnished additional evidence showing labour costs for mills in France, Switzerland, Prussia, Baden, Naples and America, while Ashworth and Pooley, and Birley and Hoole, used comparative figures from Ghent. According to their evidence, wages were 30–50% lower in the continental factories. On this basis, they were able to argue that if a ten-hour bill were introduced, the lost production would all be captured by overseas competition.

Hoole drew attention to the Swiss cotton industry, which, given its import of cotton through the Freeport at Geneva, can be better understood as part

---

89   Anon., 'The Fieldens of Todmorden', *Fortunes Made in Business: A Series of Original Sketches Biographical and Anecdotic from the Recent History of Industry and Commerce*, vol. 1 (London, 1884), p. 420.
90   For an overview of these arguments, see J. Tomlinson, 'Thrice denied: "Declinism" as a recurrent theme in British history in the long twentieth century', *Twentieth Century British History* 20 (2009), 227–51.

of a more extensive lobby for free trade.[91] Witness after witness in the anti-regulation lobby alerted the parliamentary commissioners to the danger of foreign competition. Robert Hyde Greg presented figures that showed spinning wage costs to be 50% higher in Manchester than Switzerland.[92] Even so, these arguments were not universally believed. Unsurprisingly, Ashley was one who remained to be convinced. He argued that the melancholy forebodings given in evidence at committees of 1816, 1818 and 1819 of loss to the foreigner were not fulfilled. The claimed loss of profits since 1819 was belied by a subsequent large increase in factories and arguments of MPs like Fielden and the members for Salford, Ashton and Blackburn.[93] The unanimity of the masters opposing regulation on these points[94] is also suggestive of collusion.

Having listened to their evidence, and finding it wanting, Cowell now became the chief critic of the anti-regulation lobby. He discounted all the evidence of Ashworth, Greg and Hoole, and did so on the grounds of their misleading use of accounting information, as noted earlier with respect to the treatment of fixed and circulating capital by Birley and Hoole. In his report, Cowell declared that if the evidence of Ashworth and Pooley were correct about lower wages at Ghent, 'the wonder is that the English spinners should not have been totally ruined long ago', also noting that Belgian spinners were lobbying their government for protection against English competition.[95]

Cowell supposed costs were lower in England because the mule length was wider by a greater proportion than the differential in daily wages. Acknowledging evidence that foreign workers were paid less by the hour than British workers, he pointed out that these representations failed to consider productivity differentials, noting that the typical British spinner minded three times the number of spindles compared to a German spinner. Cowell's comparison was frustrated by the failure of the Ashworth Brothers, Greg, and Hoole to supply data that

91   Hoole, *Letter to the Rt. Hon. Lord Althorp*, p. 14, argued the government should immediately repeal duty on raw cotton and other duties on consumption. The Swiss cotton industry was probably singled out for its free trade associations because it used Genoa for raw cotton imports, not because it posed a serious threat to Lancashire.

92   *Factories Inquiry Commission, Supplementary Report*, BPP, 1834, 167, Part I, Cowell's Preface, p. 399: Costs were 1.855d/lb in Manchester and 1.236d in Switzerland. Cowell estimated the differential as 38% (the ratio of 4:2.9); ibid., p. 394.

93   Ashley, *Ten Hours' Factory Bill*, pp. 10, 14.

94   Cf. comparative data, *Factories Inquiry Commission*, BPP, 1833, 450, D1, ev. E. Ashworth and J. Pooley, pp. 679–80; 450, D2, ev. R. H. Greg, pp. 789–94; 450, D1, ev. H. Birley and H. Hoole, pp. 726. On the 30–50% claim, see 450, D1, ev. E. Ashworth, p. 678; 450, D1, ev. Pooley, p. 679; 450, D2, ev. R. H. Greg, pp. 783; 450, D1, ev. H. Birley and H. Hoole, p. 726. On the consequences for foreign competition, see 450, D1, ev. E. Ashworth and J. Pooley, p. 678; 450, D1, ev. H. Birley and H. Hoole, p. 730; 450, D2, ev. R. H. Greg, pp. 782–3.

95   *Factories Inquiry Commission, Supplementary Report*, BPP, 1834, 167, Part I, Cowell's Preface, p. 401.

he knew they must have access to, namely the wage cost in terms of payment for work done.[96]

In an attempt to remedy this information gap, Table 5 shows comparative spinning costs in Mulhausen[97] and Lancashire. Mulhausen featured in evidence provided to the 1833 Commission by Edwin Rose, an operative machine-maker whom Cowell considered an independent and reliable witness, and whose testimony he drew upon to establish a comparison with Lancashire.[98] The table shows the number of spindles per mule and operatives per pair of equally sized mules for the typical mill producing coarse 40s yarn, based on evidence collated in Cowell's preface. The total wages per team of three (in both cases a spinner and two juvenile assistants) were obtained from the same source.[99] Making reasonable assumptions about output per week based on the data contained in Table 3, the example cited by Ashley of a typical mill producing 36s yarn and the average mill size according to the number of spindles,[100] it is possible to compute the wage cost in d/lb of output. As a check it can be noted that the number of personnel of 120, split approximately 40:80 between spinners and piecers, corresponds reasonably to the establishment breakdown from the 1833 survey tables.[101] Table 5 computes comparative figures for Mulhausen, holding mill size and output constant with the Lancashire average,[102] but allowing the number of mules to vary according to respective mule length.

Table 5 shows that the cost per pound was indeed lower in England than in Mulhausen, at 0.99d compared with 1.35d, or c.36%. The only reason is the difference in efficiency arising from mule length since, in Table 5, the cost per pound is computed, holding all other factors constant. According to Greg, the machinery he observed at Mulhausen 'was good and on the newest principle'.[103]

96   Cowell's frustration was justified. His report (ibid., pp. 383–4) noted that spinners in Manchester used detailed payment schedules arranged by mule length and yarn fineness count (Hanks per pound).

97   Mulhausen (Mulhouse), with 500,000 spindles in 1828, was the centre of the cotton trade in Alsace, described as the 'Lancashire of France'; Hammond and Hammond, *Rise of Modern Industry*, pp. 47–8.

98   *Factories Inquiry Commission, Supplementary Report*, BPP, 1834, 167, Part I, Cowell's Preface, p. 394.

99   See, in particular, ibid., p. 395.

100   Ashley, *Ten Hours' Factory Bill*, p. 9.

101   AP, Quarterly stock book, Eng. MS, 1201, e.g. for November 1845, per Table 4 above, is £808. *Factories Inquiry Commission, Supplementary Report*, BPP, 1834, 167, Part I, Cowell's Preface, example Mills A, B, C, pp. 387–8.

102   Similar sized factories operated at Mulhausen, for example Naegely's mill, with 37,000 spindles; A. Ure, *The Philosophy of Manufactures; or, an Exposition of the Scientific, Moral, and Commercial Economy of the Factory System of Great Britain* (London, 1835), p. 84.

103   *Factories Inquiry Commission, Supplementary Report*, BPP, 1834, 167, Part I, Cowell's Preface, p. 400. Cowell used this assumption based on evidence from Robert Hyde Greg from a mill at Salerno, recognizing that if technically equivalent, the Mulhausen mules were inferior due to their lower capacity.

Table 5. Comparative spinning costs, Mulhausen and Lancashire, c.1834

	Mulhausen	Lancashire
Spindles per mule	200	375
Spindles per team	400	750
Operatives per mule set:		
Spinners	1	1
Juvenile assistants	2	2
Total	3	3
Wages per day (d)	48	66
Wages per week (d)	288	396
Spindles per capita	133	250
Output per week (lb)	16000	16000[1]
Spindles	30000	30000[2]
Mule pairs	75	40
Output per set	213.33	400
Wage cost (d/lb)	1.35	0.99
Wage cost per week (£)	90	66
Total spinning dept personnel	225	120

Notes:
1   Ashley, *Ten Hours' Factory Bill*, p. 9, average output per week for an establishment spinning 36s yarn.
2   Based on data in *Factories Inquiry Commission*, BPP, 1834, 167, p. 396 for the number of spindles and the number of mills in Bolton, implying an average size of 34,000 spindles per mill.

Sources: Compiled from data in *Factories Inquiry Commission, Supplementary Report*, BPP, 1834, 167, Part I, Cowell's Preface, pp. 382–401.

The differential arises notwithstanding the higher wages paid per team of one spinner and two juvenile piecers, at 48s per day in Mulhausen compared with 66s per day in Lancashire, or 37.5%.

The evidence from Table 5 confirms the ephemeral nature of the threat of overseas competition and also shows that the proposed regulation of the working week would not damage profits in the context of technological improvement. Indeed mule widening provided the opportunity for increasing both wages and profits. The wage lists, which provided detailed breakdowns of payments by mule length, suggested this was precisely what occurred, showing clearly that the proportionate reduction in payment per pound was less than the increase in output that would determine the total wage.[104] Comparing Table 5 and Table 3, it is evident that the 36% increase in cost necessary to invoke the threat of competition from Mulhausen would imply a working week of 69 hours and a profit rate of 0% if the compromise figures are suitably adjusted.[105] Anything less than 69 hours, as suggested by proposed legislation would, therefore, appear to threaten the ruin that the mill owners claimed.

In other words, their claims were only supportable based on an oversimplified abstraction and by discounting the effects of the higher productivity of the Lancashire mules. Based on this evidence, it must be doubted whether Lancashire mill owners sincerely believed their rhetoric about the threat of foreign competition. Indeed, factors such as mule length, speeds, number of operatives, hours worked and wage rates were well known, as was the capital cost of machinery, computed on a per spindle basis.[106] Given such transparency, and the continued rapid entry of new firms and the fortunes made in the business pointed out by Ashley, it is unlikely that fear of foreign competition was genuine and was created more for lobbying purposes. It can thus be discounted as a legitimate reason for opposition to factory reform.

Even so, the industry dynamics illustrated above, and in particular in Table 3, offer a possible competition-based explanation of mill owner behaviour. Because technology was advancing rapidly, manifested in terms of faster and wider mules, incumbent firms faced continuing threats from new entrants. Once constructed, mills could not always be adapted to accommodate longer mules, and it was costly to do so if it involved the scrapping and replacement of expensive and still-productive smaller mules. New entrants, on the other hand, could erect purpose-built factories to accommodate wider mules. Incumbent firms, therefore, faced corresponding competitive disadvantage and pressure to work longer hours. Other things being equal, a firm using 324 spindle mules would need to work 22% longer than a firm using 396 spindle mules to achieve the same output and the same value-added, however, divided between capital and labour.[107]

---

104   Ibid., pp. 383–4; Manchester lists of prices, 5 March 1831 and 20 March 1829.

105   Assumptions are as in column [3] of Table 3 with an increase of 37.5% to total (wages) cost, resulting in a working week of 68.7 hours if profit including interest on fixed capital is equal to zero. To achieve a 5% return would imply a working week of 82 hours.

106   These were the variables most commonly referred to in the 1833–34 inquiries (*Factories Inquiry Commission*, BPP, 1833, 450, D2, ev. R. H. Greg, H. Birley and H. Hoole, and *Factories Inquiry Commission, Supplementary Report*, BPP, 1834, 167, Part I, Cowell's Preface) and in the 1840s debates (Ashley, *Ten Hours' Factory Bill*; Fielden, *Hansard's Parliamentary Debates*, 18 March 1844, vol. 73, c. 1236).

107   Such motivations are consistent with the literature that has considered the disadvantage apparently suffered by smaller, more remote water-powered mills as a consequence of the 1833 Act, specifically by looking at the differential pattern of prosecution. See Nardinelli, 'The successful prosecution of the Factory Acts', pp. 428–30.

The anti-regulation lobby anticipated the efficiency-based arguments. Writing in 1837, in direct response to Cowell, Robert Hyde Greg suggested that mule widening did not cheapen production because the number of stoppages multiplied in direct proportion to the length of the machine, and all costs, including piecers' wages, would vary accordingly. Spinners' wages would not, but according to Greg, these made up only a small proportion of the total.[108] If Greg believed his analysis, he would have little to fear from British competition in a regulated environment and much to fear from foreign firms paying low wages and working long hours. It should also be noted that Greg was now using arguments based on the variability of cost, rather than highlighting the risk of fixed capital investment. Even so, Greg was still without an explanation for the rapid expansion of production in Lancashire and only partially dealt with Cowell's more detailed evidence and argument. Cowell showed the effects of mule widening on personnel in three mills, which combined would reduce the number of adult spinners by seventy-five and increase the number of child piecers by fifty-seven.[109] The total labour cost-saving was £93 15s, which would increase the rate for the retained workers but also increase their productivity, thereby further cheapening the cost of the finished goods, and thus explaining the rapid advance of the industry into new markets.[110] In comparison to the mill owners' claims then, Cowell's evidence and analysis was more detailed and corresponded more closely to empirical reality. His report came once the 1833 Act had been passed for political motives but was influential in framing the debates that continued into the 1840s[111] when these arguments eventually prevailed.

Aftermath of the Ten Hours Act

In the discussion so far, the objections of the mill owners to labour regulation have been examined in detail. Their pessimistic interpretations of the industry's position and its prospects under a ten-hour regime were based on suspect figures and, in the end, failed to thwart the legislation. Had the anti-regulation

---

108   Greg, *The Factory Question*, pp. 101–2.
109   *Factories Inquiry Commission, Supplementary Report*, BPP, 1834, 167, Part I, Cowell's Preface, pp. 387–8. Mill A, 25 pairs combined into 13 pairs of 636 per mule, 12 of the 25 adult spinners dismissed and 9 additional piecers employed; Mill B, 20 pairs of mules combined into 10 pairs of 648 per mule, 10 adult spinners dismissed and 7 additional piecers employed; Mill C, 103 pairs of mules combined into 50 pairs of 648 per mule, 53 adult spinners dismissed and 41 additional piecers employed.
110   Ibid., pp. 388–9.
111   For example, *Mechanics Magazine* published a digest of Cowell's analysis in 'Proofs that Wages on the Continent are not lower than in England' (21 (1834), 52–7). It was also readily assimilated by economists, for example, H. C. Carey, *Principles of Political Economy* (Philadelphia, PA, 1840), p. 145.

Table 6. Average profits after the Ten Hours Act

Firm/Mill	Years	Return %
Ashworth/New Eagley	1849–1854	12.003
Ashworth/Egerton	1849–1854[1]	12.724
Greg/Quarry Bank	1852–1859	14.470
Greg/Albert	1849–1860	9.622
Fielden	1852–1860	10.405
Horrocks Miller	1849–1854[2]	16.795
Average	1849–1860	11.848
Average	1836–1847	6.575
Average	1797–1847	10.535

Notes:
1   No data 1851, 1852.
2   No data 1853.
Sources: CIFD.

lobby, then, merely 'cried wolf'? A final test of their case can be conducted by reviewing the evidence afforded by mill profits after the Ten Hours Act had been passed. Table 6 shows average profitability in the period following the Act for individual business units. The average for these mills is compared with the performance of the industry for a comparable period before the Act and over the longer run.

The evidence suggests that the Ten Hours Act did little to obstruct the profitable activities of mill owners. Indeed, average profitability in the period following the Act was higher than in a similar period before and also higher than the long-run average. The Gregs and the Ashworths, the most strident opponents of the Act, saw their mills prosper under the new regime. Ashworth's New Eagley Mill returned an average of just over 12% in the eleven years after the Act compared with 5.545% in the eleven years before.[112] A loophole allowed the use of shifts to keep mills running for twelve hours and beyond, but a further Factory Act outlawed this in 1853,[113] and there is no evidence that mills were more profitable in the early 1850s than the late 1850s. Average profit rates in the period 1849–53 were 12.9% compared to 11.1% in the period 1854–60, which included the depression year of 1857 when the average profit

112   As calculated from AP, Stock Book, Eng. MS, 1201.
113   An Act further to Regulate the Employment of Children in Factories, 1853, 30 & 31 Vict. c. 103.

rate was only 4.3%. Greg's Albert Mill recorded much higher profits in this later period.[114]

Of course, there were confounding factors associated with movements in the trade cycle and market conditions. Although these were by no means all positive during the 1850s, indeed there were some sharp downturns,[115] the data in Table 6 tell us nothing about what the profits would have been, had the Act not been passed. What is clear, however, comparing the averages by period in Table 6, is that the rate of profit increased in the 1850s over and above levels in earlier periods that had already attracted significant capital into the industry. Technical efficiencies were realized through a wave of new factory investments, extensions to existing mills, and improvements in machinery.[116] In part, this may have been a function of the requirement to deploy workers efficiently once the option to increase production by extending the working day had been ruled out.[117] In short, the legislation did not prevent the further expansion of the industry and did not prevent mill owners from earning adequate returns to justify additional investment.[118]

Horrocks Miller was a notable success in this period, with profits averaging 16.8%. A possible reason was that the firm paid lower wages than elsewhere in the industry. It did so because it offered guaranteed employment through booms and slumps, and did not participate in industry-wide short-time movements. Horrocks dominated the industry in Preston, which was the most concentrated in Lancashire. Under the firm's leadership, the first employer's association, the Masters' Association of Preston, was founded in the 1830s.[119]

The development of employers' associations and the consequent enforcement of industry-wide price and wage agreements became an essential and enduring feature of cotton industrial organization. These associations were based on town or district level agreements, reflecting differing conditions of specialization and access to networks of contacts. They were also a response to the business cycle, which as Figure 4 shows, continued to promote volatility in the rate of profit. As noted in the previous section, Cowell's 1833–34 calculations were based on tables of agreed piece rates for differing counts of yarn. Meanwhile, from the 1830s onwards, employers who refused to join short-time arrangements during

---

114 Calculated using Table 4 sources. The rate of profit at Albert Mill in the period 1854–60 was 12.3%.

115 J. R. T. Hughes, *Fluctuations in Trade, Industry and Finance: A Study of British Economic Development, 1850–1860* (Oxford, 1960), chapter 4.

116 Ibid., pp. 78–9.

117 Marx, *Capital I*, p. 635.

118 See also, G. T. Jones, *Increasing Return: A Study of the Relation between the Size and Efficiency of Industries with Special Reference to the History of Selected British & American Industries, 1850–1910* (Cambridge, 1933).

119 M. Huberman, *Escape from the Market: Negotiating Work in Lancashire* (Cambridge, 1996), p. 125.

slumps were exposed in the press and blacklisted.[120] Depressed conditions in 1857 led to an organized short-time movement instigated by the mill owners. A lack of stocks at Liverpool threatened a shortage and the prospect of higher prices, underlining the potential risk of dependence on Liverpool and the slave-owning south of the USA. Organized short time, emanating from a coalition of Manchester mill owners, began in 1857 and led to the establishment of the Cotton Supply Association.[121] These developments, and similar organized behaviour by employers such as the regulation of wages through lists, represented self-imposed deviations from the purer versions of laissez-faire whose leaders had fought so hard to maintain during the Factory debates.

All these business risks were compounded by the interruption of Lancashire's primary source of cotton supply during the American Civil War. After 1865, investment requirements for new mills became more significant as the efficient scale increased. 'Very large profits', wrote a correspondent for *The Economist* magazine in 1871, 'would be required to tempt capital into so speculative a trade.'[122] The comment was made in the context of the most recent labour dispute to affect the trade, which factory legislation had done nothing to quell.

For the labour movement, reaction to industrialization went beyond factory legislation, and, from the 1830s, the Ten Hours movement was only part of a broad-based social movement, which by 1850 was based increasingly on notions of working-class enfranchisement rather than exclusion and class conflict.[123] Given the protection offered to women and children in the Ten Hours Act, limited liability emerged as a reform that would address the further political grievances of working-class men.

As the next chapter will explore in more detail, limited liability would democratize the market and benefit the schemes promoted by Christian Socialists and co-operative pioneers such as E. V. Neale.[124] Neale advocated the conversion of capitalist enterprises, with wage earners controlling their business through share-ownership with associated rights to share in the profits and to take part in management.[125] In combination, co-operation and limited liability were to transform significant sections of the cotton textile industry in the decades after the Factory Acts.

---

120   Ibid., p. 124.
121   Hughes, *Fluctuations in Trade, Industry and Finance*, pp. 91–2.
122   'Co-operative Manufacture', *The Economist*, 6 May 1871, 533.
123   J. M. Ludlow and L. Jones, *Progress of the Working Class, 1832–67* (London, 1867). D. Loftus, 'Capital and community: Limited liability and attempts to democratize the market in Mid-19th Century England', *Victorian Studies* 45 (2002), 93–120.
124   Loftus, 'Capital and community', p. 98.
125   Edward Vansittart Neale (1810–92); A. Bonner, *British Co-operation* (Manchester, 1971), p. 114; E. V. Neale, 'The Division of Profits', *The Co-operator*, October 1861, pp. 86–7.

Conclusions

Although Senior's theory was flawed, insofar as some costs were variable, the presence of any fixed costs arising from their investments inevitably worried the cotton entrepreneurs. Fixed capital investment on the scale required by the capital-intensive, second phase of industrialization was a new phenomenon and, as the evidence surrounding Table 3 suggests, the associated risk provided their principal motivation in resisting legislation. In summary, the rate of profit was higher than the anti-regulation lobby cared to admit, even with carefully arranged and consistently pessimistic evidence. Nevertheless, regulation and the impact of fixed-cost effects meant that the consequential cut in profit would be higher than either the pro-regulation or anti-regulation lobby realized, even though the consequential rate of profit would not lead to the collapse of the industry in the face of foreign competition.

So, it followed that when legislators finally enacted the ten-hour day in the 1847 Factory Act, there is no evidence that the rate of profit reduced as a consequence. Indeed the industry continued to expand, principally because capital improvements generated further productivity gains like those pointed out by Cowell, such that the industry continued to be attractive for new investment. All of which is consistent with one of the main empirical findings that the working week could be restricted while still maintaining an adequate rate of return on capital. In short, the ten-hour working day was compatible with an average rate of profit above 10%.

The absence of an established and accepted theory of profit added complexity to the debates surrounding factory legislation, notably when the protagonists used accounting evidence to support their arguments. Without accepted standards of accounting for items such as depreciation and only inchoate theories of the rewards for enterprise, there was considerable room for interpretation. Indeed, poor understanding of accounting limited the quality of analysis conducted by contemporaries. Absence of sanction for proprietors exaggerating figures was based on ignorance of accounting, and entrepreneurs could say what they liked about their accounts and expect to be believed. Cowell was an exception and conducted a skilled analysis, reinterpreting their figures. He was ignored by legislators in the 1830s, but not by the wider public, and his conclusions began to underpin a groundswell of support for legislation in the 1840s. With this exception, inaccurate accounting obstructed regulators, while their general tolerance of cavalier abstractions of accounting data is suggestive of a highly inefficient capital market. The industry's ability to sustain a legislated shorter working week after 1847 is testimony meanwhile to the relatively high, if unstable, rate of profit.

4

Industrial Democracy and Co-operative Finance

Any interference in the regulation of free labour, never fails to excite a spirit of restlessness and insubordination, inimical to the habits of sobriety and industry among the operatives, by raising expectations that cannot be fulfilled.[1]

The most pleasing part of the matter is, that the very people who were considered to be the least prudent and the least frugal of the working classes, are continually making great savings, and employing them in the most judicious and productive manner.[2]

In 1791, a manager at Bank Top mill in Manchester purchased the first bales of imported American cotton. The manager making the purchase was Robert Owen.[3] Six decades later, vast imports of American cotton and the co-operative principles advocated by Owen contributed to a further expansion of the cotton industry. Immediately after the Ten Hours Act, and indeed in subsequent decades, the regulation of working hours, it seemed, did little to temper enthusiasm for new and, with further advances in technology, more productive cotton mills. Self-acting mules and power looms were improved, and some preparatory processes were automated.[4] In turn, productivity advanced, and importantly, was now shared in the form of increased real wages.

Cotton workers now had the opportunity to turn away from the oppressive factory system and invest in their mill projects. McKay's vision, quoted above, made assumptions about working-class behaviour that were the exact opposite of those made by the opponents of factory regulation in the lead-up to the Ten Hours Act. Witness after witness called in opposition to factory reform at the parliamentary inquiries had warned of the fecklessness, drunkenness, and other forms of antisocial behaviour that would result from any relaxation

---

1 *Select Committee on the State of the Children Employed in the Manufactories of the United Kingdom*, BPP, 1816, 397, ev. Henry Houldsworth, p. 479.
2 Charles McKay, 'Working men and factories', *The London Review*, issue 3, 21 July 1860, 51–2, at p. 52.
3 'The beginnings of the cotton trade', *Manchester Guardian*, 29 November 1884, p. 9.
4 G. Timmins, 'The cotton industry in the 1850s and 1860s: Decades of contrast', *The Golden Age: Essays in British Social and Economic History, 1850–1870*, ed. I. Inkster *et al.* (Abingdon, 2017), pp. 61–74, at p. 68.

of factory discipline. Genuine moral indignation no doubt motivated some of these claims, but as the last chapter showed, the anti-regulation entrepreneurs also had economic justifications for long hours and the threat of lost profits. Specifically, they were fearful of the risk associated with large-scale and personal, fixed-capital investment in a cyclical industry. Might then collective social capital, mobilized from the savings of the cotton operatives, respond differently to the challenges of market instability, about to be made worse by the onset of the American Civil War? Alternatively, might collective capital succumb to the same pressures as private capital?

These questions were put to the test in newly industrializing parts of the county. After 1850, factory production migrated away from Manchester, with its high property costs.[5] With Manchester concentrating increasingly on commerce and distribution, industrial activity spread into the Irwell and Rossendale valleys, and fuelled the expansion of Oldham, Rochdale and surrounding towns. Two significant and apparently contradictory developments gave rise to the emergence of these districts as the centres of joint-stock industrial organization. First, and most important, was the tradition of co-operation in the district. Co-operators developed the necessary institutions, including friendly societies, retail associations and production societies. Second, was the introduction of permissive Companies Act legislation, which allowed the deployment of capital on the joint-stock principle, while also accommodating co-operative values. These institutional changes allowed earlier principles advocated by paternalist employers and utopian socialists, like Robert Owen, to be carried on independently and, as this chapter will explain, with significant effect in the Lancashire cotton industry.

The chapter examines the origins of co-operation and joint-stock organization in Lancashire. It considers the profitability of firms that adopted co-operative principles to varying degrees and thereby explained how the savings of local people were drawn into industrial finance. It describes the system of democratic financial organization as a further model of growth and operation of a substantial section of the cotton industry. It assesses the importance of these experiments for further growth and ultimate decline of the cotton industry in Lancashire.

Early co-operatives and limited liability

There was a long tradition of co-operation in cotton production, with the most significant experiments instigated by benevolent employers. After Robert

---

5 P. Maw, T. Wyke and A. Kidd, 'Canals, rivers, and the industrial city: Manchester's industrial waterfront, 1790–1850', *EcHR* 65 (2012), 1495–1523.

Owen terminated his involvement at Chorlton in 1799 and handed over to Birley and Hornby, he had then moved to New Lanark Mills. As managing partner, Owen instigated a programme of radical reforms. There had been little oversight of the workforce for some years, and Owen set about reforming them, constructing a model society founded on socialist principles and appealing to the better part of human nature. Utilitarian philosopher, Jeremy Bentham, and the Quaker, William Allen, were subsequently admitted to partnership. Out of the profits, a maximum of 5% was paid as a return on capital with the remainder applied to the religious, educational and moral improvement of the wider community.[6]

Societies sprang up in many parts of Lancashire, most strongly influenced by the ideas of Robert Owen. A co-operative trading company was established in Oldham as early as 1795 with the purpose of bulk-purchasing food to reduce its cost. Some small employers who were also labour leaders suddenly adopted 'Owenite socialism' in the 1830s, reflecting the simultaneous pressures from the customers of their wholesale businesses and increasing working-class agitation.[7] The earliest co-operative societies stressed the power of knowledge and the provision of practical and useful education to their members.[8] 'Union and saving' meanwhile, would be the basis of capital accumulation.

In contrast to the laissez-faire opponents of the Ten Hours Act, the co-operative movement was founded on the classical labour theory of value.[9] '[T]he workman is the source of all wealth ... Who has raised all the food? ... Who spins all the yarn and makes all the cloth?', declared the *Lancashire Co-operator* in 1831.[10] All co-operators could readily agree on that point, but they found the question of the distribution of surplus less easy to resolve. Organizers of cotton mill co-operatives, first in Rochdale and then in Oldham, confronted by practical necessity experimented with various solutions. Their success and failure is the story of a new model of business organization that carried the industry to its pinnacle in 1914.

Following the Ten Hours Act, working-class savings increased, prompting associated demands for investment opportunities. Real wages, which had been stagnant up to 1840, now began to rise in line with productivity growth.[11] A wave of strikes in the early 1850s resulted not just in significant advances in wages, but also more comprehensive regulation of wages through agreed

---

6 H. R. Fox Bourne, *English Merchants* (London, 1886), pp. 404–5.

7 B. Jones, *Co-operative Production* (Oxford, 1894); J. Foster, *Class Struggle and the Industrial Revolution: Early Industrial Capitalism in Three English Towns* (London, 1974), pp. 136–7.

8 A. E. Musson, *Trade Union and Social History* (London, 1974), pp. 185–7.

9 'Rise and progress of the Rochdale limiteds', *Rochdale Observer*, 10 May 1890.

10 Musson, *Trade Union and Social History*, pp. 174–6.

11 R. C. Allen, 'Engels' pause: Technical change, capital accumulation, and inequality in the British industrial revolution', *Explorations in Economic History* 46 (2009), 418–35, figure 1.

regional lists.[12] By 1860, the flood of post-famine Irish immigration into Liverpool and Lancashire had begun to dry up, leading to labour shortages in the mills.[13] For self-acting mule spinners, wages were typically 21d per hour in 1859 compared with 17d per hour in 1839.[14]

Radical movements found it impossible to draw a line between personal and collective improvement, between imitation of the middle class and conspiring towards its defeat. The self-help-based system of co-operative production advocated by Samuel Smiles, and in Oldham by William Marcroft, became an interim solution to this dilemma.[15] Accessible social benefits gave a further impetus to the working-class co-operative movement. Where factories were once burned and machinery destroyed, by the 1860s Rochdale was a 'model town'. Co-operation now facilitated the education that the factory system denied and promoted industrial peace. Economic and social improvements led to the emergence of the 'labour aristocracy' of self-acting mule minders, exemplified by that John Bright-inspired co-operator, 'Rochdale Man'.[16]

To channel the new working-class savings that resulted, institutional change was needed. Campaigners sought alternatives to the Factory System, which following the debates of the 1830s and 1840s, they naturally regarded as oppressive, exclusive and dominated by the interests of private capital.[17] In 1850, a House of Commons Committee was established, chaired by Robert Slaney MP, to consider and suggest means of obviating obstacles and giving facilities to safe investments for the savings of the middle and working classes.[18] In Lancashire, as in London, there was a demand for investment opportunities from the middle classes and artisans that limited liability companies were thought likely to provide.[19] Supporters of the proposals, including Christian

---

12   A. Shepherd and S. Toms, 'Entrepreneurship, strategy, and business philanthropy: Cotton textiles in the British industrial revolution', *BHR* 93 (2019), 503–27.

13   McKay, 'Working men and factories', p. 52.

14   'Report by A. Redgrave, Esq.', *Reports of the Inspectors of Factories*, BPP, Half year ending 30 April 1860, p. 31. The increase in wage rate outweighed the reduction in working hours from 69 to 60 hours.

15   E. Hobsbawm, *The Age of Capital, 1848–1875* (London, 1975), p. 264.

16   J. M. Ludlow and L. Jones, *Progress of the Working Class, 1832–67* (London, 1867); P. Joyce, *Work, Society and Politics: The Culture of the Factory in later Victorian England* (Aldershot, 1991), pp. 57–8. P. Joyce, *Visions of the People: Industrial England and the Question of Class, c.1848–1914* (Cambridge, 1994), p. 58.

17   Jones, *Co-operative Production*, pp. 46–7.

18   *Royal Commission on Assimilation of Mercantile Laws in the United Kingdom and Amendments in Law of Partnership, as regards Question of Limited or Unlimited Responsibility*, BPP, 1854, 653, First Report, appendix, ev. James Andrew Anderson, p. 507.

19   J. B. Jefferys, 'Trends in Business Organization in Great Britain since 1856, with Special Reference to the Financial Structure of Companies, the Mechanism of Investment and the Relations between the Shareholder and the Company' (Ph.D. dissertation, University of London, 1938), p. 93.

socialists, argued that allowing artisans in cotton spinning to club their funds together and improve their lot was a better alternative to the 'reign of terror' of 'millocratic tyranny'. In doing so, they built on the heightened working-class consciousness promoted by the Chartist movement.[20] They were also sensitive to the absence of outlets for the profitable investments of accumulated capital.[21]

Limited liability could become a powerful instrument, it was argued, for the building of local communities tied together by a common project and shared interest through shared investment. Societies in Bacup, Padiham and Rochdale, engaged in production to satisfy the wants of their members, sought legal protection of their investments and the facility of transferable shares.[22] Limited liability would enable the establishment of 'associations of working men working for common profits', which would allow a man to control the investment of his labour.[23] In the higher reaches of the Rossendale Valley, associations of artisans hoped that the joint-stock form of organization would provide the means of escape from the thraldom of capital.[24] When established financial institutions refused them credit, they became all the more enthusiastic advocates of the corporate model. With the Joint Stock Companies Act 1856, and the advent of the limited liability principle, many in Lancashire regarded it as an adjunct of co-operation and as a means of reinforcing such working-class investment.[25]

Even so, joint-stock finance was slow to spread at first in Lancashire and there was no boom in new companies until 1860. After that, the number of incorporations was not significant year-on-year by comparison with other industries. One reason was that Manchester had established itself as a citadel of private enterprise, laissez-faire and of opposition to the joint-stock organization.[26] Indeed much of the opposition to the proposals for limited liability put

20   *Royal Commission on Assimilation of Mercantile Laws*, BPP, 1854, 653, First Report, appendix, ev. Mr Commissioner Fane, p. 664. P. Hampson, 'Working-class capitalists: The development and financing of worker owned companies in the Irwell Valley, 1849–1875' (Ph.D. dissertation, University of Central Lancashire, 2015), p. 3. P. Hampson, 'Industrial Finance from the Working Classes in later Nineteenth-Century Lancashire', *The Local Historian* 48/2 (April 2018), 119–33.

21   Jefferys, 'Trends in Business Organisation', p. 41.

22   D. Loftus, 'Capital and Community: Limited liability and attempts to democratize the market in Mid-19th Century England', *Victorian Studies* 45 (2002), 93–120, at p. 108; *Report from the Select Committee on Investments for the Savings of the Middle and Working Classes*, BPP, 1850, 508, ev. L. Jones, qq.970, 980, pp. 91–3.

23   Ibid., ev. J. Millbank, qq.510–11, p. 48.

24   R. E. Tyson, 'William Marcroft', *Dictionary of Business Biography*, ed. D. Jeremy (London, 1984–86), vol. 4, p. 121.

25   D. Farnie, *The English Cotton Industry and the World Market, 1815–1896* (Oxford, 1979), pp. 216–17, 249. The Joint Stock Companies Act, 1856 (19 & 20 Vict. c. 47) allowed joint-stock companies to operate on the principle of limited liability.

26   Farnie, *English Cotton*, pp. 62, 212, 215–16.

forward by the Mercantile Laws Commission came from Northern metropolitan industrialists, including the Liverpool and Manchester Chambers of Commerce, and also from the proud class of mill owners reluctant to surrender personal credit for their economic achievements and the social status that came with it.[27]

It was not the intention of lawmakers or of the business interests in Manchester to promote social experiments in co-operation. The company legislation of the 1850s and 1860s followed the permissive and deregulatory fashions so characteristic of the mid-Victorian economy. Indeed, with the abolition of compulsory accounting and audit provision in the Joint Stock Companies Act 1856, the period up to 1900 was marked by a complete absence of statutory regulation under general company law.

Nonetheless, the absence of defined rules on shareholder rights provided just such an opportunity in nearby Rossendale, Rochdale and Oldham. Specifically, under the terms of the Companies Act 1862, companies had the option to adopt the democratic one-shareholder-one-vote decision rule.[28] Indeed, the use of graduated voting was quite widespread as firms incorporated in the USA and Britain in the period 1862–1900.[29] Even so, the Oldham experiment with shareholder democracy was unique. There are no other examples of the 'one-shareholder-one-vote' rule, co-operative principles of member participation and stock market quotation coinciding for such a large number of manufacturing companies. For Oldham companies, this was an opportunity to avoid some of the restrictions of the Industrial and Provident Societies Act, passed in the same year. To qualify as a 'society', the Act required that finished goods be supplied to members. Such arrangements were thus inappropriate for mills spinning yarn, which was only an intermediate product. Such societies were also not particularly useful for businesses with commitments to permanent fixed-capital investments, since their rules allowed unlimited capital withdrawals.[30]

Company promoters in Oldham and the surrounding district, including Rochdale, therefore took advantage of the Companies Act rules and became a centre of co-operation and joint-stock finance simultaneously. A key advantage was the use of low-denomination shares, issued at £1 or even 5s, such that 'the poor would flock in and take ones and twos', raising enough money for a 'judicious undertaking' and providing the basis for their participation in its management.[31] The subsequent popularity of share-ownership was therefore

27   Jefferys, 'Trends in Business Organisation', p. 41.
28   Companies Act 1862, 25 & 26 Vict. c. 89. Democratic voting systems were compatible with Table A in the 1862 Companies Act.
29   C. A. Dunlavy, 'Corporate governance in late 19th century Europe and the US: the case of shareholder voting rights', *Comparative Corporate Governance: The State of the Art and Emerging Research*, ed. P. D. K. Hopt *et al.* (Oxford, 1998), pp. 5–40, at pp. 29–32.
30   Industrial and Provident Societies Act, 25 & 26 Vict. c. 87.
31   'Capital', *The Co-operator*, 15 October 1861, p. 86.

rooted in demand for working-class saving and investment opportunities, and the co-operative principle upon which many Lancashire business organizations had been founded since the 1840s. It was in Oldham in particular that the development of factories on co-operative principles, based on the mobilization of working-class savings, had a significant impact on industrial capitalism in Lancashire. The subsequent development of 'working-class limiteds' provided the outlet that was needed.[32]

These ideas, in the context of permissive company legislation, led to a wave of new joint-stock company promotions in certain localities. An early and successful co-operative, registered under the provisions of the Joint Stock Companies Act 1844 as a limited liability company, was the Bacup Joint Stock Company, founded in 1849. Its original board consisted of working-class directors, including cotton mill operatives. In 1854 it was reconstituted as the Bacup and Wardle Commercial Company.[33] In nearby Rochdale, after establishing their famous retail co-operative in Toad Lane in 1844, the Rochdale Pioneers also quickly moved to expand into cotton manufacture. The Rochdale Co-operative Manufacturing Society, which became known as the Mitchell Hey Mill, was established as an industrial co-operative in 1854. All the promoters were also members of the Society, including Thomas Collier, William Cooper, and Abraham Greenwood. Exceptionally, the mill's promoters registered it as a Friendly Society, not a limited liability company.[34]

The establishment of these producer co-operatives had a wide impact. They enthused Karl Marx in a way that retail and other societies did not. Reflecting the influence of Marx, the Inaugural Address of the International Working Men's Association, published in 1864, article 5(c), co-operative labour stated: 'We recommend to the working men to embark in co-operative production rather than in co-operative stores. The latter touch but the surface of the present economical system, the former attacks its groundwork.'[35] At Mitchell Hey, all employees were shareholders and received a share of the surplus as a bonus to labour.[36] The rule was that two-thirds of profits were distributed as

32   T. Ellison, *The Cotton Trade of Great Britain: Including a History of the Liverpool Cotton Market and of the Liverpool Cotton Brokers' Association* (London, 1886), p. 134; B. Potter, *The Co-operative Movement in Great Britain* (London, 1893; reprinted Aldershot, 1987), pp. 126–33.
33   Jones, *Co-operative Production*, pp. 252–3; Hampson, 'Working-class capitalists'; Joint Stock Companies Act 1844, 7 & 8 Vict. c. 110.
34   'Rise and progress of the Rochdale limiteds: Introduction and a sketch of Mitchell Hey', *Rochdale Observer*, 10 May 1890.
35   K. Marx, *Inaugural Address and Provisional Rules of the International Working Men's Association* (London, 1864).
36   'Rise and progress of the Rochdale limiteds', *Rochdale Observer*, 10 May 1890; J. M. Ludlow, 'On some new forms of industrial co-operation', *Good Words* 8 (April 1867), 240–8. *The Observer*, 12 July 1863, p. 3.

a bonus to labour. At a time of labour shortage, commentators regarded the bonus to labour as a useful mechanism for securing extra hands.[37] 'Thus', wrote Charles McKay, commenting on these and other businesses, 'throughout the great manufacturing districts of the North, the improvement of the workpeople by joint-stock enterprise, which was much desired by philanthropists, but considered to be hopeless, is taking place on a large and extended scale.'[38]

The new investors at Mitchell Hey and elsewhere were attracted in part by a more general boom. Over forty spinning and manufacturing companies, with mainly working-class shareholders, were launched towards the end of the 1850s and made 'fabulous' profits in 1860–61. Strong domestic demand, expansion of the China and Indian markets, albeit short-lived in the case of India, contributed to buoyant trading conditions.[39] Nine companies, most of them Rossendale Valley co-operatives, averaged returns of 28.25% during this boom.[40] The Bacup and Wardle Commercial Company recorded half-year profits of £10,722, an annual equivalent return on capital of 42.88%. In the previous four half-years, dividends were at the rate of 31, 44, 50 and 62 annual equivalent percentages, respectively. Paid-up shares of £12 10s traded were trading at £26 in 1861.[41] 'The prosperity and success of the New Bacup and Wardle Commercial Company', wrote Sir John Kincaid in a Factory Inspectors report, 'seem to have given rise to the new companies that are now formed in my immediate vicinity and preparing large factories to carry on their business.'[42] In a similar vein, high profits at Mitchell Hey had contributed to the influx of new shareholders.[43]

Ironically, as a result of success, the co-operative principle lost some of its original purity as the industry expanded further. In 1860, the Mitchell Hey society required fresh capital for a new mill. Investment was now attracted from another class of shareholders who objected to the payment of dividends to labour. These new shareholders, hungry for dividends, overturned the bonus.[44] As workers at other mills, they contended that they had no similar right to these bonuses, and in 1862, after two previous unsuccessful votes, succeeded in abolishing the labour bonus principle.[45]

---

37 'Bonus to labour', *The Co-operator*, 15 October 1866, p. 89.
38 McKay, 'Working men and factories', p. 52.
39 J. Watts, *Facts of the Cotton Famine* (Manchester, 1866), p. 341. Farnie, *English Cotton*, pp. 131, 138.
40 Calculated using buy and hold returns from data in Watts, *Facts of the Cotton Famine*, pp. 342–3.
41 Return calculated from 'Local news', *The Midland Workman and General Advertiser*, 26 October 1861, p. 8. See also Jones, *Co-operative Production*, p. 253.
42 *Reports of the Inspectors of Factories*, BPP, Half-year ending 30 April 1858, Sir John Kincaid, quoting Mr Patrick, p. 12.
43 Jones, *Co-operative Production*, p. 262.
44 Ibid.
45 'Rise and progress of the Rochdale limiteds', *Rochdale Observer*, 10 May 1890.

Commentators had meanwhile noticed the durability of the co-operative mills during difficult times, particularly after the outbreak of the American Civil War in 1861 and the onset of the 'cotton famine'. In response, mills throughout Lancashire instituted short-time working. There were specific fears for the new co-operative mills, which were perceived to be undercapitalized because of their tendency to pay out dividends and labour bonuses meant they were without significant reserve funds.[46]

For one co-operative at least, Mitchell Hey, these issues were unproblematic. The mill did not experience any serious problems, and not only ran full time but also successfully raised the further capital to build a second mill.[47] The abolition of the labour bonus did nothing to undermine what was a signally well-managed company. New investors, having achieved this change in corporate governance, were thus in a position to compromise on other co-operative principles. Specifically, short time could be avoided as a result of no longer paying the bonus. So although co-operators lamented the loss of the principle of the labour bonus, they drew consolation from the ability of the mill to offer full-time employment during the cotton scarcity and to donate to the cotton relief fund.[48] In other words, the superior profits of a democratically run business provided the opportunity to operate on full time when other mills shortened their hours or even closed altogether.

It was against the backdrop of these events that co-operation became entrenched in the nearby Oldham district. After 1862, and the abolition of the labour bonus, the experience of Mitchell Hey revealed how co-operation could be adapted to the limited liability system. No one was allowed to hold more than forty shares. As a result, the society's 13,371 shares were owned by over a thousand investors, the majority of whom were working class.[49] Although Mitchell Hey was still registered as a Friendly Society, co-operators in Oldham now realized how this general model could be applied to limited liability companies.

The Oldham Industrial Co-operative Society was founded in 1858 with the object of building a co-operative mill, which was a landmark development in the history of Oldham. William Marcroft and 'a few friends from Rochdale, Oldham, and Middleton' agreed the details at the Jumbo tea party meeting on 12 August 1860. The new mill, they decided, would be organized on democratic principles, while registered under the provisions of joint-stock company legislation.[50] The plans for the mill were ambitious and would contain 60,000 mule

46 *The Co-operator*, June 1863, 40, August 1863, p. 42.
47 Ibid. 'Rise and progress of the Rochdale limiteds', *Rochdale Observer*, 10 May 1890.
48 Ibid.
49 Ibid.
50 P. Redfern, *The Story of the C.W.S., The Jubilee History of the Co-operative Wholesale Society, Limited, 1863–1913* (Manchester, 1913), pp. 19–20. The meeting was held at Lowbands Farm, Jumbo, near Oldham.

spindles. It would be ninety-five yards long, with 350 windows and be christened Sun Mill after the 'glorious orb of the day'.[51] 'If this mill is successful, it will be the commencement of making Oldham the first cotton mill town in the kingdom', wrote a contemporary correspondent.[52]

The prophecy was entirely correct, and the new mill was a milestone for the Oldham district and local co-operators. However, in terms of its scale, Sun Mill was no more substantial than the typical mills floated in the Irwell valley a few years earlier, which were capitalized in the region of £50,000–£100,000.[53] Nor was it pioneering in the sense of its democratic structure and worker participation in profit sharing, as the Bacup and Wardle, Mitchell Hey and many other firms floated ahead of the 1860–61 boom also had these features. Instead, the new mill was part of a chain of developments in which financial success at one location prompted new and adjacent initiatives. Examples of the process in Bacup and Rochdale have already been mentioned. In Oldham, the consequences had more considerable long-run significance in terms of the scale of further expansion.

A crucial ingredient in the early stages was the apparent financial success of democratically controlled companies. Contemporary commentators initiated this narrative around the time of the boom. John Watts, a prominent champion of co-operation, compared the capital of cotton companies in which shares were mainly owned by working men, but which adopted the standard plutocratic system of voting (Schedule A), with those that had adopted a one-shareholder-one-vote principle under Schedule B of the Companies Act. He found that the capital of the latter group was much more substantial. 'To my mind', he concluded, 'here is proof enough that the power of management is not confined to any class of men.'[54] Sir John Kincaid, Leonard Horner's successor as a factory inspector for Lancashire, speaking at the Social Science Congress of 1860, quoted one of his sub-inspectors, Mr Patrick, who concluded that the Bacup and Wardle's mill at Far Holm was the best-conducted establishment of his whole division.[55] During the boom of 1860–61, the high profits, dividends

---

51   *The Co-operator*, May 1862, p. 26.

52   *Daily Despatch*, 27 March 1923.

53   In 1861, typical new large mills and their respective capitals included Mitchell Hey, with £68,000, and also Bacup and Wardle with £50,000, Newchurch Spinning and Manufacturing Company, £100,000; Jones, *Co-operative Production*, p. 262; 'Local news', *The Midland Workman and General Advertiser*, 26 October 1861, p. 8.

54   'Co-operation considered as an economic element in society', paper read by Dr John Watts before the Manchester Statistical Society, reprinted, *Co-operative News*, 30 November 1872, pp. 602–3.

55   'Co-operative societies', *Lloyd's Illustrated Newspaper*, 24 February 1861, p. 5. *Reports of the Inspectors of Factories*, BPP, Half-year ending 30 April 1858, Sir John Kincaid, p. 11. The example was cited elsewhere, including by Karl Marx, writing on 'The state of British manufacturing industry', *New York Daily Tribune*, 6 August 1860.

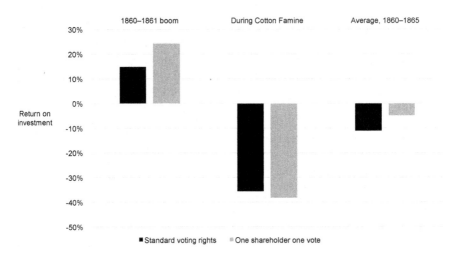

Figure 9. Democratic ownership and investment returns

Notes: Total sample size = 25 firms. 'Standard voting rights', N= 14; 'one-shareholder-one-vote', N = 11. Returns are calculated from stock price data and exclude dividends due to a lack of data. The figures are therefore useful for comparison of the two groups, assuming similar dividend payouts, but are not necessarily consistent with returns calculated from underlying accounting data.

Sources: Calculated from tables and evidence in J. Watts, 'Co-operation considered as an economic element in society', paper read by Dr. John Watts before the Manchester Statistical Society, reprinted, *Co-operative News*, 30 November 1872, pp. 602–3, and Watts, *Facts of the Cotton Famine*, p. 343.

and share prices of Bacup and Wardle, and others, attracted a great deal of attention, and no doubt further investors.

To examine the effectiveness of democratic ownership in more detail, the financial performance of differently constituted firms are compared. Figure 9 uses Watts's data to put his claims to the test. Financial returns are compared for three periods, the 1860–61 boom, the cotton famine and the average six-year return for the years 1860–65 inclusive. Consistent with Watts' analysis, Figure 9 compares two groups, those which attracted large numbers of working-class investors, but had adopted wealth-based voting rights under the Companies Act, and those which adopted a democratic one-shareholder-one-vote rule. During the 1860–61 boom, the second group enjoyed higher average positive returns, 24.27% compared with 14.79%. During the cotton famine, the profits of all firms fell dramatically, but slightly more so for the one-shareholder-one-vote group, 38.17% compared to 35.57%. For the period as a whole, consolidating the effects of these differentials, the second group was the stronger performer, with returns of −4.94% compared to −11.08%. During the cotton famine, although the negative returns for both groups were quite similar, it is noteworthy that the failure rate was much higher among the standard voting group. Of a total of fourteen firms in the sample, eight had ceased to trade by the end of the famine period.

In contrast, all eleven of the democratic firms survived. The evidence suggests that during a difficult time, these employee-controlled businesses were more effective at rationing work and payments, whether in wages or dividends. Indeed, the assertions of Watts and others that these firms were better managed would seem to have some justification in terms of financial outcomes.

Capital at first was difficult to find for the Oldham Building and Manufacturing Company Limited, subsequently renamed Sun Mill. So the leaders of the co-operative movement discouraged other projects for fear of starving the project of the required investment. When machinery ordered from Platt Brothers was delivered in 1862, the company was very short of capital and opened a public loan account, taking deposits in return for fixed interest at 5%.[56] Once local investment had been mobilized, it was then resolved that shareholders should be the first to be employed in the mill.[57]

The founders of the company inherited progressive traditions from earlier movements. Along with Marcroft, William Kenworthy was one of the inaugural directors.[58] Earlier in his career, in the 1840s, this innovating entrepreneur had campaigned for the Ten Hours Bill. Since then, in partnership with William Henry Hornby, Kenworthy had helped transform industrial relations throughout Lancashire. In contrast to Preston employers in the bitter strike of 1853–54, they offered generous wage settlements as a means of pressuring other employers to adopt uniform wage lists.[59] Marcroft was also committed to the well-being of the working class, based on ideals of producer co-operation and employee control.[60] Thus management of the company was through elected committees, for example along the lines of responsibility for different parts of the balance sheet, namely the 'Fixed Stock' and 'Saleable Stock' committees.[61] Employee shareholders were obliged to follow the instructions of the manager, for as Dr John Watts suggested, 'there must be one hand, one eye and one mind', and if employees had grievances with a poor manager they were to raise the issue with the directors.[62] From the inception of the mill, the directors were seen as the accountable representatives of the employee-shareholders. Unlike Mitchell

56 Jones, Co-operative Production, p. 287.
57 Sun Mill Papers, Board minutes, 6 January 1863, SM/1/1.
58 Jones, Co-operative Production, p. 282.
59 Shepherd and Toms, 'Entrepreneurship, strategy, and business philanthropy'.
60 Tyson, 'William Marcroft', p. 121.
61 R. E. Tyson, 'The Sun Mill Company: A Study in Democratic Investment, 1858–1959' (MA dissertation, University of Manchester, 1962), p. 230.
62 Dr John Watts, a leading co-operative activist, in his address at the foundation stone laying ceremony for Sun Mill, February 1861. Jones, Co-operative Production, p. 284.

Hey, Sun Mill only paid bonuses to selected senior employees, preferring to reward the rest of its staff with higher dividend payments.[63]

In addition to ideological inspiration, the apparent financial success of Sun Mill, as measured by its dividends, sparked similar projects in other districts of south-east Lancashire. Farnie notes that Sun Mill was the 'parent' of the unprecedented mill-building boom centred on Oldham in 1873–75.[64] A correspondent for *The Economist*, writing in 1871, pointed out the present high rate of profit of 30%. Contemporary commentators regarded excessive profits as problematic for two reasons. First, they encouraged wage claims that could be justified on the grounds of affordability. Second, they prompted speculation and, indeed, speculative mill building.[65] As Jones put it: 'The continued success of Sun Mill, with the tremendous profits made in 1870, set the Oldham district on fire.'[66] Beyond that, Sun Mill's core product was 32s coarse yarn, which supplied markets for printings and shirtings, particularly in India, and helped 'maintain a steady prosperity' in Oldham over the next two decades.[67]

The high profits at Sun Mill of the early 1870s were, however, something of a myth. The 30% figure quoted by *The Economist* had been earned only on the equity portion of the capital. Figure 10 compares the return on share capital only with the return on all capital including loans. The return on all the permanently invested capital for 1871, including the loan account, reached a maximum of only 16.15%. Although a respectable rate when compared to long-run industry averages, similar results were only attained in the adjacent years of 1870 and 1872. Loan finance accounted for around half the total capital.[68] The effect was to leverage the return on equity capital to much higher rates. As William Nuttall, an influential co-operator put it, writing in 1872: 'Working men are learning to borrow at five percent and make ten more by it.'[69] At Sun Mill, the effects can be appreciated by comparing the return on equity and the return on total capital in Figure 10, which shows that shareholder returns were greatly amplified by the use of debt finance. As a contemporary observer explained:

63   *Report to Board of Trade on Profit Sharing*, London, 1894, Report by Mr D. F. Schloss, C.7458, p. 596.

64   Farnie, *English Cotton*, p. 249.

65   'Co-operative manufacture', *The Economist*, 6 May 1871, p. 533; J. Watts, 'On strikes and their effects on wages, profits and accumulations', *Journal of the Statistical Society* 24 (1861), 498–506, at p. 505.

66   Jones, *Co-operative Production*, p. 291.

67   'Rise and progress of the Rochdale limiteds: The Crawford Spinning Company', *Rochdale Observer*, 17 May 1890.

68   In 1871, called up share capital was £50,000 and reserves £4,587, and loan capital was £54,283. Calculated from: *Co-operative News*, 23 November 1871, p. 598 and Tyson, 'Sun Mill'.

69   W. Nuttall, 'The Sun Mill', *Co-operative News*, 23 November 1871, p. 598.

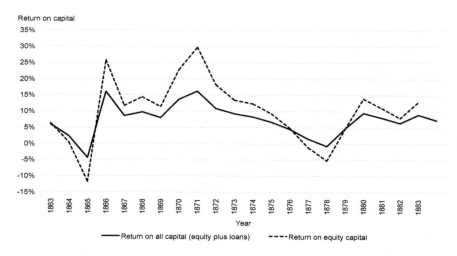

Figure 10. Return on capital, Sun Mill, 1863–83

Notes: Return on all capital is profit before interest divided by share capital and reserves plus loan capital; return on equity capital is profit after interest divided by share capital and reserves.

Sources: CIFD.

> if a company can manage to pay the banker and mortgagee five percent upon three fourths of their working capital, and can make in a good year sixteen and a quarter percent upon the whole, they may possibly, if they don't care for providing a reserve or contingency fund, pay their shareholders fifty percent.[70]

The immediate advantage of debt was, therefore, that it could be used to justify dividends well above underlying profits, which was very useful for a new business looking to expand through new share issues.

Even so, such high dividends seem counter-intuitive for a business seeking further growth. While paying dividends totalling £37,620 on a share capital of £50,000 in the period 1871–72, the firm commenced investment in a new mill. No doubt the high dividends of those years sent exactly the right signal to eager new investors. The new share capital was subscribed in equal measure with an expansion of the loan account. As the second mill was constructed, total capital increased from £100,637 in 1870 to £162,630 by 1875. In the same period, share capital increased from £50,000 to £75,000 and loan capital from £46,018 to £77,939.

These methods of financing differed fundamentally from earlier norms. As we have seen in previous phases of growth, entrepreneurs typically eschewed loan finance, other than bills of exchange to fund the working capital cycle. In these models, partnerships accumulated wealth privately and made relatively

---

70 Watts, *Facts of the Cotton Famine*, p. 342.

little use of structured debt finance. The use of loan accounts differentiated the expansion of cotton spinning in Oldham from the earlier model 1–4 growth phases up to 1850. Loan accounts were now used to capture the savings of middle and working-class investors to finance mill construction. Investors could deposit money in the loan account of any particular mill, usually withdrawable on demand. However, because the loan account was used to finance fixed as well as working capital, directors had to ensure a balance between deposits and withdrawals. Transactions were monitored accordingly, as detailed, for example, in a report of the quarterly meeting of the Croft Bank Spinning Company.[71] To assist in the balancing process, interest rates could be adjusted as necessary. For new mills, loan and share capital were called in tandem, like the arrangements of Sun Mill, the equal balance of loan and equity finance was a standard feature.[72] By these means, co-operative investors created structured finance for the building and operation of cotton mills.

Firms that managed their financial structure carefully were well regarded. Sun Mill had leveraged high dividend payments, true, but the balance between equity and debt was maintained consistently during the 1860s and early 1870s. A contemporary observer, writing in 1875, cautioned investors:

> To represent a concern as yielding a large return to shareholders when it is worked to a great extent with loan capital, the amount paid up on share capital being comparatively small, is to propagate a deception. Such deception has, however, been of immense value to the professional promoters of companies and traffickers in shares; but it is getting pretty well worn out.[73]

Excessive leverage was not always a problem, particularly where shareholders simultaneously invested in the loan account of their own company.[74] Even so, there is little doubt that debt-financing practices amplified the boom slump cycle.

A further significant difference between this new system of finance and earlier models was in the pattern of capital accumulation. Prior accumulations of the wealth of earlier industrialists allowed access to extensive credit-based networks and funded partial and stepwise automation of the value chain, thereby expanding capital further. Pre-1850 private firms therefore also provided sufficient wealth for the Birleys, Philips, Gregs and others to divest capital for different purposes. These included investments in joint ventures and purchases

71   'Proceedings of existing limited liability companies', *Oldham Standard*, 17 April 1875.
72   For example, during the construction of the Hollinwood Spinning Company; *Oldham Standard*, 17 April 1875.
73   'Local limited liability enterprise. Facts and considerations for shareholders', *Oldham Standard*, 10 July 1875.
74   As they were encouraged to do by the directors of the Westwood Spinning Company, where the loan account had risen to over £37,000 against called up share capital of just over £17,000; *Oldham Standard*, 15 July 1876.

of shares and influence in the expanding railway network. In Oldham, no public company contemplated any such accumulations. All profits were paid out to shareholders immediately as dividends and only small accumulations on reserve accounts were tolerated. Again, Sun Mill led the way. Between 1863 and 1883, the company earned profits after interest totalling £128,587, of which over 91% (£117,342) was paid out as dividend. During this period the average balance on the reserve fund was under £4,000. The purpose of these reserve funds was not to finance new investments in either fixed or working capital but to reassure investors by maximizing dividend payouts.

Shareholders in Sun Mill had every right to be nervous. As Figure 10 shows, the use of debt finance significantly amplified the volatility of their returns. In its early years up to 1865, Sun Mill suffered from bad trade and bad debts, and a relatively unprofitable investment in weaving.[75] Writing in 1871, a correspondent noted that the profits of the mill during the previous four years were 'not very much to boast of'.[76] Notwithstanding the founding principles, the mill was under the same trading pressures as other firms and management reacted by cutting corners. In 1874, the company was fined under the provisions of the Factory Acts for failing to observe dinner-break rules for child workers.[77] Underlying return on total capital was quite similar to other firms. For example average profits at New Eagley were 12.48% between 1863 and 1875, compared to 8.51% at Sun Mill for the same period.[78]

Nonetheless, dividend rates of 30% and more were easily sufficient to attract local capital into the mill investment boom that followed. Large appetite for investment from the local population meant that similar projects could be quickly developed. William Marcroft laid the foundation stone at Royton Mill in 1871 and others, including Greenacres, Green Lane, Oldham Twist, Royton and Central, followed soon after.[79] Co-operative societies were significant investors. In 1871, Oldham Co-operative stores had invested £72,785 in seventeen industrial societies and joint-stock companies.[80] Industrial societies, in turn, in the form of pyramid financing, invested in co-operative spinning mills. For example, the Oldham Industrial Co-operative Society had lent £11,732 to Sun Mill by 1875 and further substantial sums to other mills and businesses established on similar principles.[81]

---

75 Jones, *Co-operative Production*, p. 288.
76 'The Oldham lock-out', *Manchester Guardian*; 6 May 1871, p. 9.
77 'Breaches of the Factory Acts', *Manchester Guardian*; 8 January 1874; p. 4.
78 Calculated from CIFD.
79 Jones, *Co-operative Production*, pp. 282–92. Average dividends for the first 10¾ years of operation were 12½% (p. 289).
80 'Co-operation in Oldham', *Co-operative News*, 1871, vol. 1, p. 2.
81 'Oldham Joint Stock Movement', *Manchester Guardian*; 11 February 1875, p. 4. Total lending by the society was £45,437 and around £16,000 of this was invested in the loan accounts of five further cotton mills.

Revolution in corporate governance

Mitchell Hey and Sun Mill were set up as producer co-operatives, in which workers owned shares in their own companies. However, this did not last. As new mills were floated on a large scale, there was an increasing tendency for operatives to buy shares or deposit in the loan accounts of companies other than their own. To some extent, this was a rational mitigation of risk on their part. In the cyclical slumps of the 1840s and 1850s, operatives bore most of the risk of losing income as a result of flexible wage contracts and piece payment systems. By the 1870s, the leading feature of Oldham capitalism was the mass participation of workers in share-ownership of the majority of the local economy. Although by this time few workers owned shares in their own companies, cotton operatives were significant contributors to the share lists of other companies floated under the limited liability acts.[82]

Shareholder democracy was born. When William Gladstone, then Chancellor of the Exchequer, visited Sun Mill in 1867, he was told that only four out of one thousand shareholders were also employees. He pointed out 'this company is not really a co-operative one, but an association of small capitalists'.[83]

Nonetheless, these new governance structures retained many of the principles and features of co-operation. Characteristically, there was broad public participation at company meetings, in new issues, and the buying and selling of existing shares. Active participation at meetings was an important feature of the co-operative movement,[84] which the early working-class limiteds emulated. Democratic governance, under the rules of the Companies Act, allowed the application of co-operative principles to the management and control of the companies. Quarterly meetings used the 'one-member-one-vote' rule, with outcomes determined by a show of hands. Democratic norms were enforced by mechanisms such as limits on maximum shareholdings, proxy holdings and institutional anonymous or nominee investors.[85]

By more recent standards, and by contrast with the private firms elsewhere in Lancashire and other sectors of the economy, the lot of the typical director was thus an unhappy one. Directors' salaries kept to about one-tenth of those earned in other industries in companies owned by more 'upper-class' shareholders.[86] Low remuneration did not absolve directors from shareholder criticism, which

82   S. J. Chapman, *The Lancashire Cotton Industry: A Study in Economic Development* (Manchester, 1904), p. 231.
83   Tyson, 'William Marcroft', p. 121.
84   Foster, *Class Struggle*, p. 222.
85   R. Smith, 'An Oldham Limited Liability Company 1875–1896', *BH* 4 (1961), 34–53, at p. 41. Shareholder participation and democracy were evidenced by the strong resistance to proxy voting. For example, there was a heated debate on this issue at a quarterly meeting of Leesbrook Spinning Co. Ltd; *Oldham Chronicle*, 19 January 1889.
86   Potter, *The Co-operative Movement*, pp. 126, 132.

was intense, and they were keenly held to account for their actions. Following the incorporation of Sun Mill under the 1862 Companies Act, it was agreed that directors would be paid 6d per week and be fined 4d if they were absent.[87] '6d a week!' read the headline of an article written sixty years later, contrasting the 'amazing' difference between directors' salaries then and now.[88] Even when managerial labour was in short supply, replacement directors were readily available from at least two identifiable sources: existing directors from other firms who had perhaps fallen foul of their shareholders[89] and from the growing pool of technically educated, skilled operatives.[90] Adult education was another important prop of the co-operative movement, and in the 1880s Lancashire had a dominant lead in the provision of City and Guild's technical education. Technical education and the rise of skilled labour groups explain the pool of potential replacement directors and the weak bargaining power of the fledgling managerial class, the former reflecting the co-operative tradition and the latter, changes in factory organization. Directorships were, therefore, often hotly contested. One such contest at a meeting at the Higginshaw Spinning Company was likened to 'a miniature Waterloo'.[91]

Well-educated shareholders were naturally effective at scrutinizing directors using accounting information. Farnie notes, 'Such shareholders proved to be the strictest of economists and were prepared to oust a whole board which failed to produce an acceptable balance sheet, displaying as much ruthlessness as the Athenian Ecclesia or the leaders of the French Revolution towards their unsuccessful generals.'[92] Volunteer shareholders performed audits, taking their responsibilities seriously, as part of a moral duty for the sake of the wider co-operative movement.[93] Decisions on accounting choices, such as depreciation policy, were subject to debate and overruled, particularly if dividends might be impacted.[94]

The demand for dividends, which followed naturally from the cash requirements of working-class investors, also meant that directors had little freedom of action in terms of free cash flow and accumulated reserves. There was a perception in Lancashire that the companies' only purpose was to pay dividends

87 Jones, *Co-operative Production*, pp. 282–90.
88 *Daily Despatch*, 27 March 1923.
89 Tyson, 'Sun Mill', pp. 219–21.
90 S. J. Chapman and F. J. Marquis, 'The Recruiting of the Employing Classes from the Ranks of the Wage-Earners in the Cotton Industry', *Journal of the Royal Statistical Society* 75 (1912), 293–313, at p. 306
91 *Oldham Chronicle*, 30 December 1893, p. 8.
92 Farnie, *English Cotton*, p. 266.
93 S. Toms, 'The rise of modern accounting and the fall of the public company: the Lancashire cotton mills 1870–1914', *Accounting, Organizations and Society* 27 (2002), 61–84.
94 *Second Report of the Royal Commission on the Depression of Trade and Industry*, BPP, 1886, C.4715, ev. A Simpson, q.5489 and Appendix A(9), p. 378.

and nothing more, earning Oldham the nickname of 'Diviborough'.[95] A correspondent to the Oldham Chronicle complained of the 'insanity' of a 30%
dividend declared by Leesbrook Spinning Company:

> By declaring 30 per cent they deceive the public and, I think, themselves, for
> at their start they are going into the old error of not depreciating enough and
> paying away every available farthing in dividend. Every shareholder should
> surely know by now that depreciating more, and dividing less, makes any
> concern richer.[96]

Such factors undoubtedly discouraged the participation of passive, disinter-
ested, or 'naïve', investors. Shareholder activism and attendance at quarterly
meetings meant that few shareholders held fully diversified investment
portfolios. Instead, heightened risk intensified their vigilance in monitoring
the management of specific companies. Also, the practice of calling up only
a proportion of the nominal value of share capital removed some of the
protection of limited liability and created the risk of additional calls, thereby
adding to shareholder vigilance. Where directors posed the threat of calls, the
shareholder response was often hostile.[97]

These shareholders, were, for the most part, operatives employed at nearby
mills. Following the abolition of labour bonuses, cotton workers had a greater
incentive to seek out investments in other mills. The threat of strikes and
short-time working, and accompaning loss of wages, also meant that some
diversification of risk was sensible.[98]

For these reasons, the development of a share market was a necessary adjunct
of the second phase of co-operation, which commenced around 1870 with
the new mill-building boom. The organization of the stock market was in
keeping with the traditions of co-operation and the localization of investment.
William Nuttall, a luminary of the co-operative movement, now became an
active promoter of new mills, a share broker and accountant. Markets in shares
sprang up in neighbouring towns; in Ashton, for example, shares were traded
on a Tuesday night at the Feathers Inn and the Pitt and Nelson Hotel.[99] By 1875,
thirty-five mills had their share prices quoted in the local newspapers. Shares
were also traded in a further thirty-two mills in the course of erection. Further

---

95   Farnie, *English Cotton*, p. 263.
96   *Oldham Chronicle*, 4 April 1887.
97   For example, *Oldham Chronicle*, 28 December 1895, p. 8.
98   For example, in the eighteen-week strike of 1889, Sun Mill and Neville Mill employees lost
over £3,400 in wages. *Royal Commission on Labour Minutes of Evidence, Appendices (Group
C) Volume I. Textiles*, BPP, 1892, C.6708–VI, p. 261.
99   J. F. Wilson, A. Webster and R. Vorberg-Rugh, *Building Co-operation: A Business History
of The Co-operative Group, 1863–2013* (Oxford, 2013); W. A. Thomas, *The Provincial Stock
Exchanges* (London, 1973), p. 146; *Oldham Standard*, 17 April 1875, p. 8.

quotations were listed for cotton mills in nearby towns, including those which had featured in the early days of co-operation, like the Bacup and Wardle. Miscellaneous firms were also listed, providing the opportunity for local people to invest outside of the cotton industry.[100] However, all in all, investment opportunities were overwhelming skewed to local firms in the cotton industry, many of which also offered democratic voting rights.

Parallel developments of market institutions had the potential to assist the worker-owners of mills in other ways. The purchase of raw cotton was risky, and the formation of the Liverpool Cotton Brokers Association in 1841 led to improved market regulation. Notwithstanding improved organization and oversight, the Liverpool market remained vulnerable to swindlers and market operators. The shortages of American cotton created by the outbreak of the American Civil War led to a rise in imports from India. As one commentator complained: 'This last year, we shall have paid India not less than a million sterling for dirt and rubbish ostensibly sold as cotton', whose 'filthy state is owing partly to intentional fraud and partly neglect'. These problems were added to 'by want of care in the classification of cotton'.[101] In 1866, the completion of the first transatlantic cable facilitated the development of an organized futures market, overseen by the Brokers' Association. Cotton spinners, meanwhile, increasingly dealt directly with brokers.[102] They could now, theoretically at least, more effectively insure against price fluctuations. There were also better protections against adulteration and other swindles associated with misrepresenting the contents of cotton consignments, and the problems of 'bad spinning' that followed.

Ownership, performance and the trade cycle

Limited liability and the principles of co-operation facilitated an extraordinary growth in spinning capacity, financed by working-class savings. The dislocation of French and German competition during the Franco-Prussian War of 1870–71, and the expansion of weaving capacity in north-east Lancashire to meet the demand for shirtings in India and China, created new opportunities for cotton spinning in the Oldham district. The expansion of the 1873–75 mill-building boom, when sixty new mills were floated, tended to reinforce the early patterns established at Mitchell Hey and Sun Mill. Indeed, the majority of new capital, around 75%, came from working-class investors.[103] As before, the dividends

---

100   Ibid.
101   'Indian and American Cotton', *Glasgow Herald*, 8 March 1862.
102   Ellison, *Cotton Trade of Great Britain*, pp. 181, 274–5; G. von Schulze-Gaevernitz, *The Cotton Trade in England and on the Continent* (London, 1895).
103   Ellison, *Cotton Trade of Great Britain*, pp. 106–7; 135. Farnie, *English Cotton*, pp. 249–50.

paid by established companies created a strong impetus for further expansion. In 1874, the Bacup and Wardle Company was once again paying 48% dividends, with the Rossendale Cotton Spinning and Manufacturing Company not far behind at 42%. In Oldham, the more recently floated mills, including the Central and Royton Spinning Companies, with dividends of 38% and 40% respectively, outstripped Sun Mill which was now only paying 10%. Working-class investors in Oldham and around seized all opportunities. Low-denomination shares, called in even smaller instalments, encouraged such behaviour. In Preston, by contrast, the instinct of the private capitalist was to 'decline business on the first opportunity'.[104]

The system of finance in Oldham, built on co-operative principles and the institution of limited liability, led to an unprecedented expansion of the industry. By 1876, total investors in Oldham numbered 10,000, or one in five of the population.[105] Newly floated mills created large shareholder bases of working-class investors[106] They also attracted investment from other co-operative societies. Oldham Equitable Co-operative Society took up two hundred shares of the Equitable Spinning Company and one hundred in the Glodwick and Thornham Spinning Companies, while placing £3,000, £3,000 and £1,000 respectively on deposit with the loan accounts of each company.[107] At the inauguration of the new Industry Mill in 1875, the mill engine was christened the 'Oldham', as a tribute to the 3.375 million spindles now controlled by the working class of Oldham.[108] Between 1873 and 1883, almost a quarter of new capital raised was in Oldham alone, with much more invested in the surrounding district.[109] As the Rossendale co-operatives, then Mitchell Hey and Sun Mill, had signalled the virtues of the new system to eager investors, these later flotations offered the prospects of similar high returns.

Were investors justified in making these financial commitments? The evidence suggests yes. Table 7 and Figure 11 compare the returns on investments in the form of total return (capital gain plus dividend) and dividend yield for democratic, 'one-shareholder-one-vote' companies to those with standard plutocratic rules. Democratic companies also typically issued shares in low denominations, usually of less than £5, and often of £1. Plutocratic companies, by contrast, mostly used denominations of £10 or higher, often up to £50.

104   'Echoes of the Press', *Co-operative News*, 22 August 1874.
105   Tyson, 'Sun Mill', pp. 221–2.
106   Belgian, Shiloh and Thornham were typical companies with large numbers of working-class shareholders. Respectively, these companies had 639, 295 and 406 shareholders and average shareholdings of 22, 17 and 18 (Board of Trade, Dissolved Companies, BT31, 14469/7869, 14486/8310 and 14494/8449).
107   Toms, 'The rise of modern accounting', pp. 67–8 and table 2; J. C. Taylor, *The Jubilee History of the Oldham Industrial Co-operative Society Limited* (Manchester, 1900), p. 75.
108   *Textile Manufacturer*, June 1877, p. 180.
109   Ellison, *Cotton Trade of Great Britain*, pp. 134–5.

Table 7. Comparative returns, democratic and plutocratic companies, 1875–85

	Average, 1875–85		N
	Total shareholder return	Dividend yield	
Democratic	1.85%	6.89%	20
Plutocratic	−3.61%	4.37%	12
Difference	5.46%	2.52%	
All firms	1.00%	5.12%	32

Note: Total shareholder return is the difference in share price (P) plus dividends in pence (d) divided by the share price at the beginning of each year (t): $(P_t–P_{t-1} + d)/P_{t-1}$. The dividend yield is the dividend in pence divided by the share price at the end of the year: d/P_t. Returns and together dividend yields are calculated from weekly share price and dividend lists in the *Oldham Standard* and *Oldham Chronicle*.

Source: Adapted from Toms, 'Producer co-operatives and economic efficiency' p. 872, table 2.

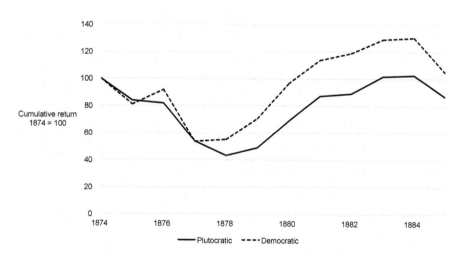

Figure 11. Total shareholder returns, democratic and plutocratic companies, 1874–85

Source: Adapted from Toms, 'Producer co-operatives and economic efficiency', p. 870, figure 6.

For most working-class investors, therefore, the only choice was to invest in democratic companies.

In general, these investments paid off. Certainly, investors in democratic companies did rather better in the period 1874–85. On average, they enjoyed returns over five percentage points ahead of plutocratic companies. They also enjoyed typically higher dividends. The differentials that emerged following the promotion boom of the early 1870s to some degree, therefore, mirrored the earlier successes of the co-operative mills. Contemporary commentators attributed the reasons for early financial success in part to the effects of social ownership on the efficient governance of mills and superintendence of production. Thomas Ellison, writing in 1886, quoting a contemporary report, highlighted the

> daily discussions which take place amongst the shareholders as to why dividends are small or otherwise, have led almost every intelligent operative to become more economical with materials, more industrious and to see what effect his individual efforts have on the cost of the materials produced. In fact, the bulk of the working class operatives of Oldham have more knowledge of the buying of cotton, working it up, and selling the manufactured good than most private employers had ten years ago ... The competition between the managers of one company and those of another, and also between the directors of different companies and the pride which each body of share-holders take in their own mill is leading to improvements ... so that *it is almost impossible for the management of any mill owned by working men to be seriously defective for any length of time* [emphasis added].[110]

Despite the relative success of the democratic investment model, it is also noteworthy that the collective performance of the Oldham limiteds during this period was disappointing. Returns averaged only one percentage point during this period. Bearing in mind that the companies were also typically paying out 5% interest on 50% of their total capital, these returns were still well below the averages earned by private mills in the first half of the century.

Lack of profitability was a consequence of growth, not a barrier to it. Like the earlier booms and slumps, the effect of upswings was to draw new capital into the Oldham district but thereby creating an immediate problem of overpro-duction. The rapid expansion of capacity led to complaints of flooded markets, for example, in 1877.[111] There were appeals for collective action to suspend further mill-building projects. No new mills were floated in 1877–79. Existing mills refused, however, to accept short-time working arrangements, preferring to accept lower-priced contracts that would cover their short-term marginal

110   Ibid., p. 138.
111   Jones, *Co-operative Production*, pp. 295–7.

costs. The City of Glasgow bank failure and the credit squeeze that followed in 1878 only made matters worse.[112]

As markets recovered, there was a new mill-building boom in the early 1880s. This time new activity was focused around Rochdale rather than Oldham. The boom featured the cluster of mills in New Hey and Milnrow using the new ring-spinning method, discussed in more detail in chapter 6. In Rochdale, in 1881, business and civic leaders expressed their concerns about the town's lack of progress relative to nearby Oldham and appointed a committee to address the issue. The result was a new spinning company, the Crawford, established on an unprecedented scale. Initial nominal capital was £100,000, increased to £200,000 the following year, such that the company built two new mills in 1882–83, totalling 154,464 spindles. Scale economies, and lower local taxes and land costs, meant that the new capacity could be installed at a record low cost of 19s per spindle, offering a potential competitive advantage over other mills in the area. In the event, the firm paid a high initial dividend shortly after its launch of 12½% in May 1884.[113] After that its profits were average.[114]

Although these developments took advantage of limited liability to raise large amounts of capital from local investors, they also had much in common with the networked partnerships of the first half of the nineteenth century. The committee that led to the promotion of the Crawford was influenced by the businessmen who had already played a leading role in the establishment of the Milnrow ring spinners. They then went on to promote another large new mill, the Rochdale Spinning Company, built on land adjacent to Crawford in 1884, capitalized at £100,000. Four further companies followed.[115] The promoters of the Crawford company were, for the most part, already directors of existing cotton and related companies. They included John Bright, John Turner, W. T. Heap and Alderman Samuel Tweedale. Bright, Tweedale and Turner had been active in the early days of Rochdale co-operation, but the consequence was that they now sat on the boards of multiple companies. Samuel Tweedale had served as mill manager at John Bright & Brothers and gained technical experience with Accrington cotton machinery manufacturers Howard & Bullough. He was subsequently a founding director of machinery manufacturers, Tweedale and Smalley, which were also equipment suppliers

112 Ellison, *Cotton Trade of Great Britain*, p. 135; 'Overproduction', *Manchester Guardian*; 7 January 1884, p. 4.

113 'Rise and progress of the Rochdale limiteds: The Crawford Spinning Company', *Rochdale Observer*, 17 May 1890. 'The cotton spinning trade', *Manchester Guardian*, 10 March 1884, p. 4.

114 In the first five years of its operation, Crawford's return on capital averaged 6.37%, compared with an industry average of 6.27%. Calculated from CIFD.

115 'Rise and progress of the Rochdale limiteds: The Rochdale Spinning Company', *Rochdale Observer*, 24 May 1890.

to John Bright & Brothers and the Milnrow ring spinners, where Tweedale also served as a director.[116]

Another feature of the Crawford project was how it fitted a broader pattern of growth. As markets expanded and technology developed, the extension of existing mills was problematic. Instead, the preference was to construct new mills, bespoken to the requirements of the latest machinery to be installed. In this fashion, promoters could construct mills on an efficient scale with land cost minimized. As a result, individual mills were not required to accumulate capital and instead could use profits to meet the requirements of local investors for dividends.

The Oldham district experiment was unique. It combined co-operation not just with limited liability but also with a liquid stock market. By 1886 the Lancashire stock market, centred around the Oldham district, had seventy-one quoted companies, rising to over a hundred quoted companies before 1900, and was, therefore, the third-largest provincial exchange in the country after Glasgow and Liverpool in terms of the number of quoted companies. Unlike the Glasgow, Liverpool and London markets, however, all the quoted companies were manufacturers, representing a substantial proportion of the local economy, which was dominated by these cotton-spinning companies.

The Rochdale boom of the early 1880s was the last wave of new co-operatively organized mills. The boom-slum cycle of the industry was problematic for all spinning and manufacturing firms, but particularly so for the co-operative mills. Neither active participation in company meetings nor improvements in market institutions could insulate investors from the risks. In 1876–79 a slump followed the mill-building boom of the early half of the decade, with further downturns in 1884–85 and 1891–96.[117]

One of the most significant outputs of the co-operative movement of the mid nineteenth century was the emergence of a new class of company promoters. William Nuttall was an early example. As a pioneer of co-operation, he was a promoter of the Oldham Twist Spinning Company and Sun Mill, and he claimed associations with twelve Oldham co-operative companies in total by 1875. He went on to promote companies in other industries.[118] Samuel Ogden Ward, at one time committed to the co-operative movement, amassed director-ships in several companies during the 1880s and 1890s. In doing so, he broke

---

116 W. Cooper, *History of the Rochdale District Co-operative Corn Mill Society* (London, 1861), p. 9; 'Milnrow ring spinning companies', *Rochdale Observer*, 28 June 1890; 'Masters of cutting edge in design', *Manchester Evening News*, 21 March 2006; 'Rise and progress of the Rochdale limiteds: The Crawford Spinning Company', *Rochdale Observer*, 17 May 1890.

117 Farnie, *English Cotton*, pp. 266, 275; S. Toms, 'The English cotton industry and the loss of the world market', *King Cotton: A Tribute to Douglas Farnie*, ed. J. Wilson (Lancaster, 2009), pp. 58–76, at p. 70.

118 J. Saville and R. E. Tyson, 'Nuttall, William (1835–1905)', *Dictionary of Labour Biography*, ed. K. Gildart and D. Howell (Basingstoke, 2010), vol. 13, p. 257.

the rule that committee members should hold only one office by serving as a director in several companies at the same time.[119] Thomas Gartside resigned as secretary of the Royton Industrial Co-operative Society after nearly twenty years' service in 1896. By 1900, he was serving on the board of four local spinning companies: Shiloh, Holly, Park & Sandy and Vine.[120]

Indeed, the steep downturn of the early 1890s proved to be the end of the co-operative experiment with joint-stock organization. Promoters of new mills, envious of the dividends and cash generation capacity of the established mills, but with less commitment to the principles of co-operation, were able to make use of the ready market in shares. Multiple directorships were now commonplace. Companies promoted by John Bunting, for example, which included Empire, Summervale and Times, were more narrowly controlled. Bunting and other mill promoters typically sat on the boards of all their companies, once floated. By 1890 Bunting was serving on the board of half a dozen companies and also writing a weekly report on share trading in the *Oldham Standard*.[121]

Companies floated after 1890 had much more concentrated ownership. Fewer shareholders controlled more shares between them, while the number of operative shareholders in the average mill declined from 22% of the total share capital in companies floated in 1874–76 to around 10% by 1897. Company promoters, who no longer had anything in common with co-operative principles, were blamed for the depressed condition of the industry in the 1880s. They were accused of using laudatory prospectuses to guarantee high initial share prices and then selling their own holdings soon after flotation, which tended to defraud the longer-term investor, making large profits for themselves in the process.

It was not just in the share market that concentrations of wealth posed problems for the co-operative mills. Powerful market manipulators increasingly dominated the Liverpool cotton market, making cotton buying risky. Liverpool merchants increasingly colluded to work the market to their advantage. In 1881, Shiloh mill stopped production for a week as a consequence of a corner operated by a syndicate in the Liverpool cotton futures market.[122] Corners like this one in the 1870s organized by Ranger and by the Steensrand syndicate of Liverpool merchants in 1887, had an increasing impact and promoted further

119 From reports of company meetings (*Oldham Standard*, various issues, 1888/9), Ward served on the boards of the Werneth, Coldhurst, Henshaw Street, Northmoor and Broadway Spinning Companies. Taylor, *Jubilee History*, pp. 112 and 125. Other examples of multiple directorships in Oldham included Thomas Henthorn (1850–1913), Harry Dixon (1880–1947), William Hopwood (1862–1936), Ralph Morton (1875–1942), John S. Hammersley (1863–1933) and Sam Firth Mellor (1873–1938). D. Gurr and J. Hunt, *The Cotton Mills of Oldham* (Oldham, 1998), pp. 9–10.
120 Anon., *The Shiloh Story* (Royton, 1974).
121 D. Farnie, 'John Bunting', *Dictionary of Business Biography*, ed. D. Jeremy (London, 1984–86), vol. 1, pp. 506–9.
122 'Oldham cotton companies', *Blackburn Standard*, 26 November 1881.

instability.[123] Buyers also faced risks associated with fraud, typically the sale of non-existent cotton or the forging of cheques and bills of exchange.[124] Private spinners, who were sceptical of the Oldham model, questioned the ability of amateurish Oldham managers to deal effectively with this challenging market. While they bought carefully, they claimed, representatives of the limited companies did their business in minutes and spent the rest of the time having picnic parties at New Brighton.[125]

The tendency for directors to act beyond the remit of a dwindling band of active shareholders was dramatically illustrated in a series of speculations on the Liverpool cotton market. Following large profits made by syndicates in 1889, Oldham investors came to believe that they too could benefit from speculation. At the Boundary Cotton Spinning Company quarterly meeting, members criticized directors for not speculating.[126] Subsequent misjudgements meant that many companies were left holding stocks of 'dear cotton'. Meanwhile, the fall in silver prices made their products more expensive in export markets.[127] The result was a significant profit crisis and share price slump that persisted until 1896.

A further set of developments that undermined the co-operative spirit of the earlier mills was the growth of trade unions and industry-level bargaining. The cotton trade unions became much more potent in the latter decades of the nineteenth century. Co-operatively owned mills had long had an ambivalent relationship with the unions. For example, they had strong incentives to join industry employer associations, including the Cotton Masters. Employers' associations became increasingly crucial in Oldham, as they already had become in Preston and elsewhere, in response to the labour disputes, especially during the 1850s (see chapter 3). Membership gave the mills access to negotiated rates with the railway companies, support for the enforcement of forward contracts on manufacturers and reduced vulnerability to speculative activity in cotton and yarn markets.

At the same time, membership created pressure to support collective action on wages and short time, leading to dilemmas for co-operative officials. As early as 1875, when the Oldham Master Spinners' Association moved to impose a lockout during a strike, Marcroft called a special meeting of the Central Cotton Spinning Company, proposing a resolution requiring shareholder approval for action in support of the Masters' Association. Such reactions grew increasingly

123 Tyson, 'Sun Mill', p. 271.
124 'Alleged Cotton Fraud', *Manchester Courier and Lancashire General Advertiser*, 5 June 1874, p. 5; 'The Charge of Fraud against a Liverpool Cotton Broker', *Manchester Courier and Lancashire General Advertiser*, 8 November 1879.
125 *Oldham Standard*, 26 December 1891.
126 *Oldham Standard*, 23 November 1889.
127 *Oldham Standard*, 7 February, 14 February, 28 February, 23 May 1891; 12 March 1892.

tricky as industry agreed wage lists negotiated by industry federation and trade unions became the norm from the mid-1880s onwards. Union members and organizers treated worker-shareholders with suspicion on the shop floor.[128] Industrial disputes affecting previously democratically managed companies, for example, the card room strikes at Sun, Hey and Neville mills in 1889, spread to 143 mills with the backing of the Masters' Association for organized short time.[129]

In the slump of the early 1890s, the deepest since the cotton famine, firms accumulated losses and prospects of future dividends became remote. Poorer, working-class investors sold their shares as wages fell and their savings were eroded. Democratic firms suffered particularly badly in this slump.[130] There was a disproportionate fall in dividend payouts. By the mid-1890s shares had fallen to low values and provided an opportunity for investors to purchase control of the firms cheaply. By securing voting blocks in this way, investors were able to abolish democratic methods of control, for example, the one-shareholder-one-vote rule, shareholder audit and limitations of directors' salaries. The Brooklands dispute of 1893, the most bitter in the history of the industry, redrew the traditional lines of class conflict. Despite their defeat, operatives preferred the security offered by union dues to the risk of share-ownership as the industry spiralled into the deepest of slumps in 1896.

The reasons for the decline of democratic ownership in the Oldham district were less prevalent elsewhere. In remoter areas, the advantages of trade union organization and uniform wage lists were mitigated by differential transport costs. Communitarianism, whereby key factory posts and shop-floor promotions could be secured by democratic election, also persisted in smaller factory villages and communities. As in Oldham, multiple directorships evolved, and investors would hold shares in local companies. However, to preserve the perceived advantages of social ownership, communitarian mills placed restrictions on share transfer. Working-class ownership persisted into the 1920s in villages like Harle Syke, near Burnley, and at co-operative mills like the New Bacup and Wardle.[131] Meanwhile the producer co-operatives in Oldham did not in the end attack the groundwork of the capitalist system, as Marx had expected. Rather they were squeezed by an intensification of class conflict in the slump of the 1890s, by the exigencies of the stock market on the one hand and the development of effective trade union organization on the other.

128 *Royal Commission on Labour Minutes of Evidence, Appendices (Group C) Volume I. Textiles*, BPP, 1892, C.6708–VI, ev. William Mullin, p. 726.
129 Tyson, 'Sun Mill', p. 267.
130 S. Toms, 'Producer co-operatives and economic efficiency: Evidence from the nineteenth-century cotton textile industry', *BH* 54 (2012), 855–82, figure 3.
131 J. Southern, 'Cotton and the community: Exploring changing concepts of identity and community on Lancashire's cotton frontier c.1890–1950' (Ph.D. dissertation, University of Central Lancashire, 2016), pp. 60, 114; Hampson, 'Working-class capitalists', p. 76.

Conclusions

By the end of the nineteenth century, the co-operative experiment in south-east Lancashire was over. After 1850, cotton mill operatives' lives had been transformed by the co-operative experiment. From being socially excluded, overworked indentured servants, protected only by the Factory Acts, they became active participants in the management of the largest and most efficient cotton mills in Lancashire, and by the same token, the world. However, cotton remained the riskiest of trades. New institutions, such as the futures market in Liverpool, and indeed the stock market that gave rise to the co-operative limited liability movement, tended to accentuate rather than reduce the vagaries of the trade cycle. With ownership comes risk, and the retreat from social ownership was effectively turned into a rout by the events of the 1890s.

The concentration of wealth and share-ownership, mainly after 1880, set the scene for further transformations in the joint-stock economy of south-east Lancashire and beyond, before and after the First World War. The mobilization of middle- and working-class savings which had financed the railway and other mid-Victorian booms also underpinned the further expansion of the cotton industry. Expansion of mill capacity, in south-east Lancashire in particular, between 1850 and 1880, represented a further step growth in the industry. Unlike the period before 1850, which had been dominated by networks of individual entrepreneurs, this new growth phase was based on a model of industrial democracy. As such, it was broadly successful. The co-operative movement successfully adapted limited liability principles to mobilize large amounts of capital from local communities. Hitherto these communities had been excluded from all but the most alienating aspects of factory labour by dominant entrepreneurs, be they philanthropists or tyrants. Under the new system, factory operatives participated in the management of cotton companies, albeit not usually those where they were directly employed. Directors were the servants of these increasingly well-educated shareholders.

Moreover, democratically governed firms typically outperformed their plutocratic rivals. However, the model did not last. The bonus to labour had ended in 1862. Thirty years later, most other features of industrial co-operation were also disappearing, buffeted by the pressures of international markets and the sometimes dysfunctional role of broader financial institutions. These changes contributed to undermining the democratic shareholding movement and began to squeeze the residual characteristics of co-operation. The movement was moribund by the mid-1880s, while the centralization of ownership reflected trends taking place across wider sections of the industry. Chapter 5 takes up the story of the reasons for these changes and their long-run impacts.

5

Industry Growth and Financial Networks

Earlier chapters have documented how the cotton textile industry in Britain emerged from regional financial and trading networks. From the onset of manufacturing, until the beginning of the nineteenth century, fixed capital requirements were small and working-capital requirements were easily satisfied by established local and regional credit markets. Automation was limited to specific processes in the value chain leading to spurts in growth, profit and capital accumulation for the partners of innovative firms. National markets, meanwhile, did not stand still and had the potential at least to supply capital to Lancashire firms on an extended scale, particularly after limited liability became widespread. As the previous chapter has shown, local middle- and working-class savings provided much of the capital that was needed. Lancashire textiles it seemed, notwithstanding continued economic growth, had little use for limited liability banking or indeed any financial institutions that did not evolve to service the specific needs of the cotton industry. The raw cotton market in Liverpool and the markets for yarn and cotton cloth in Manchester were the most important. How sustainable were these separate growth trajectories of industrial and financial institutions, and what were the implications for long-run economic performance? In general terms, how did the growth of the Lancashire textile economy fit with the rest of the British economy as it expanded in parallel? The chapter explores these questions.

As the cotton industry grew, the capital requirements of individual businesses also increased, creating options for entrepreneurs in terms of accessing finance. Second-generation mills with their larger capital bases were increasingly reliant on alternative networks to secure funding. For Lancashire-based networks, Manchester emerged as the most important centre for accessing merchant, and later finance, capital through regional stock exchanges.[1] Although a more substantial financial centre, London seemingly had little to offer in terms of financial resources for further expansion in subsequent waves of industrial

---

[1] Liverpool was also important. Pressnell notes that the majority of private banks in Liverpool emerged from wholesalers; L. S. Pressnell, *Country Banking in the Industrial Revolution* (Oxford 1956), p. 49. In Manchester, the railway boom created financial alliances between merchant and banking houses, and promoted the expansion of share dealing; Y. Cassis and P. Cottrell, *Private Banking in Europe: Rise, Retreat and Resurgence* (Oxford, 2015), p. 141.

development. As the nineteenth century progressed, Lancashire and London remained on separate trajectories of development. There has been much debate as to the degree of separation, but most acknowledge there was some distance.[2] Manufacturers more generally were excluded from the expansion of the Empire in favour of the interests of the City of London.

Consequently, the City increasingly specialized in bonds and overseas issues. The proceeds, and fees associated with such activities, were much larger than the average industrial flotation in Lancashire.[3] An exception was the railways, where cotton and other industrials were generally effective at securing access to the London stock market to complete the national network by 1900.[4] In another development, by this time some sections of the cotton industry had formed large trusts,[5] so that London finance was still a viable option, in theory at least, for these new larger firms. However, as will be demonstrated below, most of these very large firms consciously shunned London in favour of regional networks. The chapter aims to explain why this was the case and thereby inform the broader debate about the separation of London and the industrial economy.

This short historical sketch suggests that the City of London's separation from the industrial economy in the north of England, which has characterized the twentieth century and remains an issue today, has deep historical roots. As a set of financial institutions, London was not necessarily to blame. Indeed, few in the nineteenth century would have recognized there was even a problem. As we have seen in previous chapters, local and regional sources of finance were, in any case, more than adequate. Nonetheless, a crucial consequence of separation is that the historical process of London's evolution as the major, and now dominant, financial centre in the UK, by definition excluded certain parts

2 For example, the debate between Cain and Hopkins and Daunton, and the related issue of the relative political influence of Lancashire as illustrated by the bimetallism debate. P. J. Cain and A. G. Hopkins, *British Imperialism* (London, 1993); M. J. Daunton, '"Gentlemanly Capitalism" and British Industry, 1820–1914', *Past and Present* 122 (1989), 119–58; E. H. H. Green, 'Gentlemanly Capitalism and British Economic Policy, 1880–1914: The Debate over Bimetallism and Protectionism', *Gentlemanly Capitalism and British Imperialism: The New Debate on Empire*, ed. R. E. Dumett (London, 1999), pp. 44–67.

3 D. Kynaston, *The City of London II: The Golden Years, 1890–1914* (London, 1995); P. Cottrell, *Industrial Finance*. P. L. Cottrell, *Industrial Finance, 1830–1914: The Finance and Organization of English Manufacturing Industry* (London, 1980).

4 For example, the activities of Sir Edward Watkin, who, as director of the London and North Western railway, represented Liverpool mercantile interests to secure an extra line between Liverpool and Manchester. S. Amini and S. Toms, 'Elite directors, London finance and British overseas expansion: Victorian railway networks, 1860–1900' (unpublished working paper, University of Leeds, 2019).

5 For sketches of the main transactions, see H. Macrosty, *The Trust Movement in British Industry* (London, 1907).

of the economy, thereby limiting and continuing to limit its vital function: to redistribute funds to where they will find the highest social return.[6]

It was not the case that London investors necessarily found industrial ventures too risky. Michie notes that London investors' overseas portfolios shifted significantly from less risky government issues to more risky plantations, factories and mining between 1895 and 1914. Established manufacturing firms did not necessarily need new finance, as they could rely on previous generations of accumulated capital.[7] However, the long-standing nature of textile production by 1870 did neither stop the new larger mills in Oldham and Bolton seeking regional stock exchange finance, nor inhibit the trust movement of the 1890s.[8] Both of these developments deviated significantly from the intergenerational model of personal capitalism,[9] or the disintegrated, atomized and destructively competitive structure[10] stressed in previous histories of the British textile industry.

What then are the specific reasons for the separation between first capital for industrial expansion and then corporate capital to fund mergers in textiles, and the financiers of the City of London? How did the separation come about? The general argument below is that the industry developed network relationships such that it became self-sufficient financially in the take-off and initial growth phases. In the maturity phase, larger mills were financed mostly through local pools of capital, but the preference for such capital was fixed by network interrelationships established in earlier stages of development. As a consequence, as the industry expanded through the nineteenth century, it accessed more finance through established networks of connected individuals. The choices, or network preferences, of these individuals, were crucial. In documenting these preferences, the chapter answers the general question: what were the human factors that determined business network evolution and that explain the characteristics of the industry through its life cycle, including its rate of growth?

To address the general question, and its specific implications, the chapter is structured as follows. In the first section below, three overlapping kinds of literature are considered. These are: first, theories of networks and their evolution; second, theories concerning the development of financial centres;

6   The key function as described by R. Goldsmith, *Financial Structure and Development* (New Haven, CT, 1969), p. 400.

7   P. L. Cottrell, *Industrial Finance, 1930–1914: The Finance and Organization of English Manufacturing Industry* (London, 1980), pp. 269–70. R. Michie, 'Options, Concessions, Syndicates, and the Provision of Venture Capital 1880–1913', *BH* 23 (1981), 147–64.

8   D. Farnie, *The English Cotton Industry and the World Market, 1815–1896* (Oxford, 1979); Macrosty, *The Trust Movement.*

9   A. D. Chandler, *Scale and Scope: The Dynamics of Industrial Capitalism* (Cambridge, MA, 1990).

10   W. Lazonick, 'Competition, Specialization, and Industrial Decline', *JEH* 31 (1981), 1–8.

and third, the research on industry structure and economic performance, including entrepreneurship and entrepreneurial failure. The latter is important because the analysis of networks potentially complements, but does not necessarily fit into, neat descriptors of 'personal', 'family', 'corporate' capitalism, or correspond to an industrial structure dichotomy of integration or specialization. The economic and business history literature that overlaps with these three areas is integrated via the framework so that, finally, prior interpretations of the rise and fall of the Lancashire textile industry are contextualized and the new interpretation offered here specified. The chapter then goes on to consider empirical evidence on the formation and evolution of networks using a chronological approach. The general argument, summarized in the concluding section, is that financial networks rather than technological networks of collaboration became progressively more important as determinants of industry structure. In parallel, these networks developed regional centres of gravity, separate from the leading financial centre in London.

Networks and financial centres

The literature has consistently asserted that networks are economically significant, in terms of transaction cost reduction, for example, through lower contracting and information costs.[11] There has been some debate about the extent to which the social aspects of networks promote trust-based economic activity, or conversely, represent some degree of market failure.[12] Empirical studies have produced evidence across a range of networking characteristics, including economic, social, religious, political, cultural and familial linkages, but typically only focusing on selected dimensions. More holistic approaches have argued that all these factors are potentially critical explanatory determinants of decisive economic change, such as diversification of business interests.[13] These developments should be explained iteratively, stressing historical evolution and based on the precise specification of network characteristics.[14] Other interpretations have suggested that network characteristics and their growth are determined by transaction cost reduction through the process of hierarchy or

11   M. Casson, 'Institutional economics and business history: A way forward?', *BH* 39 (1997), 151–71.
12   O. E. Williamson, 'The Economics of Organization: The Transaction Cost Approach', *American Journal of Sociology* 87 (1981), 548–77; M. Granovetter, 'Economic Action and Social Structure: The Problem of Embeddedness', *American Journal of Sociology* 91 (1985), 481–510.
13   R. Pearson and D. Richardson, 'Business networking in the industrial revolution', *EcHR* 54 (2001), 657–79, at pp. 658–9.
14   J. F. Wilson, and A. Popp, 'Business networking in the industrial revolution: some comments', *EcHR* 56 (2003), 355–61.

market substitution, and the transparency or opacity of the social relationships involved.[15]

Our study of the Lancashire textile industry has the potential to illustrate how these ideas might be taken a stage further, relating networking characteristics to two possible sources of competitive advantage. These are, first, linkages that promote control of the value chain, which might include network-type relationships that substitute for what otherwise would be formal integration, vertical or horizontal. Also included here are collaborations on technology, production and marketing processes. Second, there are linkages based on financial markets, whether credit or capital markets, which provide access to capital or reduce the transaction cost of acquiring capital.

Competitive advantage is based on the accrual of rent from either source, by the dominant firm, or firms, within the network. On the one hand, abnormal returns accrue from the control of the value chain associated with market or technical dominance at its crucial stages. On the other hand, abnormal returns arise from the control of, or discounted access to, financial markets. Rents are Ricardian, such that dominant firms can allocate them within the network, thereby controlling financial returns available to other network firms. Network evolution is also path dependent, such that the accrual of superior profits in one generation impacts on the diversification of the network in the next. The pattern of diversification reflects incumbents' and entrants' preferences to link with specific nodes defined according to the underlying duality. Their opportunities, in turn, depend on the evolution of financial markets and institutions, and the ability of networks to access and potentially control them.

The development of the industrial economy during the nineteenth century was paralleled by some degree of integration of financial markets. However, financial market and institutional development tended to lag, presenting industrialists with some degree of choice across several regional and metropolitan financial centres which mirrored the regional specific, unbalanced distribution of economic activity after the industrial revolution. Writing in 1973, Kindleberger noted that there had been little interest in the geographical location or relationships among financial centres. He also suggested that a lack of local knowledge may inhibit investment by central financial institutions.[16] The reciprocal idea, that local business leaders may lack understanding of, and access to, primary finance channels could potentially be added now as further explanation. Such exclusion may indeed be problematic where clustering of activities in financial centres and facilitation of information exchange tends to

---

15   S. Toms and I. Filatotchev, 'Corporate governance, business strategy, and the dynamics of networks: A theoretical model and application to the British cotton industry, 1830–1980', *Organization Studies* 25 (2004), 629–51.

16   C. P. Kindleberger, *The Formation of Financial Centers: A Study in Comparative Economic History* (Princeton, NJ, 1974), pp. 1, 14.

reduce the transaction costs arising from such asymmetries.[17] In other words, Lancashire, as an industrial district, missed opportunities to benefit from the provision of cheaper financial services available in London.

Branch banking, allowing a central head office to channel funds from the suburbs into industrial areas, offered a further potential solution as bank finance concentrated at the end of the nineteenth century.[18] By this time, to summarize the arguments of Kindleberger, through the spread of railroads, comprehensive branch networks development, the introduction of limited liability laws and the dangers of lending specialization by industry sector, there was a durable logic to the centralization of finance in London.[19]

However, branch networks do not provide sufficient explanation for the separation of London and industrial capital in Lancashire. Michie notes a further hierarchical separation between 'high' and 'low' finance.[20] Branch banking, a form of the latter, was well developed in the regions, but provided only working capital, as opposed to longer-term structured finance. These regional and hierarchical separations were recognized by policymakers in 1931, in the form of the so-called 'Macmillan gap', in part as a response to the depressed conditions of staple industries after the First World War. Despite the efforts of policymakers and financial institutions, essential aspects of the gap persist today.[21] The evidence related below demonstrates why recognition of the separation between London and regional industries was somewhat belated.

Considering earlier phases of evolution of the textile industry as an example also allows us to identify further factors not recognized in the financial centres literature. Most notably, referring back to Kindleberger, the role of information as a centripetal force in the location of financial activities seems to apply much less in the case of textiles. By 1900, textile production remained a simple process relative to newer and higher-technology industries. Textile markets, of course, included insurance and commodity futures trading, but these functions were widely replicated in other contexts in the City of London and they could, given the right circumstances, have been easily supplied to Lancashire firms. Instead, textile firms relied on local and regional financial institutions. Economic, transaction cost-type arguments alone, therefore, seem to offer an insufficient explanation of the separate development of Lancashire and London.

Social networks offer a further possible explanation in two dimensions.

---

17 T. Gehrig, 'Cities and the geography of financial centers', CEPR Discussion Paper No. 1894 (London, 1998).

18 W. F. Crick and J. E. Wadsworth, *A Hundred Years of Joint Stock Banking* (London, 1936), pp. 329–45.

19 Kindleberger, *The Formation of Financial Centers*.

20 R. Michie, *Guilty Money: The City of London in Victorian and Edwardian Culture, 1815–1914* (London, 2009), p. 10.

21 S. Amini, K. Keasey and R. Hudson, 'The equity funding of smaller growing companies and regional stock exchanges', *International Small Business Journal* 30 (2012), 832–49.

First, City networks may have consciously shunned industrial investment opportunities. Rubinstein notes that by c.1850, there were two middle classes centred separately on commerce and London, and a smaller group based on manufacturing in the north of England. Relatively few wealthy individuals were based in Manchester, notwithstanding its commercial importance relative to the industrial towns, which had higher representations of such individuals. London's wealth predated industrialization and its established networks provided plenty of opportunities for its investors throughout the industrial era.

Nevertheless, there was a social basis for the separation of industry and finance. As aristocrats abandoned the land, they preferred finance to industry as a means of securing their fortunes.[22] Relatedly, industrialists may have experienced social barriers to accessing London finance, in the form of exclusion from relevant networks.

A second, alternative dimension is that industrial networks may have consciously shunned the City of London. As an established centre, London was no doubt technically capable of supplying any financial service demanded by Lancashire. However, suppose no such demand existed. Had Lancashire already secured self-sufficient access to suitable channels of finance, this may have indeed been the case.

Indeed, there is much to suggest that personal or highly individualized capitalism prevailed in Lancashire. Chapters 1 and 2 have outlined some leading cases of networks of individuals and the chief financial characteristics of the associated models of growth. The broader literature has regarded the personal model of capitalism as a mixed blessing. According to one argument, it invigorated Lancashire through the integration of innovation into factory settings during the industrial revolution, but later became a break on further expansion, inhibiting investment and growth.[23] Conversely, as earlier chapters have shown, previous decades of growth and path dependencies created a diversity of industrial organizations, ranging from individual entrepreneurs to financial networks to co-operative enterprises. These created a range of further investment opportunities.[24] As the industry expanded in the nineteenth century, so too did subregional specialization by product and process, as the scope of the market grew,[25] creating a further range of investment opportunities.

Specialization inhibited scale and reinforced personal control, resulting in allegations of entrepreneurial failure by the end of the nineteenth century.

22 Kynaston, *City of London II*. This was particularly true after the onset of agricultural depression in 1873; P. Anderson, 'Origins of the present crisis', *New Left Review* 23 (1964), 26–53.
23 Chandler, *Scale and Scope*.
24 S. Toms, 'Windows of opportunity in the textile industry: The business strategies of Lancashire entrepreneurs, 1880–1914', *BH* 40 (1998), 1–25.
25 S. Kenny, 'Sub-regional specialization in the Lancashire cotton industry, 1884–1914: A study in organizational and locational change', *Journal of Historical Geography* 8 (1982), 41–63.

According to these allegations, Lancashire entrepreneurs failed to make the required investments in new spinning and weaving technology, and were prevented by the separation of these functions; a theme returned to in more detail in chapter 6. Notwithstanding their physical separation, spinning, weaving and other production and distribution functions, were co-ordinated. *Market* relationships gave rise to social networks, for example, through the functioning of the Manchester Royal Exchange,[26] to some extent institutionalizing the otherwise atomized structure of the industry.

The literature on alleged entrepreneurial failure has not addressed the issue of financial networks directly. The above review has demonstrated that in addition to prior explanations of the ownership, governance and performance in the cotton textile industry, a further potential interpretation can be based on path-dependent networks increasingly dominated by financial interrelationships. There is evidence that such relationships assisted survival strategies in textiles in the second half of the twentieth century.[27] If so, then it may have been the case that this form of networked financial capitalism underpinned the subregional specialization that emerged in product markets during the nineteenth century.

If entrepreneurs were effectively networked and able to access financial resources through such networks, then the nature of barriers preventing co-ordinated investment in different branches of the industry must be reassessed. These literatures between them raise the question of whether financial networks offered a potential solution to the alleged inappropriate structure of the industry. If they did, why did they not respond with the supposed technical solutions to declining competitiveness? In the next section, the case of an evolving network, with a timeline stretching from the industrial revolution to the trust movement of the late nineteenth century and beyond, is used to address these questions.

Network evolution: cottage industries to textile trusts

The evidence presented here is set out as an extended multi-firm, multi-actor case study, to trace a small firm of the early industrial period via a social network evolution to the trust movement of the late nineteenth century. The story begins with the small partnership already introduced in chapters 1 and 2, Nathaniel Dugdale & Brothers and its initial deployment of primitive technology, and

---

26 M. B. Rose, *Firms, Networks and Business Values: The British and American Cotton Industries since 1750* (Cambridge, 2000), p. 73.
27 I. Filatotchev and S. Toms, 'Corporate governance, strategy and survival in a declining industry: A study of UK cotton textile companies', *Journal of Management Studies* 40 (2003), 895–920; Toms and Filatotchev, 'Corporate governance, business strategy, and the dynamics of networks'.

ends with the emergence of a dominant Lancashire–Scotland axis, led by J. & P. Coats. The narrative is constructed from diverse archival sources, including business-level financial records and contemporary publications. It follows an approximate chronological story.

As demonstrated in chapters 1 and 2, up to c.1830, increased productivity in spinning meant that a relatively small capital investment could sustain a more extensive network of outworking handloom weavers. Nathaniel Dugdale & Brothers, as detailed in chapter 1, used small outlays in fixed capital to sustain a web of connected outworkers, who in turn housed significant handloom-weaving capital. The resulting profits fuelled the growth of the firm and facilitated the expansion of its activities to control further aspects of the value chain.

The structure of the network, through family and business connections, provided opportunities for growth. These came in equal measure from technical collaborations and financial connections. Chapter 1 explained how the outworking network featured places founded on family-based relationships: Nathaniel's family home at Great Harwood, Oakenshaw at Clayton le Moors, the location of his former employment at Taylor, Fort & Bury's Broad Oak print works, and James Thomson's Primrose print works at Clitheroe and Lowerhouse Mill, where Thomson had once been a tenant. Dugdale was prompted to take over Lowerhouse from Thomson in 1811 by the decision to integrate forward into calico printing. Nathaniel's brother Adam took over Broad Oak print works, Accrington, in partnership with Thomas Hargreaves.[28] These partnerships provided collateral to underwrite the loans. Utilizing such relationships, Hargreaves & Dugdale expanded their network via the connection with Salis Schwabe & Co. of Middleton, near Manchester, while John Dugdale built up contacts with merchants in Liverpool and Manchester. Representatives of these firms also served on the boards of new railway companies from the 1840s onwards. Industrial and commercial activities were thus underpinned by financial connections between businesses and were reinforced through personal intermediation.

James Thomson, meanwhile, followed a similar strategy also based on technical innovation and marketing networks. The basis of his firm of Thomson & Chippendall's profitable expansion was through scientific expertise and experimentation, and effective marketing based on partnerships with merchants. As noted in chapter 2, Thomson invested significantly in patent and product development and design through a Paris-oriented network of local contacts. Among the talented staff was Walter Crumm, who worked for James Thomson before setting up his own business. Both Thomson and Crumm studied scientific

28   O. Ashmore, *The Industrial Archaeology of North-west England* (Manchester, 1982), p. 179; R. Ainsworth and R. S. Crossley, *Accrington through the Nineteenth Century* (Accrington, n.d.), p. 18; G. Turnbull, *A History of the Calico Printing Industry of Great Britain* (Altrincham, 1941), p. 97.

subjects at universities in Glasgow, which underpinned their network connections and assisted their business careers. Empirical evidence from other contexts
suggests that university scientists with links to industrial firms have more
significant social capital and higher propensity to become entrepreneurs as a
consequence.[29]

Successful firms in the first phase of industrialization, like the Dugdale–
Hargreaves–Schwabe collaboration and the associated endeavours of Thomson
& Chippendall, formed the basis of larger combinations subsequently. These
developments were the genesis of connections between the Manchester and
Glasgow branches of the cotton textile industry. On the death of Robert
Hargreaves in 1854, his firm was transferred to F. W. Grafton & Co. and
subsequently became a leading company in the Calico Printers' Association.[30]
These later developments, as will be explained below, strongly impacted on
the concentration of this section of the industry centred on the Lancashire–
Scotland axis, supported by connections established by mid-century.

Indeed, the nature of these connections is worthy of detailed investigation,
not least because the literature has hitherto stressed the separate development of
Lancashire and Scotland. Howe notes the parochial origins of most Lancashire
entrepreneurs and likewise, Slaven found that the overwhelming majority of
Scottish cotton masters were born in Scotland. Apart from Robert Owen, who
had travelled extensively between Manchester and Scotland, sharing technical
and managerial knowledge, Henry Houldsworth (1770–1853) was the only
exception.[31] Although born in Nottingham, Houldsworth became the owner of
one of the largest mills in Manchester by 1800. He delegated the management
of the Manchester mill to his brother Thomas and concentrated his energies on
cotton-spinning partnerships in the suburbs of Glasgow, with a steam-powered
mill at Anderston and a water-powered mill at Woodside. He maintained
business connections in both locations, and subsequently became Chairman
of the Manchester and Leeds railway. His son John (1807–60) became head of
spinning in his father's cotton business but also devoted attention to iron ore
and railways, including the Caledonian Railway, which connected to the family
iron ore business at Coltness.[32]

29   D. B. Audretsch and J. R. Hinger, 'From entrepreneur to philanthropist: Two sides of the same
coin?', *Handbook of Research on Entrepreneurs' Engagement in Philanthropy: Perspectives*, ed.
M. L. Taylor, R. J. Strom and D. O. Renz (Cheltenham, 2014), pp. 24–32, at pp. 29–30.
30   Turnbull, *History of the Calico Printing Industry*, p. 78.
31   A. Cooke, *The Rise and Fall of the Scottish Cotton Industry, 1778–1914: The Secret Spring*
(Manchester, 2010), pp. 47–8, 183–4; A. C. Howe, *The Cotton Masters, 1830–1860* (Oxford, 1984);
A. Slaven, 'Entrepreneurs and business success and business failure in Scotland', *Enterprise and
Management: Essays in Honour of Peter L. Payne*, ed. D. H. Aldcroft and A. Slaven (Aldershot,
1995).
32   In 1816, Houldsworth's mill was the third largest in Manchester, by employment. *Select
Committee on the State of the Children Employed in the Manufactories of the United Kingdom*,

Subsequent generations of the Dugdale–Hargreaves–Schwabe network complemented and enhanced the Houldsworth connections between Lancashire and Scotland. William Henry Houldsworth (1834–1917), was educated at St Andrews and married Elisabeth, the daughter of Walter Crumm, James Thomson's collaborator at Glasgow and leading technical employee at Thomson & Chippendall. The marriage took place in Glasgow in 1862 and thereby connected Houldsworth to relevant Glasgow family networks by technical collaboration, birth, and marriage.[33]

Notwithstanding these connections, William Henry Houldsworth's immediate business priorities were in Lancashire, where he established the Reddish Spinning Company at the Houldsworth Mill complex at Stockport in the period 1863–72, financed by share capital in which the family retained 60% control. His strategy was to install efficient machinery to achieve high productivity and, as a consequence, dominate the market. He had a philanthropic approach to management and promoted educational and social activities for his employees.[34] His vision had been realized by the time of his retirement as Chairman in 1908 from what by then had become the Fine Cotton Spinners' & Doublers' Association, the largest manufacturing employer in the country.[35] However, Houldsworth's activities were not limited only to the Fine Cotton Spinners' & Doublers' Association, and continued through his more extensive business network.

The Houldsworth–Crumm–Thomson network demonstrated strong connections between Lancashire and Scotland. Textile and finishing businesses featured prominently, but the network was also strongly characterized by family connections and portfolio-style investments in otherwise unrelated firms. Institutional connections were also meaningful, and all the network components benefited from interests in infrastructure, particularly railways and, increasingly, financial

BPP, 1816, 397, ev. Henry Houldsworth, pp. 464–5; ibid., p. 610. 'Tenth Half-yearly Meeting of the Manchester and Leeds Railway Company', *Manchester Courier and Lancashire General Advertiser*, 18 September 1841, p. 6; Henry Hounds Houldsworth was a partner in the Coltness Iron Company. 'Railways Amalgamation Bill', *Glasgow Herald*, 3 July 1861.

33   J. H. M. Laslett, *Colliers Across the Sea: A Comparative Study of Class Formation in Scotland and the American Midwest, 1830–1924* (Urbana, IL, 2000), p. 78. J. R. Kellett, *The Impact of Railways on Victorian Cities* (Toronto, 1969), p. 222; E. Gordon and G. Nair, *Public Lives: Women, Family, and Society in Victorian Britain* (New Haven, CT and London, 2003), p. 50; A. C. Howe, 'Houldsworth, Sir William Henry, First Baronet (1834–1917), Cotton Industrialist and Politician', *Oxford Dictionary of National Biography* (Oxford, 2004), https://doi.org/10.1093/ref:odnb/40813, accessed 6 April 2020.

34   'Sir W. H. Houldsworth and his Workpeople', *Manchester Courier and Lancashire General Advertiser*, 7 November 1887, p. 6.

35   R. N. Holden, 'The architect in the Lancashire cotton industry, 1850–1914: The example of Stott & Sons', *Textile History* 23 (1992), 243–57; M. Cowle, *Dirty Politics: A Trilogy of Blasphemies* (Manchester, 2010); Howe, 'Houldsworth'. Houldsworth's company was the lead firm in the amalgamation.

connections. The character of these evolved networks meant that at the close
of the nineteenth century, textile entrepreneurs faced a choice between securing
finance from London or regional financial markets. For the Houldsworth–
Crumm–Thomson network, the specifically relevant regional alternatives
for accessing finance were the provincial stock markets of Manchester and
Glasgow.

These preferences were exercised as the finishing and thread sectors of the
industry underwent rapid consolidation. Commentators noted that these
amalgamations were 'trusts' framed on American lines.[36] In some respects,
for example, in price-fixing, the leading players in these combines resembled
Cornelius Vanderbilt's methods of controlling railroad and freight rates. Unlike
Vanderbilt, Carnegie and others, who came from humble origins, the members
of the Manchester–Glasgow textile axis were second- and third-generation
descendants of successful textile entrepreneurs and included talented techni-
cians, in some cases with university backgrounds. The strength of this network,
therefore, reflected earlier successes and Britain's first-mover advantages dating
back to the industrial revolution. Once established, the network would now go
through a further phase of expansion and consolidation, based on the financial
centres of Manchester and Glasgow.

The emergence of the Coats network, 1890–1914

Trusts, or terminable combinations, as developed in the textile trades, facilitated the standardization of contracts and selling arrangements, and prevented
exclusive deals for customers, for example, involving secret rebates. The impetus
for the movement was the depression that followed the boom of 1870–75 and
the development of similar practices in the USA. Several British combines
now emerged from pre-existing sales associations. The trust paid high prices
on admission, to compensate existing owners for the loss of independence.[37]
In practice, the textile combinations typically incentivized component firms
by allowing them to retain local management teams superintended by representative boards of directors. At the same time, conflicts of interest were
occasioned between component firms and the association. The earliest mergers
were Horrockses Crewdson (1887) and J. & P. Coats (1890).[38] A further series
of combinations followed: English Sewing Cotton (1897), American Thread
(1900), the Fine Cotton Spinners' & Doublers' Association (1898), the Calico
Printers' Association (1899) and the Bleachers' Association (1900). Except

---

36   *Reynolds's Newspaper*, 17 December 1899.
37   Macrosty, *The Trust Movement*, p. 6.
38   Ibid., pp. 16–17, 126.

for Horrockses, these combinations floated their shares on the London and regional stock markets, although London ceased to be relevant for fundraising following the initial floats.[39]

The unexpected result of these combines was the emergence of J. & P. Coats as the leading firm. Coats' dominance was exercised not just in the thread and finishing sectors, as is well known, but also through financial connections with the other significant combines through regional financial networks and markets. There were three critical dimensions. First, Coats was the only firm that utilized connections via London and the metropolitan social elite. Second, Coats enjoyed very high profitability relative to the other combines floated at around the same time. Third, Coats used its financial strengths arising from these sources to reinforce the network connections, principally between Manchester and Scotland, that had emerged over previous generations. Each of these three dimensions is now considered in turn.

On 8 August 1890, Coats made a new share issue converting the existing firm into a limited company. Unlike the floats that followed later in the decade, the Coats board of 1890 had a distinctly elite flavour. There were three aristocratic directors, each with secure connections to non-textile elements of broader business networks: Sir James Whitehead (baronet), Lord Mayor and High Sheriff of London;[40] Sir James King (baronet), Deputy Chairman of the Caledonian Railway; and Sir William Arrol, of the civil engineering firm Arrol Brothers of Glasgow. The firm set up a London office at the time of the float, and the shares were also brokered in Glasgow and Montreal, the value of the preference and debenture stock classes per the prospectus was £1,333,340 each.[41] Both were oversubscribed, attracting total applications of £15 million.[42] The ordinary shares opened at 1½–1¾ premium.[43]

Notwithstanding this very successful share issue, Coats resisted becoming a London-centric company and its financial centre of gravity remained in its Scottish heartland. The vendors retained one-third of the capital, the maximum allowed under the rules of the London Stock Exchange.[44] The London office was only a temporary arrangement and the main head office continued to be in Paisley. A further amalgamation followed in 1896 when Coats purchased its chief rivals, which had hitherto collaborated in the Central Thread Agency and which exploited economies mainly through the control and administration of

39 *Investors Monthly Manual*, various issues.
40 Whitehead was also a Director of Pawsons & Co. Ltd, the London-based clothing and wholesale warehouse business. Prospectus: 'Public Companies', *The Times*, 8 August 1890, p. 11; *The Economist*, 1 March 1873, p. 260.
41 Prospectus: 'Public Companies', *The Times*, 8 August 1890, p. 11.
42 'The Money Market', *The Times*, 16 August 1890, p. 11.
43 'The Money Market', *The Times*, 12 August 1890, p. 9.
44 'The Money Market', *The Times*, 8 August 1890, p. 9.

selling agents.[45] These acquisitions provided Coats with a dominant position in the distribution stage of the value chain.

The Fine Cotton Spinners' & Doublers' Association was formed as an association of cotton firms spinning average counts of 120 or higher, in addition to doubling firms. Coats was a significant shareholder in the Fine Cotton Spinners' & Doublers' Association from the outset, with 200,000 ordinary shares. This investment was made to secure some control over raw material in the form of cotton yarn,[46] but also reflected financial network connections through director interlocks. As noted earlier, the Houldsworth family had interests in the Caledonian Railway, as did the Coats director, Sir James King, the railway's Deputy Chairman.[47] By this time a baronet and Conservative MP, Sir William Houldsworth was, as noted, also the Chairman of the Fine Cotton Spinners' & Doublers' Association.[48] The prime movers in forming the Association were Mr Scott Lings (also of Houldsworth's Reddish Spinning Company) and Herbert Dixon (of A. & G. Murray).[49] Dixon had modernized A. & G. Murray by investing in new technology and later became Managing Director of the Association. On the formation of the Fine Cotton Spinners' & Doublers' Association, constituent firms like Murrays were wound up and conveyed to the new amalgamation.[50] Apart from Houldsworth, there were no other peers or elite directors on the executive or general boards, which were made up of representatives drawn from the Association's constituent mills.

The Fine Cotton Spinners' & Doublers' Association's prospectus was issued in May 1898 and applications closed on 11 May. The Association's head office was in Manchester and its shares were listed on London and regional markets. The total value of the issue was £4 million (£2 million ordinary shares and £2 million preference shares), with a further £1 million in debentures, and was therefore large enough for London to be interested. The issue of the ordinary share capital was three times oversubscribed, but there was less interest in the debentures and preference shares, which were more marginally oversubscribed.[51] The equities opened trading at 1s 6d premium (on 10s called up).[52] The company moved quickly for a stock exchange settlement and London

---

45   Macrosty, *The Trust Movement*, p. 6; M. Blair, *The Paisley Thread Industry and the Men who Created and Developed it: With Notes Concerning Paisley, Old and New* (Paisley, 1907), p. 63.
46   Macrosty, *The Trust Movement*, p. 127.
47   Prospectus: 'Public Companies', *The Times*, 8 August 1890, p. 11.
48   Howe, 'Houldsworth'. In 1877 Houldsworth was chosen to represent the Conservative party alongside Mr Hugh Birley. *The Standard*, 20 June 1877, p. 3.
49   *Pall Mall Gazette*, 15 March 1898.
50   I. Miller and C. Wild, *A & G Murray and the Cotton Mills of Ancoats* (Lancaster, 2007).
51   *Pall Mall Gazette*, 14 May 1898.
52   *Belfast News-Letter*, 1 June 1898.

quotation post issue,[53] but Manchester was the primary market for its financial dealings.[54]

Further issues of uncalled capital and share issues to existing investors allowed the Fine Cotton Spinners' & Doublers' Association combine to expand further. In 1904, an additional preference share issue financed the purchase of the Great Lever Spinning Company in Bolton, the Wingate Spinning Company in Westhoughton and the Lumb Spinning Company in Manchester.[55] In 1911 the company launched a rights issue, underwritten by the directors, to finance the acquisition of cotton plantation facilities in the Mississippi Delta. The early stages of this venture involved some financial assistance and collaboration with Horrockses and the Calico Printers' Association, and reflected some frustration with other sections of the cotton industry who were engaged in apparently wasteful attempts to set up new sources of cotton supply in Africa.[56]

As these investments unfolded utilizing existing pools of investors, the Coats connection underpinned the already developing preference of the Manchester-based Fine Cotton Spinners' & Doublers' Association for Scottish financial links, notwithstanding its initial issue of shares in London. It is noteworthy that all the combines of the trust movement that subsequently featured in the Coats financial network, including the Fine Cotton Spinners' & Doublers' Association, listed Manchester as the primary location of commercial dealings. For Coats, Glasgow was the first listed location, ahead of London.[57] Through its links with London and its financial connections to the other combines, Coats was effectively able to function as an investment banker to the network.

Coats was now in a commanding position and able to influence the other combinations in the merger wave. The first of these was the English Sewing Cotton Company, which floated in 1897. There were no Lords on the board, although there were several Justices of the Peace. In the absence of active connections to London elites, J. & P. Coats acted as a broker for the firm via its London office. Other brokers were listed in Glasgow, Dublin and Manchester. Apart from the Coats holding, most of the interest was from numerous new

---

53 *Pall Mall Gazette*, 23 June 1898. Shares were quoted in London, Manchester, Glasgow, Belfast, Dublin, Bradford and Nottingham. Prospectus, 'The Fine Cotton Spinners' and Doublers' Association, Limited', *The Times*, 7 May 1898, p. 6.

54 *Investors Monthly Manual*, December 1903.

55 'The Fine Cotton Spinners' New Issue', *Financial Times*, 2 March 1904, p. 2.

56 The focus of this critique was the British Cotton Growing Association: 'Fine Cotton Spinners & Doublers', *Financial Times*, 27 May 1911, p. 3; J. E. Robins, *Cotton and Race Across the Atlantic: Britain, Africa, and America, 1900–1920* (Rochester, NY, 2016), p. 260, n. 41.

57 For example, *Investors Monthly Manual*, December 1903, entries for American Thread (p. 755), Calico Printers' Association and J. & P. Coats (p. 759), English Sewing Cotton and Fine Cotton Spinners' & Doublers' Association (p. 761) and other issues, *passim*.

retail investors.[58] The prospectus noted that the company aimed to maintain the trade of the component firms by promoting friendly relationships with other manufacturers. These included J. & P. Coats, which the prospectus noted, had a 'perfectly friendly' attitude and would apply for 200,000 shares in English Sewing Cotton. Constituent firms, which included Edmund Ashworth & Sons, Egerton, near Bolton, and Bagley & Wright, Oldham, had suffered low profits in recent years, not disclosed in the prospectus, as a consequence of 'excessive undercutting'.[59] As early as June 1898, in parallel with speculation about good early profits and dividends, rumours circulated that Coats was interested in purchasing English Sewing Cotton.[60]

Like J. & P. Coats, English Sewing Cotton invested significantly in the USA, acquiring capacity there to avoid import tariffs.[61] In 1900 English Sewing Cotton set up the American Thread Company, in which it owned all the paid-up common stock of the American firm.[62] The firm was, therefore, British in all but name, with preference and debenture stocks quoted in Manchester, reflecting the significant interest of English Sewing Cotton and also of J. & P. Coats.[63] Trading results in the American firm were poor, and as a consequence, it was dependent on loans from English Sewing Cotton, which in turn used a loan from J. & P. Coats, offered at a preferential rate of interest.[64] Shareholders complained that English Sewing Cotton extracted all spare cash from American Thread in the form of dividends.[65] In 1907 the firm ceased to issue balance sheets because these would disclose valuable information to competitors.[66] Immediately before this point, financial performance was poor, with the firm returning only 3.2% on capital in 1905 and 2.7% in 1906.

US diversification, then, did little to assist English Sewing Cotton, notwithstanding the attempt to extract financial resources through dividends. After 1898, the new British combine, including its US subsidiary, could do nothing to resolve the problem of low profitability in its constituent firms. In the period 1898–1914, the firm's average profit was 6.2% compared to 17.0% for J. & P. Coats in the same period. A possible reason was that the English Sewing Cotton had, according to Rose, a cumbersome management structure that typified the

---

58 'English Sewing Cotton Company', *Financial Times*, 9 December 1897, p. 4.
59 Prospectus: 'English Sewing Cotton Company Limited', *The Times*, 2 December 1897, p. 4.
60 *Financial Times*, 14 June 1898, p. 4.
61 'The Thread Combines', *Financial Times*, 2 January 1900, p. 3. On Coats's US involvement, see M. Wilkins, *The History of Foreign Investment in the United States to 1914* (Cambridge, MA, 1989), pp. 361–3.
62 'The American Thread Report', *Financial Times*, 2 July 1902, p. 2.
63 'The Thread Combines', *Financial Times*, 2 January 1900, p. 3.
64 'Dividends and Reports', *Financial Times*, 1 July 1903, p. 2.
65 'American Thread Company', *Financial Times*, 10 May 1907, p. 7. Letter to the editor from a Londonderry debenture and preference shareholder.
66 'American Thread Company', *Financial Times*, 1 July 1907, p. 2.

unsuccessful pre-war holding company model.[67] By 1902 the firm required a financial reconstruction. J. & P. Coats provided a loan at below-market rates, which also allowed English Sewing Cotton to offer a lifeline to its American Thread subsidiary.[68] Coats later took over its overseas and then its domestic operations.[69] Through this process, the dominant position in the distribution node of the value chain, which Coats had established through the Central Thread Agency, was now reinforced through the control of the English Sewing Cotton distribution operation. Although this provided an immediate response to the English Sewing Cotton pre-interest loss of over £150,000 (−3.7% of capital) in 1902 in the form of new capital, subsequent rates of profit remained typically around the long-run average of 6% before 1914.

Another of the combines that soon needed support from the Coats-led financial network was the Calico Printers' Association. Launched in 1899, the Calico Printers' Association reflected the influence of the Houldsworth–Crumm–Thomson network and its historical links with J. & P. Coats. The firm's prospectus was issued 13 December 1899 and Francis Frederick Grafton, of the successor firm to Hargreaves and Dugdale from the mid nineteenth century, was listed as the Chairman. Again, none of the executive or general board were peers. Even so, although there were no elite directors, the firm had the advantage of political and social connections through the Lancashire network. A leading firm in the combine was the Thornliebank Company Ltd, whose Chairman, William Graham Crumm, as noted above, shared business connections with James Thomson and was connected by marriage to the Houldsworth family.[70]

The Calico Printers' Association was a genuinely Lancashire–Glasgow combine. It included thirteen merchants and forty-six printing firms, with twenty-two of the participant firms based in Glasgow and the remaining thirty-seven near Manchester. The firm's registered office was in Manchester and shares were to be traded initially in London, Manchester and Glasgow.[71] The issue was immediately successful, being two times oversubscribed, and the shares traded at a post-issue premium of 4s 9d.

67   Rose, *Firms, Networks and Business Values*, p. 174; J. F. Wilson, *British Business History* (Manchester, 1994), p. 107.

68   'Dividends and Reports', *Financial Times*, 1 July 1903, p. 2.

69   P. L. Cook and R. Cohen, *The Effects of Mergers: Six Studies* (London, 1958), p. 135. Coats controlled the English Sewing Cotton distribution operation and the sale of sewing silk threads on behalf of Messrs Lister & Co. of Bradford; Blair, *The Paisley Thread Industry*.

70   William Graham Crumm's role included acting as trustee for the debentures; see Prospectus: 'The Calico Printers' Association, Limited', *The Times*, 14 December 1899, p. 3.

71   Ibid. Shares at this stage had 7s 6d called up. Total capital issued by the Calico Printers' Association was £8.2 million. The purchase price of the concerns taken over was £8,047,031, with a certified value of £7,693,504, with profits on equity capital (post depreciation) of £355,826 over the previous five years, thus averaging 4.6% of capital excluding goodwill.

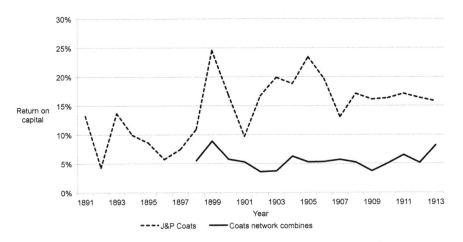

Figure 12. J. & P. Coats and satellite combines, profitability, 1891–1913

Sources: Calculated from CIFD.

Notwithstanding the successful launch of its shares in late 1899, the firm did not perform well financially. Its £1 shares rose to 25s and 26s soon after issue but fell to 14s by September 1900.[72] The firm got into managerial difficulties and was restructured in 1902. A new executive board was formed to rescue the ailing business, including O. E. Philippi of J. & P. Coats, John Stanning of the Bleachers' Association and Frank Hollins of Horrockses Crewdson.[73] A consistent pattern of J. & P. Coats' involvement in financial support and restructuring in the combines is emerging; more will be said about the latter two firms subsequently.

In summary, the story of the merger wave firms considered thus far is of a financial network centred on J. & P. Coats. Coats had been the first firm to raise significant capital in 1891 and used its elite directors and London connections to achieve this. The firm then consolidated its position away from London on its traditional Manchester–Glasgow axis. Coats, through its networked connections, now became a prime mover in the reorganization of significant sections of the industry through the four further new combines: the Fine Cotton Spinners' & Doublers' Association, English Sewing Cotton, American Thread and the Calico Printers' Association.

As the above analysis shows, these satellite firms had prior connections, which they chose to utilize to secure financial resources in preference to seeking out new relationships through London. The new combines had the scale to

72   Cook and Cohen, *The Effects of Mergers*, p. 158.
73   Rose, *Firms, Networks and Business Values*, p. 174.

Table 8. Textile combines, comparative profitability, 1891–1913

	Return on capital employed	
	Average 1891–1897 (%)	Average 1898–1913 (%)
A. J. & P. Coats and general comparatives		
J. & P. Coats	8.97	17.02
Coats network combines: average		5.56
Cotton industry: average	5.94	9.09
B. J. & P. Coats network combines:		
Calico Printers' Association		3.45
English Sewing Cotton		6.16
American Thread		6.05
Fine Cotton Spinners' & Doublers' Association		6.17
C. Other Combines:		
Bleachers' Association		4.97
Horrockses Crewdson	14.37	11.31

Notes: Return on capital employed is defined as profit before interest divided by total long-term capital (ordinary shares plus reserves plus preference shares, debentures, and other long-term loans).

Sources: Calculated from CIFD.

interest London-based intermediaries in new issues potentially, but they lacked the necessary connections. Unlike Coats, their boards did not include elite directors with useful links to the City. Instead, their directors were influential through connections to northern political and civic networks, and in parallel, through connections to a previously evolved Manchester–Glasgow axis under the auspices of J. & P. Coats. Consequently, as the new combines hit financial trouble in the early 1900s, Coats further increased its control of their operations and their capital.

To assess the economic effects of industry restructuring, the return on capital employed was calculated for the relevant firms. Figure 12 shows the return on capital for Coats compared to an aggregate of the four firms that were subsequently invested in by Coats or provided with financial assistance during and after the amalgamation wave of 1897–1900: American Thread, Fine Cotton Spinners' & Doublers' Association, Calico Printers' Association, and English Sewing Cotton. Table 8 shows further comparisons divided into subperiods before and after the merger wave, 1891–97 and 1898–1913, between Coats and an index comprising the British cotton industry generally, the four satellite firms (panel A), the individual performances of those firms (panel B) and returns of other combined firms, Horrockses Crewdson and the Bleachers' Association (panel C).

The figures show that in the period before the merger wave, Coats's profits were adequate but not spectacular. They were ahead of the cotton industry generally, typified by the smaller specialized mills of Lancashire, which were locked into stagnant export markets before 1896.[74] Conversely, they lagged Horrockses, which averaged over 14% returns during this period. After the merger wave, the situation changed radically. At just over 17%, Coats' profits in the 1898–1913 period were substantially higher than any other firm or benchmark, notwithstanding the generally favourable trading conditions, including the spectacular boom enjoyed by the industry generally in the period 1904–07. As Figure 12 shows, the profits of Coats were persistently higher than the other firms in its immediate network and under its close influence. It is undoubtedly the case that the profitability of J. & P. Coats was much higher following the merger wave of 1898–99 than before, while the profitability of all the other firms within the Coats network remained sufficient to keep them afloat, but at the same time stubbornly low (Figure 12). Ricardian rents were, it seemed, extracted by Coats as the dominant firm in the network. The difference in profits between Coats and English Sewing Cotton is illustrative. Given the overarching control of English Sewing Cotton by J. & P. Coats, financially and over its primary source of competitive advantage in distribution, and the similarity of their activities otherwise, the superior profitability of J. & P. Coats may well have reflected nothing more than its dominance within the financial network.

The network of interlocking directors emanating from Coats had a central-izing effect on the control of the sector,[75] and the connections of all four of these firms extended the power of a relatively small number of individuals across an essential segment of the industry. Manchester and Glasgow were the focal points of the network, with London excluded.

Other combines: Horrockses and the Bleachers' Association

As discussed earlier, the rescue of the Calico Printers' Association by Coats in alliance with representatives of two other combines effectively widened the network further to include Horrockses Crewdson and the Bleachers' Association. Significantly, unlike the other combines discussed earlier, although

74 Toms, 'Windows of opportunity'.
75 Rose, *Firms, Networks and Business Values*, p. 174.

associated with Coats, they were not dependent upon the Scottish combine. It is, therefore, appropriate to analyse the evolution of these firms separately to trace the reasons for their preferences in voluntarily assisting the Coats-led network.

Frank Hollins' choice to join in the Coats network was significant as it signalled a new stage in Horrockses progressive move away from London and reorientation to its northern network. Horrockses had initially expanded from its Preston base by setting up an associated partnership in London. The partnership was structured so that the Horrocks family and their associates retained control, and in 1860, following retirements and deaths of other partners, Thomas Miller became the sole proprietor.[76] Frank Hollins, who later emerged as the chief executive, had previously been a partner at Sovereign Cotton Mill, Preston. Both of these companies also had offices in London and Manchester.[77]

The Horrockses merger began two years earlier in 1885 when the unincorporated Preston firm Horrockses, Miller & Co. reached an arrangement with the adjoining firm of Hollins Brothers, creating the largest cotton firm in the country.[78] A subsequent amalgamation in 1887 brought together the existing partners of Horrockses, Miller & Co. and the members of the Bolton firm Crewdson Crosses & Co. (Limited).[79] Hence no new shares were issued to the public. The chairman was Mr F. Styles and the board members with responsibility for the Preston mills were Frank Hollins, Sidney A. Hermon, S. O. Hermon and W. W. Galloway. The Manchester branch of the business was controlled by Isaac Crewdson Waterhouse and Alfred Crewdson, the Bolton mills by Edward and then Carlton Cross, and the London interest by W. B. Secretan.[80] The directors of the company consisted therefore entirely of local business leaders with specialist knowledge of the Preston, Manchester and Bolton branches of the firm.

Essentially a series of amalgamations, in which pre-existing independent businesses achieved some continuity in the merged firm, the Horrockses mergers thus had much in common with strategic amalgamations of partnerships of the early and mid nineteenth century, discussed in chapters 1 and 2. The scale of the Horrockses operation, however, meant that this model now needed adapting, such that the new board was the representative of the component firms. As a consequence, in its board structure at least, Horrockses had much in common

76 'Messrs. Horrockses, Crewdson, and Co. and the Cotton Manufacture', *Manchester Times*, 25 November 1892.
77 *Preston Guardian*, 8 June 1878.
78 'Messrs. Horrockses, Crewdson, and Co. and the Cotton Manufacture', *Manchester Times*, 25 November 1892.
79 *The Standard*, 29 April 1887, p. 6. Both companies had offices in London and Manchester.
80 A. C. Howe, 'Sir Frank Hollins', *Dictionary of Business Biography*, ed. D. Jeremy (London, 1984–86), vol. 3, pp. 313–17.

with the larger combinations that followed. The combination meant that what was already Britain's largest cotton-manufacturing firm after the 1885 merger, now became even more significant, with a capital of £773,000.

Hollins focused his business strategy on mitigating the firm's dependence on London. Most notably this approach included the construction of a new warehouse in Manchester. An important reason for the investment was that Hollins considered the London staff, inherited from the 1887 merger, to be unreliable.[81] To further assist its marketing operation, the firm invested heavily in brands. In parallel to the development of the selling and retail capacity, production was also expanded with the construction of the new Centenary Mill (completed in 1896) and the acquisition of the Fishwick Mills through the absorption of the Swainson Birley partnership in 1900.[82] The main problem faced by this new, vertically integrated combine was the difficulty of selling into remote and challenging markets, in particular, Latin America. The firm had to rely on London agents to do this, notwithstanding the investment in Manchester, and this proved expensive.[83]

Even so, the preference for brands over standard contracts was generally a successful one for Horrockses. Before the combinations of the late 1890s, it was the most profitable of the merged firms, earning almost twice the average rate of return on its assets compared with J. & P. Coats (Table 8). It is noteworthy that it was only after the merger wave of the late 1890s that Coats became an industry leader in terms of its profitability, superseding Horrockses. Even so, Horrockses remained a robust financial performer compared to the other combines.

As the firm accumulated capital, the scope of its activities widened through selected investments in other businesses. These included the British Cotton Growing Association and the British Northrop Loom Company.[84] In short, then, the emergence of the Horrockses combine was based on the centralization of production assets in the north. A more diverse, brand-oriented distribution network was also controlled from Lancashire as far as possible. With the accumulation of capital, Horrockses built financial connections through investments in other firms, including in 1902, the Calico Printers' Association.

The final prominent firm in the network that evolved as a consequence of the trust movement was the Bleachers' Association. An executive board led the Association, chaired by Herbert Shepherd Cross. As the MP for Bolton and

---

81   Ibid., p. 315.

82   S. Toms, 'The profitability of the first Lancashire merger: The case of Horrocks, Crewdson & Co. Ltd, 1887–1905', *Textile History* 24 (1993), 129–46, at p. 135.

83   S. D. Chapman, *Merchant Enterprise in Britain* (Cambridge, 2004), pp. 200, 304–5.

84   In addition, Hollins was a director of the Manchester & County Bank, the London & North Western Railway and a supporter of the Manchester Ship Canal. Howe, 'Sir Frank Hollins', pp. 315–16.

Chairman of Thomas Cross & Co. Bolton, Cross complemented the dominant political and business interests of Horrockses in Preston and Bolton. Cross now became Chairman of the Bleachers' Association, a combine of fifty-three concerns. Remaining members of the executive or general boards were made up of representatives drawn from the Association's constituent mills.[85] Its prospectus was issued in July 1900 and applications closed on 25 July. According to the prospectus, its registered office was to be in Manchester and its shares to be traded in London, Manchester, and Glasgow. The share issue was not a success and, as a consequence, the vendors took up the ordinary shares.[86] As a result, the firm had few residual connections through London but continued to grow its connections in the north and more firms applied to join the combine after the first issue.[87] The consequence was steady, if unspectacular, profits for the new combination (Table 8).

In summary, the trust movement had a significant effect on the structure of an essential part of the textile industry. The evolution of the network, through technical collaborations, but more substantively through financial connections, resulted in an interconnected system of nominally independent businesses. The controlling network was firmly centred on Lancashire, particularly Manchester (through Horrockses, the Bleachers' and the Fine Cotton Spinners' & Doublers' Association) and Scotland (through J. & P. Coats), but not London. Indeed, once floated, and even on flotation in some cases, there is little evidence that these new textile giants caught the imagination of the London investor. The consolidation of Horrockses in Manchester and Preston, the failure of the Bleachers' issue and the bailout of the Calico Printers' Association reinforced the independence of the Manchester–Scotland axis from London finance. By 1902 the key firms and substantial capital were controlled by a relatively small group of connected individuals. Coats was the dominant firm, in terms of its physical scale as a multinational conglomerate, but also in terms of its network influence. Unlike the other firms, the Coats board featured several directors who were members of the aristocratic elite and enjoyed international connections.

For the other dominant firms in the group, particularly the Manchester-centred group of Horrockses, the Bleachers' and the Fine Cotton Spinners' & Doublers' Association, political connections were meaningful and were exercised through the Conservative party. In the case of Horrockses, as noted earlier, political connections were established by previous generations

85 Prospectus: 'Bleachers' Association, Limited', *The Times*, 23 July 1900, p. 6. Cross was a partner in Thomas Cross & Co. of Mortfield Bleach Works, Bolton. J. J. Mason, 'Herbert Shepherd Cross', *Dictionary of Business Biography*, ed. D. Jeremy (London, 1984–86), vol. 1, pp. 845–6.
86 'Bleachers' Association. I.', *Manchester Courier and Lancashire General Advertiser*, 31 August 1901, p. 5.
87 *Glasgow Herald*, 22 August 1900.

of partners in the composite firms.[88] John Kynaston Cross, of what became Horrockses Crewdson, was Tory MP for Bolton, and Herbert Shepherd Cross of the Bleachers' Association served as one of the town's MPs from 1885 to 1906.[89] William Henry Houldsworth of the Fine Cotton Spinners' & Doublers' Association served as Tory MP for Manchester.[90]

The Manchester–Glasgow axis described by these interconnected firms was easily the largest and most powerful network. There were, however, similar if smaller networks. Like English Sewing Cotton, United Turkey Red attracted significant investment from Scotland and had strong links with Lancashire. It was successfully launched soon afterwards, in 1898, raising £1.5 million through private subscription.[91] United Turkey Red combined three firms in the Vale of Leven, centred on Dumbarton: Archibald Orr Ewing & Co., John Orr Ewing & Co. and William Stirling & Co.[92] United Turkey Red opened a branch at Manchester as red yarn merchants in c.1880.[93] The only large firm outside the main Calico Printers' Association and United Turkey Red combines was Accrington-based F. Steiner & Co. Ltd, which had its advantages in terms of process innovation in Turkey Red dyeing, patents and scale in its distribution network.[94] As noted in chapter 2, Lancashire firms like Thomson & Chippendall had played an essential role in developing the Turkey Red process.

The characteristic feature of all these networks was their orientation to technical processes, usually patentable, or applied to design through copyright, and the finishing process, with its associated scale economies. Notwithstanding technical collaborations, by the end of the nineteenth century, financial ties were the dominant feature of these networked combinations.

Conclusions

The network preferences of the orchestrators of the combinations reviewed in the evidence presented above can be summarized as follows. Technical collaborations, underpinned by family connections, were the rationale for developing and extending networks up to the mid nineteenth century. The

---

88   John Horrocks was elected Tory MP for Preston in 1802, which coincided with his brother Samuel becoming local Chief Magistrate, who then succeeded John as MP. John Kynaston Cross, MP for Bolton, 1874–75 and Under-Secretary for India, 1883–85. 'Messrs. Horrockses, Crewdson, and Co. and the Cotton Manufacture', *Manchester Times*, 25 November 1892; 9 December 1892.

89   Mason, 'Herbert Shepherd Cross', pp. 845–6.

90   Hollins later became a baronet (in 1907); Howe, 'Sir Frank Hollins'.

91   'Scotch Industrial Notes', *Financial Times*, 15 January 1898, p. 5.

92   *Financial Times*, 1 November 1897, p. 3.

93   *The Scottish Commercial List* (London, 1880–81).

94   Cook and Cohen, *Effects of Mergers*, p. 152; on the Steiner process, see E. Knecht and J. B. Fothergill, *The Principles and Practice of Textile Printing* (London, 1912).

control of these embryonic production and distribution networks, as shown in chapter 2, resulted in impressive financial returns for the firms in the central nodes. With the consequent accumulation of capital, these networks extended through diversification into textile-related activities, but also banks, railways and overseas interests. Scale economies in distribution provided the rationale for the amalgamations of the late nineteenth century.

Prior accumulations of capital and pre-existing network connections limited the dependence of these amalgamated firms on the London capital markets. J. & P. Coats, with its elite connections, might have fallen back on London, had the need arisen. In practice, through the preferences of firms that were less financially successful, it headed a network based on the regional financial centres of Manchester and Glasgow. Given the scale of the mergers, the general absence of involvement by London finance is, at first sight, surprising.

However, the long-run evolution of the networks, as described in the evidence above, illustrates the reasons for the orientation of the associated combined firms to the regions. Indeed, the centralization of production and ownership networks around these regional centres had a long history, borne out of technical collaborations; design-led production, high profitability and capital accumulation within connected family networks and regional financial markets. The separation that appeared between London and the regions had long-run consequences, particularly after 1920, when regional financial structures experienced systemic failure. We return to this theme in chapter 7.

The networked capitalism that emerged in the long nineteenth century defies description as purely family, managerial or financial capitalism, although in certain respects it combined all these features. In doing so, the leading firms in the networks combined innovative investment with financial amalgamation that resulted in large profits. To some extent, these profits came at the expense of the less successful, bailed-out firms whose activities were sustained by the Coats-led financial colossus. The Coats-led network used its dominance in distribution to control more extensive networks that included upstream producers. In doing so, it anticipated features of industrial structure that were to become more widespread by the late twentieth century. In this later period, the success and survival of fabric and textile manufacturers came to depend on the allocation of sufficient margin by retail giants.[95]

95 S. Toms and Q. Zhang, 'Marks & Spencer and the Decline of the British Textile Industry, 1950–2000', *BHR* 90 (2016), 3–30.

PART II: APOGEE AND DECLINE

6

Entrepreneurs, Technology and
Industrial Organization

The attitude of Lancashire manufacturers towards novelties is decidedly
sceptical. Each wants to see the new thing well tested by somebody else before
he tries it. Six years ago the average small manufacturer regarded anyone who
approached him to urge the adoption of a new kind of machine with pity. He
looked upon you as a crank, a person with a 'bee in his bonnet', and if you
tried to argue with him he would not listen to your reasons, but would, as
likely as not, turn on his heel and leave you talking. But now there is a great
change. Now such a man will listen to you – for a moderate time – and say
that no doubt your invention is 'bound to come', although he himself will
not, except in rare cases, do anything to assist its coming.

An anonymous English inventor, c.1903.[1]

In 1903, following a tour of the cotton manufacturing districts of the USA,
Thomas Young wrote an extensive account contrasting the positive and negative
attitudes of American and Lancashire entrepreneurs towards new technology.
No doubt, some Lancashire entrepreneurs displayed these attitudes. However,
the expansion of the Lancashire textile industry up to 1914 was not based on the
investment decisions of a stereotypical entrepreneur. Instead, as previous chapters
have shown, different types of entrepreneur created and became embedded in
different models of industrial organization. Perhaps their only common feature
was, like entrepreneurs anywhere, they straddled multiple organizations and
institutions. The early cotton entrepreneurs transformed prior business structures
to operate in multiple partnership networks, which often extended to important
infrastructure development projects. Elsewhere in Lancashire, the exclusion of
the operative class from the political process and the alienation of the Factory
System led to a new wave of social enterprise founded on the principles of
co-operation. In parallel, the locally financed enterprises of the earlier phases
of the industrial revolution evolved into multi-business and multi-plant enterprises, and the giant trusts of the early twentieth century.

---

1   T. M. Young, *The American Cotton Industry: A Study of Work and Workers* (New York,
1903), p. 140.

Such diversity alone should caution against blanket accusations of entrepreneurial failure. It is undoubtedly true that Lancashire faced pressure from overseas competition after 1870. However, this was nothing new. As chapter 3 has shown, some mill owners wheeled out the threat of foreign competition whenever legislators raised the prospect of restrictive legislation. After 1870, the lobbying traditions of Ashworth and Greg were continued through the political activities of cotton industrialists such as Edward Tootal Broadhurst and writers such as Thomas Ellison.[2] During trade depressions, including the protracted downturn of the early 1890s, these authors highlighted the adverse impact of protection in export markets, but the superiority of British products in 'open markets' was strongly emphasized.[3] These arguments were reinforced after the industry recovered from the traumas of the 1890s, and a new wave of mill building began.[4] Notions of failure and decline were generally absent from the accounts of those writing before the First World War.

Subsequently, however, Lancashire has borne the full brunt of the declinist narrative. Two general trends inform this story. The first is that Lancashire entrepreneurs should have emulated the methods of their competitors, most notably, the US Fordist industrial model as advocated by Alfred Chandler, but failed to do so. The second, which is a critique of the first, is that entrepreneurs were entirely rational in the face of changes in the world market, making appropriate investments as the industry grew and divestments as it contracted. In this liberal, free trade characterization, entrepreneurs could only really be criticized for not divesting quickly enough. Had they followed the advice of Chandler and others, and adopted the Fordist model, this would only have made matters worse. In the event, they did not adopt it and can be rehabilitated, at least for failing to follow bad advice.

Even so, for many historians, the cotton industry symbolized Britain's more comprehensive shortcomings as a manufacturing nation. For some, this failure had nineteenth-century origins.[5] Entrepreneurs generally, and Lancashire entrepreneurs, in particular, became technologically conservative. Their attitudes

2   P. F. Clarke, *Lancashire and the new Liberalism* (Cambridge, 2007). T. Ellison, *The Cotton Trade of Great Britain: Including a History of the Liverpool Cotton Market and of the Liverpool Cotton Brokers' Association* (London, 1886), p. 113.

3   Examples include: ibid., p. 116; R. Marsden, 'Optimistic views of the cotton trade', *Textile Mercury*, 15 April 1893, pp. 275–6, at p. 275; S. J. Chapman, 'The report of the tariff commission', *Economic Journal* 15 (1905), 420–7, at p. 420.

4   Ellison, *Cotton Trade of Great Britain*; G. von Schulze-Gaevernitz, *The Cotton Trade in England and on the Continent* (London, 1895); S. J. Chapman, *The Lancashire Cotton Industry: A Study in Economic Development* (Manchester, 1904); see also, D. Farnie, 'Three Historians of the Cotton Industry: Thomas Ellison, Gerhart von Schulze-Gaevernitz, and Sydney Chapman', *Textile History* 9 (1978), 75–89.

5   For example, B. Elbaum and W. Lazonick, eds, *The Decline of the British Economy* (Oxford, 1987). W. Lazonick, *Business Organization and the Myth of the Market Economy* (Cambridge, 1993).

manifested as 'iron-clad arguments against re-equipment'.[6] In cotton, the self-acting mule, which had revolutionized spinning productivity after 1830, now became the 'stubborn' mule, as other nations developed alternative production methods. Failure to make similar changes in Lancashire has provided many critics with an obvious explanation for the failures of the industry.[7] In spinning, this meant effectively replacing mule spindles with ring spindles, and in weaving, replacing power looms with automatic looms. In contrast to developing industries in competitor countries, most notably Japan and the USA, Lancashire entrepreneurs tended to retain mules and power looms.[8]

The issue of technology has perhaps been the loudest metaphor of all for the mistakes of Lancashire. With the advent of 'new economic' history, or the use of applied economics techniques to investigate historical issues, entrepreneurial failure, and associated technological conservatism, was initially called into question.[9] Subsequently, a series of interpretations readdressed the evidence concerning the additional issue of industry 'constraints', namely the rise of vertical specialization and the structure of labour relations.[10] These issues have dominated recent debates. Since the early 1990s, economic historians have re-examined aspects of entrepreneurial failure in cotton textiles, with particular reference to the issue of technological choice and alleged conservatism. In general, recent evidence from the economic history literature has supported the rehabilitation of Lancashire entrepreneurs. For example, Leunig shows that in Lancashire mule spinning was more productive and entrepreneurs' choices were therefore rational.[11] Saxonhouse and Wright show that decisive improvements in

6   D. C. Coleman and C. MacLeod, 'Attitudes to new techniques: British businessmen, 1800–1950', EcHR 39 (1986), 588–611, at p. 589.

7   For an early exposition of this view, see Young, The American Cotton Industry, p. 137; for later views of technological conservatism, see G. R. Saxonhouse and G. Wright, 'Stubborn mules and vertical integration: The disappearing constraint?', EcHR 40 (1987), 87–94; W. Lazonick, 'The cotton industry', The Decline of the British Economy, ed. B. Elbaum and W. Lazonick (Oxford, 1987), pp. 18–50; and W. Lazonick, 'Stubborn mules: Some comments', EcHR 40 (1987), 80–6.

8   D. H. Aldcroft, 'The entrepreneur and the British Economy', EcHR 17 (1964), 113–34. D. Landes, The Unbound Prometheus: Technological Change and Industrial Development in Western Europe from 1750 to the Present (Cambridge, 1969). D. McCloskey and L. Sandberg, 'From Damnation to Redemption: judgements on the late Victorian entrepreneur', Explorations in Economic History 9 (1972), 89–108. L. Sandberg, Lancashire in Decline: A Study in Entrepreneurship, Technology, and International Trade (Columbus, OH, 1974).

9   McCloskey and Sandberg, 'From Damnation to Redemption', pp. 102–3; Sandberg, Lancashire in Decline.

10   For a summary, see W. Mass and W. Lazonick, 'The British cotton industry and international competitive advantage: The state of the debates', BH 32 (1990), 9–65.

11   T. Leunig, 'New answers to old questions: Explaining the slow adoption of ring spinning in Lancashire, 1880–1913', JEH 61 (2001), 439–66. T. Leunig, 'A British industrial success: Productivity in the Lancashire and New England cotton spinning industries a century ago', EcHR 56 (2003), 90–117.

preparatory technology, in particular the Casablancas company's high drafting method, meant the mule lost its advantage on finer counts, but only from the 1920s onwards.[12] These studies confirm the view that Lancashire entrepreneurs made rational decisions in terms of their choice of technology.[13] They also tend to relocate the search for entrepreneurial failure in the 1920s rather than in the late Victorian era.

How significant was this alleged conservatism and did entrepreneurs make rational choices? Connected is the second issue, industry structure. Because the spinning and weaving branches of the industry were specialized, industry structure created a barrier to the technical challenges of re-equipment.[14] The third issue, which transcends the first three, is the pattern of entrepreneurs' behaviour, particularly their methods of accessing funds for investment, and their apparent preference for distribution and consumption over reinvestment of profits.[15] Such criticisms have been applied to entrepreneurs generally. In Lancashire in particular, a variant on this theme is that entrepreneurs were indeed rational before 1914, but the path dependency of their investment decisions immediately after the First World War, in the face of market dislocations which proved permanent, resulted in misalignment of firms and financial institutions.[16] Taken together, these issues, and their interpretation thus far in the literature, suggests that entrepreneurs failed on several levels and were culpable for the long-term collapse of a once-great industry.

These dominant accounts have effaced somewhat the possibility of alternative narratives. We have already noted the diverse character of entrepreneurship across Lancashire and beyond. It seems reasonably obvious to assume that some business leaders were more ready than others to implement technological and organizational innovations, and that they did so quite rationally. In general, the declinist narrative applied to cotton correlates performance with

12   The Casablancas High Draft Co. Ltd was set up in Manchester in 1925. G. R. Saxonhouse and G. Wright, 'National leadership and competing technological paradigms: the globalization of cotton spinning, 1878–1933', *JEH* 70 (2010), 535–66.

13   S. Toms, 'Growth, profits and technological choice: The case of the Lancashire cotton textile industry', *Journal of Industrial History* 1 (1998), 35–55.

14   For the main interpretations, see Sandberg, *Lancashire in Decline*; W. Lazonick, 'Competition, Specialization and Industrial Decline', *JEH* 31 (1981), 31–8. W. Lazonick, 'Factor costs and the diffusion of ring spinning prior to World War One', *Quarterly Journal of Economics* 96 (1981), 89–109. W. Lazonick, 'Industrial organization and technological change: The decline of the British cotton industry', *BHR* 58 (1983), 195–236. Saxonhouse and Wright, 'Stubborn mules and vertical integration'; Mass and Lazonick 'The British Cotton Industry'.

15   Aldcroft, 'The entrepreneur and the British Economy'. These issues have been the subject of wider debates regarding the British economy, including the sociological aspects of entrepreneurial failure. See M. Weiner, *English Culture and the Decline of the Industrial Spirit, 1850–1980* (London, 1981); and for a critique, see W. Rubinstein, *Capitalism, Culture, and Decline: 1750–1990* (London, 1993).

16   D. Higgins and S. Toms, *British Cotton Textiles: Maturity and Decline* (London, 2017).

market share, making the observed decline a function of capacity installation in newly industrializing overseas competitors. Such a relationship is, however, predominantly mathematical and devoid of empirical richness regarding the efficiency, or otherwise, of the Lancashire textile industry.

With these contextual issues in mind, the chapter revisits the debate on entrepreneurial failure and reassesses the view that a failure of leadership in the late Victorian period caused the subsequent protracted decline of the industry. Such a reassessment is necessarily coloured by the distinct patterns of entrepreneurship documented in previous chapters. Did all types of entrepreneur make the same mistakes concerning technology and industry structure? If not, how successful were those who adopted alternative technologies and business structures? To answer these questions requires some scrutiny of investment decisions and their financial outcomes. These are evaluated using financial evidence from the firms involved. Firm-specific evidence is reviewed and cases are examined of firms adopting new technologies in ring spinning and automatic weaving. The relative profitability and productivity of these firms are then considered. A further comparison is conducted between horizontally specialized and vertically integrated firms. It shows that, notwithstanding the criticisms of economists and some contemporaries, Lancashire did adopt new technology when and where appropriate, and only failed to do so more generally because of the sudden paralysis arising from the exogenous shock occasioned by the loss of export markets in the 1920s.

Technological change in the late nineteenth century

Before examining entrepreneurial decision-making, it is worth sketching the development of competing technologies in cotton manufacture during the second half of the nineteenth century and their pattern of diffusion in Lancashire. As will be demonstrated, these path dependencies had significant impacts on decisions to adopt new technology. Established models of production, the characteristics of required labour and associated cost structures explain the pattern of adoption and experimentation in specific businesses.

In weaving, the power loom supplanted the handloom and the domestic system most decisively in the 1840s. There were no significant alternatives to the power-loom model until 1894 with the development of the Northrop automatic loom. Such technology meant that weft could be reloaded onto shuttles without stopping the loom, thereby allowing an operative to supervise more than the four looms that became standard in power-loom weaving.[17] Although there

---

17   E. M. Gray, *The Weaver's Wage: Earnings and Collective Bargaining in the Lancashire Cotton Weaving Industry* (Manchester, 1937), p. 33. The manufacturer claimed that the weaver using

were earlier experiments, the Northrop automatic loom was only commercially available in Lancashire from 1903 onwards, mainly on the patented terms of the American parent company, following the establishment of the British Northrop Loom Company.[18] Crucially in spinning, alternatives evolved earlier and therefore presented different entrepreneurial opportunities. As will become apparent, the adoption of automatic weaving depended to some degree on parallel investment in ring spinning. It is, therefore, the decision to invest in ring spinning that is scrutinized first.

In spinning, two methods developed in parallel from the inception of mechanized manufacture. Arkwright's water frame was a system of continuous spinning, which, as explained in chapter 2, became more generally known as throstle spinning. The development of the self-acting mule in the early 1830s meant that the intermittent mule-spinning system became increasingly dominant, but still coexisted with continuous throstle spinning. The latter method was favoured from the outset by firms producing durable, even yarns.[19]

Ring spinning emerged in the mid nineteenth century as an alternative method of continuous spinning. The ring-spinning system had been developed initially and was later widely adopted in the USA. The US patent of John Thorp was adopted and patented in England within six months by George William Lee in 1829.[20] The first Lancashire experiment in ring spinning occurred in 1833–34, but the results were disappointing. Lancashire entrepreneurs already committed to continuous spinning methods, for example, in the Rochdale area, therefore turned their attention to improvements in throstle spinning. Through mechanisms to increase driving speed and reduce vibration, adaptation of this technology achieved similar efficiency improvements when compared to the ring-spinning system.[21]

Notwithstanding the relatively early date of patent registration in the USA, the ring spindle did not achieve a decisive breakthrough until about four decades later. The new Sawyer and Rabbeth spindles facilitated greater revolutions per minute, for example, by self-lubrication, resulting in higher engine efficiency.[22]

Northrop automatic looms could be up to eight times more productive than the plain loom weaver: British Northrop Loom Company, *Northrop Labour Saving Looms: A brief Treatise on Weaving and Northrop Looms*, 3rd edn (Blackburn, 1905), p. 10.

18   S. B. Saul, 'The engineering industry', *The Development of British Industry and Foreign Competition, 1875–1914*, ed. D. Aldcroft (London, 1968), pp. 186–237, at p. 195.

19   Mule spinning was intermittent, with twist inserted only on the outward movement of a wheeled carriage. For a more detailed explanation, see Sandberg, *Lancashire in Decline*, pp. 18–20; J. Nasmith, *Students' Cotton Spinning* (Manchester, 1896), p. 501.

20   D. J. Jeremy, *Transatlantic Industrial Revolution: The Diffusion of Textile Technologies between Britain and America, 1790–1830s* (Cambridge, MA, 1981), pp. 214 and 243.

21   'Ring spinning and its development', *Rochdale Observer*, 21 December 1889, 4 January 1890.

22   T. R. Navin, *The Whitin Machine Works since 1831: A Textile Machinery Company in an Industrial Village*, vol. 15 (Cambridge, MA, 1950), pp. 191–3.

These developments now resulted in rapid adoption in the USA from the 1870s and a significant shift to rings from mules.[23]

In Lancashire too, entrepreneurs began to express interest in ring spinning, once these improvements had been recognized. During the 1870s, competing claims on technology patents began to circulate for the Booth-Sawyer, and later, the more efficient Rabbeth or gravity spindle. Representatives of capital equipment manufacturers, notably Howard & Bullough of Accrington, were the first to make moves to acquire patents along with rival machine-makers, Samuel Brooks of Manchester.[24] Both firms made several visits to the USA, and they returned enthused about the ring spindle and impressed by its operation. Perhaps the most crucial visit was by Howard & Bullough representatives in 1872 since it resulted in the acquisition of patents for the Booth-Sawyer, and the commencement of commercial production using ring frames in 1874.[25] From the 1880s, based on the similar spinning method, the ring was able to supplant the throstle due to its higher speed, as facilitated by the use of a 'traveller' to guide the yarn onto the bobbin.[26] Ring spindles and throstles were both limited by driving speed and the delay and expense associated with removing, or 'doffing' the full bobbins.[27]

Entrepreneurs in spinning firms then faced not one but two technological alternatives. Thus far, the literature has only addressed the first choice, the replacement of mules by rings, and accusations of entrepreneurial failure in Lancashire rest on there being so few cases of such replacements. The second, more limited choice was to replace only throstles with rings. As the evidence presented below illustrates, Lancashire adopted rings typically where throstle spinning had previously prevailed.[28] Such a pattern of development is crucial for two reasons. First, it offers a path-dependent, technological explanation of entrepreneurial behaviour that otherwise might be interpreted as irrational. Second, the emergence of some ring-spinning companies in Lancashire after 1880 provides an opportunity to contrast the profitability of ring and mule spinning and reassess the investment decisions of entrepreneurs accordingly.

23 G. R. Saxonhouse and G. Wright, 'Rings and Mules around the World', *Research in Economic History* Supplement 3 (1984), 271–300, at p. 289.
24 *Rochdale Observer*, 4 January 1890. W. S. Murphy, *The Textile Industries: A Practical Guide to Fibres Yarns and Fabrics*, vol. 3 (London, 1910), p. 75, refers to the visit of James Blakey, the representative of Samuel Brooks, but not the others, which occurred approximately contemporaneously.
25 M. Williams and D. Farnie, *Cotton Mills in Greater Manchester* (Lancaster, 1992), p. 44; D. Farnie, *The English Cotton Industry and the World Market, 1815–1896* (Oxford, 1979), pp. 229–31. *Rochdale Observer*, 4 January 1890, p. 6; 28 June 1890, p. 4.
26 M. Copeland, 'Technical development in cotton manufacturing since 1860', *Quarterly Journal of Economics* 24 (1909), 109–59, at p. 122.
27 Murphy, *The Textile Industries*, vol. 3, p. 71.
28 *Textile Recorder*, 13 May 1897, attributed the spread of ring spinning in Rochdale to the previous tradition of throstle spinning; see also *Cotton Factory Times*, 26 March 1897.

The Oldham district, which included Rochdale, provides a valuable opportunity to examine these issues further. One interpretation of the diffusion of
textile technology suggests the division of the market as an important determinant. Certainly, ring spinning was particularly useful for the production of
coarser yarns and was widely adopted throughout the world by companies
spinning counts of below 40s.[29] It also developed actively in the Rochdale area,
which had traditionally relied on wool and worsted but, with the emergence
of the cotton industry, increasingly specialized in flannels and flannelettes, the
latter being introduced in 1883.[30]

All of these fabrics were conducive to the use of the continuous spinning
method. In the Rochdale area, there had been an established tradition of using
throstle spinning for producing the coarser warp yarns that were required.[31]
Nearby Oldham, the centre of the British coarse trade, and, dependent on Platt
Brothers for machinery supply, was notable for its retention of the mule,[32] and
greater specialization in coarser counts.[33] At the subregional level, product
specialization was increasing and not just in mule spinning. As specialization
grew, fostered by the development of the cotton and yarn markets in Liverpool
and Manchester, naturally, there were also niches available for ring spinners.[34]

Strong regional path dependency explained the establishment of the first
ring-spinning mills in the Rochdale area and so too did the tradition of
co-operative ownership. One of the early pioneers in producer co-operatives,
Samuel Tweedale, introduced in chapter 4, now turned his attention to the introduction and dissemination of ring spinning. To do this effectively, Tweedale
exploited his connections with capital equipment manufacturer John Bullough
(1837–91), of Howard & Bullough.[35] As part of his managerial role within the
firm, Tweedale had sent a relative on the visit to America in 1872 and, from

29 Sandberg, *Lancashire in Decline*, p. 59.

30 Williams and Farnie, *Cotton Mills in Greater Manchester*, p. 44.

31 Toms, 'Growth, profits and technological choice'.

32 F. Jones, 'The cotton spinning industry in the Oldham district from 1896–1914' (MA dissertation, University of Manchester, 1959), p. 18; D. Farnie, 'The emergence of Victorian Oldham
as the centre of the cotton spinning industry', *Saddleworth Historical Society Bulletin* 12 (1982),
41–53, at p. 49.

33 S. Toms, 'The finance and growth of the Lancashire cotton textile industry, 1870–1914' (Ph.D.
dissertation, University of Nottingham, 1996), in chapter 3, shows that for a sample of continuously trading Oldham firms, the average count fell from 37.2 to 34.4 between 1891 and 1913.

34 In contrast to Oldham as a whole, the wider industry had begun to shift to finer counts.
E. Helm, 'The alleged decline of the British cotton industry', *Economic Journal* 2 (1892), 735–44,
at p. 739; A. Marrison, 'Great Britain and her rivals in the Latin American cotton piece-goods
market, 1880–1914', *Great Britain and her World, 1750–1914*, ed. B. Radcliffe (Manchester, 1975),
pp. 308–48, at p. 309; 'Finer counts in Oldham and what they are indicative of', *Textile Mercury*,
16 August 1890.

35 *Rochdale Observer*, 4 January 1890; R. Kirk, 'John Bullough', *Dictionary of Business
Biography*, ed. D. Jeremy (London, 1984–86), vol. 1, p. 502.

then on, was closely involved in the new wave of ring-spinning experiments in Lancashire.

The first experiment took place at Bright Brothers, where Tweedale was mill manager, probably in 1876. A year later, Tweedale became an inaugural director of the New Ladyhouse Cotton Spinning Co. Ltd. Registered on 26 April 1877, it was the first British company dedicated to the new, improved methods of ring spinning.[36] It was a vertically specialized spinning mill on a single-storey shed pattern which replaced an older mill that had previously burned down. This contrasted with the multistoried construction of mule mills, encouraged by more expensive land in the Oldham and Manchester areas. In the New Ladyhouse Mill and similar cases in the Rochdale area, lower land prices explain the use of single-storey shed-style construction.[37] Subsequent investments at the same location in the early 1880s saw the establishment of Haugh and New Hey Mills.[38] The mills were in the township of Milnrow, south-east of Rochdale and north-west of Oldham, which collectively became known as the 'Milnrow Ring Spinners'.

The small, but highly significant Milnrow firms operated in a geographically concentrated cluster. They shared the cross-directorship structure increasingly typical of the industry elsewhere. Like the partnerships of the early nineteenth century, business groups formed, this time modified by the adoption of limited liability characteristics.[39] A good example was James Heap (1828–92). A local man, as were all the other directors and shareholders, he was chairman of all three Milnrow ring-spinning companies until his death in 1892. Like his collaborator John Bullough in Accrington, he was prominent in the Conservative party and as the principal employer, a dominant figure in the locality,[40] although mostly unrecognized in histories of the industry. In a way, this is surprising, particularly given the general assertion noted earlier of Lancashire's dogged adherence to mule spinning.[41] Because ring mills were

---

36 New Ladyhouse Cotton Spinning Co. Ltd, Financial Records, Memorandum and Articles of Association. Samuel Tweedale was an inaugural director of the New Ladyhouse Spinning Company; 'Milnrow Ring Spinning Companies', *Rochdale Observer*, 28 June 1890, p. 4.

37 Leunig, 'New answers to old questions'. New Ladyhouse Mill was subsequently emulated by larger ring mills, notably Cromer (1906), *Rochdale Observer*, 28 June 1890, p. 4; Williams and Farnie, *Cotton Mills in Greater Manchester*, p. 44; Farnie, *English Cotton*, p. 230.

38 New Ladyhouse Cotton Spinning Co. Ltd, Financial Records, Memorandum and Articles of Association; 'Milnrow Ring Spinning Companies', *Rochdale Observer*, 28 June 1890, p. 4.

39 Ibid. Similar loose structures were beginning to emerge elsewhere in Lancashire, for example the so-called 'Bunting group'; D. Farnie, 'John Bunting', *Dictionary of Business Biography*, ed. D. Jeremy (London, 1984–86), vol. 1, pp. 506–9.

40 *Rochdale Observer*, 16 April 1892.

41 More recently, economists have acknowledged that British ring spinning was significant and subjected it to some analysis. For example: Leunig, 'New answers to old questions'; F. Ciliberto, 'Were British cotton entrepreneurs technologically backward? Firm-level evidence on the adoption of ring spinning', *Explorations in Economic History* 47 (2010), 487–504; Toms, 'The finance

unusual, they attracted considerable interest from contemporary observers.[42] A local commentator described the Rochdale experiments as a 'leap in the dark, involving great risk'.[43]

The profitability of mule and ring spinning

Entrepreneurs like Tweedale, Bullough and Heap could not be accused of pure technological conservatism. Thanks to their pioneering efforts, ring and mule spinning now coexisted in adjacent parts of the same industrial district in south-east Lancashire. How then did that contest progress in terms of the relative profitability of spinning investments?

Figure 13 contrasts the performance of the Milnrow ring spinners with specialized mule companies spinning similar counts in nearby Oldham. From 1884, the Milnrow ring spinners outperformed mule spinners in nearby Oldham in all phases of the trade cycle.[44] Tracking the difference between the returns on capital for the two groups, profit to ring spinning was higher in almost any given year and averaged around 5% more than mule spinning. Furthermore, the variance of stock market returns suggested that the ring spinners were less risky.[45] Contemporary commentators noticed the strong performance of the Milnrow firms. Commenting on the profit per spindle results for 1890, in a table showing the Milnrow group at first, second and fourth positions, an *Oldham Chronicle* correspondent wrote: 'The ring spindle concerns lead the way as usual'.[46] Given such robust and acknowledged performance, it is surprising that the Milnrow companies were not expanded further in spindleage or capacity, and that they were not more widely emulated in the decades before 1914.

The evidence from the Milnrow group showed to the rest of Lancashire that there were profits to be made from the new method. Following on quickly from these initial developments, a large number of Rochdale companies now replaced their throstle spindles with rings. By 1890 there were 400,000 ring spindles in

and growth of the Lancashire cotton textile industry'; Toms, 'Growth, profits and technological choice'.

42   For example, a correspondent in the *Oldham Chronicle* noted: 'The companies at New Hey are attracting attention all over the country', 4 July 1887, p. 8.

43   *Rochdale Observer*, 28 June 1890, p. 4.

44   Their results also compared favourably to fine spinning companies such as Barlow & Jones Ltd and later those under the control of the Fine Cotton Spinners' & Doublers' Association. S. Toms, 'Windows of opportunity in the textile industry: The business strategies of Lancashire entrepreneurs, 1880–1914', *BH* 40 (1998), 1–25, table 2.

45   For the period 1884–1913, the average stock market return for ring spinners was 10.9% with a standard deviation of 11.1%, compared to mule spinners with 13.82% and 33.08% respectively. Toms, 'The finance and growth of the Lancashire cotton textile industry', p. 89.

46   *Oldham Chronicle*, 3 January 1891.

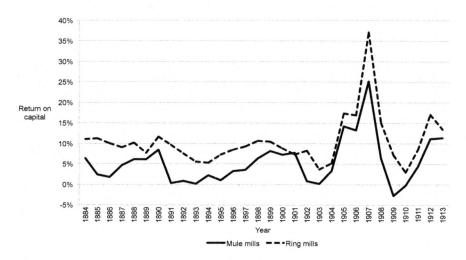

Figure 13. Comparative profitability, mule and ring spinning, 1884–1913

operation in the Rochdale area, making it the centre of a new and significant branch of the cotton industry. Of these, Howard & Bullough supplied 300,000.[47] Ring spindles provided by the six leading machine-makers up to 1890 totalled just over 792,000 (Table 9), illustrating the preponderance of one district and one capital equipment supplier in the early stages of the diffusion of the new spinning method. As Table 9 shows, in the period before 1914 ring spinning accounted for 25% of new machinery orders.

Outside of Rochdale, there were relatively few other significant ring mill constructions before the early 1900s. A fairly isolated example was Moss Side Mill in the Whitworth valley to the north of Rochdale, which was also involved in weaving, making it a rare case of a vertically integrated firm using ring spinning before 1890.[48] Among the specialized spinners, other notable exceptions were Palm Mill (1884), specializing in strong rope yarns,[49] the Nile (1898) in Oldham, Burns Ring Spinning Co. Ltd at Heywood (1891), promoted with the backing of the rival ring frame pioneer, Samuel Brooks, and the Era (1898) in Rochdale.[50] Again, Howard & Bullough were principal

47   *Rochdale Observer*, 4 January 1890.
48   The firm was small scale, employing 220 staff, with 12,000 spindles and 300 looms. B. Jones, *Co-operative Production* (Oxford, 1894), p. 279.
49   *Worrall's Cotton Spinners and Manufacturers Directory for Lancashire*; see the company's advertisement in the annual editions of the directory.
50   For a list of newly floated mills, see Jones, 'The cotton spinning industry in the Oldham district', pp. 221–3; for Palm Mill, see the company's advertisement in the annual editions of *Worrall's Cotton Spinners and Manufacturers Directory for Lancashire*; for Era Mill, see Era Ring

Table 9. Cotton spinning machinery orders by British firms, 1878–1920

Dates	Mules	%	Rings	%	Total
1878–1879	258,246	100	0	0	258,246
1880–1883	3,210,034	95	151,931	5	3,361,965
1884–1890	8,219,590	93	640,279	7	8,859,869
1891–1898	5,813,819	87	860,215	13	6,674,034
1899–1906	13,659,835	84	2,670,776	16	16,330,611
1907–1914	10,055,583	75	3,264,996	25	13,320,579
1915–1920	1,336,445	46	1,594,406	54	2,930,851

Source: Adapted from Saxonhouse and Wright, 'Rings and mules around the world', Tables 7 and 8, pp. 282–3.

supporters of the Era Mill development, where they installed 51,200 of their ring spindles. Finding employment for 450 operatives, it was described as one of the finest mills of its kind by the local newspaper.[51] It was three times the size of the prototype Milnrow firm and, as with the previous investments, backed and encouraged by capital equipment suppliers.

The trends in Table 9 also reveal how the trade cycle impacted the pattern of technology adoption and the pace of mill building in the subregional districts of Lancashire. In the 1890s, a fog of gloom enveloped the cotton industry, and many regarded its prospects as bleak.[52] The effects of the depression were mixed. Other than those noted above, there were no other significant ring mill constructions before the early 1900s.[53] In Oldham, little investment of any sort took place. Mule spindleage in the area declined from 11.4 million spindles in 1891 to 10.9 million in 1897,[54] a trend that is also apparent in Table 9. By contrast, ring spinning continued to grow, based on the replacement of throstles, notwithstanding the depressed state of the industry.

After a lag of more than ten years, the centre of the coarse spinning trade in Oldham began to emulate Rochdale to some extent. Between 1905 and 1909, a resurgence in export markets led to a new mill-building boom in south-east Lancashire. Although the majority were new mule mills, there were some significant investments in specialized ring-spinning establishments. While offering further scope for specialization, the ring spindle remained confined to

Mill Company Ltd, *History of the Era Ring Mill, 1898–1955* (Rochdale, n.d.), p. 1. *Rochdale Observer*, 4 January 1890. I am grateful to D. A. Farnie for information on the Burns Mill.
51   Era Ring Mill Company Ltd, *History of the Era Ring Mill*, p. 1.
52   'Is the cotton trade leaving the country?', *Textile Mercury*, 21 January 1893, p. 43.
53   Jones, 'The cotton spinning industry in the Oldham district', p. 223.
54   Farnie, 'The emergence of Victorian Oldham', p. 42.

the production of warp yarns. The diffusion of ring spinning was limited by packaging and transport problems for weft yarns. One investigation concluded that while this may have been a constraint in Oldham, it was not elsewhere in Lancashire since the majority of spinning companies in other districts had sufficient local weaving capacity to avoid long-distance transport if they chose to do so.[55] According to the 1906 *Enquiry*[56] quoted in this survey, Rochdale accounted for around 27% of all sub-40s yarn in Lancashire.

If Rochdale entrepreneurs had strong reasons to selectively adopt ring spinning for reasons of product and geographical specialization, these conditions were less true in nearby Oldham, where scale and efficiency factors reinforced the preference for the mule. Labour productivity was much higher in mule spinning, which had an average of 206 spindles per operative. By contrast, in the three Milnrow ring-spinning companies, the average was only 97.5 spindles per operative.[57] Labour intensity in ring spinning arose from the organization of specific processes, for example, doffing – and such tasks similarly featured in throstle spinning. An 'army of doffers' facilitated production in the throstle section of the Fielden spinning plant at Waterside.[58] The availability of such labour in throstle spinning could be readily transferred to ring spinning. Doffing was an unskilled task, customarily assigned to teams (four per machine) of young and inexperienced workers, and their employment no doubt added to the labour intensity of ring spinning.[59] Ring spinning also required more labour in roving and other preparation stages, and also other after-spinning processes, such as winding.[60] If labour cost savings did exist, they were therefore confined to the ring-spinning process itself.

In the light of evidence about the inferior productivity of ring spinning, the superior profitability of the Milnrow group appears paradoxical. A possible

55   T. Leunig, 'Lancashire at its zenith: Factor costs, industrial structure and technological choice in the Lancashire cotton industry, 1900–1913' (Ph.D. dissertation, University of Oxford, 1994), p. 44.
56   *Report of an Enquiry by the Board of Trade into the Earnings and Hours of Labour of Workpeople of the United Kingdom. No. I. – Textile Trades in 1906* (London, 1909), p. 241; Leunig, 'Lancashire at its zenith', p. 42.
57   Calculated from data in 'Milnrow ring spinning companies', *Rochdale Observer*, 28 June 1890, p. 4; G. H. Wood, 'Factory Legislation, considered with reference to the wages, &c., of the operatives protected thereby', *Journal of the Royal Statistical Society* 65 (1902), 284–324, at p. 316.
58   *Todmorden Advertiser*, 9 November 1889, p. 4.
59   J. Winterbottom, *Cotton Spinning Calculations and Yarn Costs* (London, 1921), p. 261; J. Jewkes and E. M. Gray, *Wages and Labour in the Lancashire Cotton Spinning Industry* (Manchester, 1935), p. 129.
60   C. Kenney, *Cotton Everywhere: Recollections of Northern Women Mill Workers* (Bolton, 1994), pp. 130–1. The New Ladyhouse Mill had a spindles-to-operative ratio of 79: see Toms, 'Growth, profits and technological choice', p. 42. A ring-spinning mill in France in 1882, producing 30s twist, had a spindles-to-operative ratio of 75: F. Merrtens, 'The hours and cost of labour in the cotton industry at home and abroad', *Transactions of the Manchester Statistical Society* (session 1893–4), 125–90, at p. 160. The comparable figure for British mule spinning was 205, derived from Wood, 'Factory legislation', p. 316.

reason was that there were growing niche markets for ring spinning in coarse and specialized warp yarns, and for weft yarns, as the use of automatic weaving began to spread.[61] Given the weaker productivity of ring spinning, a possible explanation of its superior profitability is that shortages promoted higher prices and hence wider profit margins. Ring spinning then offered a cheap capital, smaller-scale alternative to the mule, but it was to the latter that entrepreneurs turned in the search for economies of scale. As a consequence, the Milnrow experiments were not immediately emulated.

Higher capital intensity meant that investors could more easily realize economies of scale in mule spinning. The average size of the Milnrow mills was under 27,000 spindles. Out of seventy-four new mills commenced in the Oldham district between 1900 and 1907,[62] only eight were specialist ring spinners. Ring mills built in the 1900s were also smaller than mule mills and tended not to provide access to the scale economies of mule spinning.[63] Belgrave no. 2 mill had only 43,200 spindles, while Iris (62,568 spindles), Moston Ring (59,796) and Royton Ring (64,176) were more typical, but relatively small nonetheless. By contrast, the median mule specialist in the Oldham district was by this time of the order of 100,000–130,000 spindles. The largest, Times No. 2, at 174,000 spindles, revealed the substantial upper limits of economies of scale in mule spinning. Defenders of the mule-spinning system, who unsurprisingly included mule frame manufacturers such as Platt Brothers of Oldham, pointed to the superiority of mule-spun yarn and the practical and scientific shortcomings of ring spinning.[64]

Such biases undoubtedly influenced investment decisions in local capital markets. Chapter 4 discussed the reasons for the obsession with dividends and related demand for investment in particular local firms. In keeping with the co-operative tradition, investors were actively involved in the management of their companies and exercised detailed scrutiny of accounting information at quarterly company meetings.[65] As a result, investors were less keen to buy

---

61   In 1890, there were 400,000 ring spindles installed in the Rochdale district, producing a weekly output 17,200,000 hanks (*Rochdale Observer*, 4 January 1890), or the equivalent of forty-three per spindle. The comparable output of a mule spindle in 1893 was thirty-one hanks: T. Thornley, *Modern Cotton Economics* (London, 1923), p. 302. The district also specialized in supplying strong yarns, e.g. for tyres to the motor industry: Williams and Farnie, *Cotton Mills in Greater Manchester*, p. 44.

62   'Milnrow ring spinning companies', *Rochdale Observer*, 28 June 1890, p. 4; Jones, 'The cotton spinning industry in the Oldham district', 221–3.

63   S. Kenny, 'Sub-regional specialization in the Lancashire cotton industry, 1884–1914: A study in organizational and locational change', *Journal of Historical Geography* 8 (1982), 41–63, at p. 59.

64   'Ring spinning and its development', *Rochdale Observer*, 4 January 1890.

65   S. Toms, 'The rise of modern accounting and the fall of the public company: the Lancashire cotton mills 1870–1914', *Accounting, Organizations and Society* 27 (2002), 61–84; S. Toms, 'Information content of earnings in an unregulated market: The co-operative cotton mills of Lancashire, 1880–1900', *Accounting and Business Research* 31 (2001), 175–90; S. Toms, 'The

shares in firms with which they were technically less familiar, notwithstanding apparently superior profits. Operative investors, in particular, exercised scrutiny over their managers through such technical knowledge and would have lacked the ability to do so for firms using competing technologies in neighbouring districts. So although the dividend obsession must have reflected a degree of market inefficiency, investor behaviour was rational in the sense that high dividends reduced free cash flow and minimized monitoring costs.[66] These tendencies promoted the efficiency of established concerns, but at the same time, reinforced the path dependencies that led to new technology adoption only in specific locations.

The Oldham-centred vested interests did not stop further investments in ring spinning on an increased scale. New ring mills responded to critics like Platt by improving quality and developing higher count product ranges. While the counts spun by the Milnrow group began at 18/36s and became coarser on average at 6/36s by 1914,[67] the newer companies had average counts of 31s, including some, such as Cromer Spinning Company, producing up to 64s in Egyptian cotton and the Nile Spinning Company, 80s Egyptian, thereby entering the finer product range.[68] Product specialization and market niches undoubtedly played a part in these developments, although the ostensible constraint of sub-40s coarse specialization for ring spindles was far less applicable in the 1900s than it had been in the 1880s.

In summary, in the case of ring spinning, the evidence suggests that entre-preneurs did not fail to make the requisite investments. On the contrary, the Lancashire model of connected ownership, investment and management were quickly adaptable such that new firms could be set up and existing capacity replaced to accommodate the new methods. Moreover, investment decisions reflected prior production arrangements, geographical location, product specialization, and the supply of physical and financial capital.

In weaving, however, the barriers to investment seemed much more substantial. Automatic looms were adopted only by a small minority of firms before 1914 and typically not in the geographical specialization in centres of weaving. Of the total looms installed, a large proportion was at Ashton Brothers of Hyde.[69]

supply of and demand for accounting information in an unregulated market: Examples from the Lancashire cotton mills, 1855–1914', *Accounting, Organizations and Society* 23 (1998), 217–38.
66   Shareholders preferred the 'voice' mechanism of scrutinizing management at quarterly meetings rather than the 'exit' option of selling their shares, as defined in A. O. Hirschman, *Exit, Voice and Loyalty* (Cambridge MA, 1970). See also 'The supply of and demand for accounting information in an unregulated market', pp. 223–4.
67   *Worrall's Cotton Spinners and Manufacturers Directory*, 1891 and 1913.
68   Jones, 'The cotton spinning industry in the Oldham district', pp. 221–3.
69   A. Fowler, 'Trade unions and technical change: The automatic loom strike, 1908', *North West Labour History Society Bulletin* 6 (1979), 43–55, at p. 43; in 1911, of the total 5,409 automatic looms in Lancashire, 1,820 were installed at Ashton Bros.

Other examples of pre-1914 introductions included Tootal Broadhurst & Lee, Fielden Brothers of Todmorden and Gregs of Quarry Bank.[70]

Automation led to a wave of strikes by the weavers. These occurred at Ashton's in 1904 and again in 1908, and at Tootal's Rumworth Mill at Daubhill in 1906. Nonetheless, labour relations did not necessarily constitute a significant reason for slow diffusion; the strike at Hyde was partly at the instigation of the employers, faced as they were with high stocks and falling demand. As with the ring spindle, automatic loom adoption was related to product specialization. Ashton Brothers produced plain cloths, while the parts of north-east Lancashire that concentrated on fine goods retained the traditional power loom to work with mule-spun yarns.[71]

Again, like the ring spindle, the role of the capital equipment supplier was an essential determinant of the pattern of adoption. In the case of the automatic loom, however, the machinery company, through its patent and pricing policy, tended to act as a constraint. In contrast to the flotations of mills in the Rochdale and Oldham areas, there was little support for new weaving companies from the British Northrop Loom Company. Established in 1903, Northrop had some connections via cross-directorships between equipment supplier and manufacturer; for example, Henry Philips Greg (1865–1936), a director of Ashton Brothers, and Edward Tootal Broadhurst (1858–1922) both held directorships with the British Northrop Loom Company.[72] Industry-level evidence suggests that there was at least an association between increased adoption of ring spinning after 1902 and the establishment of the British Northrop Loom Company in 1904.[73] However, the American parent, the Draper Corporation, retained a strong influence owning two-thirds of the shares,[74] and demanding, in return for production under patent, a high level of monopoly profits. Unlike the ring spindle, whose relatively simple 'traveller' device had improved the throstle, the Northrop loom was a complex piece of equipment. One study estimates the costs of the invention at $1 million and patent control for the machine, together with improvements and attachments, became an essential part of management strategy for the parent company, which had 1,330 enforceable patents in 1907.[75] As a consequence, the prices of the looms were set high, and the expense and risk may have deterred adoption by British manufacturers. There were also concerns about difficulties

70 TP, Board Minutes, M461; FP, Board minutes, C353/1; M. B. Rose, *The Gregs of Quarry Bank Mill* (Cambridge, 1986), pp. 96–8.

71 Fowler, 'Trade unions and technical change', p. 52.

72 A. C. Howe, 'Sir Frank Hollins', *Dictionary of Business Biography*, ed. D. Jeremy (London, 1984–86), vol. 3, pp. 313–17, at p. 316; M. W. Dupree, 'Edward Tootal Broadhurst', *Dictionary of Business Biography*, vol. 1, pp. 452–5, at p. 452.

73 Ciliberto, 'Were British cotton entrepreneurs technologically backward?'

74 Saul, 'The engineering industry', p. 195.

75 W. Mass, 'Mechanical and organizational innovation: The Drapers and the automatic loom', *BHR* 63 (1989), 876–929, at pp. 901, 906–12.

with the workpeople and disruption to the piecework system, which entrepreneurs regarded as essential for competitive advantage.[76] Thus there were compelling reasons other than industry structure for the slow diffusion of automatic looms.

The discussion thus far has highlighted several interesting trends. The diffusion of ring spinning was associated with product and geographical specialization, manifesting itself prominently at first in one district, Rochdale. A decisive impetus came from one capital equipment supplier, Howard & Bullough, which, on acquiring the patents, sold the majority of the earlier frames. Ring spinning was carried out in a significant and increasing minority of establishments in the 1889–1914 period in other districts as well as Rochdale, but in virtually all cases in vertically specialized mills producing warp yarn. Vertically integrated firms, albeit unconstrained regarding the deployment of machinery in spinning and weaving branches, only rarely adopted the ring spindle and automatic loom simultaneously.

Like ring spinning, automatic weaving was associated with growing geographical diversity, product specialization and the establishment of market niches. In spinning, there had been a hundred years of competition between continuous and intermittent methods, and the adoption of the ring reflected the tradition and replacement of throstle spinning in specific districts. In weaving, however, the transition from the power loom was a straightforward question of automation. In ring spinning, capital equipment manufacturers played a crucial supporting role in the establishment of the technique and several British firms were supplying the domestic and export market for ring spindles by 1914. By contrast, capital equipment manufacture of automatic looms was monopolized and hence less supportive of cotton manufacturers.

Furthermore, automatic loom diffusion lagged ring spinning for reasons of technical development. The British Northrop Loom Company was established thirty-one years after Howard & Bullough first acquired ring-spinning patents from the USA. Ring spinning and automatic weaving also had potentially differential consequences for labour relations. Workers used to throstle spinning had no reason to oppose the introduction of the ring spindle on technology grounds alone, whereas the automatic loom was a more radical disrupter of traditional methods. Consequently, first adopters of automatic looms like Tootal, experienced problematic labour relations, for example, the Daubhill automatic loom strike of 1906.[77] They were also reliant on ring spinning specifically for weft yarn, which was in short supply. Indeed the majority of new ring-spinning capacity developed in the early 1900s was for warp and specialized yarns.[78]

---

76 'The Tariff Commission and the cotton industry', *Manchester Guardian*, 6 June 1905, p. 8.
77 Toms, 'Windows of opportunity'; Toms, 'The finance and growth of the Lancashire cotton textile industry'.
78 S. J. Procter and S. Toms, 'Industrial relations and technical change: Profits, wages and costs in the Lancashire Cotton Industry, 1880–1914', *Journal of Industrial History* 3 (2000), 54–72. For

Vertical integration strategies

The discussion in this chapter so far has examined the reasons why entrepreneurs chose, in specific circumstances, to invest in ring spinning and automated weaving technology. The apparent need to introduce them simultaneously, in nearby or collocated buildings, as at Ashton Brothers and Fielden Brothers, raises the question of Lancashire's horizontally specialized structure, and whether it acted as a barrier to the simultaneous introduction of ring spinning and automatic weaving. According to this argument, the spinning and weaving branches both resisted the introduction of new technology because of their structure.[79] Vertical specialization prevented co-ordinated decision-making between spinning and weaving mills necessary for the replacement of power looms with automatic looms because the spinning companies could only supply yarn suitable for the former.[80] Thus, in Britain, specialist ring spinners were only able to compete in the production of warp yarns, since whether spinning mills used rings or mules for warp, the yarn still had to be rewound from bobbins onto beams before weaving.[81]

It is, therefore, useful to note examples of diffusion among vertically integrated companies in other parts of Lancashire, where the vertical specialization constraint did not apply. If entrepreneurs were concerned to remove the obstacles to using ring spinning for weft yarn, they could have either installed rings in existing integrated concerns that could also take advantage of developments in automatic weaving, or built brand-new integrated factories.

Individual firm behaviour offers a useful test of these arguments. Nonetheless, in most cases, companies that adopted automatics were also vertically integrated. The exception was Quarry Bank, which abandoned spinning in 1894.[82] Integration removed the ostensible constraint of co-ordination of weft yarn production on rings with the acquisition of automatic looms. One company that almost uniquely followed the strategy of simultaneous investment in ring spinning and automatic looms on an extended scale was Ashton Brothers. Other vertically integrated companies that introduced some aspects of new technology included Fielden Brothers, Horrockses Crewdson and Tootal. As

examples of early experiments in ring-spun weft yarn, see the case of Fielden Brothers; S. Toms, 'Integration, innovation, and the progress of a family cotton enterprise: Fielden Brothers Ltd, 1889–1914', *Textile History* 27 (1996), 77–100. Toms, 'The finance and growth of the Lancashire cotton textile industry'.

79   Lazonick, 'Competition, Specialization and Industrial Decline'; Lazonick, 'Industrial organization and technological change'; Lazonick, 'The cotton industry'.

80   Lazonick, 'Competition, Specialization and Industrial Decline', pp. 33–4. M. Frankel, 'Obsolescence and technological change in a maturing economy', *American Economic Review* 45 (1955), 296–319, at p. 313.

81   Lazonick, 'Stubborn mules: Some comments', p. 82.

82   Rose, *The Gregs of Quarry Bank Mill*, p. 92.

noted above, all of these firms made investments in new technology before 1914 in some form.

As with ring and mule spinning, it is useful to evaluate the financial performance of these firms, to evaluate the rationale of their investment decisions. Figure 14 compares the rates of return on capital for the four vertically integrated innovators against an industry benchmark. In the period 1899–1913, the average was 8.81%. In the same period, Ashton Brothers mirrored the industry benchmark quite closely, averaging 7.41%, marginally underperforming in any typical year. It was during this period that Ashtons made very substantial investments in automatic looms, which according to Figure 14, did not pay off, despite the market continuing to expand before 1914.

Of all the innovating firms in Figure 14, Fielden was the worst performer. Between 1884 and 1913, the average annual rate of profit for all firms was 7.62% and, in the same period, Fielden Brothers averaged only 2.19%. The firm, led by Edward Fielden, had made a significant investment in ring spinning but only conducted limited experiments with automatic looms. The firm's Todmorden base was close to Rochdale and Milnrow, and for similar reasons, scrapped its throstles in favour of rings in 1889–90.[83] However, there were significant differences. There were disadvantages associated with being a combined mill peripheral to the emerging centres of spinning and weaving specialization, such as the physical constraint of old buildings, dependence on a coarse and plain product range, and lack of access to joint-stock finance.[84] Fielden Brothers was a long-standing concern and suffered a disadvantage from its investment in buildings that were old and less suited to ring spinning, in contrast to the purpose-built ring-spinning sheds of Rochdale and Oldham.

Nonetheless, in such situations, the ring spindle was more adaptable than the ever-widening mule frame. It was no surprise, therefore, that Robinwood Mill, in the Calder Valley at Lydgate near Todmorden, abandoned mule spinning, replaced its throstles and specialized in ring spinning from the 1890s onwards. At Fielden Brothers, many of the ring frames purchased in the 1890s for Lumbutts Mill and in the 1900s for Robinwood Mill were for weft spinning onto pirns. In one case, the purchase was made simultaneously with automatic looms.[85] The decision appears to be the only known example of Lancashire entrepreneurs putting into practice what their critics have accused them of failing to do. Even so, it underperformed the rest of the industry before and after Fielden introduced these changes.

Without casting doubt on the ultimate reasons for the adoption of the automatic loom, the evidence of corporate behaviour induces scepticism as to whether it represented a decisive breakthrough before 1914. In the Fielden

83   FP, Directors minutes, C/353/1.
84   Kenny, 'Sub regional specialization', pp. 41–63.
85   FP, Directors minutes, C/353/1, 2 March 1909, p. 334.

Figure 14. Vertical integrated innovative firms, comparative profitability, 1884–1913

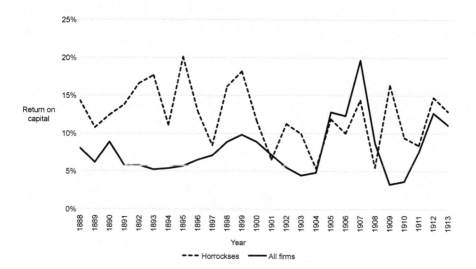

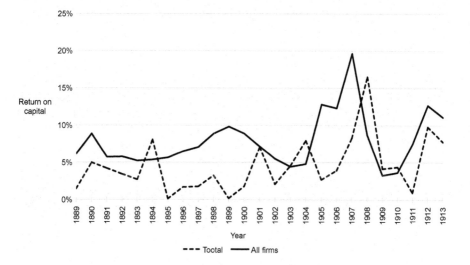

case, the fourteen automatics purchased in the period 1907–14 represented only a tiny proportion of total weaving capacity, whereas by 1914, 94% of its spinning capacity was accounted for by ring frames as replacements for earlier throstles. Vertical integration per se did not prevent this experiment taking place but equally cannot account for the lack of more widespread introduction. At the other vertically integrated companies, there was no apparent evidence of simultaneous use of the looms with ring weft spindles.

The newly merged firm of Horrockses Crewdson & Company Ltd, led by Frank Hollins, was the strongest vertically integrated performer. In the period 1888–1913, the average rate of profit in the industry was 7.90%, and the corresponding figure for Horrockses was 12.33%. The firm performed particularly well during the 1890s, a period when the rest of the industry remained in a prolonged depression. To achieve a return of 20% at the depth of the depression in 1895 was a particularly remarkable result. Not only that, the company enjoyed robust growth and Hollins made substantial investments in ring spinning, which again replaced the now obsolete throstle spindles. However, by contrast with the examples so far, there was also a tendency to replace ageing mules with rings as part of the plant replacement cycle (Table 10). True, the company did construct a specialist mule mill in 1895 of nearly 80,000 spindles, but otherwise, the ring spindle became increasingly important. In replacing some mules with rings as part of its investment strategy, Horrockses was something of an exception. More generally, as we have seen, the throstle, not the mule, was the primary victim of the development of the ring.

The diversity of machinery at Horrockses, including the simultaneous commitment to rings and mules, reflected increased diversity in the product range. By 1900 the company was producing a wide selection of goods, many of which were for the domestic market, with a growing emphasis on product quality.[86] As a consequence, Horrockses was able to command higher margins on its finished products, although this came at the price of reduced manufacturing efficiency, with the associated requirement to hold a broader range of stocks for use in shorter, differentiated production runs.

Tootal Broadhurst & Lee followed a similar strategy, based on branded products, but with a greater dependence on exports, and less apparent achievement and financial success. In the period 1889–1913, the average rate of profit for the industry was 7.89%. The comparable figure for Tootal was only around half the industry benchmark average at 4.54% and also much less than the equivalent for

---

86   D. C. M. Platt, *Latin America and British Trade 1806–1914* (New York, 1975), p. 166. Amalgamated Cotton Mills Trust Ltd, *Concerning Cotton: A Brief Account of the Aims and Achievements of the Amalgamated Cotton Mills Trust Limited and its Component Companies* (London, 1921). A section on Horrockses stressed its commitment to quality. The Centenary Mill investment, being exclusively committed to mule spinning, would have been at the leading edge of this strategy.

Table 10. Horrockses Crewdson, installed spindleage, 1887–1905

Number of spindles			
	1887	1905	Net investment
Mule spindles	118,002	173,752	54,662
Ring spindles	14,220	58,464	44,424

Notes:
1   Excluding the 78,572 mule spindles installed at Centenary Mill, there is a robust trend to replace mules with rings on a routine basis at existing sites.
2   There was no investment of any kind between 1906 and 1914.

Source: CVR, Machine Book.

Horrockses. These contrasts were particularly stark in the 1890s, when Tootal diversified into new markets, especially in the Americas, continental Europe and the home market. Bad debts in some of these markets left the firm technically bankrupt in 1894.[87] These problems persisted until 1900 when the firm's profits began to improve, although they remained unspectacular compared to other firms.

Tootal was more explicitly committed to investments in automatic looms than Horrockses, but the investments failed to pay off. The problematic labour relations that followed have already been noted and, like Horrockses, Tootal suffered manufacturing inefficiency as a result of the diversity in products and marketing. Henry Lee (1817–1904) was an enthusiastic and active mill manager who attempted to solve this problem. Coupled with withdrawal from the Coats-dominated sewing thread market, Tootal retained its essential North American markets by establishing channels for branded products direct to the retailer, a policy similar to Horrockses.[88] Departments were organized around export and other markets, and given considerable flexibility. In particular, they were allowed to place orders directly with the mills. Senior management controlled each department via the assignment of stock limits authorized by directors at committee level.[89]

Despite the determination of Tootal management and the more extensive commitment to new technology, Horrockses remained the more successful of the two firms. Indeed, Horrockses, with its diverse product range and diverse technology, was the most successful of all the integrated firms. Even so, integration was a problematic strategy for most firms before 1914.

87   TP, Minutes of general meetings, M.461, Minute book No. 2, auditors reports, 9 October 1894 and 22 October 1895.
88   A. C. Howe, 'Henry Lee and Joseph Cocksey Lee', *Dictionary of Business Biography*, ed. D. Jeremy (London, 1984–86), vol. 3, pp. 703–14, at pp. 708–9; TP, Board Minutes, M.461, Minute book no. 1, 8 March 1888.
89   TP, General Management Committee Minutes, M.461, Minute book no. 1, 19 November 1888.

Integration, specialization and performance

Table 11 shows the relative profitability of vertically integrated and specialized firms according to spinning technology for the period 1884–1913, and for subperiods as indicated by the trade cycle. The year 1896 was a turning point in this respect, with the twelve years before then reflecting mostly depressed conditions, contrasted with the boom periods that featured more prominently thereafter. Figure 15 illustrates the course of the trade cycle and the differential impact on the profitability of specialized spinners and vertically integrated firms.

While vertically integrated firms at least experimented with new technology in weaving, specialized firms, whether in ring or mule spinning, nonetheless typically outperformed them in financial terms. As Table 11 and Figure 15 show, specialized spinners enjoyed superior profitability. Only in times of relative depression, for example, in the protected downturn of the early 1890s, was integration a superior strategy. Powered by Horrockses results, on average, vertically integrated companies did relatively better in the 1890s than in the 1900s. Another advantage of vertical integration was the lower standard deviation of return, suggesting that such firms could use their market power to stabilize production and inventory levels.

Even so, there were many compelling reasons why entrepreneurs preferred to float specialized rather than integrated concerns. First, as the trends in Table 11 and Figure 15 illustrate, to specialize was more profitable during periods of boom. Specialized companies generally performed much better than those companies that perhaps attempted to achieve internal throughput economies through the adoption of vertically integrated structures.

Entrepreneurs also resisted vertical integration because they could enjoy its benefits through informal networks without the cost of creating complex organization structures.[90] An example was the contacts built by most firms with the Liverpool and Manchester markets; particularly the use made by Oldham spinners of Liverpool warehouse operators as cotton stockholders.[91] Shiloh Spinning Company established a close relationship with Melladew & Clarke, Liverpool cotton brokers, which was cemented further when the firm's founding director, T. E. Gartside, dispatched his younger son, James, to their offices for training in raw cotton selection.[92] As noted earlier, linkages with capital equipment manufacturers assisted the supply of required machinery and

---

90 Toms, 'Windows of opportunity'; D. Higgins and S. Toms, 'Firm structure and financial performance: The Lancashire textile industry, c.1884–c.1960', *Accounting, Business & Financial History* 7 (1997), 195–232, at pp. 216–17.
91 D. A. Farnie, *The Manchester Ship Canal and the Rise of the Port of Manchester* (Manchester, 1980), pp. 74–5.
92 Anon., *The Shiloh Story* (Royton, 1974).

Table 11. Organization, technology and comparative profitability

	All firms	Vertically integrated	Specialized (all)	Specialized Ring	Specialized Mule
Return on capital (%)					
1884–1896	6.03	7.12	4.86	8.83	3.36
1897–1913	8.73	7.89	8.90	11.71	7.07
1884–1913	7.56	7.56	7.22	10.46	5.46
Standard deviation (%)					
1884–1896	1.38	1.97	2.26	2.08	2.70
1897–1913	4.60	2.49	6.14	7.95	6.73
1884–1913	3.72	2.24	5.17	6.12	5.52

Sources: Compiled from the CIFD database.

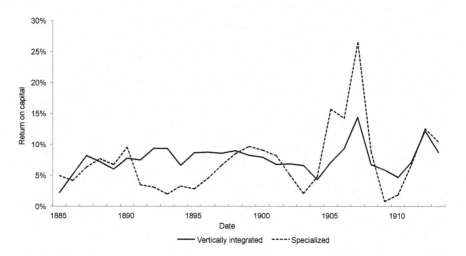

Figure 15. Comparative profitability: Vertically integrated and specialized firms
Sources: CIFD.

associated technical assistance. Furthermore, because different entrepreneurial networks dominated sub-localities and pre-existing specialization, they accordingly adopted ring spinning or automatic weaving, but not both.

Although factor costs and productivity were essential and their emphasis in recent debates is well justified, they do not fully explain performance differentials. Management of integrated companies such as Horrockses and Tootal tended to find that efficient marketing and efficient production worked in opposite directions. Investment in full product ranges limited the benefits of internal economies of scale associated with large production runs.

Nonetheless, control of the value chain, whether through networks or integration, created the possibility of sustained competitive advantage. In such cases, firms achieved higher financial returns through superior profit margins, as in the case of Horrockses.[93] To the cotton economy as a whole, marketing was more important than manufacturing efficiency and production costs remained insignificant relative to the total cost.[94]

The experience of the trade cycle underpinned all the above reasons for specialization. The British government's commitment to free trade and the gold standard were capable of exercising a dominant influence on the destiny of the industry. For example, the loss and recovery of the Indian market during the 1890s, reflecting lobbying, British electoral arithmetic and the relationship between the British and Indian governments,[95] had a decisive impact on the development of the coarse-spinning American section. First, market changes impoverished working- and middle-class investors, and centralized capital ownership. They then led to the investment boom in specialized concerns during the 1900s, backed by the new class of individualistic freelance, promotional and speculative capitalists referred to above.

To all sections of the industry, the world market was vital. Access to markets and market conditions directly impacted profitability and variation in profitability,[96] and entrepreneurs were understandably reluctant to commit themselves to the high fixed costs of big firm organization.[97] The risk associated

---

93   S. Toms, 'The profitability of the first Lancashire merger: The case of Horrocks, Crewdson & Co. Ltd, 1887–1905', *Textile History* 24 (1993), 129–46, at pp. 132–3; Toms, 'The finance and growth of the Lancashire cotton textile industry', chapter 6.

94   Higgins and Toms, 'Firm structure and financial performance', pp. 219–20; A. Marrison, 'Indian summer, 1870–1914', *The Lancashire Cotton Industry: A History Since 1700*, ed. M. B. Rose (Preston, 1996), pp. 238–64.

95   E. H. H. Green, 'Rentiers versus producers? The political economy of the Bimetallic controversy, c.1880–98', *English Historical Review* 103 (1988), 588–612. See also the further discussion in A. Howe, 'Bimetallism, c.1880–1898: a controversy re-opened?', *English Historical Review* 105 (1990), 377–91; and Toms, 'The finance and growth of the Lancashire textile industry', chapter 11.

96   Ibid.

97   A. F. Lucas, *Industrial Reconstruction and the Control of Competition: The British Experiments* (London, 1937), p. 167.

with significant changes in demand also reduced the value of internal economies of scale. Finally, the vast returns generated in the 'gold-rush time' and the days of 'easy money' in the decade before 1914,[98] had a decisive iterative influence on investor behaviour and reinforced the tendency towards specialization. Such influences prevailed particularly in coarse mule spinning during the boom of 1905–07, resulting in what proved to be an over-expansion of specialized spinning capacity.[99]

Perhaps to an extent, such entrepreneurial behaviour is to be expected for industries whose output is cyclical around an upward secular trend, as cotton was in the 1900s. Confident expectation of a new and more significant boom would no doubt have alleviated the worries of entrepreneurs whose new mills came on stream in 1908 just after the close of the greatest boom hitherto experienced by the industry.

Conclusions

In sum, the evidence shows that historical antecedents and path dependencies imparted strongly on the diffusion of technology. Entrepreneurs had little difficulty in mobilizing capital from the local sources that had funded the earlier expansion of the industry in the mid nineteenth century. Given the accumulated financial resources and flotation skills of individual entrepreneurs, and the expansion strategies of some private companies around 1900, there was nothing to stop entrepreneurs investing simultaneously in spinning and weaving capacity. Why, then, did these capital-rich entrepreneurs not simply eliminate technical interrelatedness constraints by setting up new integrated mills? In reality, there were no structural constraints and even had they been problematic, the means to eliminate them were also present before 1914, namely the fortunes and reinvestment priorities of individual entrepreneurs. In this sense, the ownership of capital and barriers to its circulation, not industrial organization, was a potential constraint and as such, as the next chapter shows, only temporarily relevant after 1920.

Specific examples of the adoption of ring spinning also vindicate entrepreneurial behaviour. Investment in spinning reflected rational technological path dependency and the superior productivity of the mule. Entrepreneurs rationally deployed their capital to expand ring spinning for specific purposes in specific geographical districts, with the required pools of labour and strategic alliances with capital equipment manufacturers. Entrepreneurs, therefore, had different routes to competitive advantage. Vertically integrated firms relied on marketing

98   B. Bowker, *Lancashire under the Hammer* (London, 1928), p. 9.
99   Toms, 'The finance and growth of the Lancashire cotton textile industry', chapter 10.

and branding rather than production economies of scale. Specialized firms pursued a different strategy, but relied upon niches to achieve the required production economies. Specialization left them vulnerable to downturns but also created the opportunity of substantial profits during booms.

The variety of entrepreneurial strategies brought undoubted success for many firms. Business leaders were quite willing to experiment with new technology where appropriate. They built on the achievements of prior generations by cementing and extending business networks, and as illustrated in the previous chapter, used them to forge large corporate structures. In general, the evidence does little to sustain accusations of entrepreneurial failure before 1914.

7

Financial Speculation, Restructuring and Survival

The meddling of garish speculation with the Lancashire cotton trade ...
proved a commercial and social calamity.[1]

Up to 1914, cotton entrepreneurs facilitated a variety of growth strategies.
They built on the technical and financial partnerships of the early industrial
revolution to construct corporate empires. Initial phase accumulated capital
was reinvested as venture capital to extend the reach of these previously local
partnerships. Regional financial institutions assisted these developments. Social
entrepreneurs, utilizing often informal stock exchanges to access local pools
of capital, evolved into a new class of financial capitalists, specializing in the
promotion of ever-larger mills during each upswing in the trade cycle. The effect
was a productive circulation of capital within Lancashire. When contemporary
commentators levelled criticism, it was at the perceived over-expansion of the
industry, which created spare capacity during downturns. Such criticism was
aimed at the problem of too much investment, rather than too little, or into
the wrong type of technology.

The previous two chapters have mapped the ingredients of the decline that
characterized British textiles in the twentieth century. In chapter 4, the evidence
shows that entrepreneurs mobilized capital using local and regional financial
institutions, which they increasingly used for speculative mill-building projects
by cliques of directors who believed they understood the cotton trade cycle only
too well. The outcome of these financing methods was the creation of groups of
mills run by interconnected directors. Chapter 5 outlined an alternative route to
growth, based on combinations of individual mills, which networked directors
floated as combines. These amalgamations also featured powerful interconnected sets of directors. Aside from a large number of small firms, specialized
mill groups and combines provided alternative models of consolidation after
1920, as Lancashire's markets began to contract. Both models continued to
reflect the features of the pre-1914 growth phase. For example, the specialized
mill groups tended to rely on the Oldham stock exchange, and also Manchester,

---

1   J. Garvin, 'Other people's money', *The Observer*, 29 September 1929, p. 5.

whereas the combines raised capital from metropolitan sources, which for the first time now included London.

Entrepreneurial choices of vertical organization and technology, as illustrated in chapter 6, were governed by path dependency and rationality, which in any case was bounded by the absence of decisive breakthroughs in spinning and weaving automation for integrated process production before 1930. This chapter brings these threads together to show how interdependency of financing arrangements and vertical organization prevented either the mill group or combine models from responding to the crisis conditions that prevailed in the interwar years.

In doing so, it contributes to a historiography that has also been coloured by the process of industrial decline. Hypotheses purporting to explain decline have been influential in economics, and indeed politics, and most of them have been applied, or apply, to the cotton industry. Obsession with manufacturing decline in the 1970s and 1980s has influenced interpretations of pre-1914 Lancashire and left its recent historiography dominated by questions of economics and industrial organization.[2] Historians of the cotton industry have thus been influential in the formation of views about the British economy as a whole and the commonly addressed question of British economic decline in the twentieth century.

During this phase, there were a series of transitions from a regionally embedded industrial system, supported by access to external economies of scale in the form of transport, institutions and markets, to increasing dependence on more remote but powerful purchasers of steadily declining output. In the earlier phases of industrialization, manufacturers had little difficulty in controlling markets. Indeed much of the early impetus came from the application of merchant capital to manufacturing. In the decline phase, access to markets became more problematic. Downstream firms, with ownership interests from outside the manufacturing districts, increasingly dictated manufacturing strategies.

These processes marked the beginning of a structural shift, in which the profitability and sustainability of manufacturing depend on the power of buyers and providers of capital. Accordingly, the later phases of the life cycle of staple industries witness the progressive transfer of independence, through concentration of buyer power in large organizations, to governments, downstream buyers and metropolitan financial institutions. These processes have impacted many core industries including coal, shipbuilding, steel, defence and financial mutuals, such that regional economic organization and identity, which had been an essential by-product of industrialization, now became associated with decline and dependency.

2   W. Lazonick, 'Competition, Specialization and Industrial Decline', *JEH* 31 (1981), 31–8; W. Lazonick, 'Industrial organization and technological change: The decline of the British cotton industry', *BHR* 58 (1983), 195–236; W. Lazonick, 'The Cotton Industry', *The Decline of the British Economy*, ed. B. Elbaum and W. Lazonick (Oxford, 1987), pp. 18–50.

The cotton industry in the twentieth century, and indeed the textile industry more generally, offers a useful case study of these relationships. In its earlier phases, as previous chapters have illustrated, the cotton industry integrated manufacturing, merchanting and financial functions through entrepreneurial networks. Those networks began to fracture in the shadow of the crisis of 1920–22, as the protracted slump that followed led industry leaders increasingly to seek outside assistance. The chapter begins with an analysis of this failure, thereby also offering an alternative to the entrepreneurial failure hypothesis discussed earlier in chapter 6. It then examines the strategies of firms that did achieve some success, notwithstanding the difficult circumstances. These firms variously invested in new technology, diversified their product range and created larger structures. To pursue these strategies, firms relied on external financial markets, particularly London, to secure funds and facilitate mergers. The regional stock markets, which had mobilized capital for a wide variety of firms during the expansionary phase, declined rapidly. Government policy facilitated the concentration of the industry, first through reorganization and subsequently by subsidized scrapping schemes, backed with substitution of defence-related investment. Other regulatory policies tipped the balance of power away from manufacturers in favour of retail. New vertical manufacturing combines absorbed much of the remainder of the cotton industry, which then attempted but ultimately failed to counterbalance the power of the retailers. Alliances with such retailers, notably Marks & Spencer, offered a final strategic option for survival.

Lancashire and the trade cycle

Since its inception, as chapter 3 has shown, the Lancashire cotton industry was strongly characterized by trade cycle volatility. To Marx, writing in the early 1860s, these booms and slumps were increasing in their intensity. Figure 16 shows the pattern of profitability in the period 1861–1938. Volatility tended to decline as the nineteenth century progressed. The slump of the 1890s was in line with previous downturns in terms of low profit rates, but more protracted in that there were ten years between the booms of the late 1880s and the late 1890s. After that up to the early 1920s, volatility became much more pronounced with sharper booms and steeper slumps, in many respects the worst that had afflicted the industry. These fluctuations were driven by variations in world prices and geopolitical circumstances, but also, particularly in 1904–07, the installation of substantial new capacity in response to favourable international trading conditions. The structural break in the rate of profit after 1920 is also observable in Figure 16. These trends are now explored in more detail.

The large Oldham district, with its substantial, publicly quoted companies and heavy dependence on export markets for its coarse yarns, was particularly

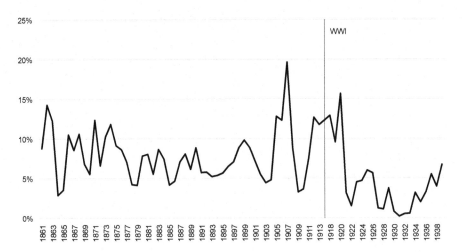

Figure 16. Profitability in the long run, 1861–1938
Source: Compiled from CIFD.

vulnerable to these cycles and was severely hit by the crisis of 1890–96.[3] Declining silver prices reduced the cost advantages in overseas markets, particularly the Indian subcontinent. Unsuccessful speculations on the Liverpool futures market compounded problems for many firms leading to a steady and prolonged fall in share prices.[4] Working- and middle-class investors were impoverished as wages fell, and their investments lost much of their value. Working-class investors sold their shares in the co-operative mills and instead placed their faith in the trade unions. A major industrial dispute, culminating in the lockout and subsequent Brooklands agreement of 1894, did nothing to rescue their situation. Indeed it linked wages more closely to the trade cycle.[5]

3   The 'Oldham District' comprised a large area of south-east Lancashire (much of present-day Greater Manchester) and included Rochdale to the north, Ashton to the south and Middleton to the west. As Farnie explains, the Oldham 'limiteds' constituted the most important group of joint-stock *manufacturing* corporations in Britain and were responsible for 12% of the *world's* cotton-spinning capacity in 1890 (emphasis added). D. Farnie, 'The emergence of Victorian Oldham as the centre of the cotton spinning industry', *Saddleworth Historical Society Bulletin* 12 (1982), 41–53, at p. 42.
4   The lowest prices since 1848 were recorded in Liverpool in March 1892 (*Oldham Standard*, 12 March 1892), and their misjudgement damaged the profits of companies that bought speculatively and left with stocks of 'dear cotton' (*Oldham Standard*, 7 February, 14 February, 28 February, 23 May 1891).
5   A. Bullen, 'The Making of Brooklands', *The Barefoot Aristocrats: A History of the Amalgamated Association of Operative Cotton Spinners*, ed. A. Fowler and T. Wyke (Littleborough, 1987), pp. 93–114.

After 1896, when currency conditions reversed, and the Indian market recovered strongly, boom conditions prevailed. Share prices in Lancashire and investor returns rose rapidly after 1896.[6] That year saw a genuine recovery in demand for direct yarn sales to the Indian market, while English investors, having been frightened off foreign stock after the Baring crisis and faced with lowered yields on Consols, could pick up cotton securities at very low values.[7] The more general improvement of the early 1900s was attributable externally to inflation and the decline of gold values. Strategically Lancashire responded by shifting to finer counts and sewing cotton, and from grey to dyed and fancy goods. By 1903, the combined effect was that important export markets had been recovered, especially India.[8] As gold prices fell, demand and profits from Lancashire spinning increased, leading to a new mill-building boom in 1904–07.

Although benefiting from broader economic shifts, Lancashire remained resolutely independent of London finance. For now, a new class of local investors stood to benefit. Typically these were entrepreneurs who, through previous involvement in the co-operative mill-building booms, had become skilled in company promotion, share-broking and auditing. These investors purchased shares cheaply and effectively took control, abolishing the democratic governance structures of one-shareholder-one-vote that had hitherto prevailed.

Local observers were concerned by their motives, hoping that their interest went beyond short-run speculative profits.[9] Investment booms followed, mostly in specialized spinning firms during the 1900s, backed by this new class of individualistic freelance promotional and speculative capitalists. The same individuals often owned these mills, but they were otherwise managed and operated as separate businesses.

In the culmination of the boom in 1907, when mills earned record profits for their shareholders, promoters attracted outside investors to new ventures financed with large amounts of debt, with significant proportions of profit distributed as dividend payments and bonus dividends. John Bunting floated the largest mill to date, the Times No. 2, in 1907 at 100,000 spindles. Bunting attracted investment from elsewhere in the immediate locality for his new ventures, for example, William Kenyon and the private spinning firm Bagley & Wright. Directors increasingly took significant blocks of shares in their own companies, such as Thomas Gartside in the Shiloh Spinning Company, and used their contacts to attract new investment.[10]

6   S. Toms, 'The finance and growth of the Lancashire cotton textile industry, 1870–1914' (Ph.D. dissertation, University of Nottingham, 1996), chapter 11.
7   *The Economist*, 1897, p. 25; E. M. Sigsworth and J. Blackman, 'The home boom of the 1890s', *Yorkshire Bulletin of Economic and Social Research* 17 (1965), 75–97, at pp. 92–3.
8   S. J. Chapman, 'The report of the tariff commission', *Economic Journal* 15 (1905), 420–7, at p. 426.
9   *Oldham Standard*, 24 September 1898.
10   *Oldham Chronicle*, 28 December 1907; S. Toms, 'The English cotton industry and the loss of the world market', *King Cotton: A Tribute to Douglas Farnie*, ed. J. Wilson (Lancaster, 2009),

During the last boom before the First World War, in 1911, some industry leaders were aware of the potential limitations of this system of finance. A bill was proposed in parliament to regulate new mill flotations. Some industry leaders, including Gartside, were concerned by the practice of calling up only part of the capital, leaving some new mills without equipment and investors vulnerable to risk from further calls of capital.[11]

To all sections of the industry, the world market was vital to profitability and variation in profitability, and entrepreneurs were understandably reluctant to commit themselves to the high fixed costs of large corporate structures.[12] The risk associated with significant fluctuations in demand also reduced the value of internal economies of scale. Finally, the vast returns generated in the days of 'easy money'[13] had a decisive iterative influence on investor behaviour and reinforced the tendency towards specialization. A consequence was the substantial further investment in coarse mule-spinning capacity during the boom of 1905–07.[14]

Perhaps such entrepreneurial behaviour is to be expected for industries whose output is cyclical around an upward secular trend, as cotton was in the 1900s. Confident expectation of a new and more significant boom would no doubt have alleviated the worries of entrepreneurs whose new mills came on stream in 1908, just after the close of the greatest boom hitherto experienced by the industry. After the end of the war in 1918, as the mills returned to civil production, the ingredients for a new and more significant boom were present. Labour and material shortages, however, restricted opportunities for a new wave of mill building. Instead, mill financiers refloated existing mills, typically at three times their pre-war values.[15]

The reconstructions and flotations fell into two broad categories. First, there were syndicates of local directors, promoters and share dealers. They had much in common with, and were often the same individuals, as those involved in the pre-war promotion booms. As explained in chapter 4, these interlocked directors built their empires on the back of the moribund industrial democracy movement in the late 1880s and 1890s. This first type of syndicate concentrated

---

pp. 58–76, at pp. 68–9; R. E. Tyson, 'The Sun Mill Company: A study in democratic investment, 1858–1959' (MA dissertation, University of Manchester, 1962); W. A. Thomas, *The Provincial Stock Exchanges* (London, 1973).

11   Anon., *The Shiloh Story* (Royton, 1974).

12   Toms, 'The finance and growth of the Lancashire cotton textile industry', chapter 11; A. F. Lucas, *Industrial Reconstruction and the Control of Competition: The British Experiments* (London, 1937), p. 167.

13   B. Bowker, *Lancashire under the Hammer* (London, 1928), chapter 3.

14   Toms, 'The finance and growth of the Lancashire cotton textile industry', chapter 10.

15   G. Daniels and J. Jewkes, 'The post-war depression in the Lancashire cotton industry', *Journal of the Royal Statistical Society* 91 (1928), 153–206, at p. 170; Thomas, *The Provincial Stock Exchanges*, p. 156.

on specialized spinning mills and raised debt finance though local loan deposit accounts and equity finance from the Oldham and Manchester stock exchanges.

The second type of syndicate was put together to refloat larger combines. These businesses were similar to, or the same as those that had originated in the merger wave of the 1890s, discussed in chapter 5. These syndicates reconstructed already large combines, absorbing further mills hitherto privately controlled, and were financed using debt and equity from metropolitan capital markets. Importantly, the City of London became involved for the first time in Lancashire on a substantial basis through this second class of transaction.

As before the war, the specialized mill groups continued to access capital from local markets, not from metropolitan or London syndicates. The financial syndicates that channelled the new investment of the 1919–20 boom were the same as those that had led the boom of 1907.[16] Multiple directorships recurred, but on a more extended scale, and all the leading players were local with substantial experience in floating and managing cotton mills. William Hopwood, for example, described as 'the Napoleon of Finance and Industry', had controlling influence in twenty mills.[17] By 1919, Sam Firth Mellor, mill promoter and share dealer, was a director of eighteen companies. One of these companies was Peel Mills, which had a significant role to play in the final transformation of Lancashire's industrial landscape, a point that will be returned to in the final chapter. John Bunting, also a share dealer, held fourteen directorships.[18] Outsiders were involved only occasionally and these included famously reckless speculators and fraudsters such as Ernest Terah Hooley and Horatio Bottomley.[19]

Syndicates were prepared to pay high prices to acquire mills and, indeed, groups of mills. The so-called 'Ashton syndicate' put together a bid of £1.5 million to acquire six mills (Atlas, Cedar, Minerva, Rock, Texas and Tudor)

16 See the survey of share registers in D. Higgins, S. Toms and I. Filatotchev, 'Ownership, financial strategy and performance: The Lancashire cotton textile industry, 1918–1938', *BH* 57 (2015), 97–121.

17 Z. Hutchinson, 'The Trusts grip cotton', *Independent Labour Party Pamphlets*, New Series, no. 28, 1920.

18 Mellor held directorships in the following mills: Argyll, Broadway; Fernhurst, Gee Cross Mill, Gorse, Greenacres, Hartford, Marland, Mars, Mersey, Monton, Moor, Orb, Peel Mills Co., Princess, Rugby, and Stockport Ring Mill. Mellor built up a substantial shareholding in many of these and other companies, for example, Argyll (7.55%), and Asia Mill (3.8%). See Higgins *et al.*, 'Ownership, financial strategy and performance'. In total, Bunting is known to have been involved in fourteen promotions: D. Farnie, 'John Bunting', *Dictionary of Business Biography*, ed. D. Jeremy (London, 1984–86), vol. 1, pp. 506–9, at p. 508.

19 Hooley was involved in the fraudulent promotion of Jubilee Cotton Mills, see *Re Jubilee Cotton Mills Ltd*, [1923] Chancery, 1, 31. Bottomley purchased a 30% stake in the Bolton Union Spinning Company, a company promoted by Alexander Young, who was also involved in the promotion of several other mills (Athens, Brunswick, Butt and Falcon Mills), during the boom. See Higgins *et al.*, 'Ownership, financial strategy and performance'.

in the Ashton-under-Lyne district. The directors of the six specialized mule-spinning mills were almost identical, which facilitated their sale as a common group.[20] The increase in the share price of one of these mills, Minerva, from 70 shillings in January 1919 to 156 shillings in November, just before the bid, was typical.[21] Fred Dawson of Oldham, a director of fifteen other companies including twelve other cotton businesses, led the syndicate. Another Minerva director, Thomas Howe, had board positions on almost precisely the same companies. The other two directors, Herbert Mills and Bertram Whitehead, had a further nine directorships between them, which in all cases were in the same companies as Dawson and Howe.[22]

Cross-directorships were vital because they facilitated lending within business groups. Sun Mill accumulated significant surpluses before and after the First World War, and the directors applied these funds to investments in other mills. Argyll Mill at Failsworth benefited from Sun Mill financial support, facilitated by William O'Neill and Edward Heaton Blackburn, who sat on the boards of both companies. In 1917, when Hall Lane Mill had difficulty repaying a loan from Sun Mill, O'Neill joined its board to provide greater security. Following the post-war recapitalizations, Sun Mill used similar methods to extend control. By 1924, Sam Firth Mellor and Fred Dawson were members of the Sun Mill board. Between them, three Sun Mill directors sat on the boards of firms controlling 1.25 million spindles.[23] In such fashion, the Sun Mill clique achieved de facto control over several mills in the district, including those controlled by the Ashton syndicate.

For the most part, particularly in the Oldham district and coarse-spinning sections, the same Lancashire-based groups which had done so well out of the 1907 boom organized the reflotations.[24] In the Oldham district, specialized mills were refloated, often at three times their pre-war value. In contrast to the groups of specialized mills floated by local operators, the reconstruction and flotation of combines attracted significant outside involvement.

These larger combines thus used a different financial model compared to the specialized spinning firms. Like the pre-war combines, they were more easily able to attract finance from metropolitan capital markets; unlike the pre-war combines, the amalgamated firms of 1919–20 drew on London finance. For example, in 1920 Sir Edward Mackay Edgar, a partner in the London finance house, Sperling & Co. formed Crosses & Winkworth Consolidated Mills, as a combination of Crosses & Winkworth Ltd and other textile firms

20   'Lancashire cotton mill sales', *The Economist*, 29 November 1919.
21   Share listings, *Oldham Chronicle*, regular weekly issues.
22   Cavendish Spinning Mill, PRO annual return form E, BT 31/33811/165932.
23   Tyson, 'The Sun Mill Company', pp. 307–19; Higgins *et al.*, 'Ownership, financial strategy and performance', Table 2.
24   Higgins *et al.*, 'Ownership, financial strategy and performance'.

including Ward & Walker, Lord, Hampson & Lord (1919) and Ainsworth Brothers Limited. Through these and other transactions, substantial sections of the industry in Preston, Blackburn and Bolton were reorganized. Crosses & Winkworth Consolidated expanded further in 1922 and floated Crosses & Heatons' Associated Mills Ltd to acquire nine further mills, mostly located in Bolton, creating a group controlling over £7.25 million of assets. The combination was financed using a new debenture issue of £1.26 million, underwritten by Edgar's investment company Sperling & Co., which collected a commission of 3%, or around £38,000 on the transaction.[25] By combining the mills in this fashion, a Lancashire-based group was able to access finance via the City of London. Hitherto, even the larger combines, including Coats, had obtained all the funding they needed through regional outlets and that remained true of the vast majority of the industry.

Again, these reorganizations followed the combine model which originated in the late 1880s. For example, Horrockses Crewdson, initially formed by a merger in 1887, and expanded through various further acquisitions discussed in chapter 5, was now absorbed into an even larger combine, the Amalgamated Cotton Mills Trust.[26] This particular combine was put together in the period 1918–20 by a coalition of financial and industrial interests from outside the cotton industry. The Chairman was Albert Kirby, Lord Fairfax, an American-born investment banker and partner in the London office of Bonbright & Co., an American finance house. Fairfax's hereditary title granted him a seat in the House of Lords.[27] Also on the board was Samuel Copley, a self-made man from Huddersfield and now Chairman of the City-based Western Australian Insurance Company. The remaining directors were Alexander Lawson Ormerod, Wilfrid Dawson and Harvey Du Cros junior, all of whom were associated with a company with a dubious history of stock market flotations, Dunlop Rubber.[28]

---

25   The acquisitions were: William Heaton & Sons (three mills), North End Spinning Co. Ltd (two mills), John Thomasson and Son, Maco Mill, Victoria Mill and the Atlantic Doubling Mill. The deal was facilitated by the sale of John Bright & Brothers to a group of London financiers: see Crosses & Heatons' Associated Mills Ltd, Prospectus, *Manchester Guardian*, 7 September 1922; *Stock Exchange Official Intelligence*, 1930; *The Times*, 9 October 1929, p. 21.

26   H. McCrosty, *The Trust Movement in British Industry* (London, 1907); Amalgamated Cotton Mills Trust Ltd, *Concerning Cotton: A Brief Account of the Aims and Achievements of the Amalgamated Cotton Mills Trust Limited and its Component Companies* (London, 1921); *Stock Exchange Official Intelligence*.

27   'Fairfax and Co.', *Financial Times*, 7 January 1925, p. 4; *Hansard's Parliamentary Debates*, House of Lords sitting, 18 November 1908.

28   Hutchinson, 'The Trusts grip cotton'. Dawson collaborated with Copley to pull off a major property deal in Huddersfield at around the same time: 'Ramsden Estate. Huddersfield', *Daily Telegraph*, 27 October 1919, p. 12; *Huddersfield Examiner*, 18 February 2011. Du Cros junior was the son of a former Dunlop director and was also involved in the reflotation of the Austin Motor Company. 'Company meetings: Austin Motor Company', *Manchester Guardian*, 23 January 1920, p. 12.

The Amalgamated Cotton Mills Trust's purpose was to buy cotton mills, which were then floated as a combined concern.[29]

The method of finance and promotion bore strong parallels to the Dunlop float of 1896. In this episode, the infamous promoter Ernest Terah Hooley purchased multiple bicycle and tyre manufacturers in the Midlands, and used London connections to push the shares.[30] For similar reasons, the Amalgamated Cotton Mills Trust board, alongside Fairfax, included other prominent financiers: James White of the Beecham Trust and A. R. Stephenson of Messrs Barnato Brothers.[31] White had been a member of the Dunlop board during the pre-war Hooley speculations. In 1916–19, he gained effective control of the Beecham Trust, as members of the Beecham family either died or resigned, becoming the major shareholder and sole active director. White used the Beecham Trust as a vehicle to purchase all the shares in the Amalgamated Cotton Mills Trust.[32] White also collaborated closely with Sir Edgar Mackay Edgar of Crosses & Heaton. Barnato Brothers had accumulated vast capital through dealing in illicit diamonds before the war and now commanded a range of international investments, mostly in Southern Africa. The head of Barnato Brothers, Solly Joel, was also the largest shareholder in De Beers.[33] White and the Beecham Trust were also significant investors in De Beers and in new share issues by the Austin Motor Company and the Dunlop Rubber Company.[34]

Elsewhere in Lancashire, financiers amalgamated mills into larger combines. Although these new combines shared much common practice with the pre-war merger movement, the effect was now to place a large section of the Lancashire cotton industry under the control of London and international finance. In contrast, the specialized mill groups continued to rely on local sources of funding. In the combines, the key players, including the promoters, were industry outsiders with little knowledge or interest in the cotton industry. It was only by creating such large combinations that Edgar and White were able to interest London-based investors. In the event, these new investors would have reason to regret their involvement with the cotton mills of Lancashire.

---

29   Amalgamated Cotton Mills Trust was registered in 1918 as a private company and converted into a public company in 1919. The cotton firms acquired during 1919 were: Robert Hyde Buckley & Sons, Ltd; John Ashworth (1902), Ltd; Mill Hill Spinning Co. Ltd, Eckersleys Cotton Trust Ltd and Acme Spinning Company Limited. 'Amalgamated Cotton Mills Trust (Limited)', *The Times*, 4 December 1919, p. 24.

30   S. Amini and S. Toms, 'Accessing capital markets: Aristocrats and new share issues in the British bicycle boom of the 1890s', *BH* 60 (2018), 231–56.

31   'Amalgamated Cotton Mills Trust (Limited)', *The Times*, 4 December 1919, p. 24.

32   Hutchinson, 'The Trusts grip cotton'; 'Beecham Trust Affairs', *Financial Times*, 13 October 1927, p. 3.

33   T. Johnston, *The Financiers and the Nation* (London, 1934), p. 95; J. Roberts, *Glitter & Greed: The Secret World of the Diamond Cartel* (New York, 2007).

34   *The Economist*, 26 July 1919, p. 140; 8 February 1919, p. 188; 29 March 1919, p. 521.

The interwar crisis

Inflated prices in the reflotations reflected what many commentators believed was a temporary dislocation. Market disequilibrium was sufficient to motivate short-term speculative objectives by promoters well versed in such practices from the pre-war booms. Their flotations achieved new valuations, which created significant fixed-cost commitments for firms in terms of depreciation charges and interest payments that they could not avoid, regardless of the downturn in operating cash flows. Added to that was an expectation of regular dividends based on pre-war levels.

Moreover, the reflotations were conducted in the full knowledge of an advance in wages of 30% across the board. The increase had been agreed as compensation for loss of earnings when, in July 1919, the working week was reduced from 55½ to 48 hours per week. Operatives benefited by around £1.5 million according to one estimate, which needs to be set in the context of the £5.6 million upward revaluation of the refloated mills, justified by expectations that 'the present boom will last several years'.[35] It is noteworthy that these changes paralleled the outcome of the Factory Act debates seventy years earlier, but without the intense lobbying based on the threat of foreign competition. Ironically international competition proved to be a much more significant problem after 1920 than it did after 1850. The attitude of mill owners after the First World War is a testament to their new-found confidence in trading conditions, which was underpinned with genuine optimism, however misplaced.

The use of existing capacity as the basis for the reflotation also locked firms into pre-1914 technology. Once the crisis hit, with new cost pressures and in the absence of free cash flow and declining share prices, firms lacked the funds needed for reinvestment and re-equipment. In this sense, the ownership structure that emerged from the reflotation boom acted as a barrier to the successful reorganization of the industry once it became apparent that the reduction in demand for Lancashire's products was long-term.[36]

The scale of the collapse in export markets in 1920–21 was unprecedented in the history of the industry. Firms exporting to India were particularly vulnerable as tariffs on imports were introduced to pay for the defence of the Raj in 1917, and were then increased in 1921, 1925 and 1931 in an attempt to cultivate support from local Indian elites.[37] The loss of demand caused a parallel

---

35 'Lancashire cotton trade in 1919', *The Economist*, 31 January 1920, p. 183.

36 I. Filatotchev and S. Toms, 'Corporate governance and financial constraints on strategic turnarounds', *Journal of Management Studies* 43 (2006), 407–33.

37 J. Singleton, 'The Lancashire cotton industry, the Royal Navy, and the British Empire, c.1700–1960', *The Fibre that Changed the World: The Cotton Industry in International Perspective*, ed. D. Farnie and D. Jeremy (Oxford, 2004), pp. 57–84, at p. 75.

collapse in profit margins and dividends. Figure 16 shows the spike in profit during the short-lived boom, and the breakdown and further falls that followed.

Although dramatic, investors could not have anticipated the subsequent and permanent collapse in the post-war market. Unlike previous cotton booms, such as those of 1907 and 1911–13, the events of 1919–21, precipitated a much more extended and severe period of depression, which had more impact on the coarse section around Oldham than the fine spinning sector centred on Bolton.[38] Exports of cotton piece goods averaged 58% of their 1913 level during the 1920s and 29% during the 1930s. For yarn exports, the corresponding figures were 80% and 66% respectively.[39] Throughout the interwar period as a whole, profit rates reflected these changes. Profit rates approximately halved, from an average return on capital of 7.52% in the period 1890–1913 to 2.59% in 1921–39.[40] As Figure 16 shows, in the latter period, profit rates rarely exceeded 5% in any given year. Once the boom was over, in the absence of co-ordinated restructuring strategies to defend remaining markets, the industry faced further protracted decline.

For many years after the post-war boom, some industry leaders refused to acknowledge the consequences of changed conditions. As might be expected, industry representatives were keen to defend the industry's performance, particularly in the crisis-ridden interwar years, and blamed governments for monetary policies that made cotton less competitive in overseas markets. They argued that the conditions of the early 1890s paralleled those of the 1920s and early 1930s.[41] There was some justification for this line of reasoning. After all, the industry had suffered protracted periods of market dislocation and prolonged slumps in the early 1800s, the 1860s and again in the 1890s.

Unsurprisingly, by the late 1920s, critical voices grew louder. The persistence of depression led industry expert Benjamin Bowker to suggest that the pre-war period had been a 'golden age' by comparison.[42] John Maynard Keynes was prominent in discussions of how to resolve Lancashire's increasingly protracted crisis. He argued that the core problem was overcapacity, but also that directors lacked the incentives to scrap machinery or even exit the industry altogether, describing them as 'boneheads ... who want to live the rest of their lives in peace'.[43] By the early 1930s, many firms had substantial debit balances on

---

38   Sir H. Clay, *Report on the Position of the English Cotton Industry* (London, 1931), pp. 8–9; Political and Economic Planning, *Report on the British Cotton Industry* (London, 1934), pp. 55–6, 58.
39   Calculated from B. Mitchell and H. Jones, *Second Abstract of British Historical Statistics* (Cambridge, 1971), and R. Robson, *The Cotton Industry in Britain* (London, 1957), statistical appendices.
40   Calculated from CIFD.
41   Federation of Master Cotton Spinners' Associations, *Measures for the Revival of the Lancashire Cotton Industry* (Manchester, 1936).
42   Bowker, *Lancashire under the Hammer*, p. 23.
43   Quoted in R. Streat, *Lancashire and Whitehall: The Diary of Sir Raymond Streat*, vol. 2 (Manchester, 1987), p. 181.

their reserve accounts.[44] In many cases, these translated into significant and unplanned overdrafts. As significant numbers of cotton firms accumulated losses, the indebtedness of the cotton firms threatened the stability of the banks. Particularly affected were those such as Williams Deacon's Bank and the Union Bank of Manchester, which had significant exposure to the cotton industry and the broader economy of northern England.[45] However, rather than face a significant bad debt problem in the event of liquidation of the weaker firms, the banks chose instead to keep the firms afloat, in the hope of them undercutting competitors and trading out of difficulty. Firms shared remaining production through organized short time.

The Clynes Report of 1929 acknowledged the problem of debt overhang and the barrier created to raising new capital to finance re-equipment and the closer integration of spinning and weaving. It proposed a new organization, the Lancashire Cotton Corporation which, with the support of the Bank of England, would acquire financially distressed mills. Some units would be closed down, but technically efficient mills would be freed of debt and potentially expanded.[46] Between 1929 and 1931, the Bank advanced capital of £920,000, which the Lancashire Cotton Corporation used to acquire approximately ten million spindles and a hundred firms, mainly in the depressed coarse-spinning section. Frank Platt, who had been involved in the 1919–20 boom and retired prematurely on the proceeds, was appointed as managing director of the new combine in 1932.[47]

Notwithstanding this intervention, for Keynes and other critics of the industry the problem was too much capacity. As a result, fixed costs were spread across too many firms, and rationalization of surplus capacity was prevented.[48] Much of the subsequent historiography of the industry has endorsed Keynes' position.[49]

---

44 Of a sample of 161 companies listed in *Tattersall's Annual Cotton Trade Review* of 1931, 101 had debit balances on their reserve accounts, which for some mill companies exceeded £140,000: Atlas (£252,000), Astley (£170,000), Palm (£147,000), Butts (£146,000), Ace (£144,000).

45 The bank's lending accounted for 13.8% of spindles using American cotton and its total advances to forty spinning companies was £3.7 million by the end of 1928. Political and Economic Planning, *Report on the British Cotton Industry*, p. 59; R. S. Sayers, *The Bank of England 1891–1944*, vol. 3: *Appendices* (Cambridge, 1976), p. 253. J. H. Bamberg, 'The government, the banks and the Lancashire cotton industry, 1918–1939' (Ph.D. dissertation, University of Cambridge, 1984), pp. 308–9.

46 *Economic Advisory Council, Committee on the Cotton Industry* (Clynes Report), BPP, 1929–30, Cmd. 3615, XII.825, pp. 20–1.

47 J. H. Bamberg, 'Sir Frank Platt', *Dictionary of Business Biography*, ed. D. Jeremy (London, 1984–86), vol. 4, pp. 716–22. Thomas, *The Provincial Stock Exchanges*, p. 157; J. H. Bamberg, 'The rationalization of the British cotton industry in the interwar years', *Textile History* 19 (1988), 83–101, at p. 94.

48 J. M. Keynes, *The Return to Gold and Industrial Policy II, Collected Works* (Cambridge, 1981), pp. 601, 605; Bamberg, 'The rationalization of the British cotton industry', pp. 94–6.

49 J. H. Porter, 'The commercial banks and the financial problems of the English cotton industry, 1919–1939', *The International Review of Banking History* 9 (1974), 1–16; Bamberg, 'The rationalization of the British cotton industry'; R. Marchionatti, 'Keynes and the collapse of

If Keynes' analysis was correct, it lends weight to the arguments about the failure of the Lancashire entrepreneurial class discussed in the previous chapter. As demonstrated, there is little evidence of irrational entrepreneurial decision-making before 1914. However, it could perhaps still be argued that things were different post-1920, such that with the problem of overcapacity and the sunk investments in mule spinning and power-loom weaving, entrepreneurial stubbornness was now the main obstacle to successfully repositioning the cotton industry in the long run.

Indeed the Keynesian narrative assigns collective responsibility for failure to entrepreneurs as a class. For Keynes, the problem lay with incumbent directors, and the banks, that he held responsible for their inability to restructure the industry. Keynes famously accused the bankers of acting like 'professional paralytics' and 'a species of deaf-mutes'.[50]

How far is it justifiable to blame entrepreneurs collectively? The accusation might be reasonable if all entrepreneurs conformed to the Keynes stereotype. However, as earlier chapters have shown, Lancashire entrepreneurs were a heterogeneous group. In the difficult circumstances of the 1920s and 1930s, were there nonetheless some success stories and were they sufficient to exonerate the much-maligned mill owners?

Interwar successes and failures

As had been the case before 1914, the most successful firms, in financial terms at least, were the Milnrow Ring Spinners. Each of the original firms – Haugh, New Ladyhouse and New Hey – comfortably exceeded the average rate of return.[51] Year on year, each firm's returns on capital were similar, reflecting collaborative arrangements for purchasing, transport and distribution. As before 1914, the three firms shared common directorships. Similar arrangements were in force elsewhere in Rochdale and in 1930 there was a merger between the Clover, Croft and State Mills. In 1934, the three Milnrow firms merged to become New Hey Rings, thereby cementing the previous voluntary arrangement.[52]

Equally successful was the Era Ring Mill in Rochdale, which gained a

---

the British cotton industry in the 1920s: a microeconomic case against laissez-faire', *Journal of Post Keynesian Economics* 17 (1995), 427–45. S. Bowden and D. M. Higgins, 'Short-time working and price maintenance: Collusive tendencies in the cotton-spinning industry, 1919–1939', *EcHR* 51 (1998), 319–43.

50 Keynes, *The Return to Gold and Industrial Policy II*, p. 605.

51 Average profits were respectively 9.21, 8.32 and 10.24%, compared with the average for all firms of 2.59%. Calculated from CIFD.

52 'Spinning companies amalgamate', *Manchester Guardian*, 15 March 1930, p. 24; 'Another Rochdale combine', *Manchester Guardian*, 25 July 1934, p. 18.

reputation as one of the most up-to-date mills in Lancashire. Originally floated in 1898 as a project backed by Howard & Bullough, the mill was subsequently extended to house 120,000 ring spindles, making it one of the largest of its kind. Unlike many companies in the 1920s, the mill was free of debt. It used the capital raised in the boom to invest outside the industry, in government and municipal securities, creating a fund of financial assets worth over £130,000. In 1928 the firm used this surplus to reduce its capital by half, thereby undoing the overcapitalization of the post-war boom. In doing so, it repaid £90,000 to its shareholders.[53] In other words, cash flow was steady, although the rate of profit was lower than it would have been had the firm not watered its stock in the 1919–20 boom. Even without the financial investments, Era was the most successful of the ring spinners and, indeed, most other Lancashire firms in the interwar period. It averaged 9.18% profit during the period and this rate increased significantly after the capital reduction.[54] These results demonstrated that specialist Lancashire ring spinners could be competitive in coarse counts, even in the challenging conditions of the interwar period.

Other specialist ring spinners enjoyed more modest returns compared to Era and the Milnrow group. Iris, Ellenroad and Cromer all earned average profits in the range of 4–6%. Even so, in common with the other ring spinners, they typically built substantial credit balances on reserve and were free of debt. Taken together, however, they outperformed the rest of the industry. Figure 17 shows the relative rates of profit. As the trend shows, the fluctuations in the general level of profit were similar, but the ring spinners enjoyed a consistent premium in all years. In the period 1926–38, this averaged 2.89%.[55] During the 1930s, the gap was widening and was likely explained by improvements in ring-spinning technology. The automation of intermediate processes like high-speed winding and the development of high drafting were particularly significant, and made the productivity advantages of ring spinning much more apparent.[56] In

53   Era Ring Mill Company Ltd, *History of the Era Ring Mill, 1898–1955* (Rochdale, n.d.); 'Mill capital reduction', *Manchester Guardian*, 11 April 1928, p. 10; 'Capital returned to shareholders', *Manchester Guardian*, 3 October 1928, p. 14.
54   Calculated from CIFD.
55   Calculated from CIFD. The seven specialized ring spinners in the sample averaged profits of 5.18% compared to 2.29% for a sample of all other types of firm, including typically specialized mule spinners and vertical combines.
56   S. Toms, 'Growth, profits and technological choice: The case of the Lancashire cotton textile industry', *Journal of Industrial History* 1 (1998), 35–55; S. Toms and M. Beck, 'The limitations of economic counterfactuals: The case of the Lancashire textile industry', *Management & Organizational History* 2 (2007), 315–30. H. Catling, *The Spinning Mule* (Newton Abbot, 1970), p. 189; S. Noguera, *Theory and practice of high drafting* (privately published, 1936), pp. 20–3; L. H. C. Tippett, *A Portrait of the Lancashire Textile Industry* (Oxford, 1969); G. R. Saxonhouse and G. Wright, 'Stubborn Mules and Vertical Integration: The disappearing constraint?', *EcHR* 60 (1987), 87–94, at p. 92; Toms, 'The finance and growth of the Lancashire cotton textile industry', chapter 5.

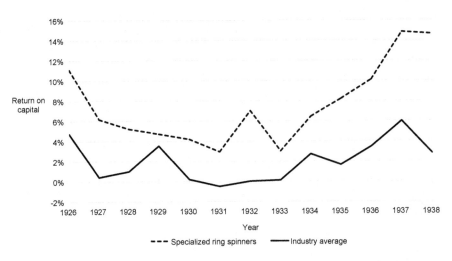

Figure 17. Comparative profitability, specialized ring spinners, and other firms, 1926–38

Source: CIFD.

1932 a survey noted three cases of ring-spinning mills replacing low-draft with high-draft spinning, resulting in average improvements in labour productivity of 49.3%.[57] In 1936 industry lobbyists noted that high draft, bigger lifts and larger rings paved the way for the replacement of mules with ring spindles.[58]

These improvements offered direct advantages to specialized ring spinners but also had the potential to facilitate the integration of spinning and weaving processes. Ashton Brothers of Hyde, now under the chairmanship of Henry Philips Greg, was able to build on his connections to the British Northrop Loom Company and its strong pre-war track record as an innovative business.[59] Frank Smallshaw, spinning manager at the firm's Throstle Bank Mill, developed an automatic bunching motion which allowed ring spinning directly onto pirns for use on automatic looms.[60] Innovations like this helped ensure that Ashtons was the most successful of the larger combines during the interwar period.

The Ashton Brothers' strategy provided a working example of the type of integration now aspired to by policymakers in the formation of the Lancashire Cotton Corporation. Company advertising stressed the firm's ability to deliver large orders quickly and at low-cost, thanks to its investment in three thousand

---

57 Board of Trade, *An Industrial Survey of the Lancashire Area* (London, 1932), p. 135.
58 CP, Ernest Varley Haigh, 'Memorandum on the Cotton Spinning Industry Bill', CHAR 2/289, p. 24.
59 *Investors Monthly Manual*, December 1921, p. 761.
60 A. Ormerod, *Industrial Odyssey* (Manchester, 1996), pp. 15–16.

Figure 18. Ashton Brothers, comparative profitability, 1921–39
Source: CIFD.

automatic looms.[61] Even so, the profits of Ashtons did nothing to inspire confidence in the likely financial success of a strategy based on integration, and certainly not before 1930. As Figure 18 shows, Ashton Brothers' profits tracked the rest of the industry quite closely, and if anything, underperformed slightly.[62] Although Ashtons improved in the 1930s, the benefits of technological innovation associated with integrated production did not translate readily into enhanced financial returns. Elsewhere in the weaving section, in Burnley and Nelson, for example, high indebtedness prevented investment in automatic looms, with employers instead preferring the labour-intensive 'more looms' strategy. The intention was to increase the number of looms per operative from the traditional four up to eight, but the consequence was a series of strikes and lockouts in the early 1930s.[63]

Success stories were, for the most part, confined to the specialized firms, including, perhaps most surprisingly, in the specialized mule-spinning section. The American coarse section was particularly badly hit by the loss of export markets, but even there, some firms performed well. The original producer

61   Board of Trade, *British Fair Catalogue*, Dept. of Overseas Trade (London, 1929).
62   From 1921 to 1931, Ashtons averaged 1.04% compared with 2.95% for the rest of the industry; in the period 1932–39, the corresponding figures were 6.70% and 3.20%. Calculated from CIFD.
63   J. Southern, 'Cotton and the Community: Exploring changing concepts of identity and community on Lancashire's cotton frontier c.1890–1950' (Ph.D. dissertation, University of Central Lancashire, 2016), p. 144.

co-operative, Sun Mill, now managed on conventional lines, enjoyed profits averaging 7.53%, more than the average ring spinner, and well ahead of the average for the industry as a whole of 2.29%.

The reasons for this success were financial rather than a matter of purely productive efficiency. A typical survival strategy for the more successful firms was to invest the surplus cash raised in the 1919–20 boom in other businesses or financial assets. The returns on these investments provided a cushion and profit boost during the difficult years of the 1920s and helped pay down any outstanding debt finance. By the early 1930s, these firms had typically cashed in their investments and used the proceeds to reduce share capital. Era, Sun, Clover and Croft Mills all followed this strategy. Loans to municipal authorities were cashed in to finance the merger in the case of Clover and Croft Mills.[64]

Where debt was problematic for many Oldham companies, it was an asset for others. Like Era, by the mid-1920s, Sun Mill had significant investments outside the business amounting to £100,000. In the tradition of the venture-capital-type strategies of the early successful entrepreneurs, the Sun Mill directors invested in other cotton firms. The largest loan was £50,000, secured on the assets of Minerva Mill, Ashton-under-Lyne. Having failed to secure an agreement to be absorbed by the Lancashire Cotton Corporation, the shareholders agreed to put Minerva into liquidation in May 1930, giving Sun Mill as a secured creditor de facto control. The Sun Mill directors were well connected and now received £75,000 in settlement from the Lancashire Cotton Corporation, which took over the assets of Minerva in 1931. The proceeds were applied to reduce the capital of Sun Mill from £150,000 to £75,000.[65] It is worth noting that Sun Mill was making good profits, exceeding £30,000 in each of the years 1927–29, which, excluding the financial assets and their associated income, represented a good return on capital.[66] In 1931, the Lancashire Cotton Corporation was receiving advances from the Bank of England to buy out cotton mills and close them down. The generous settlement of the Minerva debt, therefore, amounted to a bonus for Sun Mill, an already successful company.

Unlike Sun Mill, and most of the industry, the specialized mule-spinning firm Shiloh committed to further investment in modern plant and equipment. In 1926, it constructed a brand-new mill, the Elk, which along with Park and Royton Mills, now became part of the Shiloh group. For several years the Royton-based group remained outside industry-wide price agreements. In 1934, the Shiloh directors, led by Gartside, relented and accepted the need for collusion on pricing. Their negotiations with the rival Royton-based Cheetham

64 'Amalgamation at Rochdale', *Manchester Guardian*, 20 May 1930, p. 14.
65 'Minerva Spinning Company', *Manchester Guardian*, 27 May 1930, p. 18; 'A successful company', *Manchester Guardian*, 10 November 1931, p. 12.
66 CIFD.

group, resulted in the Royton Coarse Count agreement.[67] Shiloh's profits were low in the 1920s and lower still in the 1930s once these new arrangements were in place. Even so, the firm outperformed other specialized mills year by year and on average during these decades.[68]

Where opportunities were available to achieve financial successes in the problematic decades of the 1920s and 1930s, these were mostly taken by specialized firms. Whether successful or not, the specialized firms were characterized by interlocking control of regional directorates which facilitated mergers, collusion through price agreements, output and profit-sharing, selective mill closure and, where needed, access to venture capital. By contrast, the larger combines were almost uniformly unsuccessful. The limited financial returns of Ashton Brothers, notwithstanding an innovative strategy, have already been noted.

An innovative strategy of a different kind was developed by the large combine, Tootal Broadhurst & Lee. As the directors of Sun Mill had abolished the bonus to labour fifty years earlier, it was now introduced as 'good business' sense by the executive of one of Lancashire's largest firms, Sir Kenneth Lee. Each year, the value of the labour bonus was determined by the dividend paid to ordinary shareholders, which could be taken directly as wages or as shares in the company. The firm also made significant investments in pensions and education, such that there would be no waste of young life. The bonus to labour was substantial in financial terms, amounting to £47,000 in 1937, the equivalent of around 3% return on capital. Between 1919 and 1939, the firm met the threshold necessary to trigger the employee bonus every year excepting 1921 and 1931. Factoring the bonus, the firm was the most profitable of the larger combines. Moreover, the firm's cash flow was sufficient to redeem the entirety of its debenture stock in 1934.[69] Where Sun Mill had failed, Tootal Broadhurst & Lee succeeded in aligning the incentives of its employees.

Of the remaining combines, the Fine Cotton Spinners' & Doublers' Association and Barlow & Jones were more successful. These firms had raised significant amounts of fresh capital from the London and Manchester stock markets when floated in the amalgamation boom of 1898–1900 and had built up further reserves in the intervening profitable years before 1920. Hence the scale of their refinancing activities was lower than comparable companies such as Amalgamated Cotton Mills Trust and Crosses & Winkworth Consolidated

---

67 The so-called 'Cheetham Group' consisted of the Bee, Fir, King, Lion, Thornham and Ash (of Shaw), and was initially launched by John Brown Tattersall. Anon., *The Shiloh Story*.

68 In the period 1926–38, Shiloh's profits were 3.46% compared with 1.30% for other specialized mills. Calculated from CIFD.

69 CIFD; 'Copartnership in cotton industry', *Manchester Guardian*, 4 March 1938, p. 14. The bonus was paid where the firm paid a dividend of more than a threshold of 7½% on its ordinary shares and was set at twice the difference between the actual dividend and the threshold.

Mills. They therefore required less debt finance. In 1912 the Fine Cotton Spinners' & Doublers' Association's total loan capital was £9,633,000, increasing to £12,633,000 by 1921, which although a considerable increase of 30%, was small compared to the typical average for a refloated company.[70] Similar circumstances favoured the Bolton-based, fine-spinning combine Barlow & Jones. The firm averaged profits of around 6% during the interwar period as a whole, more than double the industry average, although it was a relatively poor performer after 1926,[71] notwithstanding significant investments in modern machinery. Even so, the firm was sufficiently profitable to pay down a half or its preference capital in a restructuring in 1931.[72] Nonetheless, difficult trading circumstances squeezed profits further. In a statement issued in 1934, the Chairman, Mr T. D. Barlow, attributed the decline in the company's fortune to changing customer tastes and the threat of Japanese competition.[73]

The most notable failures in the interwar period were the large combines floated by London finance houses. These were most notably Crosses & Heatons and the Amalgamated Cotton Mills Trust, promoted by a closely linked group of London-based investors. Crosses & Heatons' Associated Mills, the Bolton-based combine, consisted of nine pre-war mills, again with relatively modern equipment of 709,000 mule-equivalent spindles.[74] The recapitalization deal used securitized finance, such that promoters were able to realize profits on the issue, leaving outside investors taking most of the risk,[75] and ultimately bearing the losses when the firm subsequently performed very poorly in financial terms. The firm recorded double-digit percentage losses in 1928, and again in 1933, and underperformed the industry index in almost all other years.[76]

The effect of the promotions was to confirm mutual suspicion and distrust between Lancashire and the City of London, which was also illustrated by the flotation and subsequent financial performance of the Amalgamated Cotton Mills Trust. In 1919, the new Chairman of the Amalgamated Cotton Mills Trust, Lord Fairfax, thanked James White of the Beecham Trust, for being 'a tower of strength in shaping your company into its present strong position'.

70   D. Higgins and S. Toms, 'Financial distress, corporate borrowing, and industrial decline: The Lancashire cotton spinning industry, 1918–38', *Accounting, Business & Financial History* 13 (2003), 207–32. The figures for the Fine Cotton Spinners' & Doublers' Association are calculated from the SER, annual accounts, London Guildhall Library.

71   CIFD.

72   'Barlow & Jones: Proposed Return of Half the Pref. Capital', *Manchester Guardian*, 22 July 1931, p. 14.

73   'Barlow & Jones, Ltd: Changes in Consumers' Habits', *Manchester Guardian*, 27 February 1934, p. 17.

74   These mills were valued into the new combine at £2.456 million; *Manchester Commercial Guardian*, 7 September 1922.

75   Higgins *et al.*, 'Ownership, financial strategy and performance'.

76   In the period 1921–39, the firm averaged profits of only 0.5% per annum; Calculated from CIFD.

At the same time, Fairfax was also keen to play down impressions that the combine was dominated by London interests, stressing that every firm in the amalgamation was under the control of a Lancastrian director. He also pointed out that the financial advisory committee, which sat in London, was strongly influenced by gentlemen from Lancashire and Yorkshire.[77] Fairfax, no doubt, had in mind the very same James White, the son of a Rochdale bricklayer and cotton factory worker in his youth, and Wilfrid Dawson and Samuel Copley, both of Huddersfield origin, now turned property speculators and City bankers.[78]

Having been provided with the necessary finance by the Beecham Trust, the strategy of the Amalgamated Cotton Mills Trust was to invest in mills, which, according to technical advisers, would complement existing strengths. Horrockses Crewdson, the more substantial part of the new combine, had pursued such a strategy quite successfully before 1914. Horrockses had a reputation in the quality end of the market and relatively modern machinery. Moreover, Horrockses had combined ownership of all stages of production, such that yarn was supplied directly to its weaving sheds, which in turn supplied its making-up factory in Manchester. The vertical structure allowed Horrockses to promote its goods through marketing and advertising into retail outlets in the home market.[79]

Horrockses, along with smaller, previously independent west Lancashire companies, was now absorbed by the newly formed Amalgamated Cotton Mills Trust. Notwithstanding the pre-war success of the Horrockses model, the combination failed to earn anything but the smallest profits throughout the interwar period, barely breaking even in most years.[80] The financial results reflected the Amalgamated Cotton Mills Trust's economic structure. It was mostly an investment trust and collected dividends from its subsidiary investments such that it could maintain a positive balance on its reserve account.

In guaranteeing that it could service its financial liabilities, the Amalgamated Cotton Mills Trust placed a great deal of pressure on its subsidiary companies. These firms, including Horrockses, had independent debt capital, raised with guarantees provided by the Trust. Servicing this debt was problematic in the face of declining operating margins and the requirement to pay dividends to the Trust. In 1930, Horrockses was forced to defer interest payments on its debentures and the Amalgamated Cotton Mills Trust sought release from its guarantee. Horrockses was restructured shortly afterwards with £1.4 million written-off assets and conversion of some of the debentures into non-cumulative preference shares. A further pending write-down excused Fairfax from reporting

77 'Amalgamated Cotton Mills Trust', *The Times*, 4 December 1919, p. 24.
78 T. A. B. Corley, 'White, James (1877–1927)', *Oxford Dictionary of National Biography* (Oxford, 2004); *Huddersfield Examiner*, 18 February 2011.
79 'Horrockses, Crewdson, & Co., Ltd', *Manchester Guardian*, 20 December 1935, p. 16.
80 The average return on capital in the period 1921–38 was just 1.40%. Calculated from CIFD.

the losses in Horrockses in 1931 and he excluded Horrockses from the compu-
tation of a £222,024 loss for the rest of the group, most of which was due to
an extraordinary write-down of stocks.[81]

The restructuring of 1931 was the first step towards Horrockses becoming an
independent business once again. To do so meant removing the constraints of
London finance imposed by the 1919–20 reconstruction. The firm had already
reduced capital in 1927, following falls in the price of raw cotton and significant
stock write-downs.

Meanwhile, the Amalgamated Cotton Mills Trusts' chief financial backer, the
Beecham Trust, had already collapsed in 1927 following White's failed oilfields
speculation in collaboration with Sir Edgar Mackay Edgar, and his subsequent
suicide.[82] The cancellation of the preference shares in the 1931 reconstruction
ended the Amalgamated Cotton Mills Trusts' dominant control over board
appointments.[83] In 1935, Horrockses was demerged from the Amalgamated
Cotton Mills Trust and relaunched as an independent company. The capital
was now reduced to £1 million, split equally between ordinary stock and
debentures. Before the first reconstruction in 1927, the equivalent figure was
£5.5 million, which provides some barometer of not just the scale of the initial
overcapitalization, but also the amount of capital subsequently absorbed in
fixed charges and dividends. The new Chairman, Ernest Varley Haigh, stressed
that the effect of the reconstruction would be a relief of £70,000 net debenture
interest, which could instead be invested in working capital. In turn, this would
facilitate maintenance of output at higher and more profitable levels.[84]

Haigh's expectations were substantially fulfilled in subsequent years.
Volumes increased significantly in absolute terms and relative to the rest of the
industry in both domestic and overseas markets. New markets were developed
in North America and the loss-making garment operation in Manchester was
made profitable. Problems remained, most notably in Central Europe where the
firm's Austrian subsidiary was closed down in response to difficulties caused
by quotas and employment regulations.[85] Nonetheless, the company achieved
something of a turnaround as a result of becoming independent.

81 'Interest payment deferred', *Financial Times*, 22 October 1930, p. 7; 'Amalgamated Cotton
Mills Trust', *Financial Times*, 21 December 1931, p. 7; 'Interim Dividends', *Financial Times*,
12 December 1931, p. 6.
82 'Horrockses Crewdson', *Financial Times*, 19 January 1927. Johnston, *Financiers and the
Nation*, p. 95.
83 'Amalgamated Cotton Mills Trust', *Financial Times*, 21 December 1931, p. 7.
84 Capital was reduced to £4.1 million in 1927 and £2.5 million by 1932. 'Horrockses Drastic
Capital Plan', *Financial Times*, 26 April 1935; 'Horrockses, Crewdson, & Co., Ltd', *Manchester
Guardian*, 20 December 1935, p. 16.
85 'Horrockses, Crewdson, & Co., Limited: A Year of Progress', *Manchester Guardian*,
22 December 1936, p. 18; 'Horrockses, Crewdson, and Company, Limited', *Manchester Guardian*,
21 December 1937, p. 18.

The history of the Amalgamated Cotton Mills Trust and Horrockses illustrates the combined adverse effects of recapitalization and overcapacity, and their interaction. Horrockses had a successful business model before 1914 which did not work as part of the Amalgamated Cotton Mills Trust combine. Overcapacity in the industry generally meant Horrockses was vulnerable to price-cutting competition, but the requirement to service debt and pay dividends to the Amalgamated Cotton Mills Trust starved it of funds for working capital so that it could not exploit its scale and efficiency advantages. Funds that could have been invested in Lancashire were, for the first time, used to prop up the share price of a combine financed by London investors. In common with other Lancashire businesses in the interwar period,[86] financial restructuring was an essential prerequisite for successfully turning around Horrockses Crewdson.

As had been the case before 1914, Horrockses' success was based around a coherent vertical structure, but this was not always replicated by the other large combines. Problems arose from organizational structure and production planning. These were particularly notable at the Lancashire Cotton Corporation, where acquisitions had been determined by financial considerations and the convenience of pre-existing networks of interconnected directors. As a consequence, the merged units lacked logic and created significant management problems. The firm was an amalgamation of mostly unintegrated firms that nonetheless required the co-ordination of output. During the 1930–32 depression, management problems in the early days of the Lancashire Cotton Corporation were added to by first, the sheer scale of a business operating in an industry characterized by relatively small order size and second, the pedagogic planning problems endemic in centrally allocating these orders to a large number of operating factories.[87] A boardroom battle led to the abandonment of centralized management control in 1932 and its replacement with a profit-centre structure. Platt's emergence as managing director ensured that the company remained a relatively decentralized federation of vertically specialized units.[88]

In sum, amalgamations centralized capital and facilitated the retention of control by incumbent directors, while preserving specialized physically separated units. As a result, the large combines were not suitable for delivering technologically integrated production. The same was true of mergers of smaller groups of specialized spinning mills. They were, however, able to co-ordinate pricing and exercise considerable market power. After 1933, for example, Platt launched the first of a series of price maintenance schemes to cover the medium 'American' section, with the support of the banks, which did not succeed

---

86 Filatotchev and Toms, 'Corporate governance and financial constraints on strategic turnarounds'.
87 G. A. Bennett, 'The present position of the cotton industry in Great Britain' (MA dissertation, University of Manchester, 1933), p. 77.
88 Bamberg, 'Sir Frank Platt', pp. 717–19; *The Economist*, 8 October 1932.

straight away but subsequently, and once more widely accepted, spread to other sections of the industry.[89]

Despite greater industry co-ordination, performance differentials mitigated its effectiveness. Where efforts were made to secure industry-wide solutions to the problem of overcapacity, financially successful and struggling firms now adopted different lobbying strategies. In 1936, the Cotton Spinning Industry Bill proposed a scrappage scheme based on quota to reduce surplus capacity, which was to be financed by a levy on all firms. The better-performing firms opposed the measure, such as Era Ring Mill, and the Shiloh group, including Elk and Park Mills and Royton Spinning Company. Oliver Jacks of Ashton Brothers co-ordinated the opposition to the Bill.[90] Although a majority of 57% of employers favoured the Bill, such support, according to their opponents, merely reflected the interests of the banks.[91] Ernest Varley Haigh, of Horrockses Crewdson, supported the Bill, albeit in guarded terms, favouring intervention per se, but based on a government subsidy that could finance re-equipment rather than using the proposed levy on cotton firms.[92] The supporters of the Bill prevailed and in 1936 an Act was passed, providing a compulsory levy on the trade to purchase and scrap 'redundant' spindles. The Act resulted in the scrapping of 641 million spindles by the time the Spindles Board was wound up in 1942.[93]

The passage of the Act coincided with a recovery in profit rates for many cotton firms. Other facts besides scrapping surplus capacity contributed to the improvement. Lancashire Cotton Corporation paid its first-ever dividend in 1938, nine years after its formation. The directors attributed the increased profits to the successful operation of pricing agreements, which helped guarantee good margins and further inter-firm collaborations to improve product quality.[94] The Fine Cotton Spinners' & Doublers' Association also achieved its best profit for eight years in 1938.[95]

The critical problem that remained was that the loss of export markets denied access to scale economies and the possibility of greater production efficiency. At the Ottawa Conference in 1932, a system of bilateral tariffs within the British Empire was agreed upon, recognizing that there could be no return to the gold standard. Industry leaders, therefore, retained some hope that a currency depreciation would prompt a recovery, as had happened previously

89   Bamberg, 'The government, the banks and the Lancashire cotton industry', pp. 308–12.
90   CP, Cotton Spinning Industry Bill, CHAR 2/289, Correspondence, pp. 1–8.
91   CP, Cotton Spinning Industry Bill, CHAR 2/289, Opposition Committee Memorandum, pp. 8–9.
92   CP, Cotton Spinning Industry Bill, CHAR 2/289, Correspondence, pp. 1–8.
93   Anon., The Shiloh Story; Cotton Industry (Reorganisation) Act 1936, 26 Geo. 5 & 1 Edw. 8 c. 21.
94   Manchester Guardian, 7 January 1938; 'Value of price agreements in cotton industry', Manchester Guardian, 28 January 1938, p. 13.
95   Manchester Guardian, 14 May 1938.

in 1896.[96] In the absence of such conditions, they instead focused their efforts on recovering these markets. In 1937, they published a pamphlet entitled 'Lancashire's remedy'. The document represented an attempt at industry self-government and became the basis for the proposed Cotton Industry Enabling Bill. The pamphlet advocated an industry levy to fund technical and scientific research and greater co-ordination of effort between producers and distributors, to make it possible to produce and sell in bulk.[97] Self-government failed, partly as a result of opposition from independent firms, reluctant to pay levies to benefit those less efficient. The provisions were watered down when legislation was finally introduced in 1939 and was, in any case, not implemented due to the intervention of wartime arrangements.[98]

During the interwar period, the evidence shows that many firms were efficiently organized with modern technology and committed to further innovation. At the same time, several firms had surplus capital, which they invested in financial assets. There was no evidence, therefore, that there was a shortage of capital or a lack of commitment to investment for the productive opportunities that were available. Even so, all firms suffered to some extent by reduced opportunities in export markets. 'Lancashire's remedy' typified several failed attempts at collective entrepreneurship on the part of industry leaders. Although profit rates were low throughout the 1920s and 1930s, they were not uniformly so, partly reflecting the differential impact of financial restructuring in the 1919–20 boom and that financially stronger firms had little incentive to join in collective schemes to rescue the industry.

Business as usual: 1945–60

The Second World War and the boom conditions that prevailed immediately afterwards finally cleared the financial overhang of the reflotations. Remaining firms were once again typically debt-free and for many, therefore, there was a short period when Lancashire continued on its traditional model of organization. In the period 1930 to 1960, there were new developments in technology which meant, in textiles, the possibility of mass production on an integrated basis replaced craft production for the first time. During this period, therefore, there was an opportunity to restructure the industry along these lines if specific barriers could be overcome.

The events of the interwar period showed that British government trade

---

96 I. Drummond, *British Economic Policy and Empire, 1919–1939* (Abingdon, 2006). Federation of Master Cotton Spinners' Associations, *Measures for the Revival of the Lancashire Cotton Industry*.
97 'Cotton trade reforms', *Financial Times*, 7 December 1938, p. 7.
98 Cotton Industry Reorganisation Act 1939, 2 & 3 Geo. 6 c. 54.

policy increasingly determined the industry's fortunes. Of course, this was nothing new. Before 1914 the British government's commitment to free trade and the gold standard were capable of exercising a dominant influence on the destiny of the cotton industry. Chapter 6 has noted the importance of political lobbying in the pre-1914 period, reflecting the importance of the cotton industry in British elections and the associated requirement to maintain demand for its output in overseas markets, especially India. Lancashire's influence in these respects had a decisive impact on the expansion of the coarse-spinning American section centred on Oldham before 1914. The consequence of this expansion was that the industry was saddled with overcapacity in the interwar period. The Ottawa Agreements of 1932 afforded some protection in Dominion and later Commonwealth markets. After 1945, new countries were in the process of industrialization, further developing their textile industries, including Commonwealth countries such as India, Pakistan and Hong Kong. British foreign policy aimed at preserving influence in these countries through promoting economic development. Moreover, protection for Lancashire against import penetration became more difficult after Britain joined the General Agreement on Tariffs and Trade in 1948.[99] In 1950, Britain ceased to be a net exporter of cotton piece goods.[100]

After 1945, industry output was around half its pre-war level. Post-war shortages fuelled boom conditions, which lasted until 1951. As Figure 19 shows, the rate of profit exceeded anything achieved in the interwar period after the speculative boom of 1919–20. At first sight, this is surprising since, after 1953, and the rapid onset of further import penetration and loss of markets, surplus capacity once again became a problem. Unlike the 1930s, when pricecutting was a problem, there was now a more widely accepted arrangement for minimum prices in the form of the Yarn Spinners Association, which prevented selling below cost, from British producers at least.[101]

Not only could firms use these profits to eliminate residual debt finance, but they could also afford to re-equip. Moreover, a substantial proportion of the capital required for re-equipment was financed by the government, serving an agenda of modernization and scale economies. The 1948 Cotton Spinning Re-Equipment Subsidy Act, known as the Cripps scheme, offered re-equipment subsidies amounting to 25% of the cost of new machinery, conditional on amalgamation.[102] By 1959, the industry had spent at least £100 million on re-equipment.[103]

99   Robson, *The Cotton Industry in Britain*, pp. 6–26.
100 D. Farnie, 'The role of merchants as prime movers in the expansion of the cotton industry, 1760–1990', *The Fibre that Changed the World: The Cotton Industry in International Perspective, 1600–1990s*, ed. D. Farnie and D. Jeremy (Oxford, 2004), pp. 15–55, at p. 47.
101 CH, Annual Report and Accounts, Lancashire Cotton Corporation, 1953, Chairman's statement (John H. Grey).
102 Cotton Spinning (Re-equipment Subsidy) Act 1948, 11 & 12 Geo. 6 c. 31.
103 *Hansard's Parliamentary Debates*, House of Commons Debate, 4 June 1959, vol. 606, cc. 376–494, Sir John Barlow MP, c. 407.

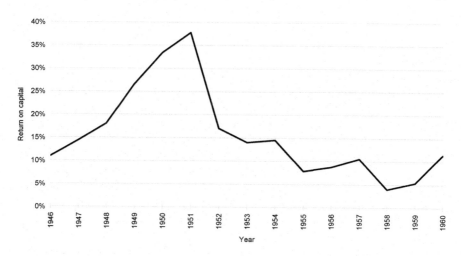

Figure 19. Profitability, 1946–60
Sources: Calculated from CIFD.

The effect of these incentives, and trading conditions more generally, was to accelerate the replacement of mule spindles with ring spindles. Dart Mill of Bolton carried out such a policy in the 1950s. In common with other mills, the firms made large profits up to 1952, but with average returns falling typically to single-figure percentages for the remaining years of the decade. Even so, the directors felt that their major investment in new ring spindles was justified. Overall profits were lower because although demand for ring yarn was strong, it was more erratic for mule yarn. The company found it difficult to guarantee steady employment for mule spinners, many of whom left the industry. At the same time, it proved impossible to attract young workers to train as mule spinners.[104]

The Shiloh group of mills was another of the firms to benefit from the provisions of the 1948 Act. Shiloh Mills invested £150,000 and four mills in the Gartside group were amalgamated to form the Royton Textile Corporation, which spent a further £300,000 on re-equipment. Much of this investment was in new ring spindles.[105]

Another important focus was on the improvement of labour conditions. Domestically, the British cotton industry experienced labour shortages. Other industries offered a more stable future and better wages, while memories of the interwar years were still fresh in the mill towns. Shiloh invested in

104 CH, Annual Reports and Accounts, Dart Mill, 1950–1959, Chairman's statements, Bolton Archives and Local Studies, Dart Mill, FET1/16/56.
105 The Grape, Holly, Park & Sandy and Vine Mills were merged into the Royton combine, Anon., *The Shiloh Story*.

dust-extraction machinery and created wider spacing in its mills. Reflecting the earlier co-operative tradition, it introduced a bonus to labour in the form of a profit-sharing scheme set pro rata to earnings.[106] Similar developments stressing the prime importance of employee welfare occurred elsewhere, for example, at Era Ring Mill, again to attract and retain scarce workers.[107]

The Milnrow ring spinners, now combined into the New Hey Rings group, had consistently outperformed the rest of the industry year-on-year and decade-on-decade for almost sixty years. After 1945, the group lost its competitive advantage. Its profits were now regularly below the rest of the industry and averaged only 5.14% between 1949 and 1955. The firm specialized in coarse counts which were now vulnerable to import competition. It responded by closing one of its mills in 1956, the Haugh, and concentrated production at the remaining sites. These mills received new investment in the form of electrification in 1958 but were closed down under the incentives provided by the 1959 Cotton Industry Act.[108]

Cliques of interconnected directors continued to dominate the industry. Such connections were used to manipulate markets. The Lancashire Cotton Corporation had taken the initiative by setting up price maintenance schemes. The Yarn Spinners' Agreement established fixed margins for varying types of yarn based on the future value or the replacement cost of production, including agreed allowances for depreciation. Members of the agreement were not allowed to sell below the fixed margin.[109] The purpose of the agreement was thus to prevent a return to the problem of undercutting, or 'weak selling', based on marginal cost pricing that occurred in the interwar years, and to provide sufficient cash flow to promote re-equipment. By creating the opportunity for longer, stable production runs, the scheme supported full employment and reduced the risk of losing workers to other industries in the event of short time or temporary closure due to fluctuations in demand.[110]

However, as before the war, there was the risk of collective schemes of self-government being undermined by divisions within the industry. Not every firm joined in and the associated threat weak selling, by firms outside the Yarn Spinners' Agreement, created pressure for the Lancashire Cotton Corporation to take over competing firms. Smaller weak-selling firms, on the other hand, welcomed approaches from the Lancashire Cotton Corporation, as the exit value for sale of the business was often higher than the realizable value of old premises and equipment.[111]

---

106   'Company Meetings, Shiloh Mills, Ltd', *Manchester Guardian*, 22 December 1950, p. 7.
107   Anon., *The Era Idea* (Rochdale, n.d.).
108   'Textile imports close mill', *Financial Times*, 31 July 1956; 'Company Affairs', *Manchester Guardian*, 29 January 1958, p. 10; 'New Hey Rings', *Financial Times*, 3 September 1959.
109   'Trading agreements for yarn and medicines', *The Times*, 17 September 1958, p. 17.
110   Restrictive Practices Court, *The Times*, 28 October 1958, p. 7.
111   LCCR, Board Minutes, 21 February 1952; 25 November 1955; 7 December 1955.

During the 1950s, the Lancashire Cotton Corporation engaged in a series of negotiated takeovers, exploiting its network of interconnected directors. Having paid off its pre-war debt, the firm now proceeded to 'cherry-pick' the best mills as takeover targets. For example, Shiloh's J. B. Garside was a director of A. A. Crompton and of Durban Mill. Directors of Durban Mill were also directors of Willow Bank Mill, both acquired by the Lancashire Cotton Corporation. It also engaged in unrelated diversification, acquiring brickmaking and electrical companies, partly aimed at retaining managerial talent within the business.[112] For the Lancashire Cotton Corporation, the strategy was a successful one and the firm averaged profits of 17.17% during the period 1946–60.[113]

Even so, beyond these informal business connections, the premiums paid on acquisition for these firms had little economic rationale. For example, when the Eagle Spinning Company was taken over by the Lancashire Cotton Corporation in 1956, J. B. Whitehead was a director of the former company for several years before being appointed to the Lancashire Cotton Corporation board as well in 1955. Shareholders received a premium compared to the realizable value of their investments. For example, the Lancashire Cotton Corporation paid £795,000 for Durban and Eagle, representing an 8% premium on their combined market value of £733,000. The Corporation paid a similar premium to acquire Argyll Mill in 1953. Cyril Lord, Fine Cotton Spinners' & Doublers', and Shiloh pursued similar strategies.[114] In 1958, the Amalgamated Cotton Mills Trust launched a bid for British Van Heusen. Again, the rationale was similar: both firms had common directors and the bid valuing Van Heusen at £1.6 million was described as 'generous'.[115]

Through these activities, a Lancashire version of managerial capitalism emerged in the 1950s. Firms became more substantial in terms of the number of units and specific factory units were often re-equipped. Through the takeover of Van Heusen, the Amalgamated Cotton Mills Trust extended its reach beyond Lancashire, acquiring the goodwill of nationally famous brands and making-up units in the south-west of England and in South Africa.[116] In general, however, the horizontally specialized plant remained the norm.

Although the industry had once again reduced in size in terms of the number of firms, the character of re-equipment for the survivors now depended on longer, stable production runs and a level playing field in international trade. The takeovers were managerially motivated but emerged from the networks

---

112 LCCR, Annual Report and Accounts, 1962.
113 Calculated from CIFD.
114 I. Filatotchev and S. Toms, 'Corporate governance, strategy and survival in a declining industry: A study of UK cotton textile companies', *Journal of Management Studies* 40 (2003), 895–920.
115 'British Van Heusen', *The Economist*, 8 November 1958, p. 554.
116 'The British Van Heusen Company', *Financial Times*, 18 July 1956, p. 7.

and inherited patterns of behaviour established in Lancashire during previous financing and refinancing activities. The City of London was not a feature of these regional agreements and friendly deals. Lancashire remained an isolated regional economy and its political bargaining power dissipated gradually as newer sectors of the economy became more critical than textiles.

Throughout the 1950s, industry leaders lobbied for further government assistance, and against threats to remove the Yarn Spinners' Agreement, which provided guaranteed margins and reduced the risk associated with expensive re-equipment. In reality, however, the scheme was irrelevant for the survival of the industry as a whole because it merely transferred profit from weaving to spinning, leaving weaving vulnerable to international competition.[117] The Restrictive Practices Court overturned the Yarn Spinners' Agreement in 1958, with the immediate consequence of a fall in margins 'to such levels that few mills could operate at a profit'. When in force, the Yarn Spinners' Agreement had transferred profit from weaving to spinning,[118] but its abolition created pressure from the influential spinning lobby for more drastic interventions.

Industry leaders also lobbied for protection from what was perceived as unfair overseas competition. However, protective tariffs did not sit well with broader British foreign policy objectives that aimed to promote economic development in the Far East and elsewhere, which allowed duty-free imports from India, Pakistan, and Hong Kong.[119] Loss of markets created further problems with overcapacity.

In 1959, a year after the end of the Yarn Spinners' Agreement, the government introduced a new Cotton Industry Act aimed at resolving the industry's problems once and for all.[120] The legislation provided subsidies either for firms to leave the industry altogether or for re-equipment of the remaining companies.[121] The Cotton Industry Act marked a watershed in the pattern of restructuring. Before 1959, acquisitions typically destroyed value for the acquiring shareholders but proceeded nonetheless due to the interconnectedness of the directors and the continued dependence of firms on local sources of finance.[122] Now, weaker firms tended to exit, whether voluntarily or with

---

117   J. Singleton, *Lancashire on the Scrapheap* (Oxford, 1991), p. 201.
118   LCCR, Annual Report and Accounts, 1959, Chairman's statement (R. M. Lee), p. 12. J. Singleton, 'The decline of the British cotton industry since 1940', *The Lancashire Cotton Industry: A History Since 1700*, ed. M. B. Rose (Preston, 1996), pp. 296–324, at pp. 313–14. See also A. Sutherland, 'The RPC and cotton spinning', *Journal of Industrial Economics* 8 (1959), 58–79.
119   'The Federation of Master Cotton Spinners' Associations Ltd', *The Times*, 26 March 1958, p. 18.
120   Cotton Industry Act (1959), 7 & 8 Eliz. II; D. Higgins and S. Toms, 'Public subsidy and private divestment: The Lancashire cotton textile industry, c.1950–1965', *BH* 42 (2000), 59–84.
121   For detail on the provisions of the Act, see C. Miles, *Lancashire Textiles: A Case Study of Industrial Change* (Cambridge, 1968).
122   Higgins and Toms, 'Public subsidy and private divestment'.

the assistance of the 1959 Act. Survivors, meanwhile, invested more in new fixed assets and made greater use of cheaper debt capital. Most crucially, they obtained institutional support for new share issues, as in 1919, creating combinations large enough to interest the City of London once again.

Planning for cotton: 1961–72

In the period after 1960, the remainder of the cotton industry, and indeed the British textile industry as a whole, adapted rapidly to a new pattern of organization, dominated by integrated combines. Two essential strands paved the way for the dominance of the new model. The first was the replacement of the traditional marketing structure. National retail organizations replaced merchant houses and their international connections to export markets.

Notwithstanding the rapid decline of the once export-dominated cotton industry, merchant and retail organizations could not afford to let it disappear entirely and had an interest in protecting their sources of supply through direct or quasi-vertical integration. One of the reasons for the build-up of powerful vertical groups was to act as a counterbalance to the increasing dominance of retailers in the domestic market. Large-scale investments by manufacturers were problematic in the face of cyclical demand, which was compounded by further shifts in the balance of power away from manufacturers.

Moreover, merchants did not deal with the same risk as manufacturers in the face of declining export markets, as they could switch their expertise to importing.[123] As more rationalization occurred, particularly by the 1960s, merchants feared that too much capacity had been lost and sourced more orders abroad, leading to a surge in imports and further difficulty for the surviving manufacturing firms.[124] Merchants were mistrusted and blamed for protecting their profits at the expense of the rest of the industry.[125]

The second important strand was the replacement of the insider regional financial structure with London-based external finance. As has been demonstrated earlier, local cliques of directors dominated regional financing methods that had grown up in the successive booms before 1920. Between the wars and after 1945, these groups had promoted amalgamations and re-equipment, at intervals benefiting from government assistance. Combines exercised a significant influence but were never able to exert absolute control over the whole industry. Smaller independent groups remained important and drew on local financial and social connections.

123 Farnie, 'Merchants as prime movers', p. 47.
124 Anon., *The Shiloh Story*.
125 *Hansard's Parliamentary Debates*, House of Commons Debate, 1 July 1963, 'Textile industry', Anthony Greenwood (Rossendale).

By the 1960s, the independent model was increasingly unsustainable. Traditional cotton mills that survived the 1959 Act recorded low average profits in the years following, typically under 5%, and were closed down or taken over. For example, Werneth, a long-standing Oldham spinning company, averaged 4.58% before closing in 1969. Shiloh averaged only 2.39% during a similar period, and Cromer and Era followed the same pattern.[126] By 1965, there were only twenty-five companies left on the Oldham list, the last year it appeared separately.[127] The decline of regional stock exchanges in Oldham and Manchester paved the way for more substantial scale mergers, this time backed by the City of London. As has been demonstrated earlier, local cliques of directors dominated regional financing methods and promoted friendly mergers as the industry declined in the 1930s and again in the 1950s. By the 1960s, the market for corporate control, which sometimes featured hostile takeovers, developed rapidly and was increasingly dominated by transactions orchestrated by London-based financial institutions. An estimated £340 million was spent acquiring textile businesses in the form of cash and shares.[128]

The entry of new combines in the early 1960s brought together City and regional interests for the first time. Following the Cotton Industry Act, the remainder of the textile industry was characterized by merger activity. In this period, the UK developed the most concentrated and integrated of the world's major textile industries.[129] At this time, the remainder of the cotton industry, and indeed the British textile industry as a whole, adapted rapidly to a new pattern of vertical organization.[130] In the period 1962–64, the previously dominant Lancashire firms – the Lancashire Cotton Corporation, Fine Cotton Spinners' & Doublers' Association, and Combined English Mills – were taken over by Courtaulds with some involvement from ICI. Some firms, including Courtaulds, Smith & Nephew and Shiloh, also diversified beyond the textile sector.[131] Courtaulds took over the rump of the Lancashire textile industry, while Coats Viyella grew into a textile conglomerate through a series of mergers

---

126   Calculated from CIFD.

127   Thomas, *The Provincial Stock Exchanges*.

128   J. A. Blackburn, 'The vanishing UK cotton industry', *National Westminster Bank Quarterly Review* (November 1982), 42–52, at p. 42.

129   G. Shepherd, 'Textiles: New ways of surviving in an old industry', *Europe's Industries: Public and Private Strategies for Change*, ed. G. Shepherd, F. Duchêne and C. Saunders (London, 1983), pp. 26–51, at pp. 29–30.

130   Higgins and Toms, 'Public subsidy and private divestment'; R. Millward, 'Industrial and Commercial Performance since 1950', *The Cambridge Economic History of Modern Britain, Volume 3: Structural Change, 1939–2000*, ed. R. Floud and P. Johnson (Cambridge, 2004), pp. 123–67.

131   Filatotchev and Toms, 'Corporate governance, strategy and survival'.

in other textile sectors.[132] The wider textile industry feared for its sources of supply, whether arising from further closures of limitations on imports.[133]

For the mainstream spinning and doubling industry, the Courtaulds takeover of the Lancashire Cotton Corporation and other firms in 1964 was the most significant development. With its downstream capacity in synthetics, Frank Kearton, Courtaulds' chief executive, argued that vertical control could promote efficiency through capital-intensive investment based on shared knowledge up and down the value chain. Kearton's arguments were based on the success of the US textile industry,[134] which had never developed the extensive horizontal specialization characteristic of Lancashire. Courtaulds' intervention thus offered an opportunity to implement the vertical strategy that Lancashire has been so roundly criticized for avoiding.[135] In 1968 Courtaulds controlled 199 production units in spinning and doubling employing over 47,000 people.[136]

In 1963, ahead of their subsequent election victory that owed much to Lancashire marginal constituencies, the Labour party launched its 'Plan for Cotton'. The policy statement promised favourable renegotiation of GATT agreed on quotas with India, Pakistan and Hong Kong, in addition to a further subsidy for re-equipment and integration.[137] Once in office, the Wilson government established the Textile Council, whose function was to enforce import regulation and oversee a new study into productivity. Even so, to many, the government seemed indifferent to the fate of the industry. Weak prices in cotton at this time contrasted with surging demand in synthetic fibres and the traditional sector faced further competition from the new warp knitting industry.[138] The government policy towards Commonwealth competitors continued, particularly during negotiations in 1966–67, with significant sacrifices of the UK industry made in favour of quotas of ever-increasing

132   G. Owen, *The Rise and Fall of Great Companies: Courtaulds and the Reshaping of the Man-made Fibres Industry* (Oxford, 2010); D. Higgins and S. Toms, 'Financial institutions and corporate strategy: David Alliance and the transformation of British textiles, c.1950–c.1990', *BH* 48 (2006), 453–78.

133   L. Briscoe, *The Textile and Clothing Industry of the United Kingdom* (Manchester, 1971), pp. 168–9.

134   Owen, *Rise and Fall of Great Companies*, pp. 64–5.

135   Lazonick's critique in particular: see W. Lazonick, 'The cotton industry', *The Decline of the British Economy*, ed. B. Elbaum and W. Lazonick (Oxford, 1987), pp. 18–50; and W. Mass and W. Lazonick, 'The British cotton industry and international competitive advantage: The state of the debates', *BH* 32 (1990), 9–65.

136   M. Cannell, 'Rise of Shiloh: Bucking the trend in the UK spinning industry', *Textile Outlook International* 69 (1997), 60–75, at p. 60.

137   'Labour's plan for cotton', *The Times*, 20 July 1963.

138   'Imports doom super mill', *Lancashire Evening Post*, 8 January 1968; 'Action needed now on the cotton towns', *The Times*, 9 January 1968, p. 19.

imports.[139] However, the government had not entirely given up on Lancashire. Wilson's apparent indifference to the traditional cotton mills, such as Tulketh Mill which closed in 1968, was based in part on a determination to concentrate the industry and integrate it with the artificial fibre sector.[140]

In the light of government ambivalence and increased involvement from the City, how successful was the experience of vertical integration? Figure 20 compares the profitability of the new combines with what was left of the traditional cotton sector. The new combines were much more successful financially, and consistently so, up to 1974. During this period, the conventional and mostly specialized mills experienced meagre profit rates, typically in the range of 2–6% and exited the industry or were taken over. The remainder of the sector remained troubled by the legacy of its disintegrated structure. There were weak links between marketing and production, which disadvantaged the cotton sector, especially.[141] The external economies of scale that had benefited earlier models of industrial organization were increasingly absent post-1950.[142] The production-led, dominant-firm strategy underestimated the importance of marketing and specialization, and remained vulnerable to eventual trade liberalization.[143] At the same time, buyer power became more concentrated in retail organizations, which bypassed cotton wholesalers and began to establish direct links with downstream textile manufacturers.

The Cotton Industry Act did little to rescue the fortunes of the Lancashire Cotton Corporation. Profits reached historically low levels in 1962 and 1963, with a return on capital below 2% in both years. Ronald Lee complained that the severity of the recession was unprecedented for an industry that could no longer fall back on the defences of the Yarn Spinners' Agreement. Market uncertainty and the availability of more general tax allowances reduced the value of cotton industry-specific investment allowances. The chairman of Amalgamated Cotton Mills Trust (now British Van Heusen) expressed the same sentiment. New machinery necessitated round-the-clock shifts, but this model was only sustainable if a particular share of the home market could be guaranteed and protected from imports being sold at less than the cost of production.[144]

139   A. Ormerod, 'Textile manufacturing: Smokestack industry or an essential sector of the national economy?', *Journal of the Textile Institute* 90 (1999), 93–103.

140   '500 lose jobs as textile mill closes', *The Times*, 9 January 1968, p. 15; 'Lancashire must help itself', *Lancashire Evening Post*, 8 January 1968.

141   Millward, 'Industrial and commercial performance since 1950', p. 139; Lazonick, 'The Cotton Industry', p. 39.

142   S. Broadberry, 'The Performance of Manufacturing', *The Cambridge Economic History of Modern Britain. Volume 3: Structural Change, 1939–2000*, ed. Floud and Johnson, pp. 57–83, at p. 80.

143   Shepherd, 'Textiles: New ways of surviving', p. 46.

144   LCCR, Annual Report and Accounts, 1961, Chairman's statement (R. M. Lee), p. 13; 'British Van Heusen's Difficulties', *Financial Times*, 7 March 1963, p. 16.

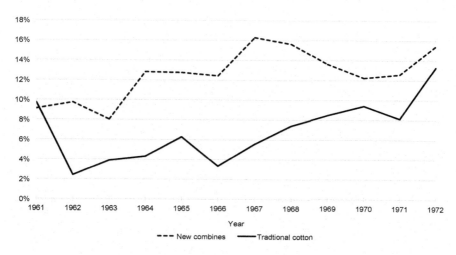

Figure 20. Profitability, new combines and the traditional cotton sector, 1961–72

Source: Calculated from CIFD.

The expiration of such agreements created too much uncertainty. Under agreements with Commonwealth countries, automatic increases in quota were allowed if Lancashire's order books reached fifteen weeks.[145] However, the protocols themselves imposed limitations on scale economies available to the more efficient Lancashire firms. In response, the Lancashire Cotton Corporation held back on re-equipment and announced the closure of a further five mills.[146]

The experience of Ashton Brothers was illustrative of the extra pressures that traditional Lancashire producers faced in the new environment and financial model. As illustrated in chapter 6, Ashtons had long been committed to innovation and vertical integration, and was independent of the cliques and regional financial institutions of Lancashire. In the 1950s, the investment in new technology, such as shuttleless weaving, continued. Allan Ormerod, the managing director, increasingly regretted the pressures that the stock market imposed. In common with other industry leaders, he also lamented the failure of British governments to follow through the provisions of the 1959 Act with stricter limits on imports. Even so, Ashtons relentlessly pressed on with modernization. The consequence was a fall in margins, prompting Ormerod to bemoan the stock market's obsession with financial returns that now left the firm vulnerable to takeover. To pre-empt matters, Ormerod voluntarily entered negotiations

145　On the fifteen-week agreement, see 'No supplementaries', *The Economist*, 16 December 1961, p. 1164.

146　LCCR, Annual Report and Accounts, 1962, Chairman's statement (R. M. Lee), pp. 12–13.

with Courtaulds in 1968. In a deal brokered by Jacob Rothschild, Ashtons was taken over and became part of the Courtaulds Northern Weaving Division.[147]

Smith & Nephew was another firm that expanded using stock market-backed acquisitions during the 1960s. Between 1950 and 1961, the firm attracted increasing institutional investment, allowing it to increase its capital base significantly. As a consequence, when it acquired Brierfield Mills and Glen Mills the firm immediately installed modern machinery, making it the most efficient in the industry.[148] Being mostly a health-care provider, Smith & Nephew was somewhat peripheral to the textile industry.

Other firms developed survival strategies based on distinctive brands. For example, the Fine Cotton Spinners' & Doublers' Association adopted a more vertical integration, not just acquiring other relatively profitable companies (Asia and Maple), but also investing in research and development to create trademarks and branded finished goods.[149] Mountain and outdoor equipment provided further opportunities for product development and branding.[150]

The British government supported the Courtaulds strategy through regional assistance programmes and by otherwise ignoring the de facto monopoly enjoyed by the firm.[151] Evidence confirms that the productivity of UK textiles was also better than other manufacturing sectors at this time.[152] Through shift working, mills averaged 81 hours per week with some units achieving 120 hours and with an aspiration for 168 hours.

Improvements in productivity reflected investment and modernization across the sector. A report published by the Textile Council in 1969 showed that in a sample of twenty-two mills, the best twelve had increased productivity by 35% in two years. Significant investment in new technology, such as open-ended spinning and shuttleless weaving, resulted in a 72.4% increase in productivity in the period 1963–73.[153]

Lancashire's political representatives blamed restrictions on British exports imposed by Commonwealth countries and stronger quota restrictions in the USA and Western Europe. These circumstances might have been used to British

---

147   Ormerod, *Industrial Odyssey*, pp. 197–205.
148   Filatotchev and Toms, 'Corporate governance, strategy and survival', p. 914. The number of shareholders increased from 730 to 8700, controlling 2.5 million and 30.4 million shares respectively at the two dates, of which 0.94 million and 13.6 million were controlled by institutional investors: CH, Smith & Nephew, Annual Reports and Accounts.
149   Filatotchev and Toms, 'Corporate governance, strategy and survival'.
150   M. C. Parsons and M. B. Rose, 'Communities of knowledge: Entrepreneurship, innovation and networks in the British outdoor trade, 1960–90', *BH* 46 (2004), 609–39.
151   D. Ricks, 'An overview of government influence', *The Global Textile Industry*, ed. B. Toyne *et al.* (London, 1984), at pp. 123–6.
152   S. Broadberry and N. Crafts, 'UK productivity performance from 1950 to 1979: A restatement of the Broadberry–Crafts view', *EcHR* 56 (2003), 718–35, at p. 719.
153   Textile Council, *Cotton and Allied Textiles: A Report on Present Performance and Future Prospects* (Manchester, 1969).

advantage had early negotiations to join Europe's Common Market succeeded. As early as 1957, with the formation of the European Free Trade Area, a Lancashire spokesman feared that the arrangement might become a gateway for cheap imports from former European colonies.[154] As it was, a German commentator writing in March 1964 noted that Britain's policy amounted to the blind sacrifice of its industry in favour of Commonwealth interests. European governments meanwhile supported their industries concurrently and in the Common Market, at least, there was a cautious approach to external imports.[155] In other cases, some dumping activities that negatively affected British industry, for example, by Portugal and also Pakistan, were based on direct government subsidies. Others were based on price discrimination. In the case of India, prices were 30% below UK national levels. According to MP Charles Fletcher-Cooke's statement in the House of Commons:

> It is, I think, well known that at present there is a practice in many of the countries which send textile goods to us of concentrating first on one part of the industry here, hoping to knock it out, and then on another part, and so on, until every section has been destroyed.

Hong Kong, in particular, was the target of such criticisms and substantial diplomatic efforts were made to secure sustainable agreements on imports.[156]

Part of the criticism was that generous quotas were being offered within an international development policy to Commonwealth countries such as Malaysia, notwithstanding their relatively small domestic industries. Quotas were, in any case, unenforceable due to the absence of precise product categorization and rights of carry-over of unused allowance from previous years. There was also a perceived lack of reciprocity: for example, British exports to Canada were subject to duty, whereas Canadian imports into Britain were duty-free under Commonwealth preference.[157]

Complaints from Lancashire's traditional producers were nonetheless justified to some extent. In a detailed letter to the *Guardian* newspaper, which he based on a detailed statistical analysis, Allan Ormerod, managing director

---

154 LCCR, Annual Report and Accounts, 1958, Chairman's statement (R. M. Lee), p. 13.
155 Ormerod, 'Textile Manufacturing', p. 96. The German authority cited by Ormerod was Dr F. Richter.
156 *Hansard's Parliamentary Debates*, House of Commons Debate, 1 July 1963, 'Textile industry', Charles Fletcher-Cooke (MP for Darwen, qq.107–8); 'Cotton Imports Criticized', *The Times*, 24 June 1965; Kayser Sung, 'Textiles resilient', *The Times*, 20 September 1968, p. 38; 'Lancashire prepares to fight for its textile future', *The Times*, 8 November 1971, p. 21.
157 *Hansard's Parliamentary Debates*, House of Commons Debate, 1 July 1963, 'Textile industry', Charles Fletcher-Cooke (Darwen); John Leavey (Heywood and Royton); Fred Blackburn (Stalybridge and Hyde); Ernest Thornton (Farnworth); Sir John Barlow (Middleton and Prestwich); Dan Jones (Burnley). 'Cotton Imports Problem, New threat by Canada', *The Times*, 17 March 1965, p. 18.

of Ashton Brothers, pointed out that Lancashire's productivity gains were impressive compared with many other industries in Europe, the USA, India and the Far East. The British textile industry, he concluded, 'is the only textile industry in the world which is not considered to be an integral part of the national economy'.[158]

By 1970 more firms had left the industry or been taken over by the combines. In the early 1970s, however, there is some evidence for a recovery in the profits of the remaining independents. Shiloh, which now advertised itself as 'an independent force in Lancashire textiles', reported improved profits.[159] Rochdale-based John Bright & Brothers also benefited from improved trading conditions. Closer integration and internal sourcing created stability in production, making possible further investments and efficiency improvements. The strategy, which resulted in improved financial returns, was also underpinned by a successful merger with Preston and Bottomley, a Manchester-based industrial textile manufacturer, facilitated by Kleinwort Benson.[160]

Notwithstanding these successes, the remaining independent firms continued to face the twin threats of undercutting by imports and by the combines. A report by the Textile Council recommended further rationalization of the independent sector. However, with many firms making good profits, there was little support for the rationalization plans from within the independent sector, nor from the textile trade unions.[161] Instead, industry leaders like Sir Frank Kearton, writing in 1969, favoured further integration, particularly of production and marketing, underpinned by additional investments in productivity and scale economies, and trade protections to guarantee market stability. By 1972, negotiations for British entry into the EEC were well advanced, prompting a new round of uncertainty.

Conclusions

Throughout the period after 1919, up to British entry into the EEC in 1973, Lancashire faced increased global competition and loss of markets. However, the sector as a whole and firms within it had very different experiences. The 1920s and 1930s were the most difficult decades. Speculative activity accentuated the problems caused by overcapacity and prevented firms from restructuring

---

158   Ormerod, *Industrial Odyssey*, pp. 185–9.
159   Shiloh Spinners, *The Times*, 19 June 1970, p. 22; 'Better Trend for Shiloh', *Financial Times*, 15 June 1972, p. 26.
160   Return on capital increased to 11.9% in 1969 and 13.5% in 1970 (calculated from CIFD). 'Preston & Bottomley gets £1.4m offer', *The Times*, 2 July 1968, p. 26; 'John Bright Group', *The Times*, 22 June 1971, p. 16.
161   R. W. Shakespeare, 'Textiles still stormy', *The Times*, 11 February 1970, p. 3.

or better exploiting economies of scale to drive down their unit costs. In the post-1945 period, the elimination of debt overhang removed a constraint for many firms that had previously prevented investment.

After 1960, in particular, vertical integration created access to economies of scale and greater market stability allowed impressive gains in productivity. The City of London assisted the process, brokering deals and facilitating mergers, while the traditional, local financial institutions of Lancashire disappeared. Government policy encouraged concentration and supported investment through regional assistance, tax breaks and direct subsidy. Crucially, trade policy, reflecting broader strategic interests, left the British domestic market vulnerable to import penetration from Commonwealth competition, thereby undermining what might have been achieved from productivity alone. For similar reasons, British entry to the EEC, therefore, had the potential to undermine other European textile industries.

In the event, European textiles survived, and British textiles did not, and the reasons are explored in the next, final chapter.

Epilogue

> Textiles still makes a significant contribution to the UK economy, both in terms of economic output and employment, whilst also providing considerable support to the UK Exchequer.
>
> Alliance Project Team, 2015[1]

According to the 'gentlemanly capitalist' thesis, throughout its history, the Lancashire textile industry's interests were ignored by politicians in favour of the City of London. It was for this reason that the gold standard had been at the centre of British policy towards India in the nineteenth century. Similarly, the Ottawa agreements of the 1930s were designed to underpin the financial obligations of dominion countries.[2] Even so, until the 1960s, at least, as the previous chapter has shown, Lancashire had some significance at least insofar as its marginal constituencies could decide Westminster elections. Successive governments promoted industrial modernization and export industries to support the balance of payments.[3] So, although the cotton industry was of dwindling significance even in Lancashire, and trade negotiations had broader strategic objectives, influenced by foreign policy and Commonwealth priorities, the combination of protection with a supportive industrial policy provided stable investment conditions for the remainder of the cotton industry.

These circumstances promoted vertical integration of cotton production in the 1960s and 1970s. As noted in previous chapters, critics of the industry argued that such a structure had been necessary for a long time.[4] That remains a matter of debate, but the experience of the combines from the 1960s onwards, as shown in the last chapter, suggests that vertical structure and investment in the latest technology could promote financial success, at least for a time.

However, the changed circumstances of the mid-1970s posed new threats to the vertical model. Surplus capacity, which had plagued Lancashire since the slumps of the late nineteenth century and during the protracted interwar

1   Alliance Project Team, *Repatriation of UK textiles manufacture* (Manchester, 2015), p. 11.
2   P. J. Cain and A. G. Hopkins, *British Imperialism: 1688–2000* (London, 2014), pp. 83–7, 342–3.
3   Ibid., pp. 632–5.
4   W. Lazonick, 'The cotton industry', *The Decline of the British Economy*, ed. B. Elbaum and W. Lazonick (Oxford, 1987), pp. 18–50.

crisis, now became a problem impacting all advanced economies. Vertically integrated firms faced higher fixed costs and inflexibility, and therefore needed some guarantee of market share. The success of this strategy was, in part, therefore, a result of government protection, which reflected the evolving relationship between the USA and the European Economic Community (EEC), and also structural imbalances in the international economy. As trade policy was liberalized further after 1980, these imbalances became more acute, and the survival of textile production in advanced economies, including Britain, much more problematic.

Survival strategies suited to the circumstances of the late twentieth century reflected models of organization discussed in earlier chapters. The conglomerate model, which had advanced through merger since the 1890s, was promoted through further consolidation. The independent model too, offered the prospect of further refinement through leveraging embedded skills and resources into niche markets. Shiloh, Lancashire's last surviving independent spinning firm, illustrates the effectiveness of this model. Each of these models is discussed in turn later and the chapter evaluates their effectiveness, prefaced and contextualized by a discussion of the effects of entry into the European Economic Community and the subsequent globalization and liberalization of trading arrangements. The chapter ends by demonstrating the importance of history and the role of the textiles on the post-industrial landscape of Lancashire.

Cotton textiles and the UK entry to the European Common Market

On 1 January 1973, following a series of negotiations, Britain entered the EEC. Notwithstanding the apparent benefits of membership, Britain's relationship with the EEC, and what later became the EU, has always been problematic. Before and immediately following the new arrangements, Lancashire's representatives amplified their long-held concerns that trade policy would not provide the stable market conditions required to justify substantial investments in capital equipment. The debate was not merely a matter of free trade versus protection. All developed economies controlled imports to some degree across most sectors, and politicians in developing countries promoted subsidized exports, or 'dumping', in equal measure. Instead, it was a matter of achieving quota-based settlements in line with the desired capacity of domestic industries, including cotton and other textiles.

Previously established agreements on textile quotas formed the backdrop to British negotiations to enter the EEC in 1973. Notwithstanding the apparent advantages of vertical integration, the US textile industry felt the need for protection from lower-cost producers, which led its representatives to put pressure on the government.[5] The US initiative which followed, restricted imports of cotton, leading overseas producers to shift to synthetics. As a consequence, protection for cotton was rolled up with an extended Multi Fibre Arrangement.[6] Similar measures were now introduced in Europe, resulting in a Multi Fibre Arrangement between the USA and EEC in 1973, based on quotas subject to annual increases of 6%.[7]

Textile interests on either side of the negotiations between Britain and Europe perceived significant risk. British textile industry representatives, Edmund Gartside of Shiloh and John Brierley of Ash Spinning Company, believed that European countries protected their markets effectively using unofficial arrangements that were not available to British producers. They also feared competition from Mediterranean countries, such as Morocco, Tunisia and Turkey, which had access to European markets as associate countries. The Textile Industry Support Campaign (TISC), led by Gartside, was supported by 70% of employers and warned of thousands of job losses if Britain entered the EEC.[8] At the same time, the threat of textiles imported without control from British Commonwealth countries concerned the EEC negotiators.[9]

In the event, following UK entry, the EEC facilitated significant increases in quotas of 25% from the Mediterranean associate countries as early as 1975. Moreover, it was EEC practice to treat cotton yarn as raw material and, therefore, on a 'common liberalization' list.[10] Indeed the EEC's obligations to these associate countries were paramount and limited its freedom of action to take defensive action to preserve the cotton and textile sectors in Britain and other core EEC countries. As chairman of the TISC, Gartside warned that Turkish factories, supported by government export subsidies of 40%, were being set up for the specific purpose of penetrating the British market.[11]

There was no further growth in productivity after 1973, suggesting that market uncertainty placed limits on the further exploitation of scale-based economies. Between 1973 and 1981, production and employment fell in tandem (56.3% compared to 57.3%), although there were further improvements in

---

5   J. Singleton, 'The decline of the British cotton industry since 1940', *The Lancashire Cotton Industry: A History Since 1700*, ed. M. B. Rose (Preston, 1996), pp. 296–324, at p. 312; V. K. Aggarwal and S. Haggard, 'The politics of protection in the US textile and apparel industries', *American Industry in International Competition: Government Policies and Corporate Strategies*, ed. J. Zysman and L. Tyson (Ithaca, NY, 1983), pp. 249–312.

6   M. B. Rose, 'Politics of protection: An institutional approach to government–industry relations in the British and United States cotton industries, 1945–73', *BH* 39 (1997), 128–50.

7   Aggarwal and Haggard, 'Politics of Protection', pp. 253–4, 265, 296.

8   A. Smith, 'EEC entry will hit Lancs. Jobs', *Financial Times*, 12 May 1972, p. 16.

9   J. Trafford, 'Textile industry seeks answer to plea for parity with EEC', *Financial Times*, 19 April 1972, p. 19; 'Textile industry fear over EEC entry grows', *The Times*, 15 June 1972, p. 25.

10   J. Trafford, 'Lancashire fears a flood of Asian yarn', *Financial Times*, 22 May 1972, p. 35.

11   R. David, 'Cheap cotton imports pose a "threat" to U.K. Industry', *Financial Times*, 22 March 1974, p. 14.

the 1980s.[12] As a result, in Lancashire there was an increase in short-time working and redundancies, affecting around twenty spinning and weaving mills, prompting support from trade union and cotton political interests for the anti-Market campaign ahead of the referendum on EEC membership on 5 June 1975.[13]

Notwithstanding these new and problematic international trading relationships, British textile producers, including the remaining Lancashire firms, were still capable of accessing specific markets. These included Commonwealth countries and specialist fabric production. Some strategic options therefore remained, through further reorganization, fixed capital investment and exploiting niche markets. British government policy bolstered these strategies. In 1977 the Callaghan Labour government requested a commitment to zero import growth, specifically to assist the cotton-spinning sector in Lancashire. When the EEC turned down the request, the government extended the Temporary Employment Subsidy to support the industry.[14]

Given these competing influences, how well did the surviving textile firms perform once Britain had acceded to the EEC? Figure 21 shows the overall rate of return on capital for a sample of surviving companies in the period 1973–82. The dates in Figure 21 are selected to include the early years of EEC membership up to and including the effects of the recession of 1981. The graph also indicates the performance of Courtaulds, the largest producer of textile goods, including cotton, during this period.

Between 1973 and 1982 the profitability of all firms averaged 11.6%. These profits were typically, therefore, as good as any other period post-1945 and much better than the interwar period. The relatively higher earnings in the six years or so after 1973 suggest that entry into the EEC did not significantly impact the financial performance of surviving firms. It should be noted that not all firms in the sample survived until 1982. Moreover, across the industry as a whole, exits were much more pronounced in the recessionary period of 1979–82 than in the years following entry to the EEC.

By the mid-1980s, in response to changes in global trading rules, British governments no longer countenanced protection for domestic textile industries. The 1988–94 Uruguay Round led to textiles falling under the jurisdiction of

---

12   G. Shepherd, 'Textiles: New ways of surviving in an old industry', *Europe's Industries: Public and Private Strategies for Change*, ed. G. Shepherd, F. Duchêne and C. Saunders (London, 1983), pp. 26–51; V. N. Balasubramanyam, 'International trade and employment in the UK textiles and clothing sector', *Applied Economics* 25 (1993), 1477–82.
13   K. Gooding, 'Curb on imports of cotton yarn', *Financial Times*, 21 December 1974, p. 22; R. David, 'Pledge on textile imports is given to Eurocoton', *Financial Times*, 13 March 1975, p. 10; P. Hill, 'EEC go ahead for rise in cotton yarn imports raises protest in Britain', *The Times*, 5 March 1975, p. 17; S. Fleming, 'Cotton spins a tale of woe', *Financial Times*, 21 May 1975, p. 11.
14   R. David and P. Clark, 'UK to keep tough stand on cotton yarn imports', *Financial Times*, 3 November 1977, p. 8.

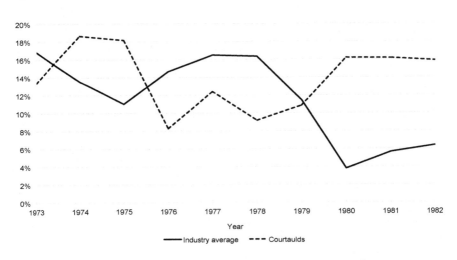

Figure 21. Profitability, Courtaulds and other cotton industry firms, 1973–82

the World Trade Organization. An essential part of the more comprehensive process, the Munich summit of July 1992 signalled the end of Multi Fibre Arrangement quota protection for UK firms.[15] The resulting Agreement on Textiles and Clothing specified a ten-year phase-out of the Multi Fibre Arrangement, beginning in 1995.[16]

Before that recession, the industry experienced a slower attrition rate. When the Oldham spinning company Joseph Clegg exited the sector in October 1974, citing cheap import competition, it was the first mill closure in two years. As in previous downturns, other mills avoided exit by using short-time working.[17] Where firms did exit, EEC trade practices were often the focus of criticism. Industry representatives regarded EEC associate countries like Greece, Turkey, Yugoslavia and Portugal as a new and more significant problem than Commonwealth countries, where the EEC had already taken some action.[18] Further increases to EEC-associate-member Mediterranean countries were granted subsequently, giving rise to complaints from British cotton and textile representatives.[19]

They coupled protests with requests for help, justified by the efficiency of the

15   *Guardian*, 9 July 1992.
16   D. Spinager, 'Textiles beyond the MFA phase out', *World Economy* 22 (1999), 455–76.
17   P. Hill, 'EEC go ahead for rise in cotton yarn imports raises protest in Britain', *The Times*, 5 March 1975.
18   R. Vielvoye, 'Cheap imports blamed for textile mill closure', *The Times*, 17 October 1974, p. 19.
19   P. Hill, 'EEC go-ahead for rise in cotton yarn imports raises protest in Britain', *The Times*, 5 March 1975, p. 17.

remaining mills and their commitment to further modernization. John Bright made substantial capital investments in 1977 on the back of steady profits and in anticipation of a recovery in markets.[20] In the event, profits dipped sharply in the following year, falling from 12.5% to 7.2% return on capital.[21] The firm specialized in tyre and carpet yarns, and was dependent on the domestic market. It was also vulnerable to swings in the price of raw cotton on international markets. Adverse movements in both hit profits badly in 1977–78, resulting in capacity closure[22] and leaving the firm vulnerable to takeover, which occurred a year later.

The largest firm, Courtaulds, outperformed the rest of the industry during the period. It earned an average rate of profit of 13.9%, and the difference was most pronounced during the recessionary years of 1979–82. For Courtaulds and most other textile firms up to 1979, the performance was broadly comparable to the decade before entry into the EEC (see chapter 7, p. 244 and Figure 20).

It was not until the recession of 1980 that the industry experienced another significant downturn. During that year, there was a wave of mill closures and widespread short-time working, with 100,000 jobs lost in the textile and clothing industry as a whole. Extensive import penetration from low-cost producers resulted in an accelerated programme of mill closures, the rationalization of spinning and weaving capacity by Courtaulds, and ICI's hurried divestment of Carrington Viyella to David Alliance's Vantona group.[23] Members of Parliament with significant textile production in their constituencies, including Lancashire, complained about depressed home trade, further import competition (including from US producers who were benefiting from subsidized energy prices), and a lack of action from a government committed to free trade.[24]

The demise of the conglomerates

An important reason for the success of the conglomerates that emerged through the mergers of the 1960s and 1970s was that, to some extent, they created countervailing power against the retailers. There were strong vertical linkages in all the main groups as part of a conscious strategy, which in the case of the Calico Printers' Association, meant forward integration into retailing. The vertical approach provided the basis for new productivity-enhancing investment by Courtaulds, which failed in part due to the lack of emphasis on flexibility

20 'Optimism at John Bright', *Financial Times*, 23 June 1977, p. 33.
21 Calculated from CIFD.
22 'John Bright More Than Halved', *Financial Times*, 1 June 1978, p. 28.
23 See, for example, A. Ormerod, 'The decline of the UK textile industry: the terminal years, 1945–2003', *Journal of Industrial History* 6 (2003), 1–33, at p. 31.
24 'Moves through EEC more likely to get results', *The Times*, 27 February 1981, p. 11.

and design.[25] Even so, these large groups had strong negotiating power with the retailers.

Following the recession of the early 1980s, the balance of power shifted increasingly from textile producers in favour of high street, retail fashion chains. Large retailers, like Marks & Spencer, provided the stability that export markets could not, allowing producers to take advantage of guaranteed and substantial bulk orders, thereby recouping their investment in new machinery. Even so, there were problems, which created pressures for further rationalization.

Dependence on retailers created new instabilities in the supply chain, particularly for fabric producers. For example, if Marks & Spencer invited garment makers to tender for a contract, each bidder would request a quotation from the producer further up the supply chain. Each garment maker would state that they had an Marks & Spencer order, leading their suppliers to place orders with fabric producers. The result was an increase in fibre capacity, but also overproduction.[26]

Although arrangements with retailers had the potential to sustain a substantial domestic textile sector, they represented a new danger to the remnants of the Lancashire cotton industry that had been absorbed by the conglomerates in the 1960s and 1970s. These mills were now threatened not by import penetration and loss of export markets, but by boardroom decisions to reroute supply chains overseas.

A leading example was the arrangement between Marks & Spencer and Courtaulds which evolved in the 1970s. Overseas sourcing offered cost advantages to Marks & Spencer, but the firm lacked expertise in managing international supply chains, partly because of its heavy dependence on British domestic suppliers. Marcus Sieff of Marks & Spencer, therefore, looked to a long-term partnership with Courtaulds to deliver such expertise. By the end of the 1970s, Sieff and Frank Knight of Courtaulds were committed to a joint agenda of overseas sourcing.[27]

Bulk fabric, in particular, was now sourced overseas. Building on its general approach to the Mediterranean associate countries, European policy now encouraged the location of bulk fibre production in countries like Morocco. The Moroccan model was to import raw fibres (taking advantage of tax breaks for doing so) and re-export to Europe based on specifications laid down by a European partner. These arrangements, as used for example by Italian fashion retailer Benetton, were typically based on subcontracting, licensing agreements and joint ventures. Courtaulds now set up subsidiaries in Morocco, similarly benefiting from local and EU fiscal incentives. For example, Courtaulds

25   J. Singleton, *Lancashire on the Scrapheap* (Oxford, 1991), pp. 219–28.
26   D. Buck, *More Ups Than Downs: An Autobiography* (Spennymoor, 2001), p. 90.
27   M&SCA, Supplier File, Courtaulds (Northgate Group), E5/1/140, Knight to Sieff, 17 December 1979.

constructed Chelco in 1981 as a joint venture with Morocco's Office for Industrial Development and Moroccan private investors, and in 1988 had three factories selling to leading retailers Mothercare and British Home Stores.[28]

The arrangement with Courtaulds meant that Marks & Spencer continued to lack expertise in overseas supply-chain management, but even so, it had an increasingly dominant influence. By progressively using fewer suppliers and encouraging rationalization of its supply chain through mergers, Marks & Spencer was able to pressurize these firms to source upstream overseas production on its behalf. Marks & Spencer pressure on apparel suppliers resulted in them sourcing more fabric from overseas, even though they could misrepresent garments as made in the UK. Marks & Spencer took a proprietory interest in the design and production activities of its suppliers, promoting investment by the apparel sector in new technology such as Gerber cutting, based on a 'proprietary' interest in its 'factories' from Marks & Spencer. The close relationship between Marks & Spencer and apparel suppliers led to neglect of fabric, and a loss of control of overall product quality, which in turn impacted on design.[29]

Coats Viyella thus expanded through a series of takeover transactions, but in doing so, became more dependent on Marks & Spencer. Acquisitions included Carrington Viyella (1983), F. Miller (1984), Nottingham Manufacturing Company (1985), Coats Paton (1986), Tootal (1991) and Corah (1994).[30] Like Courtaulds, Coats Viyella developed significant strength in managing the international supply chain.[31] As a consequence, Vantona, which had been supplying 20% of its output to Marks & Spencer in 1984, became Coats Viyella, providing 50% by 1991.[32]

Further relaxation of world trade rules in the early 1990s, pressurized Marks & Spencer to push for further cost reductions and rationalizations of the supply chain.[33] Through new mergers, Courtaulds strengthened its position as the dominant supplier to Marks & Spencer.[34] By taking over other Marks & Spencer

---

28   Economic Intelligence Unit, *Mediterranean Textiles and Clothing* (London, 1989), p. 92. 'Profile of Morocco's Textile and Clothing Export Industry', *Textile Outlook International*, July 1994, p. 126.
29   Buck, *More Ups than Downs*, pp. 110–12.
30   *The Observer*, 17 October 1982; *The Times*, 16 October 1982; *Financial Times*, 24 February 1984; *The Times*, 18 May 1985; *Sunday Times*, 23 June 1985; *The Observer*, 23 June 1985; *Daily Mail*, 29 September 1986; *The Times*, 18 May 1991; *The Times*, 6 October 1994.
31   Buck, *More Ups than Downs*, pp. 114–15.
32   D. Higgins and S. Toms, 'Financial institutions and corporate strategy: David Alliance and the transformation of British textiles, c.1950–c.1990', *BH* 48 (2006), 453–78; *Glasgow Herald*, 4 July 1984; *The Times*, 18 May 1991.
33   M. Johnson, 'Marks & Spencer implements an ethical sourcing program for its global supply chain', *Journal of Organizational Excellence* 23 (2004), 3–16.
34   G. Owen, *From Empire to Europe: The Decline and Revival of British Industry* (London, 1999).

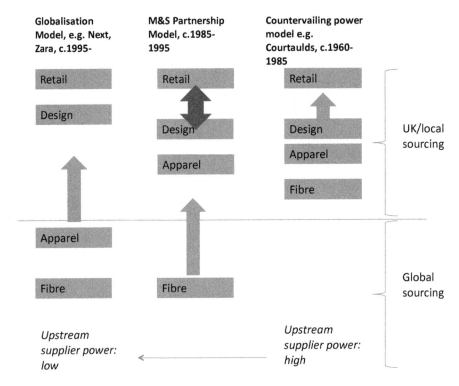

Figure 22. The international disintegration of textiles

Note: Joined blocks indicate vertical integration, vertical blue arrows, third-party arms-length sourcing, and red arrow collaboration, quasi-integration.

suppliers, Courtaulds could, when suitable, switch their production overseas. A notable case was the takeover of Claremont Garments in 1997 and the subsequent closure and relocation of its British factories to Morocco and elsewhere.[35] In 2000, Coats Viyella, disappointed by poor margins and instability from domestic contract work, divested its Marks & Spencer business. Coats's management argued that the required investment to remain linked to Marks & Spencer no longer made financial sense.[36] Courtaulds, now the last surviving large group, depended for its survival almost entirely on its relationship with Marks & Spencer.

As dominant retailers pushed fabric production and upstream commodity textile production overseas, supplier firms concentrated increasingly on design

---

35 S. Toms and Q. Zhang, 'Marks & Spencer and the decline of the British textile industry, 1950–2000', *BHR* 90 (2016), 3–30.

36 D. Harrison, 'Network effects following multiple relationship dissolution', *Proceedings of the 17th Annual IMP Conference* (Oslo, 2001), pp. 1–23, at p. 19.

and branding. This strategy was adopted most notably by Marks & Spencer's competitor, Zara, which globalized rapidly and launched in the UK in the late 1990s, using a business model of 'fast fashion'. Short lead times relied on the integration of local design and product development functions supported by global sourcing of upstream production. Under this model, cotton, along with other textile fabrics, was now subsumed in the broader global supply chain, with relatively few surviving specialist functions. Figure 22 sets out these more general trends in the final decades of a recognizable British textile industry, of which cotton was now only a small component. By 2000, what remained of the British textile manufacturing industry depended almost entirely on imported yarn.[37]

Figure 22 depicts three models, which evolved from the right to left as a function of the rise of retail and the decline of upstream supplier power (horizontal axis). In the countervailing power model of the 1960s and 1970s, textile production reached peak vertical integration, with large firms controlling all aspects of textile production. As power shifted to retail, in parallel with further trade liberalization, conglomerates began to move their fibre production overseas. The Marks & Spencer partnership model, at its purest during the 1980s, retained close co-operation with local suppliers, who were able to integrate design with the requirements of retail buying departments. Under the global sourcing model that emerged during the Multi Fibre Arrangement phase-out period of 1995–2005, all substantive textile production, including apparel, was moved offshore, substantially contributing to the final demise of cotton production in Lancashire.

Shiloh: Lancashire's last ditch

Since the 1920s, the conglomerate model had coincided with the independent model as the basis of a potential strategic response to the loss of markets. Unlike the conglomerates, which increasingly relied on London financial markets to facilitate takeover and merger activities, the independents, for reasons of historical path dependency, typically drew on Lancashire for financial and other resources. Shiloh, the last significant group of mills built up under this model, tells the story of the rearguard attempt to keep cotton spinning alive in Lancashire.

Shiloh had a long history, with the original mill founded in 1874, at the height of the Oldham district's first significant wave of mill flotation. Like the Lancashire Cotton Corporation in the 1950s, it had expanded through a series of negotiated mergers, using directors' local and regional contacts to raise the necessary finance. The amalgamation of Shiloh with Park, Roy and Royton Mills in 1953 was then

37 Ormerod, 'The UK textile industry: the terminal years, 1945–2003'.

used to secure a London Stock Exchange listing, and this represented a departure from the traditional model of relying purely on finance from within the district.[38] The Shiloh group remained under the control of the Gartside family so that, although quoted on the London stock market, it was able to resist pressures to deliver short-term financial results. Even so, Gartside family control persisted through differential classes of capital and still amounted to 30% in 1992.[39]

Using its combined resources, the firm built up markets in Europe, Scandinavia and the Commonwealth, although these accounted for only a small fraction of total turnover.[40] Shiloh took advantage of the 1959 Act to close some capacity and re-equip the rest. In the 1960s, it invested in productivity improvements while lobbying for improved protection from cheap imports.[41] Specifically, the Shiloh Chairman, Edmund Gartside, as a leading representative of smaller independent mills, called for quotas as opposed to tariffs as the only way of dealing with export incentive schemes, effectively 'dumping', administered by countries like Pakistan.[42] To deal with market volatility, the firm also began to diversify into non-textile products, mostly health care, which accounted for one-fifth of group profit by 1971.[43] Shiloh Healthcare was launched in 1970 and expanded subsequently in tandem with the decline of spinning.[44] Even so, Gartside was a stout defender of the core business. A further round of re-equipment and modernization occurred in 1975, notwithstanding the increased market penetration of imports from Turkey and elsewhere, following the UK's entry to the EEC.[45]

Domestically, Shiloh's mills were involved in supplying yarns for knitters, mainly to the Vantona group, which, in turn, through a series of mergers, became Coats Viyella, a significant supplier to Marks & Spencer by 1990. Carrington Viyella suffered substantial financial losses in the 1980–81 recession associated with debt overhang and associated rationalization costs.[46] As a result, it was the first to be acquired in the further expansion of the Vantona group under the leadership of David Alliance.[47]

38   'Cotton spinning amalgamation', *The Times*, 7 March 1953.
39   'Battle against cheap imports', *Daily Telegraph*, 3 February 1992, p. 27.
40   Anon., *The Shiloh Story* (Royton, 1974); M. Cannell, 'Rise of Shiloh: Bucking the trend in the UK spinning industry', *Textile Outlook International* 69 (1997), 60–75, at p. 66.
41   Anon., *The Shiloh Story*.
42   'Lancashire prepares to fight for its textile future', *The Times*, 8 November 1971.
43   *The Times*, 27 August 1959, p. 12; '17 firms volunteer to be productivity guinea pigs', *The Times*, 25 August 1967, p. 15; 'Shiloh Spinners', *The Times*, 26 April 1971, p. 18.
44   Cannell, 'Rise of Shiloh'; E. Rigby, 'Shiloh spins healthcare future out of textile past', *Financial Times*, 14 July 2001, p. 2.
45   E. T. Gartside, 'Textile imports', Letters to the editor, *Financial Times*, 21 November 1975, p. 23.
46   CIFD.
47   A. Moreton, 'Carrington Viyella Finds a Wealthy Partner in Vantona', *Financial Times*, 19 October 1982, p. 8.

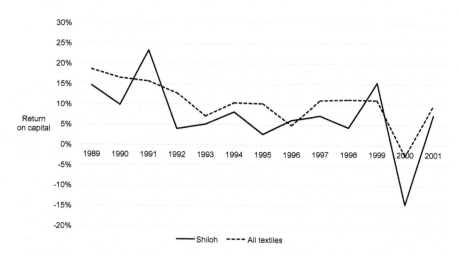

Figure 23. Profitability: Shiloh and other textile firms
Source: Calculated from CIFD.

The financial performance of Shiloh after 1989 compared to the textile sector, broadly defined, and not just confined to firms spinning cotton, is shown in Figure 23.[48] It can be seen that, for most of the 1990s, Shiloh underperformed, mostly due to high import costs and overseas competition.[49] Gartside attributed falling profits in 1991 to the erosion of margins caused by competition from subsidized imports. He complained explicitly of illegal 'dumping' by Brazil and Turkey, their governments providing discounts of 20% and 30% respectively, and Chinese imports being disguised as British by illegal relabelling. Lobbying resulted in a limited response from the Department of Trade and Industry, but did not provide a sustainable solution to what Gartside described as the absence of a 'level playing field'. For these reasons, between 1989 and 1992, thirty mills were closed, leaving only 25,000 employees left in the Lancashire textile industry. Shiloh, with its continued investment in spinning proved, for a time at least, that survival strategies could be made to work. Its remaining three mills concentrated on specialized yarns, which could be used to underpin product development in health care and specialized clothing.[50]

Notwithstanding these efforts, Gartside felt undermined by other aspects

48 CIFD. Limited financial information for Shiloh is available before 1989.
49 'Margins Squeezed at Shiloh', *Financial Times*, 1 May 1992, p. 21; 'Spinning Imports Hit Shiloh', *Financial Times*, 2 May 1991, p. 28.
50 'Battle against cheap imports', *Daily Telegraph*, 3 February 1992, p. 27; R. Tickel, 'Shiloh raises payout on first half recovery', *Daily Telegraph*, 28 October 1993, p. 27; 'Spinning Imports Hit Shiloh', *Financial Times*, 2 May 1991, p. 28.

of government policy. In 1994, he spoke out strongly against the provision of £61 million state aid for Taiwanese company Hualon to establish a factory in Belfast.[51] After 1995, as indicated in Figure 23, the performance of all firms, including Shiloh, became much worse in the new environment following the Uruguay Round.[52] Any remaining benefits that British textile firms had enjoyed under the Multi Fibre Arrangement were phased out and markets liberalized further under the terms of British membership of the World Trade Organization.

It was at this point that Shiloh, taking over two Courtaulds mills, became the largest spinner in the UK cotton sector. Speaking in 1997, Martin Taylor, the Courtaulds Textiles Chief Executive, blamed the introduction of equipment subsidies for yarn production in developing countries for the lack of a stable investment climate in Britain. By this time, Courtaulds had only thirty-five units employing 2,400 staff, albeit with output per employee around four times higher than it had been in 1968.[53]

Some textile firms, hitherto supplying Marks & Spencer, had performed well relative to the sector as a whole. In a similar vein, one of the reasons for the takeover of the two Courtaulds mills in 1997 was that Shiloh believed it could offer a reliable source of supply to Marks & Spencer. In contrast to Courtaulds, Shiloh based its strategy on flexibility and responsiveness, investing in product development based on close liaison with customers. Profits increased in 1997 due to strong performance in health care but also a contribution from the two new spinning units acquired from Courtaulds textiles.[54]

Commitments to specialist and bespoke yarns meant that the firm could not operate the traditional Lancashire model of covering raw material purchases with yarn sales.[55] The firm was also able to hedge some of the risks associated with textile price and currency fluctuations by diversifying into related health-care products.[56] However, without specific support from downstream purchases, especially the retail sector, the flexible specialization model was not sustainable. Such flexibility became the hallmark of other surviving branches of the textile industry, such that they could offset the apparent cost disadvantages, vis-à-vis overseas competition, by exploiting shorter lead times.[57]

51 'Shiloh blasts Taiwan aid', *Daily Telegraph*, 16 June 1994, p. 27.
52 Toms and Zhang, 'Marks & Spencer and the decline of the British textile industry'.
53 Cannell, 'Rise of Shiloh', pp. 61–2.
54 'Edmund Gartside, chairman and managing director of Shiloh', *The Times*, 1 May 1997, p. 33.
55 Cannell, 'Rise of Shiloh', p. 67; J. Zeitlin, 'The clothing industry in transition: International trends and British response', *Textile History* 19 (1988), 211–37, at p. 216; J. Zeitlin and P. Totterdill, 'Markets, technology and local intervention: The case of clothing', *Reversing Industrial Decline? Industrial Structure and Policy in Britain and Her Competitors*, ed. P. Hirst and J. Zeitlin (New York, 1989), pp. 155–90.
56 Cannell, 'Rise of Shiloh'; Rigby, 'Shiloh spins healthcare future out of textile past', *Financial Times*, 14 July 2001.
57 Cannell, 'Rise of Shiloh', pp. 68–9.

In Shiloh's case, weakness in the pound left the firm vulnerable to increases in import costs of raw cotton, while buyer power in the retail sector meant that increases could not be passed on. Once again, vertical specialization imposed limitations on survival strategies. Yarn sales fell by 19% in 1998,[58] leading to the closure of Elk Mill, the last mule-spinning mill to be constructed in Lancashire back in 1926, which was demolished and transformed into a retail park. The proceeds were used to complete the transformation of Shiloh into a health-care business.[59] Even so, the firm retained its spinning division with mills employing six hundred staff, which continued to struggle financially.[60] Such was the commitment of Edmund Gartside to the traditional side of the business that he subsequently led a management buyout of the textile division.[61] Gartside finally retired in 2005 when Shiloh was taken over by Synergy Healthcare and Shiloh Spinners was dissolved in 2009.[62]

The succession: finance, property and retail

Like Shiloh, Peel Mills Holdings was an amalgamation of mills put together on the regional interlock model, dating back to the activities of Sam Firth Mellor and others in the 1920s and before, described in chapter 7. However, the firm had a very different trajectory of development that, in the end, had little to do with textile production, but offered some alternative vision for post-industrial Lancashire.

In August 1972, the Peel Mills group was effectively taken over by Agremin, run by Lancashire businessman John Whittaker. At the same time, Whittaker was busy buying elsewhere and acquired Era Ring Mill in December 1972, which he promised to retain as part of a plan to expand the cotton industry but subsequently scheduled for closure. Spinning was closed in 1975 and the remainder of the winding and doubling business in 1979, which realized a cash surplus of £374,000 for Agremin.[63] Meanwhile, in 1973, Agremin had acquired Clover Croft, subsequently transformed it into a property development company.[64]

Agremin was an agent for another firm, Largs Ltd, also controlled by John

---

58   'Shiloh slips into the red', *The Times*, 5 November 1998, p. 32.
59   Rigby, 'Shiloh spins healthcare future out of textile past', *Financial Times*, 14 July 2001.
60   S. Jones, 'Textiles chief refashions shifts', *Financial Times*, 29 March 1999, p. 10.
61   B. Benoit, 'Shiloh embroiled in bitter bid row', *Financial Times*, 6 November 1999, p. 15.
62   'Edmund Gartside', Obituaries, *Daily Telegraph*, 31 July 2018; Damon Wilkinson, 'The incredible life of Lancashire's last cotton king', *Manchester Evening News*, 18 July 2018.
63   Agremin-Era Ring, *Financial Times*, 7 December 1972, p. 26; 'Agremin offer for Era Mill', *Financial Times*, 24 October 1972, p. 22; 'Textile unions in lobby to reprieve mills', *Financial Times*, 5 August 1975, p. 8; 'Emess Lighting Limited', *Financial Times*, 9 January 1980, p. 8.
64   'Bids and Deals', *The Times*, 30 August 1973, p. 18; 'Clover Croft Joins in Property Deals', *Financial Times*, 1 September 1980, p. 28.

Whittaker. Now using Largs, an Isle of Man-registered investment company, as his primary vehicle, Whittaker acquired John Bright in 1979.[65] Following a further acquisition, this time of Highams, Whittaker arranged for John Bright to be merged with other manufacturing interests including the Ash Spinning Company and then sold to Highams, and in turn, transferred to Peel Holdings. When Peel Holdings joined the London Stock Exchange in 1983, the reference to mills had been dropped from its name and it was effectively a property management company, via a majority shareholding still controlled by John Whittaker.[66]

Through Agremin and Largs in the 1970s, and then Peel Holdings in the 1980s, acquisitions of textile mills and their premises provided Whittaker with the opportunity to exploit new opportunities in warehousing and retail. Peel Holding thus also acquired infrastructure that had initially grown up around the cotton industry, including the Manchester Ship Canal in 1987 and the Mersey Docks & Harbour Company in 2005. These acquisitions provided the basis for the Atlantic Gateway project, a plan launched in 2008 to regenerate the Liverpool–Manchester corridor with new sustainable industries. Control of property assets granted Whittaker a dominant political position which he used to increasingly influence North West development strategy through regional development authorities in the late 1990s and early 2000s.[67]

There were some apparent symmetries between the creation of Lancashire as an industrial district in the models of initial expansion introduced in chapter 2, and the significant acquisition of industrial space and associated infrastructure during the final phase of decline. In performing this transformation, Peel Holdings exploited the emergence of the market for corporate control in the late 1960s, which was a precursor to an acquisition strategy of quoted mills. In combination, these influences have resulted in substantial regeneration of the Manchester and Liverpool regions in particular. Where industries are relatively dispersed spatially and subject to more private and decentralized ownership structures, similar opportunities are less likely to be present. Such differences may, in part, explain the success of regeneration in Manchester and Liverpool relative to peripheral cotton towns and, indeed, other former industrial regions. Of course, the economic performance of regions and subregions is the outcome of a host of influences, but a lesson of the history of Lancashire as an industrial district is that success follows where entrepreneurs can link local transformation with infrastructural development.

---

65 'Take-over bids and deals', *Financial Times*, 26 May 1979, p. 21.
66 'Profile: John Whittaker', *The Scotsman*, 28 March 2010.
67 D. Shaw and O. Sykes, 'Liverpool story: Growth, distress, reinvention and place-based strategy in a northern city', *Transforming Distressed Global Communities*, ed. F. Wagner, R. Mahayni and A. G. Piller (Abingdon, 2015), pp. 51–72, at p. 57; J. Harrison, 'Rethinking city-regionalism as the production of new non-state spatial strategies: The case of Peel Holdings Atlantic Gateway Strategy', *Urban Studies* 51 (2014), 2315–35.

Conclusions

As the previous chapters have shown, although the industry declined steadily after 1920, each subsequent decade offered some hope of recovery. In the 1920s and 1930s, Lancashire entrepreneurs hoped for the return of pre-war trading conditions but lacked the financial resources to re-equip in that eventuality. In the 1930s, the intervention of the Bank of England and the formation of the Lancashire Cotton Corporation provided an alternative to the model of cut-throat competition in declining markets that had prevailed in the 1920s. With much of the interwar debt paid off in the 1940s, the 1950s offered a last chance for restructuring under the traditional Lancashire model of speciali-zation supported by regional financial networks. The year 1960 was a watershed, marking the end of local control and new dependencies on decisions taken by governments, big corporations and retailers. By the 1960s, the ability to fix prices locally disappeared with the Yarn Spinners' Agreement, and regional stock markets were usurped by the intervention of the London-financed corporate giants. The 1960s offered a restructured industry a further opportunity, based on capital investment and vertical integration. The strategy worked for a while until the early 1970s but was undermined by the removal of government support for import quotas under the Multi Fibre Arrangement. In the absence of guarantees of steady production, the flexible specialization model gained some traction in the 1980s. In some respects, this was a reversion to the tradi-tional basis of Lancashire's success, although there were few production units left capable of operating the model and the strategy was dependent on the sourcing policies of major retailers.

By 2000, little remained of the Lancashire textile industry. Free trade, which had facilitated the industry's first expansion, had, through successive rounds of liberalization, closed down most of the options left other than exit. Risk, associated with fixed investments in volatile markets, that had first impelled entrepreneurs to work their factories and child workers for sixteen hours a day, now became too much even in periods characterized by protection from governments and the umbrellas of larger corporate organizations. As these protections were stripped away, so disappeared the remainder of a once-great industry. Shiloh was the last substantial Lancashire cotton business that could trace its origins to the expansion phase of the industrial revolution.

However, the story does not entirely end there. As the quotation from the Alliance Project Report at the beginning of the chapter suggests, activities are still significant and opportunities remain. Today, in emulation of its strategy, several firms continue to spin cotton-related fabrics for specific purposes. For example, Culimeta Saveguard, based at Tame Valley Mill, produces high-performance technical fibre yarns based on specialized batch production – a highly profitable strategy. Between 2010 and 2015, the firm averaged a return on capital of 16% and grew capital and turnover by over 20%.[68] In 2016, English Fine Cottons, a wholly owned subsidiary of Culimeta Saveguard, opened a new cotton spinning facility at Tower Mill, Dukinfield. First constructed in 1885, the mill was extensively renovated and equipped with modern machinery. These developments represented a substantial investment for Culimeta Saveguard and were assisted by loans from the Greater Manchester Combined Authority and the N. Brown clothing retail group, and a grant from the Textile Growth Programme, part of the EU's Regional Development Fund. They were also justified by increasing demand from clothing and textile producers wishing to demonstrate British provenance. Such products have become popular with the middle classes of Asia and Latin America, creating once again the opportunity for British spun cotton to be exported to markets that it once dominated.[69]

Initiatives at Dukinfield and elsewhere may well succeed in breathing life back into the virtually defunct British textile industry. In recent years Culimeta Saveguard has based its strategy on investment in the most modern machinery combined with traditional cotton spinning skills and expertise. The recently published Alliance Report recognizes similar opportunities, showcasing high-end apparel, luxury clothing for export, homeware for the domestic market and fast fashion, all of which can be supported by investment in full or high levels of automation. The report also recognized significant barriers, including power imbalances between producers and retailers, poor supply-chain integration, the sustainability of demand, sweatshop image and skill shortages, and lack of access to suitable finance, particularly for medium-sized enterprises.[70]

Such opportunities and problems have recurred throughout the long history of textile production in Lancashire. Unstable relationships with customers and dislocation of overseas markets in the Napoleonic Wars prevented the early cotton entrepreneurs from fully exploiting the benefits of automation. The sweatshop image was a dominant characteristic of the first factories, overcome in part by the temporary success of worker-owned co-operatives. During the process of industrial expansion, profits from core activities have been used to finance new ventures supported by a more extensive network, including other firms along the value chain. Such a system, comprising customers as well as regional and state organizations, facilitated the investment at Tower Mill.

The involvement of the latter, however, hints at a potential barrier to further

---

68   Calculated from CH, Culimeta-Saveguard Ltd, Financial Statements, 31 December 2011–31 December 2016.

69   https://culimeta-saveguard.com/textile/, accessed 9 September 2019; S. Begum, 'Cotton spinning returns to Greater Manchester thanks to £5.8m investment', *Manchester Evening News*, 2 December 2015; https://www.englishfinecottons.co.uk, accessed 9 September 2019; D. Higgins and S. Toms, *British Cotton Textiles: Maturity and Decline* (London, 2017), p. 206.

70   Alliance Project Team, *Repatriation of UK textiles manufacture*.

expansion, which is the absence of intermediate financial institutions. History reveals that these can be an essential means of mobilizing local savings to facilitate industrial development. Regional stock markets provided access to equity capital for hundreds of medium-sized cotton mills which dominated the landscape of industrial Lancashire. Even so, these markets only coexisted with the Lancashire industrial district for part of its history, roughly from the 1860s to the 1960s, and as the book has demonstrated, attracted speculators that caused the industry to grow too quickly in the expansion phase, only to produce an equally sharp downward correction in the 1920s. The alternative models were those prevailing before 1850, based on networks and influence with state institutions, or those emerging after 1960, using flexible specialization in which firms rely heavily on their internally generated financial resources. The vertical control model of the 1960s and 1970s is no longer relevant, given the small scale of the industry. In sum, none of the feasible strategies require involvement from City financial institutions and rarely in the long history of the industrial North West have such institutions played an important role. Even today, small and medium-sized enterprises face lower barriers to raising equity in London and the South East.

Moreover, where government has intervened to address this problem, it has nonetheless left gaps in financial support for medium-sized businesses.[71] Such imbalances are not insurmountable and, as history demonstrates, regional networks of entrepreneurs, in association with government organizations, may hold the key to regenerating the industrial north of England. Without such responses, in textiles or other industries, the mill towns of Lancashire remain devoid of their original purpose, unmodernized and left behind.

71   C. Mason and R. Harrison, 'Closing the regional equity gap? A critique of the Department of Trade and Industry's regional venture capital funds initiative', *Regional Studies* 37 (2003), 855–68.

Appendix 1:
Cotton Industry Financial Database – Sample Firms and Sources

Firm	Dates	Sources
Cardwell, Birley & Hornby	1777–1809; 1813–1827; 1834–1857	Stock books and ledgers, WP, Eng. MS, 1199/1–6, 1208.
Cowpe, Oldknow & Siddon	1786–1813; 1831–1847; 1873–1881	Pleasley Mill, S. Pigott, *Hollins: A Study of Industry, 1784–1949* (Nottingham, 1949), pp. 37–8, 72, 86; S. D. Chapman, *The Early Factory Masters: The Transition to the Factory System in the Midlands Textile Industry* (Newton Abbot, 1967), table 5, p. 126.
Philips & Lee	1794–1815	Philips & Lee, Abstracts of accounts (Shakespeare Birthplace Trust), DR 198/167.
S. Oldknow, Mellor Mill	1797	G. Unwin, *Samuel Oldknow and the Arkwrights* (Manchester, 1968), p. 195
Greg, Lyle & Ewart	1797–1809	GP, Partnership Accounts, 1796–1810, C5/1/2/1.
McConnel & Kennedy	1797–1807; 1813–1827	MKP, Financial records, GB133 MCK; C. H. Lee, *A Cotton Enterprise 1795–1840: A History of M'Connel & Kennedy Fine Cotton Spinners* (Manchester, 1972), appendix; P. Richardson, 'The structure of capital during the industrial revolution revisited: Two case studies from the cotton textile industry', *EcHR* 42 (1989), 484–503, Table 1.
N. Dugdale & Bros	1797–1803; 1807–1808; 1815–1823	Accounts and financial records, WP, Eng. MS, 1208.
Greg & Ewart	1798–1815	GP, Partnership Book, C5/1/2/2.
Horrockses Miller	1799–1828; 1836–1854[1]	HCP, Ledgers, DDHS 1.

Firm	Dates	Sources
J. & N. Philips	1807–1832	JNPP, Ledgers and Balance, 1807–1831, M97/2/1/1.
James Lees	1809–1818[2]	JLP, ledger and stock accounts, 1804–1820, DDRE 13/1.
Thomson & Chippendall	1811–1825	TCP, Primrose Mills, Ledger accounts, CYC 3/46–48.
Birley & Co	1811–1839	BCP, Chorlton Mill, Ledgers, 1811–1823; 1824–1840, UF-1 and 2.
S. Greg & Sons: Caton Mill	1815–1841	GP, ledger, C5/1/2/5.
S. Greg & Sons: Quarry Bank Mill	1816–1831	GP, Partnership Accounts, C5/1/2/3–4.
Ashworth Brothers: New Eagley	1818–1879	AP, Stock books, quarterly stock book, Eng. MS, 1201; R. Boyson, *The Ashworth Cotton Enterprise* (Oxford, 1970), pp. 18, 30, 68.
S. Greg & Sons: Lancaster Mill	1824–1841	GP, ledger, C5/1/2/5.
S. Greg & Sons: Ancoats Mill	1824–1827	GP, ledger, C5/1/2/5.
S. Greg & Sons: Hudcar Mill	1828–1841	GP, ledger, C5/1/2/5.
Ashworth Brothers: Egerton	1834–1840; 1845–1846	AP, Stock books, quarterly stock book, Eng. MS, 1201; Boyson, *Ashworth Cotton*, p. 30
Fielden Bros.	1836–1847, 1852–1913	S. D. Chapman, 'The Fielden Fortune. The Finances of Lancashire's most Successful Ante-bellum Manufacturing Family', *Financial History Review* 3 (1996), 7–28, table 6, pp. 22–3; B. Law, *Fieldens of Todmorden: A Nineteenth Century Business Dynasty* (Littleborough, 1995), Table XVII, p. 129; FP, Financial records, C353/475.
Bashall & Boardman	1838–1850	Bashall & Boardman Records, Ledgers, DDX819.1.
Chorlton, McIntosh	1834–1843	S. Clark, 'Chorlton Mills and their neighbours', *Industrial Archaeology Review*, 1978, 207–39, at p. 235.
Greg: Albert Mill	1849–1860	GP, Ledger, C5/1/2/8.
Mitchell Hey	1857–1861	B. Jones, *Co-operative Production* (Oxford, 1894), p. 262.

Firm	Dates	Sources
Sun Mill	1863–1913; 1949–1958	R. E. Tyson, 'The Sun Mill Company: A study in democratic investment, 1858–1959' (MA dissertation, University of Manchester, 1962), appendices 1 and 2; *Oldham Chronicle* and *Oldham Standard*, 'Commercial reports', Saturday issues, quarterly reports detailing profits, dividends, share and loan capital, April 1875–December 1913; C/DTI, 1949–1958.
Rylands and Sons	1872–1949	D. A. Farnie, 'John Rylands of Manchester', *Bulletin of the John Rylands Library* 75/2 (1993), 2–103, at pp. 71–2; SER, commercial reports, half-yearly balance sheets, 1884–1913; SEOI, 1920–1949.
Moorfield Spinning Company	1877–1913	*Oldham Standard* and *Oldham Chronicle*, 'Commercial reports', Saturday issues, quarterly reports detailing profits, dividends, share and loan capital, April 1877–December 1913; R. Smith, 'An Oldham Limited Liability Company 1875–1896', *BH* 4 (1961), 34–53.
Borough Spinning Company	1880–1883	*Oldham Chronicle* and *Oldham Standard*, 'Commercial reports', Saturday issues, quarterly reports detailing profits, dividends, share and loan capital, April 1880–December 1883.
Barlow & Jones	1884–1960	IMM, 1884–1892; SER, commercial reports, half-yearly balance sheets, 1900–13, commercial reports, annual balance sheets, 1920–1929; SEOI, 1920–1950; C/DTI, 1950–1960.
Haugh Spinning Company	1884–1913, 1926–1934	*Oldham Chronicle*, 'Commercial reports', Saturday issues, quarterly reports detailing profits, dividends, share and loan capital, April 1884–December 1913; *Rochdale Observer*, ditto, 28 June 1890 and quarterly reports April 1892–December 1914 inclusive. *Tattersall's Annual Cotton Trade Review*, 1926–1934.
New Ladyhouse Spinning Company	1884–1913, 1926–1934	*Oldham Chronicle*, 'Commercial reports', Saturday issues, quarterly reports detailing profits, dividends, share and loan capital, April 1884–December 1913; *Rochdale Observer*, ditto, 28 June 1890 and quarterly reports April 1892–December 1914 inclusive. *Tattersall's Annual Cotton Trade Review*, 1926–1934.

Firm	Dates	Sources
Werneth Spinning Co.	1884–1913; 1949–1969	*Oldham Chronicle*, 'commercial reports', Saturday issues, quarterly reports detailing profits, dividends, share and loan capital, April 1884–December 1888; WSCR, Quarterly reports to members, Misc. 42/17 and 18, April 1889–October 1912; C/DTI, 1949–1969.
Crawford Cotton Spinning Co.	1885–1913; 1926–1938	*Oldham Chronicle*, 'Commercial reports', Saturday issues, quarterly reports detailing profits, dividends, share and loan capital; SER, commercial reports, quarterly balance sheets, 1885–1913; *Tattersall's Annual Cotton Trade Review*, 1926–1938.
Dowry Cotton Spinning Co.	1885–1912	*Oldham Chronicle*, 'Commercial reports', Saturday issues, quarterly reports detailing profits, dividends, share and loan capital, April 1884–December 1913; CCA, Dowry Cotton Spinning Company, nominal ledger, LCC/Dow1 NRA29343; June 1885–December 1912.
New Hey	1887–1913; 1926–1934	*Oldham Chronicle*, 'Commercial reports', Saturday issues, quarterly reports detailing profits, dividends, share and loan capital, September 1886–June 1913; *Rochdale Observer*, ditto, 28 June 1890 and April 1892–June 1914; *Tattersall's Annual Cotton Trade Review*, 1926–1934.
Healey Wood Mill	1885–1913	Healey Wood Mill Records, Balance Sheets, Quarterly Trading and Profit and Loss Accounts and Balance Sheets, BB614, April 1907–December 1914; Dividends Ledger, April 1882–December 1914.
Horrockses Crewdson Ltd	1888–1913, 1950–1958	CVR, accounts, half-yearly balance sheets and profit and loss accounts, November 1887–October 1905; HCP, DDHS 53, balance sheets, half-yearly balance sheets and profit and loss accounts, October 1905–April 1914; C/DTI, 1950–1958.
Tootal	1889–1962, 1970–1974, 1980–1991	TP, board minutes, yearly balance sheets and profit and loss accounts, M.461, July 1888–July 1914; SEOI, 1920–1950; CDC, 1950–1962; Thomson Reuters, *Datastream*, 1980–1991.
Osborn	1890–1913	DDX 869/3/1, trade, capital, and profit and loss accounts, June 1889–December 1913.
J. & P. Coats/ Coats Viyella	1891–1941; 1970–2001	IMM, 1891–1920; SEOI, 1920–1941; C/DTI, 1970–1984; *Datastream*, 1984–2001.

Firm	Dates	Sources
Sir Elkanah Armitage	1891–1949	SER, commercial reports, yearly balance sheets, 1891–1913; SEOI, 1920–1949.
Centenary Mill (Horrockses)	1895–1913	CVR, accounts, November 1887–October 1905.
Mellodew	1896–1920	W. M. Hartley, *An Oldham Velvet Dynasty: The Mellodews of Moorside* (Lancaster, 2009), chapter 10 and appendix III.
T. & R. Eccles	1897–1913	TRER, balance sheets, DDX 868/1711, September 1897–September 1914.
English Sewing Cotton	1898–1913	IMM, 1898–1913.
Ashton Bros.	1899–1960	SER, commercial reports, half-yearly balance sheets, 1899–1913 and annual balance sheets and profit and loss accounts, 1920–1925; SEOI, 1920–1950; C/DTI, 1950–1960.
Fine Cotton Spinners' & Doublers' Association	1899–1960	SER, commercial reports, half-yearly balance sheets, 1900–13; SEOI, 1920–1950; C/DTI, 1950–1960.
American Thread	1900–1906	IMM, 1900–1906.
Calico Printers' Association	1900–1913	IMM, 1900–1913.
G. Whiteley & Co.	1900–1913	G. Whiteley & Co. Ltd Records, balance sheets, annual balance sheet and profit and loss account summary, DDX 868/21/5, September 1898–September 1914.
Bleachers' Association/ Whitecroft	1901–1913; 1949–1984	IMM, 1900–1913; C/DTI, 1949–1984.
Hollins Mill	1920–1949	SEOI, 1920–1950.
Brierfield Mills	1920–1948	SEOI, 1920–1948.
Joshua Hoyle	1920–1963	SEOI, 1920–1963.
Pear Mill	1920–1928	R. N. Holden, 'Pear Mill, Stockport: An Edwardian Cotton Spinning Mill', *Industrial Archaeology Review* 10 (1988), 162–74.
Amalgamated Cotton Mills Trust	1921–1960	SEOI, 1921–1950; C/DTI, 1950–1960.
Butts Mills	1921–1958	SEOI, 1921–1950; C/DTI, 1950–1958.
Broadstone	1922–1949	SEOI, 1922–1949; C/DTI, 1950–1958.
Crosses & Winkworth	1922–1960	SEOI, 1922–1950; C/DTI, 1950–1960.
Era Ring Mill	1925–1938; 1949–1963	SEOI, *Tattersall's Annual Cotton Trade Review*, 1925–1938, C/DTI, 1949–1963.
Argyll	1926–1928; 1952–1953	*Tattersall's Annual Cotton Trade Review*, 1926–1928; C/DTI, 1952–1953.

Firm	Dates	Sources
Asia	1926–1927; 1934–1952	*Tattersall's Annual Cotton Trade Review*, 1925–1938; C/DTI, 1949–1952.
Cromer Ring Mill	1926–1972	SEOI, *Tattersall's Annual Cotton Trade Review*, 1926–1938; C/DTI, 1949–1972.
Gladstone	1926–1928	*Tattersall's Annual Cotton Trade Review*, 1926–1928.
Irwell	1926–1928	*Tattersall's Annual Cotton Trade Review*, 1926–1928.
Iris	1926–1958	*Tattersall's Annual Cotton Trade Review*, 1926–1934, SEOI, 1934–1949; C/DTI, 1949–1958.
Maple	1926–1928; 1950–1953	*Tattersall's Annual Cotton Trade Review*, 1926–1928; C/DTI, 1949–1953.
Melbourne	1926–1928; 1949–1958	*Tattersall's Annual Cotton Trade Review*, 1926–1928; C/DTI, 1949–1958.
Mersey	1926–1928; 1949–1963	*Tattersall's Annual Cotton Trade Review*, 1926–1928; C/DTI, 1949–1963.
Mona	1926–1928; 1952–1958	*Tattersall's Annual Cotton Trade Review*, 1926–1928; C/DTI, 1952–1958.
Ocean	1926–1927; 1949–1957	*Tattersall's Annual Cotton Trade Review*, 1926–1927; C/DTI, 1949–1957.
Olive	1926–1928; 1951–1956	*Tattersall's Annual Cotton Trade Review*, 1926–1928; C/DTI, 1951–1956.
Peel	1926–1927; 1952–1969	*Tattersall's Annual Cotton Trade Review*, 1926–1927; C/DTI, 1952–1969.
Roy	1926–1928; 1949–1952	*Tattersall's Annual Cotton Trade Review*, 1926–1928; C/DTI, 1949–1952.
Shiloh	1926–1928; 1949–1969; 1989–2001	*Tattersall's Annual Cotton Trade Review*, 1926–1928; C/DTI, 1949–1969; *Datastream*, 1989–2001.
Soudan	1926–1928; 1949–1952	*Tattersall's Annual Cotton Trade Review*, 1926–1928; C/DTI, 1949–1952.
Westwood	1926–1928	*Tattersall's Annual Cotton Trade Review*, 1926–1928.
Belgrave	1927–1960	SEOI, 1927–1950; C/DTI, 1950–1960.
Swan	1927–1928; 1949–1986	*Tattersall's Annual Cotton Trade Review*, 1927–1928; C/DTI, 1949–1986.
Lancashire Cotton Corporation	1931–1963	SEOI, 1931–1950; CH, Annual report and accounts, 1950–1963.
Asia Mills	1934–1952	SEOI, 1934–1950; C/DTI, 1950–1952.
New Hey Rings	1935–1938; 1949–1955	*Tattersall's Annual Cotton Trade Review*, 1935–1938; C/DTI, 1949–1955.

Firm	Dates	Sources
Baytree	1949–1958	C/DTI, 1949–1958.
Blue Printers	1949–1959	C/DTI, 1949–1959.
Dart Mill	1949–1960	C/DTI, 1949–1960.
Durban	1949–1953	C/DTI, 1949–1953.
Ellenroad	1949–1957	C/DTI, 1949–1957.
English Calico	1949–1983	C/DTI, 1949–1983.
Falcon	1949–1959	C/DTI, 1949–1959.
Highams	1949–1983	C/DTI, 1949–1983.
Illingworth Morris	1949–1983	C/DTI, 1949–1983.
Jackson & Steeple	1949–1965	C/DTI, 1949–1965.
John Bright	1949–1977	C/DTI, 1949–1977.
North British Rayon	1949–1956	C/DTI, 1949–1956.
Park	1949–1953	C/DTI, 1949–1953.
Vantona	1949–1974; 1976–1984	C/DTI, 1949–1974; 1976–1984.
Viyella/Carrington Viyella	1949–1969	C/DTI, 1949–1969.
Whitehead	1949–1969	C/DTI, 1949–1969.
Barber Text. Corp.	1950–1960	C/DTI, 1950–1960.
Bee Hive	1950–1966	C/DTI, 1950–1966.
Comb. Eng. (Egyptian) Mills	1950–1960	C/DTI, 1950–1960.
Royton	1950–1964	C/DTI, 1950–1964.
Coldhurst	1951–1960	C/DTI, 1951–1960.
Cotton & Rayon	1951–1968	C/DTI, 1951–1968.
Eagle	1953–1955	C/DTI, 1953–1955.
Coats Patons	1961–1984	C/DTI, 1961–1984.
John Spencer	1977–1982	C/DTI, 1977–1982.
British Enkalon	1967–1971	C/DTI, 1967–1971.
Allied Textiles	1985–1999	*Datastream*, 1985–1999.
Hollas	1988–1997	*Datastream*, 1988–1997.
Courtaulds Textiles	1990–1999	*Datastream*, 1990–1999.

Notes:
1 Four missing observations interpolated 1836–54.
2 Average profits used for missing single years.
Firms are listed in order of earliest data and alphabetically.

Appendix 2: Money Equivalent Values

Date	Value (£)	Date	Value (£)	Date	Value (£)
1750	217.80	1850	132.24	1940	54.99
1760	198.36	1860	119.44	1950	33.66
1770	179.16	1870	116.93	1960	22.62
1780	176.32	1880	118.17	1970	15.20
1790	148.11	1890	126.23	1980	4.21
1800	82.28	1900	120.74	1990	2.23
1810	77.14	1910	115.71	2000	1.65
1820	94.94	1920	43.91	2010	1.26
1830	112.20	1930	64.21	2018	1.00
1840	100.07				

Source: Compiled from Bank of England, inflation calculator, https://www.bankofengland.co.uk/monetary-policy/inflation/inflation-calculator.

Bibliography

Unpublished primary sources

Bolton Archives and Local Studies
  Dart Mill Records

Churchill College, Cambridge
  Churchill Papers

Courtaulds Company Archive, Coventry
  Dowry Cotton Spinning Company, ledgers

Data Archive, Wivenhoe, Essex
  Cambridge/Department of Trade and Industry, SN2366, Databank of
    Company Accounts, 1948–1985

Companies House
  Annual Reports and Accounts, various companies.

John Rylands Library Manchester
  Ashworth Papers
  McConnel & Kennedy Papers
  Sun Mill Papers
  Wadsworth Papers

Lancashire County Record Offices (now Lancashire Archives)
  Bashall & Boardman Records
  Coats Viyella Records
  T. & R. Eccles Ltd Records
  Horrockses Crewdson & Co. Ltd Papers
  James Lees Papers
  Osborne Ltd Records
  Thomson & Chippendall Papers
  G. Whiteley & Co. Records

London Guildhall Library
  Stock Exchange Records

Manchester Central Library
    Greg Papers
    J. & N. Philips Papers
    Lancashire Cotton Corporation Records
    Tootal Papers

Marks & Spencer Company Archive

Oldham Local Studies Library
    Werneth Spinning Co. Records

Public Record Office
    Board of Trade, Dissolved Companies, BT31 file

Rochdale Local Studies Library
    New Ladyhouse Cotton Spinning Co. Ltd, Financial Records

Rossendale Museum
    Healey Wood Mill Records

Shakespeare Birthplace Trust, Stratford
    Philips & Lee, Abstracts of Accounts

Thomson Reuters, *Datastream*. Online database, https://www.refinitiv.com/
    en/products/datastream-macroeconomic-analysis, accessed 6 April 2020.

University of Florida Smathers Library
    Birley & Co. Papers

West Yorkshire Record Office
    Fielden Papers

Published primary sources

'Lancashire and Yorkshire Railway and its Connections' (1915), Lancashire
    and Yorkshire railway map, 1998-8534, Science Museum Group Collection
    Online, https://collection.sciencemuseumgroup.org.uk/objects/co439974,
    accessed 10 January 2020.
Smith's English Atlas (London, 1804).
Hansard's Parliamentary Debates, 1st–6th series, 1803–2004.
Orders in Council, 1808, BPP, 10.
Anon., *Copy of the Demise of the Manchester Exchange* (Manchester, 1810).
'A petition', *House of Commons Sessional Papers*, BPP, 1791, 33, 28 January,
    pp. 94–5.
*Select Committee on the State of the Children Employed in the Manufactories
    of the United Kingdom*, BPP, 1816, 397.

Select Committee into the Present State of Affairs of the East India Company, BPP, 1830, 646.

Report from the Committee (Sadler Committee) on the 'Bill to regulate the labour of children in the mills and factories of the United Kingdom', BPP, 1831–32, 706.

Select Committee on Manufactures, Commerce and Shipping, BPP, 1833, 690.

Factories Inquiry Commission, BPP, 1833, 450.

Factories Inquiry Commission, Supplementary Report, BPP, 1834, 167.

Select Committee on Handloom Weavers' Petitions, BPP, 1835, 341.

Return of Number of Persons Summoned for Offences against the Factories Act, 1835–36, BPP, 1836, 50.

Return of Mills in Lancaster and York, in which the System of Relays of Children has been Observed, since July 1836, BPP, 1837, 50.

Reports of Inspector of Factories, BPP, October 1845.

Report from the Select Committee of the House of Lords on the Burdens Affecting Real Property, BPP, 1846, 411 II.

Reports of Inspector of Factories, BPP, October 1846.

Return of Joint Stock Companies Registered under Act 7 & 8 Victoria, BPP, 1846, 110.

Second report from the Secret Committee on Commercial Distress, BPP, 1847–48, 584.

Supplemental Appendix to Reports from the Secret Committee on Commercial Distress, BPP, 1847–48, 395.

Report from the Secret Committee of the House of Lords Appointed to Inquire into the Causes of the Distress, BPP, 1847–48, 565.

Report from the Select Committee on Investments for the Savings of the Middle and Working Classes, BPP, 1850, 508.

Reports of the Inspectors of Factories, BPP, Half-year ending 30 April 1858.

Royal Commission on Assimilation of Mercantile Laws in the United Kingdom and Amendments in Law of Partnership, as regards Question of Limited or Unlimited Responsibility, BPP, 1854, 653.

Reports of the Inspectors of Factories, BPP, Half-year ending 30 April 1860.

Reports of the Inspectors of Factories, BPP, 31 October 1862.

Second Report of the Royal Commission on the Depression of Trade and Industry, BPP, 1886, C.4715.

Royal Commission on Labour Minutes of Evidence, Appendices (Group C) Volume I. Textiles, BPP, 1892, C.6708–VI.

Report to Board of Trade on Profit Sharing, London, 1894, Report by Mr. D. F. Schloss, C.7458.

Report of an Enquiry by the Board of Trade into the Earnings and Hours of Labour of Workpeople of the United Kingdom. No. I. – Textile Trades in 1906 (London, 1909).

Economic Advisory Council, Committee on the Cotton Industry (Clynes Report), BPP, 1929–30, Cmd. 3615, XII.825.

Board of Trade, *An Industrial Survey of the Lancashire Area* (London, 1932).

Newspapers and periodicals

Belfast News-Letter
Blackburn Standard
British Labourer's Protector and Factory Child's Friend
Bradshaw's Shareholders Guide, Railway Manual and Directory
Co-operative News
The Co-operator
Cotton Factory Times
Daily Despatch
Daily Mail
Daily Telegraph
The Economist
Financial Times
Fraser's Magazine for Town and Country
Gentleman's Magazine
Glasgow Herald
Guardian
Huddersfield Examiner
Investors Monthly Manual
Lancashire Evening Post
The Literary Panorama
London Gazette
The London Review
Lloyd's Illustrated Newspaper
Manchester Commercial Guardian
Manchester Courier and Lancashire General Advertiser
Manchester Evening News
Manchester Guardian
Manchester Times
Mechanics' Magazine Museum, Register, Journal, and Gazette
The Midland Workman and General Advertiser
The Monthly Magazine
New York Daily Tribune
The Observer
Oldham Chronicle
Oldham Standard

Pall Mall Gazette
Pigot's Commercial Directory
Preston Chronicle
Preston Guardian
Railway Chronicle
Reynolds's Newspaper
Rochdale Observer
The Scotsman
The Scottish Commercial List
The Standard
Stock Exchange Official Intelligence
Sunday Times
Tattersall's Annual Cotton Trade Review
Textile Manufacturer
Textile Mercury
Textile Outlook International
Textile Recorder
The Times
Todmorden Advertiser
Worrall's Cotton Spinners and Manufacturers Directory

Contemporary books and articles

Abram, W. A., *A History of Blackburn: Town and Parish* (Blackburn, 1877).
Ainsworth, R. and R. S. Crossley, *Accrington through the Nineteenth Century* (Accrington, n.d.).
Amalgamated Cotton Mills Trust Ltd, *Concerning Cotton: A Brief Account of the Aims and Achievements of the Amalgamated Cotton Mills Trust Limited and its Component Companies* (London, 1921).
Anon., 'Mr Horrocks', *The Repertory of Arts, Manufactures and Agriculture* 25/2 (1814), p. 1.
Anon. (attributed to John Doherty), *Misrepresentations Exposed in a Letter Containing Strictures on the Letters on the Factory Act etc.* (Manchester, 1838).
Anon., 'Answers to Certain Objections made to Sir Robert Peel's Bill', *The Factory Act of 1819*, ed. K. Carpenter (New York, 1972).
Anon., 'The Fieldens of Todmorden', *Fortunes Made in Business: A Series of Original Sketches Biographical and Anecdotic from the Recent History of Industry and Commerce*, vol. 1 (London, 1884).
Anon., *The Era Idea* (Rochdale, n.d.).
Anon., *The Shiloh Story* (Royton, 1974).

Ashley, Lord, *Ten Hours' Factory Bill, The Speech of Lord Ashley M.P.* (London, 1844).

Baines, E., *History of the Cotton Manufacture in Great Britain* (London, 1835).

Baines, E., *History, Directory and Gazetteer of the County Palatine of Lancaster*, Vols. 1 and 2 (Liverpool, 1825).

Blair, M., *The Paisley Thread Industry and the Men who Created and Developed it: With Notes Concerning Paisley, Old and New* (Paisley, 1907).

Board of Trade, *British Fair Catalogue*, Dept. of Overseas Trade (London, 1929).

Bowker, B., *Lancashire under the Hammer* (London, 1928).

British Northrop Loom Company, *Northrop Labour Saving Looms: A brief Treatise on Weaving and Northrop Looms*, 3rd edn (Blackburn, 1905).

Brown, J., 'A Memoir of Robert Blincoe' (1832), reprinted in *The Ten Hours Movement in 1831 and 1832: Six Pamphlets and One Broadside*, ed. K. Carpenter (New York, 1972).

Brydges, S. E., *A Biographical Peerage of the Empire of Great Britain*, vol. 1 (London, 1808).

Butterworth, E., *Historical Sketches of Oldham* (Oldham, 1856).

Calico Printers' Association, *Fifty Years of Calico Printing* (Manchester, 1949).

Carey, H. C., *Principles of Political Economy* (Philadelphia, PA, 1840).

Carlyle, T., *Past and Present* (London, 1843).

Chapman, S. J., *The Lancashire Cotton Industry: A Study in Economic Development* (Manchester, 1904).

Chapman, S. J., 'The report of the tariff commission', *Economic Journal* 15 (1905), 420–7.

Chapman, S. J. and F. J. Marquis, 'The Recruiting of the Employing Classes from the Ranks of the Wage-Earners in the Cotton Industry', *Journal of the Royal Statistical Society* 75 (1912), 293–313.

Clay, Sir H., *Report on the Position of the English Cotton Industry* (London, 1931).

Cooper, W., *History of the Rochdale District Co-operative Corn Mill Society* (London, 1861).

Copeland, M., 'Technical development in cotton manufacturing since 1860', *Quarterly Journal of Economics* 24 (1909), 109–59.

Craik, G. L. and C. MacFarlane, *The Pictorial History of England during the Reign of George the Third* (London, 1848).

Daniels, G. and J. Jewkes, 'The post-war depression in the Lancashire cotton industry', *Journal of the Royal Statistical Society* 91 (1928), 153–206.

Dodd, W., *A Narrative of the Experience of the Sufferings of William Dodd: A Factory Cripple* (London, 1841).

Economic Intelligence Unit, *Mediterranean Textiles and Clothing* (London, 1989).

Ellison, T., *The Cotton Trade of Great Britain: Including a History of the*

Liverpool Cotton Market and of the Liverpool Cotton Brokers' Association (London, 1886; reprinted Aldershot, 1987).

Era Ring Mill Company Ltd, *History of the Era Ring Mill, 1898–1955* (Rochdale, n.d.).

Federation of Master Cotton Spinners' Associations, *Measures for the Revival of the Lancashire Cotton Industry* (Manchester, 1936).

Fox Bourne, H. R., *English Merchants* (London, 1886).

French, G. J., *The Life and Times of Samuel Crompton of Hall-in-the-Wood, Inventor of the Spinning Machine Called the Mule* (London, 1862).

Grant, P. and A. Ashley Cooper [Earl of Shaftesbury], *The Ten Hours' Bill: The History of Factory Legislation* (Manchester, 1866).

Gray, E. M., *The Weaver's Wage: Earnings and Collective Bargaining in the Lancashire Cotton Weaving Industry* (Manchester, 1937).

Greg, R. H., *The Factory Question* (London, 1837).

Grieg, J., *The Farington Diary*, vol. II, 28 August 1802 to 13 September 1804 (London, 1923).

Hardwick, C., *History of the Borough of Preston and its Environs: In the County of Lancaster* (Preston, 1857).

Helm, E., 'The alleged decline of the British cotton industry', *Economic Journal* 2 (1892), 735–44.

Hewitson, A. ['Atticus'], *Our Country Churches and Chapels* (London, 1872).

Pigott, S., *Hollins: A Study of Industry, 1784–1949* (Nottingham, 1949).

Hoole, H., *A Letter to the Rt. Hon. Lord Althorp* (Manchester, 1832).

Hutchinson, Z., 'The Trusts grip cotton', *Independent Labour Party Pamphlets*, New Series, no. 28, 1920.

Jewkes, J. and E. M. Gray, *Wages and Labour in the Lancashire Cotton Spinning Industry* (Manchester, 1935).

Johnston, T., *The Financiers and the Nation* (London, 1934).

Jones, B., *Co-operative Production* (Oxford, 1894).

Kent, H., *Kent's Directory for 1803* (London, 1803).

Kenworthy, W., *Inventions and Hours of Labour: A Letter to Master Cotton Spinners, Manufacturers, and Millowners in General* (Blackburn, 1842).

Keynes, J. M., *The Return to Gold and Industrial Policy II, Collected Works* (Cambridge, 1981).

Knecht, E. and J. B. Fothergill, *The Principles and Practice of Textile Printing* (London, 1912).

Ludlow, J. M., 'On some new forms of industrial co-operation', *Good Words* 8 (April 1867), 240–8.

Ludlow, J. M. and L. Jones, *Progress of the Working Class, 1832–67* (London, 1867).

Macrosty, H., *The Trust Movement in British Industry* (London, 1907).

Marsden, R., *Cotton Spinning: Its Development, Principles and Practice* (London, 1884).

Marx, K., *Inaugural Address and Provisional Rules of the International Working Men's Association* (London, 1864).

Marx, K., *Capital I* (Harmondsworth, 1976).

Marx, K., *Capital III* (London, 1984).

Merrtens, F., 'The hours and cost of labour in the cotton industry at home and abroad', *Transactions of the Manchester Statistical Society* (session 1893–4), 125–90.

Morgan, J. Minter, *Remarks on the Practicability of Mr. Robert Owen's Plan to Improve the Condition of the Lower Classes* (London, 1819).

Murphy, W. S., *The Textile Industries: A Practical Guide to Fibres Yarns and Fabrics*, vol. 3 (London, 1910).

Nasmith, J., *Students' Cotton Spinning* (Manchester, 1896).

Noguera, S., *Theory and practice of high drafting* (privately published, 1936).

North, D., *Discourses upon Trade* (London, 1691).

Oastler, R., *Fleet Papers* (London, 1842).

Pitt, W., *A Topographical History of Staffordshire: Including its Agriculture, Mines, and Manufactures* (Newcastle-under-Lyme, 1817).

Political and Economic Planning, *Report on the British Cotton Industry* (London, 1934).

Potter, B., *The Co-operative Movement in Great Britain* (London, 1893; reprinted Aldershot, 1987).

Rae, J., *Statement of some new Principles on the Subject of Political Economy: Exposing the Fallacies of the System of Free Trade, and of some other Doctrines Maintained in the "Wealth of Nations"* (Boston, 1834).

Ramsay, G., *An Essay on the Distribution of Wealth* (Edinburgh, 1836).

Schulze-Gaevernitz, G. von, *The Cotton Trade in England and on the Continent* (London, 1895).

Scrope, G. P., *Principles of Political Economy* (London, 1836).

Senior, N. W. and L. Horner, *Letters on the Factory Act, as it affects the Cotton Manufacture, Addressed to the Right Honourable the President of the Board of Trade* (London, 1837).

Streat, R., *Lancashire and Whitehall: The Diary of Sir Raymond Streat*, vol. 2 (Manchester, 1987).

Taylor, J. C., *The Jubilee History of the Oldham Industrial Co-operative Society Limited* (Manchester, 1900).

Textile Council, *Cotton and Allied Textiles: A Report on Present Performance and Future Prospects* (Manchester, 1969).

Thackrah, C. T., *The Effects of the Principal Arts, Trades and Professions and of Civic States and Habits of Living on Health and Longevity* (London, 1831).

Thornley, T., *Modern Cotton Economics* (London, 1923).

Thornton, H., *An Enquiry into the Nature and Effects of the Paper Credit of Great Britain* (1802; reprinted London, 1939).

Ure, A., *The Philosophy of Manufactures; or, an Exposition of the Scientific, Moral, and Commercial Economy of the Factory System of Great Britain* (London, 1835).

Watts, J., 'On strikes and their effects on wages, profits and accumulations', *Journal of the Statistical Society* 24 (1861), 498–506.

Watts, J., *Facts of the Cotton Famine* (Manchester, 1866).

Winterbottom, J., *Cotton Spinning Calculations and Yarn Costs* (London, 1921).

Wood, G. H., 'Factory legislation, considered with reference to the wages, &c., of the operatives protected thereby', *Journal of the Royal Statistical Society* 65 (1902), 284–324.

Wood, G. H., *The History of Wages in the Cotton Trade During the Past Hundred Years* (London, 1910).

Young, T. M., *The American Cotton Industry: A Study of Work and Workers* (New York, 1903).

Secondary sources

Aggarwal, V. K. and S. Haggard, 'The politics of protection in the US textile and apparel industries', *American Industry in International Competition: Government Policies and Corporate Strategies*, ed. J. Zysman and L. Tyson (Ithaca, NY, 1983), pp. 249–312.

Albert, W., *The Turnpike Road System in England: 1663–1840* (Cambridge, 1972).

Aldcroft, D. H., 'The entrepreneur and the British Economy', *EcHR* 17 (1964), 113–34.

Allen, R. C., *The British Industrial Revolution in Global Perspective* (Cambridge, 2009).

Allen, R. C., 'Engels' pause: Technical change, capital accumulation, and inequality in the British industrial revolution', *Explorations in Economic History* 46 (2009), 418–35.

Alliance Project Team, *Repatriation of UK Textiles Manufacture* (Manchester, 2015).

Amini, S. and S. Toms, 'Accessing capital markets: Aristocrats and new share issues in the British bicycle boom of the 1890s', *BH* 60 (2018), 231–56.

Amini, S. and S. Toms, 'Elite directors, London finance and British overseas expansion: Victorian railway networks, 1860–1900' (unpublished working paper, University of Leeds, 2019).

Amini, S., K. Keasey and R. Hudson, 'The equity funding of smaller growing companies and regional stock exchanges', *International Small Business Journal* 30 (2012), 832–49.

Anderson, G. M., R. B. Ekelund Jr and R. D. Tollison, 'Nassau Senior as economic consultant: The Factory Acts reconsidered', *Economica* 56 (1989), 71–81.

Anderson, P., 'Origins of the present crisis', *New Left Review* 23 (1964), 26–53.

Ashley, W. J., *English Economic History* (London, 1892).

Ashmore, O., *The Industrial Archaeology of North-west England* (Manchester, 1982).

Ashton, T. S., *The Industrial Revolution* (Oxford, 1969).

Aspin, C., *The First Industrial Society: Lancashire, 1750–1850* (Lancaster, 1995).

Aspin, C., *The Water-Spinners* (Helmshore, 2003).

Audretsch, D. B. and J. R. Hinger, 'From entrepreneur to philanthropist: Two sides of the same coin?', *Handbook of Research on Entrepreneurs' Engagement in Philanthropy: Perspectives*, ed. M. L. Taylor, R. J. Strom and D. O. Renz (Cheltenham, 2014), pp. 24–32.

Balasubramanyam, V. N., 'International trade and employment in the UK textiles and clothing sector,' *Applied Economics* 25 (1993), 1477–82.

Bamberg, J. H., 'Sir Frank Platt', *Dictionary of Business Biography*, ed. D. Jeremy (London, 1984–96), vol. 4, pp. 716–22.

Bamberg, J. H., 'The rationalization of the British cotton industry in the interwar years', *Textile History* 19 (1988), 83–101.

Barker, T. C. and J. R. Harris, *A Merseyside Town in the Industrial Revolution: St. Helens, 1750–1900* (Liverpool, 1954).

Beattie, D., *Blackburn: The Development of a Lancashire Cotton Town* (Blackburn, 1992).

Beckert, S., *Empire of Cotton: A Global History* (New York, 2014).

Berg, M., *The Machinery Question and the Making of Political Economy 1815–1848* (Cambridge, 1982).

Berg, M., *The Age of Manufactures, 1700–1820: Industry, Innovation and Work in Britain* (New York, 2005).

Berg, M., 'Quality, cotton and the global luxury trade', *How India Clothed the World: The World of South Asian Textiles, 1500–1850*, ed. G. Riello and T. Roy (Leiden, 2009), pp. 391–414.

Blackburn, J. A., 'The vanishing UK cotton industry', *National Westminster Bank Quarterly Review* (November 1982), 42–52.

Bogart, D., 'The transport revolution in industrializing Britain: A survey', *The Cambridge Economic History of Modern Britain*, vol. 1: *1700–1870*, ed. R. Floud, J. Humphries and P. Johnson (Cambridge, 2014), pp. 368–91.

Bonner, A., *British Co-operation* (Manchester, 1971).

Bowden, S. and D. M. Higgins, 'Short-time working and price maintenance: Collusive tendencies in the cotton-spinning industry, 1919–1939', *EcHR* 51 (1998), 319–43.

Boyson, R., *The Ashworth Cotton Enterprise* (Oxford, 1970).

Briscoe, L., *The Textile and Clothing Industry of the United Kingdom* (Manchester, 1971).

Broadberry, S., 'The Performance of Manufacturing', *The Cambridge Economic History of Modern Britain, Volume 3: Structural Change, 1939–2000*, ed. R. Floud and P. Johnson (Cambridge, 2004), pp. 57–83.

Broadberry, S. and N. Crafts, 'UK productivity performance from 1950 to 1979: a restatement of the Broadberry–Crafts view', *EcHR* 56 (2003), 718–35.

Brown, D., 'From "Cotton Lord" to Landed Aristocrat: the Rise of Sir George Philips Bart., 1766–1847', *Historical Research* 69 (1996), 62–82.

Brown, E. P. and S. J. Handfield-Jones, 'The climacteric of the 1890's: A study in the expanding economy', *Oxford Economic Papers* 4 (1952), 266–307.

Buck, D., *More Ups Than Downs: An Autobiography* (Spennymoor, 2001).

Bullen, A., 'The Making of Brooklands', *The Barefoot Aristocrats: A History of the Amalgamated Association of Operative Cotton Spinners*, ed. A. Fowler and T. Wyke (Littleborough, 1987), pp. 93–114.

Burscough, M., *The Horrockses: Cotton Kings of Preston* (Lancaster, 2004).

Bythell, D., *The Hand-loom Weavers: A Study in the English Cotton Industry During the Industrial Revolution* (Cambridge, 1969).

Cain, P. J. and A. G. Hopkins, *British Imperialism* (London, 1993).

Cain, P. J. and A. G. Hopkins, *British Imperialism: 1688–2000* (London, 2014).

Calladine, A. and J. Fricker, *East Cheshire Textile Mills* (London, 1993).

Cannell, M., 'Rise of Shiloh: Bucking the trend in the UK spinning industry', *Textile Outlook International* 69 (1997), 60–75.

Cantrell, J. A., 'James Nasmyth and the Bridgewater Foundry: Partners and Partnerships', *BH* 23 (1981), 346–58.

Cassis, Y. and P. Cottrell, *Private Banking in Europe: Rise, Retreat and Resurgence* (Oxford, 2015).

Casson, M., 'Institutional economics and business history: A way forward?', *BH* 39 (1997), 151–71.

Catling, H., *The Spinning Mule* (Newton Abbot, 1970).

Chaloner, W. H., 'Robert Owen, Peter Drinkwater and the early factory system in Manchester, 1788–1800', *Industry and Innovation: Selected Essays by W. H. Chaloner*, ed. D. A. Farnie and W. O. Henderson (London, 1990).

Chandler, A. D., *Scale and Scope: The Dynamics of Industrial Capitalism*, Cambridge, MA, 1990.

Chapman, S. D., *The Early Factory Masters: The Transition to the Factory System in the Midlands Textile Industry* (Newton Abbot, 1967).

Chapman, S. D., 'Fixed capital formation in the British cotton industry, 1770–1815', *EcHR* 23 (1970), 235–53.

Chapman, S. D., 'Financial restraints on the growth of firms in the cotton industry, 1790–1850', *EcHR* 32 (1979), 50–69.

Chapman, S. D. and J. Butt, 'The cotton industry, 1775–1856', *Studies in Capital*

Formation in the United Kingdom, 1750–1920, ed. C. Feinstein and S. Pollard (Oxford, 1988), 105–25.

Chapman, S. D., 'The Fielden Fortune. The Finances of Lancashire's most Successful Ante-bellum Manufacturing Family', *Financial History Review* 3 (1996), 7–28.

Chapman, S. D., *Merchant Enterprise in Britain* (Cambridge, 2004).

Ciliberto, F., 'Were British cotton entrepreneurs technologically backward? Firm-level evidence on the adoption of ring spinning', *Explorations in Economic History* 47 (2010), 487–504.

Clapham, J. H., *An Economic History of Modern Britain*, vol. 1: *The Early Railway Age, 1820–1850* (Cambridge, 1930).

Clark, G., 'Why isn't the whole world developed? Lessons from the cotton mills', *JEH* 47 (1987), 141–73.

Clark, G., 'Factory discipline', *JEH* 54 (1994), 128–63.

Clark, S, 'Chorlton Mills and their neighbours', *Industrial Archaeology Review*, 1978, 207–39.

Clarke, P. F., *Lancashire and the new Liberalism* (Cambridge, 2007).

Cohen, J. S., 'Managers and Machinery: An Analysis of the Rise of Factory Production', *The Textile Industries*, ed. S. D. Chapman (London. 1997), pp. 96–114.

Coleman, D. C. and C. MacLeod, 'Attitudes to new techniques: British businessmen, 1800–1950', *EcHR* 39 (1986), 588–611.

Collier, F., *The Family Economy of the Working Classes in the Cotton Industry* (Manchester, 1964).

Cook, P. L., and R. Cohen, *The Effects of Mergers: Six Studies* (London, 1958).

Cooke, A., *The Rise and Fall of the Scottish Cotton Industry, 1778–1914: The Secret Spring* (Manchester, 2010).

Corley, T. A. B., 'White, James (1877–1927)', *Oxford Dictionary of National Biography* (Oxford, 2004).

Cottrell, P. L., *Industrial Finance, 1930–1914: The Finance and Organization of English Manufacturing Industry* (London, 1980).

Cowle, M., *Dirty Politics: A Trilogy of Blasphemies* (Manchester, 2010).

Crafts, N. F. R. and C. K. Harley, 'Output growth and the industrial revolution: A restatement of the Crafts–Harley view', *EcHR* 45 (1992), 703–30.

Crafts, N. F. R., 'Productivity growth in the industrial revolution: A new growth accounting perspective', *JEH* 64 (2004), 521–35.

Crick, W. F. and J. E. Wadsworth, *A Hundred Years of Joint Stock Banking*, London 1936.

Crouzet, F., *Capital formation in the Industrial Revolution* (London, 1972).

Daniels, G. W., 'The early records of a great Manchester cotton spinning firm', *Economic Journal* 25 (1915), 175–88.

Daniels, G. W., 'The cotton trade during the Revolutionary and Napoleonic wars', *Transactions of the Manchester Statistical Society* (1915/16), 53–84.

Daniels, G. W. 'The cotton trade at the close of the Napoleonic War', *Transactions of the Manchester Statistical Society* (1918), 1–29.

Daniels, G. W.,'Samuel Crompton's census of the cotton industry in 1811', *Economic Journal* 40 (Supplement) (1930), 107–10.

Daunton, M. J., '"Gentlemanly Capitalism" and British Industry, 1820–1914', *Past and Present* 122 (1989), 119–58.

Deane, P. and H. I. Habakkuk, 'The Take-Off in Britain', *The Economics of Take-Off into Sustained Growth*, ed. W. W. Rostow (London, 1963), pp. 63–82.

DeLong, J. B., 'This time, it is *not* different: The persistent concerns of financial macroeconomics', *Rethinking the Financial Crisis*, ed. A. S. Blinder, A. W. Lo and R. M. Solow (New York, 2013), pp. 14–36.

Dickinson, T. C., *Cotton Mills of Preston: The Power Behind the Thread* (Lancaster, 2002).

Dimson, E., P. Marsh and M. Staunton, 'Equity premiums around the World', *Rethinking the Equity Risk Premium*, ed. P. B. Hammond Jr, M. L. Leibowitz and L. B. Seigel (Charlottesville, VA, 2011), pp. 32–52.

Drummond, I., *British Economic Policy and Empire, 1919–1939* (Abingdon, 2006).

Dunlavy, C. A., 'Corporate governance in late 19th century Europe and the US: the case of shareholder voting rights', *Comparative Corporate Governance: The State of the Art and Emerging Research*, ed. P. D. K. Hopt, K. J. Hopt, H. Kanda, M. J. Roe, S. Prigge and E. Wymeersch (Oxford, 1998), pp. 5–40.

Dupree, M. W., 'Edward Tootal Broadhurst', in D. Jeremy (ed.), *Dictionary of Business Biography* (London, 1984–86), vol. 1, pp. 452–5.

Edwards M. M., *The Growth of the British Cotton Trade, 1780–1815* (Manchester, 1967).

Edwards, R. S., 'Some notes on the early literature and development of cost accounting in Great Britain', *The Accountant* 97 (1937), 193–5.

Elbaum, B. and W. Lazonick, eds, *The Decline of the British Economy* (Oxford, 1987).

Farnie, D., 'Three Historians of the Cotton Industry: Thomas Ellison, Gerhart von Schulze-Gaevernitz, and Sydney Chapman', *Textile History* 9 (1978), 75–89.

Farnie, D., *The English Cotton Industry and the World Market, 1815–1896* (Oxford, 1979).

Farnie, D. A., *The Manchester Ship Canal and the Rise of the Port of Manchester* (Manchester, 1980).

Farnie, D., 'The emergence of Victorian Oldham as the centre of the cotton spinning industry', *Saddleworth Historical Society Bulletin* 12 (1982), 41–53.

Farnie, D., 'John Bunting', *Dictionary of Business Biography*, ed. D. Jeremy (London, 1984–86), vol. 1, pp. 506–9.

Farnie, D. A., 'John Rylands of Manchester', *Bulletin of the John Rylands Library* 75/2 (1993), 2–103.

Farnie, D., 'The metropolis of cotton spinning machine making and mill building', *The Cotton Mills of Oldham*, ed. D. Gurr and J. Hunt (Oldham, 1998), pp. 4–11.

Farnie, D. and D. Jeremy (eds), *The Fibre that Changed the World: The Cotton Industry in International Perspective, 1600–1990s* (Oxford, 2004).

Farnie, D., 'The role of merchants as prime movers in the expansion of the cotton industry, 1760–1990', *The Fibre that Changed the World: The Cotton Industry in International Perspective, 1600–1990s*, ed. D. Farnie and D. Jeremy (Oxford, 2004), pp. 15–55.

Fetter, F. W., *Development of British Monetary Orthodoxy, 1797–1875* (Cambridge, MA, 1965).

Filatotchev, I. and S. Toms, 'Corporate governance, strategy and survival in a declining industry: A study of UK cotton textile companies', *Journal of Management Studies* 40 (2003), 895–920.

Filatotchev, I. and S. Toms, 'Corporate governance and financial constraints on strategic turnarounds', *Journal of Management Studies* 43 (2006), 407–33.

Fitton, R. S. and A. P. Wadsworth, *The Strutts and the Arkwrights, 1758–1830: A Study of the Early Factory System* (Manchester, 1958).

Foster, J. 'The Making of the First Six Factory Acts', *Bulletin of the Society for the Study of Labour History* 18 (1969), 4–5.

Foster, J., *Class Struggle and the Industrial Revolution: Early Industrial Capitalism in Three English Towns* (London, 1974).

Fowler, A., 'Trade unions and technical change: The automatic loom strike, 1908', *North West Labour History Society Bulletin* 6 (1979), 43–55.

Frankel, M., 'Obsolescence and technological change in a maturing economy', *American Economic Review* 45 (1955), 296–319.

Freeman, T. W., H. B. Rodgers and R. H. Kinvig, *Lancashire, Cheshire and the Isle of Man* (London, 1966).

Gatrell, V., 'Labour, power, and the size of firms in the second quarter of the nineteenth century', *EcHR* 30 (1977), 95–139.

Gayer, A. D., A. Jacobson and I. Finkelstein, 'British share prices, 1811–1850', *Review of Economic Statistics* 22 (1940), 78–93.

Gayer, A. D., W. W. Rostow and A. J. Schwartz, *The Growth and Fluctuation of the British Economy, 1790–1850* (Oxford, 1953).

Gehrig, T., 'Cities and the geography of financial centers', CEPR Discussion Paper no. 1894 (London, 1998).

Goldsmith, R., *Financial Structure and Development* (New Haven, CT, 1969).

Gordon, E. and G. Nair, *Public Lives: Women, Family, and Society in Victorian Britain* (New Haven, CT and London, 2003).

Granovetter, M., 'Economic Action and Social Structure: The Problem of Embeddedness', *American Journal of Sociology* 91 (1985), 481–510.

Gray, R., *The Factory Question and Industrial England, 1830–1860* (Cambridge, 1986).

Green, E. H. H., 'Rentiers versus producers? The political economy of the Bimetallic controversy, c.1880–98', *English Historical Review* 103 (1988), 588–612.

Green, E. H. H., 'Gentlemanly Capitalism and British Economic Policy, 1880–1914: The Debate over Bimetallism and Protectionism', *Gentlemanly Capitalism and British Imperialism: The New Debate on Empire*, ed. R. E. Dumett (London, 1999), pp. 44–67.

Gremson, S., I. Pringle and D. Winterbotham, *Philips Park: Its History and Development* (Bury, 2011).

Gurr, D. and J. Hunt, *The Cotton Mills of Oldham* (Oldham, 1998).

Hall, B., *Lowerhouse and the Dugdales: The Story of a Lancashire Mill Community* (Burnley, 1976).

Haggerty, S., *'Merely for money'? Business Culture in the British Atlantic, 1750–1815* (Liverpool, 2012).

Hammond, J. L. and B. Hammond, *The Rise of Modern Industry* (London, 1911).

Hammond, J. L. and B. Hammond, *The Town Labourer, 1760–1832* (London, 1925).

Hampson, P., 'Industrial Finance from the Working Classes in later Nineteenth-Century Lancashire', *The Local Historian* 48/2 (April 2018), 119–33.

Hanes, W. T. and F. Sanello, *The Opium Wars: The Addiction of One Empire and the Corruption of Another* (Naperville, IL, 2002).

Harley, C. K., 'Cotton textile prices and the industrial revolution', *EcHR* 51 (1998), 49–83.

Harley, C. K. and N. F. R. Crafts, 'Simulating two views of the British Industrial Revolution', *JEH* 60 (2000), 819–41.

Harley, C. K., 'Was technological change in the early Industrial Revolution Schumpeterian? Evidence of cotton textile profitability', *Explorations in Economic History* 49 (2000), 516–27.

Harrison, A. and B. L. Hutchins, *A History of Factory Legislation* (London, 1903; reprinted Abingdon, 2013).

Harrison, D., 'Network effects following multiple relationship dissolution', *Proceedings of the 17th Annual IMP Conference* (Oslo, 2001), pp. 1–23.

Harrison, J., 'Rethinking city-regionalism as the production of new non-state spatial strategies: The case of Peel Holdings Atlantic Gateway Strategy', *Urban Studies* 51 (2014), 2315–35.

Hartley, W. M., *An Oldham Velvet Dynasty: The Mellodews of Moorside* (Lancaster, 2009).

Higgins, D., and S. Toms, 'Firm structure and financial performance: The Lancashire textile industry, c.1884–c.1960', *Accounting, Business & Financial History* 7 (1997), 195–232.

Higgins, D. and S. Toms, 'Public subsidy and private divestment: The Lancashire cotton textile industry, c.1950–1965', *BH* 42 (2000), 59–84.

Higgins, D. and S. Toms, 'Financial distress, corporate borrowing, and industrial decline: The Lancashire cotton spinning industry, 1918–38', *Accounting, Business & Financial History* 13 (2003), 207–32.

Higgins, D. and S. Toms, 'Financial institutions and corporate strategy: David Alliance and the transformation of British textiles, c.1950–c.1990', *BH* 48 (2006), 453–78.

Higgins D., S. Toms and I. Filatotchev, 'Ownership, financial strategy and performance: The Lancashire cotton textile industry, 1918–1938', *BH* 57 (2015), 97–121.

Higgins, D. and S. Toms, *British Cotton Textiles: Maturity and Decline* (London, 2017).

Hills, R. L., *Power in the Industrial Revolution* (Manchester, 1970).

Hindle, P., *Manchester, Bolton and Bury Canal through Time* (Stroud, 2013).

Hirschman, A. O., *Exit, Voice and Loyalty* (Cambridge MA, 1970).

Hobsbawm, E., *Industry and Empire: The Birth of the Industrial Revolution* (New York, 1968).

Hobsbawm, E., *Age of Revolution: 1789–1848* (London, 2010).

Hobsbawm, E., *The Age of Capital, 1848–1875* (London, 1975).

Hodgkins, D. (ed.), *The Diary of Edward Watkin* (Manchester, 2013).

Hodson, J. H., *Cheshire, 1660–1780: Restoration to Industrial Revolution*, Chester, 1978.

Holden, R. N., 'Pear Mill, Stockport: An Edwardian Cotton Spinning Mill', *Industrial Archaeology Review* 10 (1988), 162–74.

Holden, R. N., 'The architect in the Lancashire cotton industry, 1850–1914: The example of Stott & Sons', *Textile History* 23 (1992), 243–57.

Homer, S. and R. Sylla, *A History of Interest Rates*, 4th edn (Hoboken, NJ, 2011).

Honeyman, K., *Origins of Enterprise: Business Leadership in the Industrial Revolution* (Manchester, 1982).

Howe, A. C., *The Cotton Masters, 1830–1860* (Oxford, 1984).

Howe, A. C., 'Sir Frank Hollins', *Dictionary of Business Biography*, ed. D. Jeremy (London, 1984–86), vol. 3, pp. 313–17.

Howe, A. C., 'Henry Lee and Joseph Cocksey Lee', *Dictionary of Business Biography*, ed. D. Jeremy (London, 1984–86), vol. 3, pp. 703–14.

Howe, A. C., 'Bimetallism, c.1880–1898: a controversy re-opened?', *English Historical Review* 105 (1990), 377–91.

Howe, A. C., 'Houldsworth, Sir William Henry, First Baronet (1834–1917), Cotton Industrialist and Politician', *Oxford Dictionary of National Biography* (Oxford, 2004), https://doi.org/10.1093/ref:odnb/40813, accessed 6 April 2020.

Huberman, M., *Escape from the Market: Negotiating Work in Lancashire* (Cambridge, 1996).

Hudson, P., *The Industrial Revolution* (London, 2014).

Hughes, J. R. T., *Fluctuations in Trade, Industry, and Finance: A Study of British Economic Development, 1850–1860* (Oxford, 1960).

Humphries, J., *Childhood and Child labour in the British Industrial Revolution* (Cambridge, 2010).

Jacob, M. C., *The First Knowledge Economy: Human Capital and the European Economy, 1750–1850* (Cambridge, 2014).

Janes, M., *From Smuggling to Cotton Kings: The Greg Story* (Cirencester, 2010).

Jeremy, D. J., *Transatlantic Industrial Revolution: The Diffusion of Textile Technologies between Britain and America, 1790–1830s* (Cambridge, MA, 1981).

Jeremy, D., 'The International Diffusion of Cotton Manufacturing Technology, 1750–1990s', *The Fibre that Changed the World: The Cotton Industry in International Perspective, 1600–1990s*, ed. D. Farnie and D. Jeremy (Oxford, 2004), pp. 85–127.

Johnson, M., 'Marks & Spencer implements an ethical sourcing program for its global supply chain', *Journal of Organizational Excellence* 23 (2004), 3–16.

Jones, G. T., *Increasing Return: A Study of the Relation between the Size and Efficiency of Industries with Special Reference to the History of Selected British & American Industries, 1850–1910* (Cambridge, 1933).

Joyce, P., *Work, Society and Politics: The Culture of the Factory in later Victorian England* (Aldershot, 1991).

Joyce, P., *Visions of the People: Industrial England and the Question of Class, c.1848–1914* (Cambridge, 1994).

Kellett, J. R., *The Impact of Railways on Victorian Cities* (Toronto, 1969).

Kenney, C., *Cotton Everywhere: Recollections of Northern Women Mill Workers* (Bolton, 1994).

Kenny, S., 'Sub-regional specialization in the Lancashire cotton industry, 1884–1914: A study in organizational and locational change', *Journal of Historical Geography* 8 (1982), 41–63.

Kindleberger, C. P., *The Formation of Financial Centers: A Study in Comparative Economic History* (Princeton, NJ, 1974).

Kirby, R. G. and A. E. Musson, *Voice of the People, John Doherty, 1798–1854: Trade Unionist, Radical and Factory Reformer* (Manchester, 1975).

Kirk, R., 'John Bullough', *Dictionary of Business Biography*, ed. D. Jeremy (London, 1984–86), vol. 1, p. 502.

Kynaston, D., *The City of London II: The Golden Years, 1890–1914* (London, 1995).

Landes, D., *The Unbound Prometheus: Technological Change and Industrial Development in Western Europe from 1750 to the Present* (Cambridge, 1969).

Laslett, J. H. M., *Colliers Across the Sea: A Comparative Study of Class Formation in Scotland and the American Midwest, 1830–1924* (Urbana, IL, 2000).

Law, B., *Fieldens of Todmorden: A Nineteenth Century Business Dynasty* (Littleborough, 1995).

Lazonick, W., 'Competition, Specialization, and Industrial Decline', *JEH* 31 (1981), 31–8.

Lazonick, W., 'Factor costs and the diffusion of ring spinning prior to World War One', *Quarterly Journal of Economics* 96 (1981), 89–109.

Lazonick, W., 'Industrial organization and technological change: The decline of the British cotton industry', *BHR* 58 (1983), 195–236.

Lazonick, W. and W. Mass, 'The performance of the British cotton industry, 1870–1913', *Research in Economic History* 9 (1984), 1–44.

Lazonick, W., 'Stubborn mules: Some comments', *EcHR* 40 (1987), 80–6.

Lazonick, W., 'The cotton industry', *The Decline of the British Economy*, ed. B. Elbaum and W. Lazonick (Oxford, 1987), pp. 18–50.

Lazonick, W., *Business Organization and the Myth of the Market Economy* (Cambridge, 1993).

Lee, C. H., *A Cotton Enterprise, 1795–1840: A History of M'Connel & Kennedy Fine Cotton Spinners* (Manchester, 1972).

Leunig, T., 'New answers to old questions: Explaining the slow adoption of ring spinning in Lancashire, 1880–1913', *JEH* 61 (2001), 439–66.

Leunig, T., 'A British industrial success: Productivity in the Lancashire and New England cotton spinning industries a century ago', *EcHR* 56 (2003), 90–117.

Lloyd-Jones, R. and M. J. Lewis, *Manchester and the Age of the Factory: The Business Structure of Cottonopolis in the Industrial Revolution* (London, 1988).

Loftus, D., 'Capital and community: Limited liability and attempts to democratize the market in Mid-19th Century England', *Victorian Studies* 45 (2002), 93–120.

Lucas, A. F., *Industrial Reconstruction and the Control of Competition: The British Experiments* (London, 1937).

Marchionatti, R., 'Keynes and the collapse of the British cotton industry in the 1920s: a microeconomic case against laissez-faire', *Journal of Post Keynesian Economics* 17 (1995), 427–45.

Marglin, S. A., 'What do bosses do? The origins and functions of hierarchy in capitalist production', *Review of Radical Political Economics* 6 (1974), 60–112.

Marrison, A., 'Great Britain and her rivals in the Latin American cotton piece-goods market, 1880–1914', *Great Britain and her World, 1750–1914*, ed. B. Radcliffe (Manchester, 1975), pp. 308–48.

Marrison, A., 'Indian summer, 1870–1914', *The Lancashire Cotton Industry: A History Since 1700*, ed. M. B. Rose (Preston, 1996), pp. 238–64.

Marvel, H. P., 'Factory regulation: A reinterpretation of early English experience', *Journal of Law and Economics* 20 (1977), 379–402.

Mason, C. and R. Harrison, 'Closing the regional equity gap? A critique of the Department of Trade and Industry's regional venture capital funds initiative', *Regional Studies* 37 (2003), 855–68.

Mason, J. J., 'Herbert Shepherd Cross', *Dictionary of Business Biography*, ed. D. Jeremy (London, 1984–86), vol. 1, pp. 845–6.

Mass, W., 'Mechanical and organizational innovation: The Drapers and the automatic loom', *BHR* 63 (1989), 876–929.

Mass, W. and W. Lazonick, 'The British cotton industry and international competitive advantage: The state of the debates', *BH* 32 (1990), 9–65.

Mathias, P., *The First Industrial Nation: An Economic History of Britain, 1700–1914* (London, 1969).

Maw, P., T. Wyke and A. Kidd, 'Canals, rivers, and the industrial city: Manchester's industrial waterfront, 1790–1850', *EcHR* 65 (2012), 1495–1523.

Maw, P., *Transport and the Industrial City: Manchester and the Canal Age, 1750–1850* (Manchester, 2013).

McCloskey, D. 'The industrial revolution, 1780–1860: A survey', *The Economic History of Britain since 1700*, ed. R. Floud and D. McCloskey (Cambridge, 1981), 103–27.

McCloskey, D. and L. Sandberg, 'From Damnation to Redemption: judgements on the late Victorian entrepreneur', *Explorations in Economic History* 9 (1972), 89–108.

Mendels, F. F., 'Proto-industrialization: The first phase of the industrialization process', *JEH* 32 (1972), 241–61.

Michie, R., *Guilty Money: The City of London in Victorian and Edwardian Culture, 1815–1914* (London, 2009).

Michie, R., 'Options, Concessions, Syndicates, and the Provision of Venture Capital 1880–1913', *BH* 23 (1981), 147–64.

Miles, C., *Lancashire Textiles: A Case Study of Industrial Change* (Cambridge, 1968).

Miller, I. and C. Wild, *A & G Murray and the Cotton Mills of Ancoats* (Lancaster, 2007).

Millward, R., 'Industrial and Commercial Performance since 1950', *The Cambridge Economic History of Modern Britain, Volume 3: Structural Change, 1939–2000*, ed. R. Floud and P. Johnson (Cambridge, 2004), pp. 123–67.

Mitchell, B. and P. Deane, *Abstract of British Historical Statistics* (Cambridge, 1962).

Mitchell, B. and H. Jones, *Second Abstract of British Historical Statistics* (Cambridge, 1971).

Mokyr, J., 'Editor's introduction: The new economic history and the Industrial

Revolution', *The British Industrial Revolution: An Economic Perspective*, ed. J. Mokyr (Boulder, CO, 1993), 1–127.

Musson, A. E. and E. Robinson, 'The early growth of steam power', *EcHR* 11 (1959), 418–39.

Musson, A. E. and E. Robinson, 'The origins of engineering in Lancashire', *JEH* 20 (1960), 209–33.

Musson, A. E., *Trade Union and Social History* (London, 1974).

Nardinelli, C., 'Child labor and the Factory Acts', *JEH* 40 (1980), 739–55.

Nardinelli, C., 'The successful prosecution of the Factory Acts: A suggested explanation', *EcHR* 38 (1985), 428–30.

Navin, T. R., *The Whitin Machine Works since 1831: A Textile Machinery Company in an Industrial Village*, vol. 15 (Cambridge, MA, 1950).

Ormerod, A., *Industrial Odyssey* (Manchester, 1996).

Ormerod, A., 'Textile manufacturing: Smokestack industry or an essential sector of the national economy?', *Journal of the Textile Institute* 90 (1999), 93–103.

Ormerod, A., 'The decline of the UK textile industry: the terminal years, 1945–2003', *Journal of Industrial History* 6 (2003), 1–33.

Osborn, T., *The Industrial Ecosystem: An Environmental and Social History of the Early Industrial Revolution in Oldham, England, 1750–1820*, vol. 2 (Santa Cruz, CA, 1997).

Owen, G., *From Empire to Europe: The Decline and Revival of British Industry* (London, 1999).

Owen, G., *The Rise and Fall of Great Companies: Courtaulds and the Reshaping of the Man-made Fibres Industry* (Oxford, 2010).

Parkinson-Bailey, J., *Manchester: Architectural History* (Manchester, 2000).

Parsons, M. C. and M. B. Rose, 'Communities of knowledge: Entrepreneurship, innovation and networks in the British outdoor trade, 1960–90', *BH* 46 (2004), 609–39.

Pearson, R. and D. Richardson, 'Business networking in the industrial revolution', *EcHR* 54 (2001), 657–79.

Platt, D. C. M., *Latin America and British Trade 1806–1914* (New York, 1975).

Pollard, S., 'Fixed capital in the industrial revolution in Britain', *JEH* 24 (1964), 299–314.

Pollard, S., *The Genesis of Modern Management: A Study of the Industrial Revolution in Great Britain* (Harmondsworth, 1968).

Porter, J. H., 'The commercial banks and the financial problems of the English cotton industry, 1919–1939', *The International Review of Banking History* 9 (1974), 1–16.

Pressnell, L. S., *Country Banking in the Industrial Revolution* (Oxford, 1956).

Procter, S. J. and S. Toms, 'Industrial relations and technical change: Profits, wages and costs in the Lancashire Cotton Industry, 1880–1914', *Journal of Industrial History* 3 (2000), 54–72.

Redfern, P., *The Story of the C.W.S., The Jubilee History of the Co-operative Wholesale Society, Limited, 1863–1913* (Manchester, 1913).

Redford, A., *Manchester Merchants and Foreign Trade* (Manchester, 1934).

Reid, D. A., 'The Decline of Saint Monday 1766–1876', *Past & Present* 71 (1976), 76–101.

Rennison, R. W., *Civil Engineering Heritage: Northern England* (London, 1996).

Richardson, P., 'The structure of capital during the industrial revolution revisited: Two case studies from the cotton textile industry', *EcHR* 42 (1989), 484–503.

Ricks, D., 'An overview of government influence', *The Global Textile Industry*, ed. B. Toyne, J. Arpan, D. A. Ricks, T. A. Shimp and A. Barnett (London, 1984).

Riello, G., *Cotton: The Fabric that Made the Modern World* (Cambridge, 2013).

Roberts, J., *Glitter & Greed: The Secret World of the Diamond Cartel* (New York, 2007).

Robins, J. E., *Cotton and Race Across the Atlantic: Britain, Africa, and America, 1900–1920* (Rochester, NY, 2016).

Robson, A. P., *On Higher than Commercial Grounds: The Factory Controversy* (New York, 1985).

Robson, R., *The Cotton Industry in Britain* (London, 1957).

Roll, E., *An Early Experiment in Industrial Organization: History of the Firm of Boulton and Watt 1775–1805* (London, 1930).

Rose, M. B., *The Gregs of Quarry Bank Mill* (Cambridge, 1986).

Rose, M. B., 'Social policy and business: Parish apprenticeship and the early factory system, 1750–1834', *BH* 31 (1989), 5–32.

Rose, M. B., P. Taylor and M. J. Winstanley, 'The Economic origins of paternalism: Some objections', *Social History*, 14, 1989, 89–98.

Rose, M. B. (ed.), *The Lancashire Cotton Industry: A History Since 1700* (Preston, 1996).

Rose, M. B., 'Politics of protection: An institutional approach to government–industry relations in the British and United States cotton industries, 1945–73', *BH* 39 (1997), 128–50.

Rose, M. B., *Firms, Networks and Business Values: The British and American Cotton Industries since 1750* (Cambridge, 2000).

Rubinstein, W., *Capitalism, Culture, and Decline: 1750–1990* (London, 1993).

Sandberg, L., *Lancashire in Decline: A Study in Entrepreneurship, Technology, and International Trade* (Columbus, OH, 1974).

Saul, S. B., 'The engineering industry', *The Development of British Industry and Foreign Competition, 1875–1914*, ed. D. Aldcroft (London, 1968), pp. 186–237.

Saville, J. and R. E. Tyson, 'Nuttall, William (1835–1905)', *Dictionary of*

Labour Biography, ed. K. Gildart and D. Howell (Basingstoke, 2010), vol. 13, p. 257.

Saxonhouse, G. R. and G. Wright, 'Rings and mules around the world', *Research in Economic History* Supplement 3 (1984), 271–300.

Saxonhouse, G. R. and G. Wright, 'Stubborn mules and vertical integration: The disappearing constraint?', *EcHR* 60 (1987), 87–94.

Saxonhouse, G. R. and G. Wright, 'National leadership and competing technological paradigms: the globalization of cotton spinning, 1878–1933', *JEH* 70 (2010), 535–66.

Sayers, R. S., *The Bank of England 1891–1944*, vol. 3: *Appendices* (Cambridge, 1976).

Shaw, D. and O. Sykes, 'Liverpool story: Growth, distress, reinvention and place-based strategy in a northern city', *Transforming Distressed Global Communities*, ed. F. Wagner, R. Mahayni and A. G. Piller (Abingdon, 2015), pp. 51–72.

Shepherd, A. and S. Toms, 'Entrepreneurship, strategy, and business philanthropy: Cotton textiles in the British industrial revolution', *BHR* 93 (2019), 503–27.

Shepherd, G., 'Textiles: New ways of surviving in an old industry', *Europe's Industries: Public and Private Strategies for Change*, ed. G. Shepherd, F. Duchêne and C. Saunders (London, 1983), pp. 26–51.

Siegel, J. J., 'The real rate of interest from 1800–1990: A study of the US and the UK', *Journal of Monetary Economics* 29 (1992), 227–52.

Sigsworth, E. M. and J. Blackman, 'The home boom of the 1890s', *Yorkshire Bulletin of Economic and Social Research* 17 (1965), 75–97.

Singleton, F. J., 'The Flax Merchants of Kirkham', *Transactions of the Historic Society of Lancashire and Cheshire* 126 (1977), 73–108.

Singleton, J., *Lancashire on the Scrapheap* (Oxford, 1991).

Singleton, J., 'The decline of the British cotton industry since 1940', *The Lancashire Cotton Industry: A History Since 1700*, ed. M. B. Rose (Preston, 1996), pp. 296–324.

Singleton, J., 'The Lancashire cotton industry, the Royal Navy, and the British Empire, c.1700–1960', *The Fibre that Changed the World: The Cotton Industry in International Perspective*, ed. D. Farnie and D. Jeremy (Oxford, 2004), pp. 57–84.

Slaven, A., 'Entrepreneurs and business success and business failure in Scotland', *Enterprise and Management: Essays in Honour of Peter L. Payne*, ed. D. H. Aldcroft and A. Slaven (Aldershot, 1995).

Smith, R., 'An Oldham Limited Liability Company 1875–1896', *BH* 4 (1961), 34–53.

Solar, P. M. and J. S. Lyons, 'The English cotton spinning industry, 1780–1840, as revealed in the columns of the *London Gazette*', *BH* 53 (2011), 302–23.

Spinager, D., 'Textiles beyond the MFA phase out', *World Economy* 22 (1999), 455–76.

Stone, W. E., 'An early English cotton mill cost accounting system: Charlton Mills, 1810–1889', *Accounting and Business Research* 4 (1973), 71–8.

Sutherland, A., 'The RPC and cotton spinning', *Journal of Industrial Economics* 8 (1959), 58–79.

Temin, P., 'Two views of the British industrial revolution', *JEH* 57 (1997), 63–82.

Thomas French & Sons Ltd, 'Smallwares and Narrow Fabrics. Historical Sketch (to 1944)', *Journal of the Textile Institute* 41 (1950), 751–99.

Thomas, W. A., *The Provincial Stock Exchanges* (London, 1973).

Thompson, E. P., 'Time, work-discipline, and industrial capitalism', *Past & Present* 38 (1967), 56–97.

Thorne, R. G., *The House of Commons, 1790–1820*, IV, London, 1986.

Timmins, G., *The Last Shift: The Decline of Handloom Weaving in Nineteenth-Century Lancashire* (Manchester, 1993).

Timmins, G., *Four Centuries of Lancashire Cotton* (Preston, 1996).

Timmins, G., 'Technological change', *The Lancashire Cotton Industry: A History Since 1700*, ed. M. B. Rose (Preston, 1996), pp. 29–62.

Timmins, G. and S. Timmins, *Made in Lancashire: A History of Regional Industrialisation* (Manchester, 1998).

Timmins, G., 'John Horrocks', *Dictionary of National Biography* (Oxford, 2004), https://doi.org/10.1093/ref:odnb/13807, accessed 19 September 2019.

Timmins, G., 'The cotton industry in the 1850s and 1860s: Decades of contrast', *The Golden Age: Essays in British Social and Economic History, 1850–1870*, ed. I. Inkster, C. Griffin, J. Hill and J. Rowbotham (Abingdon, 2017), pp. 61–74.

Tippett, L. H. C., *A Portrait of the Lancashire Textile Industry* (Oxford, 1969).

Tomlinson, J., 'Thrice denied: "Declinism" as a recurrent theme in British history in the long twentieth century', *Twentieth Century British History* 20 (2009), 227–51.

Toms, S., 'The profitability of the first Lancashire merger: The case of Horrocks, Crewdson & Co. Ltd, 1887–1905', *Textile History* 24 (1993), 129–46.

Toms, S., 'Integration, innovation, and the progress of a family cotton enterprise: Fielden Brothers Ltd, 1889–1914', *Textile History* 27 (1996), 77–100.

Toms, S., 'Windows of opportunity in the textile industry: The business strategies of Lancashire entrepreneurs, 1880–1914', *BH* 40 (1998), 1–25.

Toms, S., 'The supply of and demand for accounting information in an unregulated market: Examples from the Lancashire cotton mills, 1855–1914', *Accounting, Organizations and Society* 23 (1998), 217–38.

Toms, S., 'Growth, profits and technological choice: The case of the Lancashire cotton textile industry', *Journal of Industrial History* 1 (1998), 35–55.

Toms, S., 'Information content of earnings in an unregulated market: The co-operative cotton mills of Lancashire, 1880–1900', *Accounting and Business Research* 31 (2001), 175–90.

Toms, S., 'The rise of modern accounting and the fall of the public company: the Lancashire cotton mills 1870–1914', *Accounting, Organizations and Society* 27 (2002), 61–84.

Toms, S. and I. Filatotchev, 'Corporate governance, business strategy, and the dynamics of networks: A theoretical model and application to the British cotton industry, 1830–1980', *Organization Studies*, 25(2004), 629–51.

Toms, S., 'Financial control, managerial control and accountability: evidence from the British Cotton Industry, 1700–2000', *Accounting, Organizations and Society* 30 (2005), 627–53.

Toms, S. and M. Beck, 'The limitations of economic counterfactuals: The case of the Lancashire textile industry', *Management & Organizational History* 2 (2007), 315–30.

Toms, S., 'The English cotton industry and the loss of the world market', *King Cotton: A Tribute to Douglas Farnie*, ed. J. Wilson (Lancaster, 2009), pp. 58–76.

Toms, S., 'Calculating profit: A Historical Perspective on the Development of Capitalism', *Accounting, Organizations and Society* 35 (2010), 205–21.

Toms, S., 'The labour theory of value, risk and the rate of profit', *Critical Perspectives on Accounting* 21 (2010), 96–103.

Toms, S., 'Producer co-operatives and economic efficiency: Evidence from the nineteenth-century cotton textile industry', *BH* 54 (2012), 855–82.

Toms, S. and Q. Zhang, 'Marks & Spencer and the Decline of the British Textile Industry, 1950–2000', *BHR* 90 (2016), 3–30.

Toms, S. and A. Shepherd, 'Accounting and social conflict: Profit and regulated working time in the British Industrial Revolution', *Critical Perspectives on Accounting* 49 (2017), 57–75.

Toynbee, A., *Lectures on the Industrial Revolution in England* (1887; reprinted Cambridge, 2011).

Turnbull, G., *A History of the Calico Printing Industry of Great Britain* (Altrincham, 1941).

Tyson, R. E., 'William Marcroft', *Dictionary of Business Biography*, ed. D. Jeremy (London, 1984–86), vol. 4, p. 121.

Unwin, G., *Samuel Oldknow and the Arkwrights* (Manchester, 1968).

Ville, S., 'Transport', *The Cambridge Economic History of Modern Britain*, Volume 1, ed. R. Floud and P. Johnson (Cambridge, 2004), 295–331.

Wadsworth, A. P. and J. D. Mann, *The Cotton Trade and Industrial Lancashire, 1600–1780* (Manchester, 1965).

Waller, J., *The Real Oliver Twist, Robert Blincoe: A Life that Illuminates a Violent Age* (Cambridge, 2006).

Weiner, M., *English Culture and the Decline of the Industrial Spirit, 1850–1980* (London, 1981).

Whitely, J., 'The turnpike era', *Leading the Way: A History of Lancashire's Roads*, ed. A. Crosby (Preston, 1998), pp. 119–82.

Wilkins, M., *The History of Foreign Investment in the United States to 1914* (Cambridge, MA, 1989).

Williams, M., and D. Farnie, *Cotton Mills in Greater Manchester* (Lancaster, 1992).

Williams, R. B., *Accounting for Steam and Cotton: Two Eighteenth Century Case Studies* (New York, 1997).

Williams, R. B., 'Management accounting practice and price calculation at Boulton and Watt's Soho Foundry: A late 18th century example', *Accounting Historians Journal* 26 (1999), 65–87.

Williamson, O. E., 'The Economics of Organization: The Transaction Cost Approach', *American Journal of Sociology* 87 (1981), 548–77.

Wilson, J. F., *British Business History* (Manchester, 1994).

Wilson, J. F. and A. Popp, 'Business networking in the industrial revolution: some comments', *EcHR* 56 (2003), 355–61.

Wilson, J. F., A. Webster and R. Vorberg-Rugh, *Building Co-operation: A Business History of The Co-operative Group, 1863–2013* (Oxford, 2013).

Zeitlin, J. 'The clothing industry in transition: International trends and British response', *Textile History*, 19, 1988, 211–37.

Zeitlin, J. and P. Totterdill, 'Markets, technology and local intervention: The case of clothing', *Reversing Industrial Decline? Industrial Structure and Policy in Britain and Her Competitors*, ed. P. Hirst and J. Zeitlin (New York, 1989), pp. 155–90.

Unpublished theses

Bamberg, J. H., 'The government, the banks and the Lancashire cotton industry, 1918–1939' (Ph.D. dissertation, University of Cambridge, 1984).

Bennett, G. A., 'The present position of the cotton industry in Great Britain' (MA dissertation, University of Manchester, 1933).

Edwards, M. M. 'The development of the British cotton industry, 1780–1815' (Ph.D. dissertation, University of London, 1965).

Hampson, P., 'Working-class capitalists: The development and financing of worker owned companies in the Irwell Valley, 1849–1875' (Ph.D. dissertation, University of Central Lancashire, 2015).

Hart, R., 'Financing Lancashire's industrial development' (Ph.D. dissertation, University of Central Lancashire, 2006).

Jefferys, J. B., 'Trends in Business Organization in Great Britain since 1856, with Special Reference to the Financial Structure of Companies, the Mechanism of Investment and the Relations between the Shareholder and the Company' (Ph.D. dissertation, University of London, 1938).

Jones, F., 'The cotton spinning industry in the Oldham district from 1896–1914' (MA dissertation, University of Manchester, 1959).

Leunig, T., 'Lancashire at its zenith: Factor costs, industrial structure and technological choice in the Lancashire cotton industry, 1900–1913' (Ph.D. dissertation, University of Oxford, 1994).

Miller, I., *Castle Street Mill and Tame Foundry*, 59 (University of Salford, 2016).

Southern, J., 'Cotton and the community: Exploring changing concepts of identity and community on Lancashire's cotton frontier c.1890–1950' (Ph.D. dissertation, University of Central Lancashire, 2016).

Toms, S., 'The finance and growth of the Lancashire cotton textile industry, 1870–1914' (Ph.D. dissertation, University of Nottingham, 1996).

Tyson, R. E., 'The Sun Mill Company: A study in democratic investment, 1858–1959' (MA dissertation, University of Manchester, 1962).

Index

The letter 'n' indicates further information in a numbered footnote (e.g. 101 n40, which is note 40 on page 101). Similarly, 'f' refers to a numbered figure and 't' to a table.

PEOPLE, MARKETS, GOODS:
ECONOMIES AND SOCIETIES IN HISTORY

ISSN: 2051-7467

PREVIOUS TITLES

1. *Landlords and Tenants in Britain, 1440–1660:*
Tawney's Agrarian Problem *Revisited*
edited by Jane Whittle, 2013

2. *Child Workers and Industrial Health in Britain, 1780–1850*
Peter Kirby, 2013

3. *Publishing Business in Eighteenth-Century England*
James Raven, 2014

4. *The First Century of Welfare:*
Poverty and Poor Relief in Lancashire, 1620–1730
Jonathan Healey, 2014

5. *Population, Welfare and Economic Change in Britain 1290–1834*
edited by Chris Briggs, P. M. Kitson and S. J. Thompson, 2014

6. *Crises in Economic and Social History: A Comparative Perspective*
edited by A. T. Brown, Andy Burn and Rob Doherty, 2015

7. *Slavery Hinterland: Transatlantic Slavery and*
Continental Europe, 1680–1850
edited by Felix Brahm and Eve Rosenhaft, 2016

8. *Almshouses in Early Modern England:*
Charitable Housing in the Mixed Economy of Welfare, 1550–1725
Angela Nicholls, 2017

9. *People, Places and Business Cultures:*
Essays in Honour of Francesca Carnevali
edited by Paolo Di Martino, Andrew Popp and Peter Scott, 2017

10. *Cameralism in Practice: State Administration*
and Economy in Early Modern Europe
edited by Marten Seppel and Keith Tribe, 2017

Printed in the United States
By Bookmasters